D1226704

Samuel L. Morison
John S. Rowe

WARSHIPS OF THE US NAVY

JANE'S

First published in the United Kingdom in 1983 by
Jane's Publishing Company Limited
238 City Road, London EC1V 2PU

ISBN 0 7106 0206 5

Distributed in the Philippines and the USA and its dependencies by
Jane's Publishing Inc,
135 West 50th Street,
New York, NY 10020

Typesetting by D. P. Media Ltd,
Hitchin, Herts

Printed in the United Kingdom by
Biddles Limited, Guildford, Surrey

Contents

To the Royal Navy, a sister service
of unsurpassed traditions, qualities
and spirit.

Foreword

The data presented in this book are as of July 1, 1983. All photographs and drawings used are US Navy official unless otherwise noted. All opinions expressed in this book, unless a quotation, are those of the authors, who take complete responsibility for them. Opinions, questions and comments concerning this book are welcome and should be sent to either of the authors via the following address:

c/o Brendan Gallagher,
Jane's Publishing Company Ltd,
238 City Road,
London EC1V 2PU, Great Britain

The authors wish to thank Brendan Gallagher of Jane's for his great support and encouragement in aiding us to meet an advanced deadline. It is representatives like him that make it a pleasure to write for Jane's.

Samuel L. Morison
John S. Rowe
July 1983

Notes on fleet assignments

The fleet assignment (abbreviated F/S) status of each ship in the US Navy has been included in tables, appearing in a column immediately to the right of the commissioning date. The following abbreviations are used to indicate fleet assignments:

AA	Active, Atlantic Fleet
Active	Active under charter with MSC
AR	In reserve, out of commission, Atlantic Fleet
ASA	Active, in service, Atlantic Fleet
ASR	In reserve, out of service, Atlantic Fleet
BLDG	Building
CONV	Ship undergoing conversion
LOAN	Ship or craft loaned to another government, or non-government agency, but US Navy retains title and the ship or craft is on the NVR
MAR	In reserve, out of commission, Atlantic Fleet and laid up in the temporary custody of the Maritime Administration
MPR	Same as MAR, but applies to the Pacific Fleet
NRF	Assigned to the Naval Reserves Force (ships so assigned are listed in a special table, at the end of each major category, that indicates NRF home port, date assigned to NRF and which ship, if any, it replaced)
ORD	The contract for the construction of the ship has been let but construction has not yet begun
PA	Active, Pacific Fleet
PR	In reserve, out of commission, Pacific Fleet
Proj	The ship is scheduled for construction at some time in the immediate future
PSA	Active, in service, Pacific Fleet
PSR	In reserve, out of service, Pacific Fleet
RDF	Active, Rapid Deployment Force
TAA	Active, Military Sealift Command, Atlantic Fleet
TAR	In ready reserve, Military Sealift Command, Atlantic Fleet
TPA	Active, Military Sealift Command, Pacific Fleet
TPR	In ready reserve, Military Sealift Command, Pacific Fleet
TWWR	Active, Military Sealift Command, worldwide routes

Definitions

In commission: As a rule any ship, except a service craft, that is active is in commission. The ship has a commanding officer and flies a commissioning pennant. "Commissioning date" means the date of being "in commission" rather than "completion" or "acceptance into service," as used in some other navies.

In service: All service craft (dry docks and those with classifications that start with "Y"), with the exception of *Constitution*, that are active are "in service". The ship has an officer-in-charge and does not fly a commissioning pennant.

Ships "in reserve, out of commission" or "in reserve, out of service" are in a state of preservation for future service. Depending on the size of the ship or craft, a ship in mothballs usually takes from 30 days to nearly a year to restore to full operational service.

The above does not apply to Military Sealift Command.

The totals given at the head of each class table indicate the number of units of the class in the following categories: in service; building or ordered; projected. Thus, for example, there are 24 *Los Angeles*-class SSNs in service, 16 building or ordered, and 31 projected.

SUBMARINES

Strategic Missile Submarines (SSBN)

In anticipation of the commissioning of the first *Trident* SSBN, three *George Washington*-class and *Ethan Allen*-class SSBNs were reclassified SSNs while two of the *George Washington* class were decommissioned for ultimate disposal. Thus the 1975 force of 41 Polaris/Poseidon-armed SSBNs has been reduced to 31 Poseidon/Trident-armed SSBNs. To put it another way, today there are 544 Poseidon/Trident missiles in service, compared with 656 missiles some six years ago. This has caused much concern among Navy planning staffs, as delays on the Trident project make it unlikely that this shortfall will be made up in the near future. The *Ohio*, the first Trident submarine, was finally commissioned some 40 months behind schedule, with no firm deployment date in sight.

SSBNs were originally named after famous Americans, but subsequently Latin American and Hawaiian notables have been honoured, the term "American" having been expanded to include citizens of the whole Western Hemisphere. Two are named after Europeans who aided America in the War of Independence. The names of the Trident submarines honour the States of the Union. The departure is not surprising, as there are several cases in which name categories have been changed in mid-stream.

The Trident submarine project was initiated to upgrade and modernise the US SSBN force as well as to replace the fast-ageing Polaris-armed boats. However, delays have resulted in the block obsolescence of the *George Washington* and *Ethan Allen* classes, making it impossible to implement the original gradual phase-in/phase-out policy. The Trident construction programme at General Dynamics has proved to be disastrous, prompting the Navy to consider reactivating the submarine construction facilities at Portsmouth Naval Shipyard, Kittery, Me, and Mare Island Naval Shipyard, Vallejo, Calif, at a cost of between $150 and $200 million for each yard. This would take the pressure off General Dynamics and, in part, Newport News Shipbuilding, enabling General Dynamics to catch up and set itself in order, and freeing it to concentrate more on the Trident project, a high national defence priority. However, in January 1982 the Secretary of the Navy decided to terminate any further consideration of this matter. It is unfortunate that a company that was once the leading submarine builder of the United States slipped from its formerly high standards to the point of shoddy workmanship, poor quality and plain mismanagement. However, in fairness to General Dynamics, one question has to be asked: where were the Navy's inspectors when all this was going on?

James Monroe (SSBN-622) at sea in August 1969

As an alternative to Trident, design studies for a smaller SSBN have been resumed. Called SSBNX, this project was allocated $13 million in the FY-1979 budget and a similar sum in the FY-1980 budget. In the FY-1981 budget it received $12.6 million, and $80.9 million in FY-1982. Three alternatives to the existing Trident boats are currently being considered: first, a re-engined Trident boat; second, an entirely new design with 24 tubes the same size as those on the current Trident craft; and third and less favoured, the *Los Angeles*-class design with a missile section inserted, as in the case of the *Skipjack*/*George Washington* classes.

Type: Ballistic Missile Submarines (SSBN) *Number/Class:* 3+7+(15) Ohio

Name	Number	Laid down	Launched	Commissioned	Status
Ohio	SSBN-726	10 Apr 1976	7 Apr 1979	11 Nov 1981	PA
Michigan	SSBN-727	4 Apr 1977	26 Apr 1980	11 Sept 1982	PA
Florida	SSBN-728	9 Jun 1977	14 Nov 1981	18 June 1983	PA
Georgia	SSBN-729	7 Apr 1979	6 Nov 1982		BLDG
Rhode Island	SSBN-730	19 Jan 1981			BLDG
Alabama	SSBN-731	27 Aug 1981			BLDG
	SSBN-732				ORD
	SSBN-733				ORD
	SSBN-734				ORD
	SSBN-735				ORD

Builder General Dynamics Corp, Groton, Conn
Displacement surface, 16,600 tons; submerged, 18,700 tons
Length overall 560ft (170.7m)
Maximum beam 42ft (12.8m)
Maximum draught 35.5ft (10.8m)
Main machinery One pressurised water-cooled reactor (General Electric S8G). Two Westinghouse geared turbines
Screws/s.h.p. 1/60,000
Maximum speed surface, 23 knots+; submerged, 35 knots+
Armament 24 tubes for Trident C-4 (UGM-96A) MIRV missiles with 4,000-mile+ range. Four 21in bow torpedo tubes (Mk 68)
Complement 16 officers and 117 enlisted men. Operated by two crews

These are the largest Western submarines ever built. They exceed most World War Two heavy cruisers in displacement, and were designed (SCB-304) to replace the *George Washington* and *Ethan Allen*-class ships on a one-for-two basis. The *Ohio*s are built by the modular technique, to facilitate modernisation and/or conversion. At least 25 of this class are planned.

Ohio was originally assigned the hull number SSBN-711, but on 21 February 1974 it was reclassified SSBN-1. However, sanity prevailed and *Ohio* was again reclassified, to SSBN-726, on 10 April 1974. The hull number designations are reserved en bloc, SSBN-726/749. These ships owe their size to the large S8G reactor plant specially designed to power them. The core life of the reactors is about nine years. The *Ohio*s will have a quieter propulsion system than the *Benjamin Franklin/Lafayette* classes, a higher at-sea/in-port ratio, and greater systems reliability.

Ohio was designed to handle Trident I (C-4) and Trident II (D-5) missiles. The greater number of missiles and their longer range increases the submarine's effective operating area, creating more difficulties for the Soviet ASW measures. Each Trident carries 14 multiple re-entry vehicle (MIRV) warheads, allowing 14 targets to be hit by one missile.

The cost of these submarines has escalated. Nearly $912 million was requested for SSBN-733 under FY-1979. Lead item funding alone for SSBN-734 was $274.8 million. $1,543.9 million, for the construction of SSBN-735, was approved in the FY-1983 programme. Construction problems have plagued the Trident submarine programme, and it has been far from successful. Of 36,149 welds in *Ohio*, 26 per cent (2,772) were found not to have inspection records and had to be re-inspected. Of that number 33 per cent had to be re-welded. Faulty rotors also had to be replaced. As a result of these and other shortcomings, the Navy initially refused to award General Dynamics construction of SSBN-734, and is now considering alternative platforms for the Trident D-5 missile. The present programme might be curtailed as a result. A "stretched" SSN-688 design has been considered, but might not be the best solution.

Ohio (SSBN-726) on sea trials in 1981. This boat and her sisters will replace the *George Washington* and *Ethan Allen* classes one for one and then initially supplement the *Lafayette* and *Benjamin Franklin* classes (*General Dynamics*)

Type: Ballistic Missile Submarines (SSBN) — *Number/Class:* 12 *Benjamin Franklin*

Name	Number	Laid down	Launched	Commissioned	Status
Benjamin Franklin	SSBN-640	25 May 1963	5 Dec 1964	22 Oct 1965	AA
Simon Bolivar	SSBN-641	17 Apr 1963	22 Aug 1964	29 Oct 1965	AA
Kamehameha	SSBN-642	2 May 1963	16 Jan 1965	10 Dec 1965	AA
George Bancroft	SSBN-643	24 Aug 1963	20 Mar 1965	22 Jan 1966	AA
Lewis and Clark	SSBN-644	29 July 1963	21 Nov 1964	22 Dec 1965	AA
James K. Polk	SSBN-645	23 Nov 1963	22 May 1965	16 Apr 1966	AA
George C. Marshall	SSBN-654	2 Mar 1964	21 May 1965	29 Apr 1966	AA
Henry L. Stimson	SSBN-655	4 Apr 1964	13 Nov 1965	20 Aug 1966	AA
George Washington Carver	SSBN-656	24 Aug 1964	14 Aug 1965	15 June 1966	AA
Francis Scott Key	SSBN-657	5 Dec 1964	23 Apr 1966	3 Dec 1966	AA
Mariano C. Vallejo	SSBN-658	7 July 1964	23 Oct 1965	16 Dec 1966	AA
Will Rogers	SSBN-659	20 Mar 1965	21 July 1966	1 Apr 1967	AA

Builders Newport News SB and DD, Newport News, Va (SSBN-641, -644, -654, -656). Mare Island Naval Shipyard (SSBN-642, -658). General Dynamics Corp, Groton, Conn (SSBN-640, -643, -645, -655, -657, -659)
Displacement surface, 7,250 tons; submerged, 8,250 tons
Length overall 425ft (129.5m)
Maximum beam 33ft (10.1m)
Maximum draught 31.5ft (9.6m)
Main machinery One pressurised water-cooled reactor (Westinghouse S5W). Two geared turbines: DeLaval, SSBN-654, -656; Westinghouse, SSBN-641, -644, -655, -657/659; General Electric, SSBN-640, -642, -643, -645
Screws/s.h.p. 1/15,000
Maximum speed surface 20 knots; submerged, 30 knots+
Armament 16 tubes for Poseidon C-3/Trident I C-4 missiles, with 2,900/4,000-mile+ range. Four 21-in bow torpedo tubes (Mk 65)
Complement 20 officers and 148 enlisted men. Operated by two crews

Built to the same design (SCB-216) as the *Lafayette* class, this class has quieter machinery and a larger crew. Except for minor differences, this class and the *Lafayettes* are identical. SSBN-640/645 were authorised under the FY-1963 construction programme. SSBN-654/659 were authorised under FY-1964. Additional units were cancelled.

Originally armed with Polaris A-3 missiles, the *Benjamin Franklins* were converted to the Poseidon missile system. This necessitated removal of a missile tube liner to allow for the larger missile's greater circumference. The conversion data for this class has been combined into one table and placed in the *Lafayette* class section.

SSBNs are readily identified from SSNs by the "hump" in the hull extension to house the missile tubes. Ballistic missile submarines are unique in being the only USN vessels to operate with two crews, designated "Blue" and "Gold". "Blue" crew remains on shore when "Gold" is at sea in a 60-day patrol, and *vice versa*. Each submarine is fitted with three ship's inertial navigational systems (SINS) and a navigational satellite receiver.

Type: Ballistic Missile Submarines (SSBN) — *Number/Class:* 19 *Lafayette*

Name	Number	Laid down	Launched	Commissioned	Status
Lafayette	SSBN-616	17 Jan 1961	8 May 1962	23 Apr 1963	AA
Alexander Hamilton	SSBN-617	26 June 1961	18 Aug 1962	27 June 1963	AA
Andrew Jackson	SSBN-619	26 Apr 1961	15 Sept 1962	3 July 1963	AA
John Adams	SSBN-620	19 May 1961	12 Jan 1963	12 May 1964	AA
James Monroe	SSBN-622	31 July 1961	4 Aug 1962	7 Dec 1963	AA
Nathan Hale	SSBN-623	2 Oct 1961	12 Jan 1963	23 Nov 1963	AA
Woodrow Wilson	SSBN-624	13 Sept 1961	22 Feb 1963	27 Dec 1963	AA
Henry Clay	SSBN-625	23 Oct 1961	30 Nov 1962	20 Feb 1964	AA
Daniel Webster	SSBN-626	28 Dec 1961	27 Apr 1963	9 Apr 1964	AA
James Madison	SSBN-627	5 March 1962	15 March 1963	28 July 1964	AA
Tecumseh	SSBN-628	1 June 1962	22 June 1963	29 May 1964	AA
Daniel Boone	SSBN-629	6 Feb 1962	22 June 1963	23 April 1964	AA
John C. Calhoun	SSBN-630	4 June 1962	22 June 1963	15 Sept 1964	AA
Ulysses S. Grant	SSBN-631	18 Aug 1962	2 Nov 1963	17 July 1964	AA
Von Steuben	SSBN-632	4 Sept 1962	18 Oct 1963	30 Sept 1964	AA
Casimir Pulaski	SSBN-633	12 Jan 1963	1 Feb 1964	14 Aug 1964	AA
Stonewall Jackson	SSBN-634	4 July 1962	30 Nov 1963	26 Aug 1964	AA
Sam Rayburn	SSBN-635	3 Dec 1962	20 Dec 1963	2 Dec 1964	AA
Nathanael Greene	SSBN-636	21 May 1962	12 May 1964	19 Dec 1964	AA

Builders General Dynamics Corp, Groton, Conn (SSBN-616, -617, -623, -626, -628, -631, -633). Mare Island Naval Shipyard (SSBN-620, -636). Newport News SB and DD Co, Newport News, Va (SSBN-622, -625, -627, -630, -632, -635)
Displacement surface, 7,250 tons; submerged, 8,250 tons
Length overall 425ft (129.5m)
Maximum beam 33ft (10.1m)
Maximum draught 31.5ft (9.6m)
Main machinery One pressurised water-cooled reactor (Westinghouse S5W). Two geared turbines: DeLaval, SSBN-623, -635; Westinghouse, SSBN-622, -625/628, -631, -633; General Electric, SSBN-616, -617, -619, -620, -623, -624, -629, -630, -634, -636
Screws/s.h.p. 1/15,000
Maximum speed surface, 20 knots; submerged, 30 knots+
Armament 16 tubes for Poseidon C-3 Trident I C-4 missiles, with 2,900/4,000-mile+ range. Four 21in bow torpedo tubes (Mk 65)
Complement 14 officers and 126 enlisted men. Operated by two crews

James Madison (SSBN-627) after her Trident conversion

This class was built to SCB-216 design. They were made larger mainly to make them more habitable, a vital factor on long undersea patrols. The design also included improved machinery and a larger crew. Each ship cost approximately $190.5 million to build. SSBN-616, -617, -619 and -620 were authorised under FY-1961, while SSBN-622/636 were authorised under the FY-1961 supplement.

Bow planes were installed on SSBN-626 for evaluation of their effect on depth control at periscope levels. Although the planes were successful, no other ships of this class were so fitted. All SSBNs have emergency diesels, batteries, and snorkles.

The first eight ships of this class were originally armed with Polaris A-2 missiles, and the remaining ships had Polaris A-3. SSBN-620 and 622/625 were re-armed with A-3s in 1968/1970. Subsequently, all were modified to take the Poseidon C-3 (UGM-73).

Poseidon conversions

SSBN	FY/SCB	Converting yard	Assigned awarded	Conversion begun	Conversion completed
-616	73/355	General Dynamics	15 Oct 1972	15 Oct 1972	7 Nov 1974
-617	73/355	Newport News	15 Jan 1973	15 Jan 1973	11 Apr 1975
-619	73/355	General Dynamics	15 Mar 1973	19 Mar 1973	15 Aug 1975
-620	74/355	Portsmouth Naval	1 Feb 1974	1 Feb 1974	15 Apr 1976
-622	75/355	Newport News	24 Dec 1974	15 Jan 1975	14 May 1977
-623	73/355	Puget Sound Naval Shipyard	15 June 1973	15 June 1973	27 June 1975
-624	74/355	Newport News	28 Sept 1973	1 Oct 1973	23 Oct 1975
-625	75/355	Portsmouth Naval	31 Mar 1975	29 Apr 1975	29 July 1977
-626	76/355	General Dynamics	24 Nov 1975	1 Dec 1975	21 Feb 1978
-627	68/353	General Dynamics	17 Nov 1967	3 Feb 1969	28 June 1970
-628	70/353	Newport News	6 Jan 1969	10 Nov 1969	18 Feb 1971
-629	68/353	Newport News	19 Apr 1968	11 May 1969	11 Aug 1970
-630	69/353	Mare Island Naval Shipyard	23 June 1969	4 Aug 1969	22 Feb 1971
-631	70/353	Puget Sound Naval Shipyard	6 Oct 1969	3 Oct 1969	16 Dec 1970
-632	69/353	General Dynamics	8 July 1969	11 July 1969	19 Nov 1970
-633	70/353	General Dynamics	2 Jan 1970	10 Jan 1970	30 Apr 1971
-634	71/353	General Dynamics	14 July 1970	15 July 1970	29 Oct 1971
-635	70/353	Portsmouth Naval	18 Feb 1970	19 Jan 1970	2 Sept 1971
-636	71/353	Newport News	21 July 1970	22 July 1970	21 Sept 1971
-640	71/353	General Dynamics	24 Feb 1971	25 Feb 1971	15 May 1972
-641	71/353	Newport News	12 Feb 1971	15 Feb 1971	12 May 1972
-642	72/353	General Dynamics	12 July 1971	15 July 1971	27 Oct 1972
-643	71/353	Portsmouth Naval	21 Jan 1971	28 Apr 1971	31 July 1972
-644	71/353	Puget Sound Naval Shipyard	28 Jan 1971	30 Apr 1971	21 July 1972
-645	72/353	Newport News	16 July 1971	15 July 1971	17 Nov 1972
-654	72/353	Puget Sound Naval Shipyard	15 Aug 1971	14 Sept 1971	8 Feb 1973
-655	72/353	Newport News	12 Nov 1971	15 Nov 1971	22 Mar 1973
-656	72/353	General Dynamics	11 Nov 1971	12 Nov 1971	7 Apr 1973
-657	72/353	Puget Sound Naval Shipyard	27 Dec 1971	20 Feb 1972	17 May 1973
-658	73/353	Newport News	18 Aug 1972	21 Aug 1972	19 Dec 1973
-659	73/353	Portsmouth Naval Shipyard	18 Sept 1972	10 Oct 1972	8 Feb 1974

A total of twelve units of this and the *Benjamin Franklin* classes were converted to the Trident C-4 (UGM-96) missile system. Some conversions were taken in hand during regular overhaul and refuelling yard periods; the remaining ships were modified during a tender availability period, using a conversion package.

Trident missile conversion schedule

SSBN	Programme	Conversion location	Started	Completed
-627	FY-1979	Newport News SB & DD Co	3 Aug 1979	9 Feb 1982
-629	FY-1980	Norfolk Naval Shipyard	3 Apr 1980	30 May 1980
-630	FY-1980	Norfolk Naval Shipyard	30 June 1980	26 Aug 1980
-632	FY-1980	Newport News SB & DD Co	13 Jan 1980	28 May 1982
-633	FY-1980	Newport News SB & DD Co	1 July 1980	10 Dec 1982
-634	FY-1982	Norfolk Naval Shipyard	8 Sept 1981	6 Nov 1982
-640	FY-1980	Portsmouth Naval Shipyard	12 Nov 1979	18 Sept 1981
-641	FY-1979	Portsmouth Naval Shipyard	2 Mar 1979	28 Dec 1980
-643	FY-1980	Portsmouth Naval Shipyard	1 June 1980	5 Mar 1982
-655	FY-1980	Norfolk Naval Shipyard	4 Dec 1979	7 Feb 1980
-657	FY-1979	Norfolk Naval Shipyard	24 Sept 1978	4 Dec 1978
-658	FY-1979	Norfolk Naval Shipyard	3 Sept 1979	5 Nov 1979

Some SSBNs were/are being retrofitted during a special refit period, while others are in the process of being, or were backfitted, during a regularly scheduled overhaul. Conversion is completed when sea and missile firings are satisfactory.

Submarines (SSN/SS/SSAG)

Tautog, an early example of the *Sturgeon* class

In 1975, 82 submarines were on the Navy List (76 SSN/SS, one SSG, two LPSS, three AGSS). Active craft comprised 74 SSN/SS, one LPSS and three AGSS. In reserve were two SSN, one SSG and one LPSS. In addition, 26 SSNs were under construction and nine more projected. An all-nuclear-powered attack submarine force is nearly achieved. Only five conventionally powered submarines remained active, none have been built in more than 22 years, and, despite some Congressional pressure, it is unlikely that any will ever be built again.

In 1982 98 submarines were on the Navy List (91 SSN, including ten ex-SSBNs; five SS, one SSAG, one AGSS). Of these 85 SSN, five SS, one SSAG and one AGSS were active. In reserve were five SSN and one SS. In addition, 20 SSNs were under construction and at least 38 are projected between now and FY-1987.

The Carter Administration Force Level objective for attack submarines was 90. The Reagan Administration increased this number to 100, primarily of the *Los Angeles* and *Sturgeon* classes. In the FY-1982 Amendment to the construction programme, two *Los Angeles* units (*vice* one) were requested at a cost of $1.277 billion (*vice* $576 million). The Programmes for the years FY-1983 through FY-1987 call for the construction of 19 units at a cost per unit of between $670 million and $875 million. The last five-year shipbuilding programme in the Carter Administration (FY-1982/1986) for the *Los Angeles* class ships, compared with the Reagan Administration five-year programme (FY-1983/FY-1987), is as follows:

Carter/Reagan

FY-1982	1/2	**FY-1985**	1/4
FY-1983	1/3	**FY-1986**	3/4
FY-1984	1/4	**FY-1987**	-/4

Carter total = 6 units; Reagan total = 21 units.

The Reagan Administration is relying heavily on the *Los Angeles* class to reach its ultimate SSN force level of 100 ships. But it has hit an early snag with the problems at the Groton Shipyard (see *Los Angeles* section), and the plan will remain in jeopardy unless the problems resolved promptly, because Newport News is the only other shipyard capable of building submarines.

A cheaper, but marginally less capable alternative to the *Los Angeles* "boats", called "the Fast Attack Submarine (nuclear-powered) (FA-SSN)" and derisively known as "Fat Albert" was just another Carter Administration project that foundered. It failed to survive the FY-1981 budget Congressional scrutiny and was formally cancelled by the Reagan Administration. However, alternative studies to the *Los Angeles* class continue in the research and development stage.

Type: Submarines (nuclear-powered) (SSN) *Number/Class:* 24 + 16 + (31) *Los Angeles*

Name	*Number*	*Laid down*	*Launched*	*Commissioned*	*Status*
Los Angeles	SSN-688	8 Jan 1972	6 Apr 1974	13 Nov 1976	PA
Baton Rouge	SSN-689	18 Nov 1972	26 Mar 1975	25 June 1977	AA
Philadelphia	SSN-690	12 Aug 1972	19 Oct 1974	25 June 1977	AA
Memphis	SSN-691	23 June 1973	3 Apr 1976	14 Dec 1977	AA
Omaha	SSN-692	27 Jan 1973	21 Feb 1976	11 Mar 1978	PA
Cincinnati	SSN-693	6 Apr 1974	19 Feb 1977	10 June 1978	AA
Groton	SSN-694	3 Aug 1973	9 Oct 1976	8 July 1978	AA
Birmingham	SSN-695	26 Apr 1975	29 Oct 1977	16 Dec 1978	AA
New York City	SSN-696	15 Dec 1973	18 June 1977	3 Mar 1979	PA
Indianapolis	SSN-697	19 Oct 1974	30 July 1977	5 Jan 1980	PA
Bremerton	SSN-698	8 May 1976	22 July 1978	28 Mar 1981	PA
Jacksonville	SSN-699	21 Feb 1976	18 Nov 1978	16 May 1981	AA
Dallas	SSN-700	9 Oct 1976	28 Apr 1979	18 July 1981	AA
La Jolla	SSN-701	16 Oct 1976	11 Aug 1979	24 Oct 1981	PA
Phoenix	SSN-702	30 July 1977	8 Dec 1979	19 Dec 1981	AA
Boston	SSN-703	11 Aug 1978	19 Apr 1980	30 Jan 1982	AA
Baltimore	SSN-704	21 May 1979	13 Dec 1980	24 July 1982	AA
City of Corpus Christi	SSN-705	4 Sept 1979	25 Apr 1981	8 Jan 1983	AA
Albuquerque	SSN-706	27 Dec 1979	13 Mar 1982	21 May 1983	AA
Portsmouth	SSN-707	8 May 1980	18 Sept 1982		BLDG
Minneapolis-Saint Paul	SSN-708	20 Jan 1981	19 Mar 1983		BLDG
Hyman G. Rickover	SSN-709	23 July 1981			BLDG
	SSN-710	1 Apr 1982			BLDG
San Francisco	SSN-711	26 May 1977	27 Oct 1979	24 Apr 1981	PA
Atlanta	SSN-712	17 Aug 1978	16 Aug 1980	6 Mar 1981	AA
Houston	SSN-713	29 Jan 1979	21 Mar 1981	25 Sept 1982	AA
Norfolk	SSN-714	1 Aug 1979	31 Oct 1981	21 May 1983	AA
Buffalo	SSN-715	25 Jan 1980	8 May 1982	17 Sept 1983	AA
Salt Lake City	SSN-716	26 Aug 1980	16 Oct 1982		BLDG
Olympia	SSN-717	31 Mar 1981	30 Apr 1983		BLDG
	SSN-718	10 Nov 1981			BLDG
	SSN-719	9 Oct 1982			BLDG
	SSN-720				BLDG
	SSN-721				ORD
	SSN-722				ORD
	SSN-723				ORD
	SSN-724				ORD
	SSN-725				ORD
Newport News	SSN-750				ORD
	SSN-751				ORD
	SSN-752				ORD

Los Angeles (SSN-688) on sea trials in September 1976. Her wake reveals that she is under full power *(US Navy)*

Builders General Dynamics Corp, Groton, Conn (SSN-690, -692, -694, -696/710, -719, -720, -724/725, -751/752). Newport News SB and DD Co, Newport News, Va (remainder)
Displacement surface, 5,723 tons; submerged, 6,927 tons
Length overall 360ft (109.7m)
Maximum beam 33ft (10.1m)
Maximum draught 32.3ft (9.8m)
Main machinery One pressurised water-cooled reactor, S6G (General Electric). Two General Electric geared turbines
Screws/s.h.p. 1/35,000
Maximum speed surface 20 knots+; submerged, 32 knots+
Armament Four 21in amidships torpedo tubes for Subroc, Harpoon missiles and Mark 48 ASW torpedoes
Complement 12 officers and 115 enlisted men

The detailed design contract (SCB-303) for the *Los Angeles* class, and construction of the lead ship, was awarded to Newport News. These submarines were designed for maximum speed and stealth, and dive deeper than any previous USN submarines. Authorised as follows: FY-1970 (SSN-688/690); FY-1971 (SSN-691/694); FY-1972 (SSN-695/699); FY-1973 (SSN-700/705); FY-1974 (SSN-706/710); FY-1975 (SSN-711/713); FY-1976 (SSN-714, -715); FY-1977 (SSN-716/718); FY-1978 (SSN-719); FY-1979 (SSN-720); FY-1980 (SSN-721, -722); FY-1981 (SSN-723, -724); FY-1982 (SSN-725, -750); FY-1983 (SSN-751, -752). Cost of each FY-1983 unit is set at $1,420.2 million.

The S6G reactor is a modified version of the D2G installed in *Bainbridge* (CG-25). Its cores are estimated to last ten years.

Trials of *Los Angeles* have proved the success of this design, but soaring construction costs are slowing Congressional approval for additional submarines and increasing Congressional insistence upon a cheaper design. Since FY-1976, the cost per ship has averaged $221 million, but the costs of the two FY-1981 units will be $991.7 million.

Strikes, and some anticipated problems at Newport News, delayed completion of *Los Angeles*, which took five years from keel laying to completion. While construction at this yard goes well, the same cannot be said with regard to General Dynamics, where the programme is in increasing difficulty. Of 17,792 welds in *Bremerton* (SSN-698), 45 per cent had no inspection records and had to be re-inspected. Of those 2,802 (27 per cent) had to be re-welded. Moreover, it was discovered that the wrong steel was used in current and earlier submarines at Groton. Even though it had the correct strength code, the steel accepted from the founder did not have the proper structural strength. An alert workman discovered the improperly coded steel, which had been used on all *Ohio*-class submarines and all SSNs then under construction. Five ships already in commission had diving restrictions placed upon them until they could be inspected. Maximum diving depth is 1,476ft (450m).

Each unit of this class is equipped with BQQ-5 sonar, BQS-15 towed-array sonar and SSN-688-699 only) Mark 113, Mod 10 torpedo/missile fire-control system; subsequent units have the Mk 117, which will soon replace the Mk 113 in SSN-688-699. Each unit also has BPS-15 radar.

All ships of this class will carry the Tomahawk cruise missile system. SSN-688/720 will carry 12 missiles as part of the torpedo load, and SSN-721 onwards will be fitted with a vertical launch system launcher, between the outer hull and the pressure hull, to carry 15 missiles.

Owing to outside pressure, the name of SSN-705 was changed from *Corpus Christi* to *City of Corpus Christi* on 10 May, 1982. The protests centred on the fact that *Corpus Christi* meant "the body of Christ" and the protesters thought it improper to so name a weapon of war.

San Francisco (SSN-711) departing the James River, Virginia, for sea trials on 15 March 1981. Note the raised search periscope *(US Navy)*

Type: Submarine (nuclear-powered) (SSN) — *Number/Class:* 1 *Glenard P. Lipscomb*

Name	Number	Laid down	Launched	Commissioned	Status
Glenard P. Lipscomb	SSN-685	5 June 1971	4 Aug 1973	21 Dec 1974	AA

Builder General Dynamics Corp, Groton, Conn.
Displacement surface, 5,813 tons; submerged, 6,480 tons
Length overall 365ft (111.3m)
Maximum beam 31.6ft (9.6m)
Maximum draught 31ft (9.5m)
Main machinery One pressurised water-cooled reactor, S5Wa (Westinghouse). Two General Electric turbo-electric drive
Screws/s.h.p. 1/12,000
Maximum speed surface, 20 knots+ submerged, 25 knots+
Armament Four 21in amidships torpedo tubes for Subroc, Harpoon missiles (not yet fitted) and Mark 48 ASW torpedoes
Complement 12 officers and 108 enlisted men

Another step towards the quiet submarine, this experimental design (SCB-302) has turbo-electric rather than geared drive. Authorised in the FY-1968 Programme, the purpose was to test advanced silencing techniques for super-quiet operations. The propulsion is more advanced than that of *Tullibee* (SSN-597). While it is quieter than geared-turbine submarines, the turbo-electric drive submarine (TEDS) is also slower, but geared turbines are noisier. Another disadvantage is that the TE plant is larger and heavier. Other silencing techniques were incorporated into this design to test various concepts, including quieter machinery throughout. Successful features which do not affect speed were incorporated into the *Los Angeles* design. *Glenard P. Lipscomb*, sometimes referred to as "Lipscomb Fish", has full combat capabilities.

The craft is fitted with the Mark 113, Mod 14 torpedo/missile fire control system, soon to be replaced by the Mark 117, Mod 3 system, and will be retrofitted with the Tomahawk cruise missile system.

November 1974 view of *Glenard P. Lipscomb* (SSN-685). Nicknamed the "Lipscomb Fish," this single unit was built to test advanced silencing techniques. She retains full combat capability *(US Navy)*

Type: Submarine (nuclear-powered) (SSN) *Number/Class:* 1 *Narwhal*

Name	Number	Laid down	Launched	Commissioned	Status
Narwhal	SSN-671	17 Jan 1966	9 Sept 1967	12 July 1969	AA

Narwhal (SSN-671), another single unit. Built to test an improved propulsion system incorporating a natural-circulation reactor, she too retains full combat capability *(US Navy)*

Builder General Dynamics Corp, Groton, Conn
Displacement surface, 4,749 tons; submerged, 5,350 tons
Length overall 314.6ft (95.9m)
Maximum beam 33ft (10.1m)
Maximum draught 27ft (8.2m)
Main machinery One pressurised water-cooled reactor, S5G, (General Electric). One General Electric geared turbine
Screws/s.h.p. 1/17,000
Maximum speed surface, 20 knots+; submerged, 30 knots+
Armament Four 21in amidships torpedo tubes for Subroc and ASW torpedoes (Harpoon missile system to be fitted)
Complement 12 officers and 95 enlisted men

Authorised in the FY-1964 Programme, this ship is quite similar (SCB-245) to the *Sturgeon* class submarines. The improved propulsion system is equipped with a natural circulation reactor. Primary coolant pumps come second to steam turbines as the noisiest component of a pressurised water propulsion system, and their elimination results in noise reduction. The removal of associated equipment and wiring offers simplicity and precious space.

Narwhal's bow was designed to house long-range sonar, with its optimum performance. For underwater ice work, *Narwhal* is fitted with BQQ-2 sonar (BQS-6 active, BQR-7 passive), BQS-8 upward-looking sonar and the Mark 117, Mod 3 torpedo/missile fire-control system. It will be retrofitted with the Tomahawk cruise missile system.

Type: Submarines (nuclear-powered) (SSN) *Number/Class:* 37 *Sturgeon*

Name	*Number*	*Laid down*	*Launched*	*Commissioned*	*Status*
Sturgeon	SSN-637	10 Aug 1963	26 Feb 1966	3 Mar 1967	AA
Whale	SSN-638	27 May 1964	14 Oct 1966	12 Oct 1968	AA
Tautog	SSN-639	27 Jan 1964	15 Apr 1967	17 Aug 1968	PA
Grayling	SSN-646	12 May 1964	22 June 1967	11 Oct 1969	AA
Pogy	SSN-647	5 May 1964	3 June 1967	15 May 1971	PA
Aspro	SSN-648	23 Nov 1963	29 Nov 1967	20 Feb 1969	PA
Sunfish	SSN-649	15 Jan 1965	14 Oct 1966	15 Mar 1969	AA
Pargo	SSN-650	3 June 1964	17 Sept 1966	5 Jan 1968	AA
Queenfish	SSN-651	11 May 1964	25 Feb 1966	6 Dec 1966	PA
Puffer	SSN-652	8 Feb 1965	30 Mar 1968	9 Aug 1969	PA
Ray	SSN-653	4 Jan 1965	21 June 1966	12 Apr 1967	AA
Sand Lance	SSN-660	15 Jan 1965	11 Nov 1969	25 Sept 1971	AA
Lapon	SSN-661	26 July 1965	16 Dec 1966	14 Dec 1967	AA
Gurnard	SSN-662	22 Dec 1964	20 May 1967	6 Dec 1968	PA
Hammerhead	SSN-663	29 Nov 1965	14 Apr 1967	28 June 1968	AA
Sea Devil	SSN-664	12 Apr 1966	5 Oct 1967	30 Jan 1969	AA
Guitarro	SSN-665	9 Dec 1965	27 July 1968	9 Sept 1972	PA
Hawkbill	SSN-666	12 Sept 1966	12 Apr 1969	4 Feb 1971	PA
Bergall	SSN-667	16 Apr 1966	17 Feb 1968	13 June 1969	AA
Spadefish	SSN-668	21 Dec 1966	15 May 1968	14 Aug 1969	AA
Seahorse	SSN-669	13 Aug 1966	15 June 1968	19 Sept 1969	AA
Finback	SSN-670	26 June 1967	7 Dec 1968	4 Feb 1970	AA
Pintado	SSN-672	27 Oct 1967	16 Aug 1969	11 Sept 1971	PA
Flying Fish	SSN-673	30 June 1967	17 May 1969	29 Apr 1970	AA
Trepang	SSN-674	28 Oct 1967	27 Sept 1969	14 Aug 1970	AA
Bluefish	SSN-675	13 Mar 1968	10 Jan 1970	8 Jan 1971	AA
Billfish	SSN-676	20 Sept 1968	1 May 1970	12 Mar 1971	AA
Drum	SSN-677	20 Aug 1968	23 May 1970	15 Apr 1972	PA
Archerfish	SSN-678	19 June 1969	16 Jan 1971	17 Dec 1971	AA
Silversides	SSN-679	28 Nov 1969	4 June 1971	5 May 1972	AA
William H. Bates	SSN-680	24 Nov 1969	11 Dec 1971	5 May 1973	AA
Batfish	SSN-681	9 Feb 1970	9 Oct 1971	1 Sept 1972	PA
Tunny	SSN-682	22 May 1970	10 June 1972	26 Jan 1974	PA
Parche	SSN-683	10 Dec 1970	13 Jan 1973	17 Aug 1974	PA
Cavalla	SSN-684	4 June 1970	19 Feb 1972	9 Feb 1973	AA
L. Mendel Rivers	SSN-686	26 June 1971	2 June 1973	1 Feb 1975	AA
Richard B. Russell	SSN-687	19 Oct 1971	12 Jan 1974	16 Aug 1975	AA

Richard P. Russell (SSN-687). The extension at the bottom of the after end of the sail houses the prototype of the Bustle emergency communications buoy *(US Navy)*

Pintado, seen in March 1977 during trials with the DSRV-2 experimental submarine rescue craft off the coast of California. The white trim on the sail and diving planes is luminous, helping the DSRV crew to see the mother ship when operating at great depths *(US Navy)*

Builders General Dynamics Corp, Groton, Conn (SSN-637, -650, -667, -669, -673/676, -678, -679, -681, -684). General Dynamics Corp, Quincy, Mass (SSN-638, -649). Ingalls Shipbuilding Div, Pascagoula, Miss (SSN-639, -648, -652, -680, -682, -683). Portsmouth Naval Shipyard, Kittery, Me (SSN-646, -660). Newport News SB and DD Co, Newport News, Va (SSN-651, -653, -661, -663, -664, -668, -670, -686, -687). Mare Island Naval Shipyard, Vallejo, Cal (SSN-662, -665, -666, -672, -677)
Displacement surface, 3,640 tons; submerged, 4,640 tons
Length overall 301ft (91.7m) (SSN-677/684, -686, -687); 292.25ft (89m) (remaining)
Maximum beam 31.6ft (9.6m)
Maximum draught 26ft (7.9m) (SSN-672/684, -686, -687); 30ft (9.1m) (SSN-661); 28.75ft (8.8m) (remainder)
Main machinery One pressurised water-cooled reactor, S5W (Westinghouse). Two geared turbines: Westinghouse (SSN-639, -651, -653); General Electric (SSN-647/649, -652, -672/682, -684); DeLaval (remainder)
Screws/s.h.p. 1/15,000
Maximum speed surface, 20 knots+; submerged, 30 knots+
Armament Four 21in amidships torpedo tubes for four Subroc, 15 Mark 48 ASW torpedoes and four Harpoon missiles (Harpoon not in SSN-637, -647, -650, -651, -653, -661, 664, 666, -671, 674/678, -680). 12 total Tomahawk cruise missiles carried (except SSN-637, -647, -650, -651, -653, -661, -664, -666, -674/678, -680: none)
Complement 12 officers and 95 enlisted men

◀ *Hammerhead* in June 1968 *(US Navy)*

The *Sturgeons* (SCB-188A) are basically a modified *Thresher* class design with Subsafe features included. Authorisations were as follows: FY-1962 (SSN-637/639), FY-1963 (SSN-646/653), FY-1964 (SSN-660/664), FY-1965 (SSN-665/670), FY-1966 (SSN-672/677), FY-1967 (SSN-678/682), FY-1968 (SSN-683, -684), FY-1969 (SSN-686, -687).

To improve control at periscope depth, the diving planes are positioned lower on the sail. This feature, combined with the taller sails, makes this class easily recognised from previous SSNs.

Although these ships have the same propulsion system as the *Thresher* and *Skipjack* classes, they are slower because of their increased size. To accommodate the extra electronic and sonar gear, SSN-678/684, -686 and -687 are 10ft (3.1m) longer than their sisters. Because the *Sturgeon*s have highly sophisticated sonars and other electronics housed in the specially designed bow, the torpedo tubes are located amidships rather than in the traditional bow position. All carry BPS-14 search radar and will be fitted or are fitted with Mark 117, Mod 3 torpedo/missile fire-control system. They also carry BQQ-2 sonar and BQS-12 (on first 16 boats) or BQS-13 active/passive sonars. BQS-8 sonar, intended for under-ice navigation, is also carried by each boat. As each unit enters overhaul the BQQ-2 sonar is replaced with the more modern BQQ-5.

SSN-680 was originally named *Redfish*, but was renamed on 25 June 1971. Construction of *Pogy* began at New York Shipbuilding Corp., Camden, New Jersey, where it was launched. The contract, awarded on 23 March, 1963, was cancelled on 5 June, 1967, when the shipyard closed down. In January 1968 *Pogy* was towed from the Philadelphia Naval Shipyard to Ingalls Shipbuilding for completion.

On 15 May, 1969, while being outfitted at Mare Island Naval Shipyard, *Guitarro* sank pier-side in 35ft (10.7m) of water; she was raised on 19 May. Her completion was delayed 28 months by repairs and replacement of the heavily damaged electronics and electrical gear. Damage was estimated at $25 million. The court of inquiry's official verdict attributed the sinking to negligence, but in reality it was the result of inexcusable carelessness, a comedy of errors which caused the ship to sink while workers were at lunch.

SSN-666 and -670 are fitted as mother ships for the DSRV vehicle. While submerged, the mother-ship can launch the 50ft rescue submersible from the after deck and recover it. Combat capabilities of these submarines are not affected (see Service Craft for further details on the DSRV). *Guitarro* served as test ship for the encapsulated Tomahawk cruise missile system.

Type: Submarines (nuclear-powered) (SSN) — **Number/Class:** 5 Ethan Allen

Name	Number	Laid down	Launched	Commissioned	Status
Ethan Allen	SSN-608	14 Sept 1959	22 Nov 1960	8 Aug 1961	PA
Sam Houston	SSN-609	28 Dec 1959	2 Feb 1961	6 Mar 1962	PA
Thomas A. Edison	SSN-610	15 Mar 1960	15 June 1961	10 Mar 1962	PA
John Marshall	SSN-611	4 Apr 1960	15 July 1961	21 May 1962	AA
Thomas Jefferson	SSN-618	3 Feb 1961	24 Feb 1962	4 Jan 1963	AA

Antenna/periscope layout of *Thomas Jefferson* (SSBN-618), photographed the day after she was commissioned. Most of the systems identified here have probably since been replaced with newer equipment

Ethan Allen (SSN-608) in her days as an SSBN. She was the first true US SSBN to be built, the *George Washington* class being *Skipjack*-class SSN conversions *(General Dynamics)*

Builders General Dynamics Corp, Groton, Conn (SSN-608, -610). Newport News SB and DD Co, Newport News, Va (SSN-609, -611, -618)
Displacement: surface, 6,955 tons; submerged, 7,880 tons (as SSBN)
Length overall 410.42ft (125.1m)
Maximum beam 33ft (10.1m)
Maximum draught 32ft (9.8m)
Main machinery One pressurised water-cooled reactor, S5W (Westinghouse). Two General Electric geared turbines (SSN-608/610); Westinghouse (SSN-611, -618)
Screws/s.h.p. 1/15,000
Maximum speed surface, 20 knots; submerged, 30 knots+
Armament Four 21in bow torpedo tubes
Complement 15 officers and 127 enlisted men

Displacement data as SSBN

These were the first SSBNs designed as such from the keel up (SCB-180). A modified *Thresher* (SSN-593) class design, they have quieter machinery and deeper diving capabilities than the *George Washington* class. The first four ships were authorised under FY-1959 and SSN-618 under FY-1961.

As SSBNs, the *Ethan Allen*s were originally armed with Polaris A-2 (UGM-27B) missiles of 1,700-mile range. They were later modified to handle 2,500-mile range. Polaris A-3 (UGM-27C) missiles. All were fitted with the Mark 112, Mod 2 torpedo fire control system.

As SSBNs, each boat made its last strategic deployment during 1980/1981. They are now being converted to serve as SSNs in secondary roles such as ASW training, to replace SSNs like those of the *Sturgeon* class.

Conversion to the SSN role is more extensive than in the *George Washington* class survivors, which were refuelled with long-life cores and overhauled. However, their duties will be similar to those of the other class (see *George Washington* class for modifications and roles). All are fitted with the Mark 112, Mod 2 torpedo fire control system. SSN-608/610 are assigned to Submarine Squadron 17 at Bangor, Washington. *Ethan Allen* is scheduled to decommission in March 1983, when her missile compartment will be removed (see *George Washington* class for details).

SSBN-608 was reclassified SSN on 1 September, 1980, followed by SSBN-610 to SSN on 6 October, 1980, SSBN-609 on 10 November, 1980, SSBN-618 on 11 March, 1981, and SSBN-611 to SSN on 1 May, 1981.

Type: Submarines (nuclear-powered) (SSN) — *Number/Class:* 3 George Washington

Name	Number	Laid down	Launched	Commissioned	Status
George Washington	SSN-598	1 Nov 1957	9 June 1959	30 Dec 1959	PA
Patrick Henry	SSN-599	27 May 1958	22 Sept 1959	9 Apr 1960	PA
Robert E. Lee	SSN-601	25 Aug 1958	18 Dec 1959	16 Sept 1960	PA

Builders General Dynamics Corp, Groton, Conn (SSN-598, -599). Newport News SB and DD Co, Newport News, Va (SSN-601)
Displacement surface, 6,019 tons; submerged, 6,888 tons as SSBN
Length overall 381.67ft (116.3m)
Maximum beam 33ft (10.1m)
Maximum draught 29ft (8.8m)
Main machinery One pressurised water-cooled reactor, S5W (Westinghouse). Two General Electric geared turbines
Screws/s.h.p. 1/15,000
Maximum speed surface, 20 knots+; submerged, 30 knots+
Armament Six 21in bow torpedo tubes
Complement 12 officers and 100 enlisted men

The first two boats were originally authorised as *Skipjack* SSNs, and *George Washington* was originally laid down as *Scorpion* (SSN-589). This class was re-ordered as SSGNs under the SCB-180A design, the modification requiring that SSN-589 be cut in two and a 117ft (35.7m) missile section be added. SSN-589/591 and a third unnamed unit were reclassified to SSGN-598/600 on 8 April, 1958, and again reclassified on 26 June, 1958, to SSBN. The name *Scorpion* was cancelled on 1 April, 1958, and the name *George Washington* was assigned on 6 November, 1958.

These ships were authorised under the FY-1958 Supplement to the new construction programme. The original Polaris A-1 (UGM-27A) missiles were replaced with Polaris A-3 (UGM-27C) missiles during various overhaul periods. Also, the compressed air ejection system was replaced with the gas-steam ejection system.

Submarines *ex-Theodore Roosevelt* (SSBN-600) and *Abraham Lincoln* (SSBN-602) of this class were decommissioned at Bremerton on 28 February, 1981, following the removal of their missile compartments (frames M18 through M43). This was done by cutting the compartment into 40 segments during two separate periods. The after and forward ends were then welded together. These two boats were laid up because they needed refuelling. Both are to be stricken and sunk at sea. The remaining units of the class were retained because they still had at least three years' worth of fuel left. The FY-1981 budget contains funds to convert the surviving ships of this class and the five *Ethan Allens* to SSNs at a cost of about $400,000 each.

SSN conversion includes the removal of associated Polaris electronics and one SINS. The subs will then be used as training submarines, for ASW exercises for other secondary duties. SSBN-598, -599 and -601 were reclassified to SSN on 20 November, 1981, 24 October, 1981, and 1 March, 1982, respectively. *Patrick Henry* and *Robert E. Lee* are scheduled to be decommissioned in September 1983 and sunk at sea after the removal of their missile compartments. The name of SSBN-600 was cancelled on 3 November, 1981, and reassigned to CVN-71 of the *Nimitz* class.

On 9 April, 1981, *George Washington* was cruising at shallow depth in the East China Sea, 100 miles south-southwest of Sasebo, Japan. She made sonar contact with the 2,350-ton Japanese cargo ship, *Nissho Maru*, but it was too late to avoid impact. The submarine surfaced about five minutes later to offer assistance. Fog and rain made visibility poor, and the merchant ship could not be seen. Although the submarine called in an American search aircraft to help out, nothing was seen. *George Washington* then proceeded on her course, unaware that the small ship had been fatally damaged and had sunk in 15 min, taking two of her 15-man crew with her. Survivors were rescued by a Japanese destroyer which happened to be in the area 18 hr later. Damage to the submarine was minor, being limited to a 4ft-square section of its conning tower. There was no damage to the *Polaris* missiles or the nuclear power plant. The USA investigated the matter, relieving the commanding officer of his command because of "lack of command supervision and sound judgement by a member of the US Navy Service", and extended to Japan their deep regrets and profound apologies.

Robert E. Lee (SSBN-601) concluded the final Polaris patrol on 1 October, 1982, at Apra Harbor, Guam.

Type: Submarine (nuclear-powered) (SSN) — *Number/Class:* 1 Tullibee

Name	Number	Laid down	Launched	Commissioned	Status
Tullibee	SSN-597	26 May 1958	27 Apr 1960	9 Sept 1960	AA

Builder General Dynamic Corp, Groton, Conn
Displacement surface, 2,317 tons; submerged, 2,640 tons
Length overall 273ft (83.2m)
Maximum beam 23.3ft (7.1m)
Maximum draught 21ft (6.4m)
Main machinery One pressurised water-cooled reactor, S2C (Combustion Engineering Company). Two Westinghouse turbo-electric drive
Screws/s.h.p. 1/2,500
Maximum speed surface, 15 knots+; submerged, 20 knots+
Armament Four 21in amidships torpedo tubes for Mark 44 and anti-submarine torpedoes
Complement 6 officers and 50 enlisted men

Tullibee is a small, compact-designed submarine (SCB-178) built specifically for anti-submarine warfare. Authorised in the FY-1958 construction programme, it was laid down as SSKN-597, but was reclassified SSN on 15 August, 1959. The hull is of a modified, elongated teardrop shape. In the search for a "quiet" submarine, *Tullibee* is the first to have turbo-electric drive. The bow section houses hydrophones and sonar transducers, and the craft is fitted with a BQQ-2 sonar system and a Mark 112, Mod 3 missile fire-control system. BQG-4 passive sonar is also fitted.

October 1960 view of *Tullibee* (SSN-597). Her configuration has remained unchanged since this photograph was taken *(US Navy)*

Type: Submarines (nuclear-powered) (SSN) *Number/Class:* 13 *Thresher*

Name	*Number*	*Laid down*	*Launched*	*Commissioned*	*Status*
Permit	SSN-594	16 July 1959	1 July 1961	29 May 1962	PA
Plunger	SSN-595	2 Mar 1960	9 Dec 1961	21 Nov 1962	PA
Barb	SSN-596	9 Nov 1959	12 Feb 1962	24 Aug 1963	PA
Pollack	SSN-603	14 Mar 1960	17 Mar 1962	26 May 1964	PA
Haddo	SSN-604	9 Sept 1960	18 Aug 1962	16 Dec 1964	PA
Jack	SSN-605	16 Sept 1960	24 Apr 1963	31 Mar 1967	AA
Tinosa	SSN-606	24 Nov 1959	9 Dec 1961	17 Oct 1964	AA
Dace	SSN-607	6 June 1960	18 Aug 1962	4 Apr 1964	AA
Guardfish	SSN-612	13 Feb 1961	15 May 1965	20 Dec 1966	PA
Flasher	SSN-613	14 Apr 1961	22 June 1963	22 July 1966	PA
Greenling	SSN-614	15 Aug 1961	4 Apr 1964	3 Nov 1967	AA
Gato	SSN-615	15 Dec 1961	14 May 1964	25 Jan 1968	AA
Haddock	SSN-621	24 Apr 1961	21 May 1966	22 Dec 1967	PA

Pollack (SSN-603) seen in February 1964. The periscope-like unit in the leading edge of the "sail" is in fact a snorkel

Builders Portsmouth Naval Shipyard, Kittery, Me (SSN-605, -606). Mare Island Naval Shipyard, Vallejo, Cal (SSN-594, -595). Ingalls Shipbuilding Div, Pascagoula, Miss (SSN-596, -607, -621). New York Shipbuilding Corp, Camden, N.J. (SSN-603, -604, -612). General Dynamics Corp, Quincy, Mass (SSN-613). General Dynamics Corp, Groton, Conn (SSN-614, -615)
Displacement surface, 3,800 tons (SSN-613/615); 3,750 tons (remainder). Submerged, 4,470 tons (SSN-605); 4,242 tons (SSN-613/615); 4,300 tons (remainder)
Length overall 295.6ft (90.1m) (SSN-605); 292.17ft (89.1m) (SSN-613/615); 278.5ft (84.9m) (remainder)
Maximum beam 31.6ft (9.6m)
Maximum draught 28.42ft (8.7m)
Main machinery One pressurised water-cooled reactor, S5W (Westinghouse). Two geared turbines; DeLaval (SSN-606, -613/615), Westinghouse (SSN-594/596, -607, -621), General Electric (remaining)
Screws/s.h.p. 1/15,000
Maximum speed surface, 20 knots+; submerged, 35 knots+
Armament Four 21in amdiships torpedo tubes for Subroc, Harpoon missiles (SSN-594, -603, -621 only) and anti-submarine torpedoes
Complement 12 officers and 91 enlisted men

These ships are improved *Skipjacks*, designed (SCB-188) as highly manoeuvrable deep-diving attack submarines with a modified teardrop hull. They have greater depth capability than previous submarines, and were the first to combine Subroc anti-submarine capability with the BQQ-2 sonar system. Following the loss of leadship *Thresher* (SSN-593), the construction programme was delayed to incorporate Subsafe features and other improvements. Authorised as follows: FY-1957 (SSN-593); FY-1958 (SSN-594/596); FY-1959 (SSN-603/607); FY-1960 (SSN-612/615); FY-1961 (SSN-621). All are fitted with the BQQ-2 and BQR-7 sonar systems and the Mark 113 torpedo/missile fire-control systems with the exception of SSN-594, -595, -603, -607 and -621, which are fitted with Mark 117 fire-control systems. The remaining units of the class are to receive the Mark 117 system as a replacement for the Mark 113.

SSN-595, originally named *Pollack*, was renamed *Plunger* on 23 July, 1959. SSN-596 was originally named *Plunger*, but was renamed *Pollack* on 28 April, 1959, and again changed on 23 July, 1959, to *Barb*. SSN-603 was originally named *Barb*, but was renamed *Pollack* on 23 July, 1959. The reason for this name game is not known.

SSN-594, -595, and -603 were projected as a second class of SSGNs (see photograph of model). SSN-607 was to be first of a third SSGN class (SCB-166A). The entire SSGN construction programme was cancelled when the Regulus II programme was superceded by the Polaris missile programme. All of these ships were reclassified as SSNs on 21 September, 1959.

SSN-614 and -615 were launched by Groton and towed to the Quincy yard for completion. The later ships of this class have a taller sail. SSN-613/615 were modified (SCB-188M) from the original design and have longer hulls, because a 13.75ft (4.2m) section was added to correct a stability problem caused by weight growth.

On 10 April, 1963, *Thresher* (SSN-593) was engaged in deep diving tests, about 200 miles off the northeast coast of New England, when she was lost with all hands in 8,400ft of water (112 crew and 17 civilian technicians).

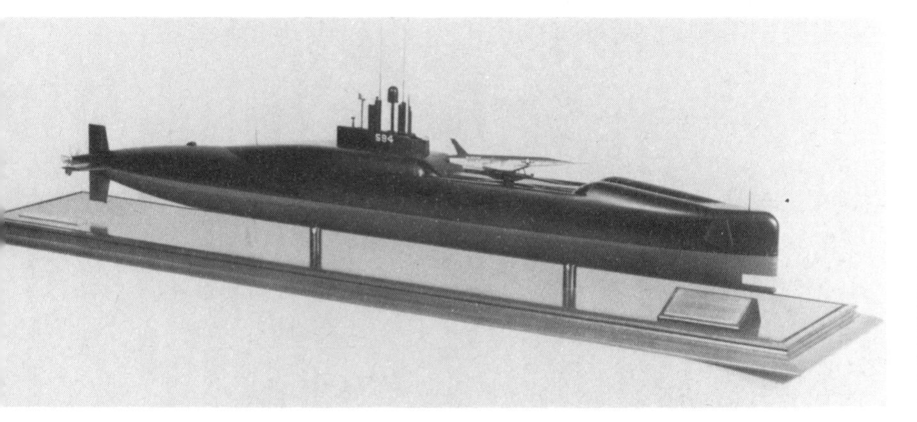

Model of *Permit* (SSN-594) in her originally designed SSGN configuration. *Plunger* (SSGN-595) and *Pollack* (SSGN-603) were to look like this, while *Dace* (SSGN-607) was to have been an improved version. Construction of the boats as SSGNs was halted when Polaris superseded Regulus, they were completed as SSNs *(US Navy)*

Type: Submarine (nuclear-powered) (SSN) *Number/Class:* 1 *Halibut*

Name	*Number*	*Laid down*	*Launched*	*Commissioned*	*Status*
Halibut	SSN-587	11 Apr 1957	9 Jan 1959	4 Jan 1960	PR

Builder Mare Island, Naval Shipyard, San Francisco, California
Displacement surface, 3,915 tons; submerged, 4,895 tons
Length overall 350ft (106.7m)
Maximum beam 29.53ft (9.01m)
Maximum draught 21.42ft (16.52m)
Main machinery One pressurised water-cooled reactor, S3W (Westinghouse). Two Westinghouse geared turbines
Screws/s.h.p. 2/6,600
Maximum speed surface, 15 knots+; submerged, 20 knots+
Armament Six 21in torpedo tubes: 4 bow (Mark 61), 2 stern (Mark 62)
Complement 10 officers and 88 enlisted men

Authorised in the FY-1956 construction programme, *Halibut* was the first submarine designed (SCB-137A) from the keel up as a missile submarine. Four near-sisters (SSGN-594, -595, -603 and -607) were completed as *Thresher*-class SSNs. Construction cost of this ship was approximately $45 million. Although it was originally planned for diesel electric propulsion (SSG), the Navy decided that *Halibut* would have nuclear propulsion.

The primary design target for this ship was to produce a stable, surface-launching, missile platform. Speed and manoeuvrability were secondary. *Halibut* was originally armed with a Regulus launcher and carried two Regulus II or five Regulus I missiles. The large missile hangar faired into the bow was almost as large as a First World War submarine. The last Regulus mission was in 1964, when the programme was terminated. Missile equipment was removed in 1965. Regulus II was a subsonic cruise missile of 1,000-mile range with a nuclear warhead. Regulus I had a little more than half that range.

Halibut was reclassified from SSGN to SSN on 15 August, 1965. As she lacked the speed and manoeuvrability of an attack submarine, her large missile compartment made her most suitable for underwater projects. After the missile equipment was removed *Halibut* was equipped to test the 50ft Deep Submergence Rescue Vehicle (DSRV), and participated in other underwater experiments. A BQS-4 sonar system is fitted.

Halibut was decommissioned at Mare Island on 30 June, 1976, and laid up at Bremerton. She is scheduled to be stricken and sunk at sea.

Halibut (SSN-587) off Hawaii in June 1968. Originally armed with Regulus, she was the only one of five planned SSGNs to be completed. The Regulus programme was terminated in 1964 and she was employed on experimental projects until decommissioned on 30 June 1976 *(US Navy)*

Type: Submarine (nuclear-powered) (SSN) *Number/Class:* 1 *Triton*

Name	Number	Laid down	Launched	Commissioned	Status
Triton	SSN-586	29 May 1956	19 Aug 1958	10 Nov 1959	AR

Until the advent of the *Ohio*-class SSBNs *Triton* was the largest submarine in the world. Originally commissioned as a radar picket submarine (note the scanner-shaped opening in the top of the sail), she became a white elephant when the Navy abandoned the SSR/SSRN concept

Builder General Dynamics Corp, Groton, Conn
Displacement surface, 5,939 tons; submerged, 6,670 tons
Length overall 447.42ft (136.4m)
Maximum beam 36.92ft (11.3m)
Maximum draught 23.83ft (7.26m)
Main machinery Two pressurised water-cooled reactors, S4G (General Electric). Two General Electric geared turbines
Screws/s.h.p. 2/34,000
Maximum speed surface, 20 knots+; submerged, 28 knots+
Armament Six 21in torpedo tubes (4 bow, 2 stern, all Mark 60)
Complement 14 officers and 156 enlisted men

Triton was authorised in the FY-1956 construction programme (SCB-132), and construction cost about $109 million. Commissioned as SSRN-586, *Triton* was for many years the world's longest submarine, until the *Ohio* class SSBNs appeared, and is the only USN submarine with two nuclear reactors.

Designed as a radar picket submarine, this ship had sufficient speed to keep up with carrier forces. She had high surface speed and good seakeeping qualities. *Triton* featured a bulbous bow, but no vertical tail fin, and was fitted with an elaborate CIC and a large radar antenna which retracted into the sail structure.

When the Navy abandoned the SSR/SSRN concept, *Triton* was reclassified SSN on 1 March, 1961. During overhaul and refuelling from July 1962 to March 1964, the extensive radar installation was largely removed. The actual conversion to SSN was made at that time.

The proposed conversion of this submarine to an underwater command ship was dropped owing to the lack of funds and technical problems. Since no logical mission seemed to exist for her, she was decommissioned at New London on 3 May, 1969, and laid up at Norfolk.

Triton achieved two firsts: she was the first submarine to circumnavigate the globe underwater, and she was also the first nuclear submarine in the world to be laid up in reserve. She is now scheduled to be disposed of by scuttling at sea.

A BQS-4 sonar system and a Mark 101, Mod 11 torpedo fire control system were fitted.

Type: Submarines (nuclear-powered) (SSN) — *Number/Class:* 5 *Skipjack*

Name	*Number*	*Laid down*	*Launched*	*Commissioned*	*Status*
Skipjack	SSN-585	29 May 1956	26 May 1958	15 Apr 1959	PA
Scamp	SSN-588	23 Jan 1959	8 Oct 1960	5 June 1961	AA
Sculpin	SSN-590	3 Feb 1958	31 Mar 1960	1 June 1961	PA
Shark	SSN-591	24 Feb 1958	16 Mar 1960	9 Feb 1961	AA
Snook	SSN-592	7 Apr 1958	31 Oct 1960	24 Oct 1961	AA

Builders General Dynamics Corp, Groton, Conn (SSN-585). Mare Island Naval Shipyard, Mare Island, Cal (SSN-588). Ingalls Shipbuilding, Pascagoula, Miss (SSN-590, -592). Newport News SB and DD Co, Newport News, Va (SSN-591)
Displacement surface, 3,075 tons; submerged, 3,513 tons
Length overall 251.73ft (76.73m)
Maximum beam 31.58 ft (9.63m)
Maximum draught 29.42ft (8.97m)
Main machinery One pressurised water-cooled reactor, S5W (Westinghouse). Two geared turbines; Westinghouse (SSN-585), General Electric (remainder)
Screws/s.h.p. 1/15,000
Maximum speed surface, 16 knots+; submerged, 30 knots+
Armament Six 21in bow torpedo (Mark 59) tubes for anti-submarine torpedoes
Complement 8 officers and 85 enlisted men

Built primarily for anti-submarine work, the *Skipjack* design (SCB-154) was very much influenced by the sustained endurance of the *Nautilus* and *Skate* classes and the high speed and manoeuvrability of *Albacore* (AGSS-569). *Skipjack* was authorised in FY-1956, and the remaining ships in FY-1957. Each submarine cost about $40 million, and they were the first submarines built by Newport News since before the Second World War. They were also USN's first high speed teardrop designed submarines. Diving planes are located on the sail structures to improve underwater manoeuvrability. The tapered sterns in this class preclude the traditional aft torpedo tubes. The successful S5W nuclear propulsion plant incorporated in most USN submarines was introduced in this class, which is fitted with a modified BQS-4 sonar system and the Mark 101, Mod. 17 torpedo fire control system.

The keel laying of *Scamp* was delayed when her materials were diverted to SSBN-599 construction. The keel for sister ship *Scorpion* was originally laid down on 1 November, 1957, but when nearing completion, she was redesignated SSBN-598 and renamed *George Washington*. She was then cut in two and lengthened 117ft (35.67m) to become the first ballistic missile submarine. The keel for a second *Scorpion* was laid on 20 August, 1958.

Scorpion (SSN-589), the sixth ship of this class, was last heard from on 21 May, 1968, when she had begun a routine Atlantic crossing while returning home from a Mediterranean deployment. After reporting that she was 27 miles off course and 40 miles behind schedule on her crossing, *Scorpion* was never heard from again. She was listed as "overdue and presumed lost with all hands" on 27 May, and officially declared lost, with her entire crew of 99 men, on 6 June, 1968. On 30 June that year, *Scorpion* was struck from the NVR. An intensive search by *Mizar* (AGOR-11) located her hull in 10,000ft (3,048m) of water about 400 miles southwest of Azores.

Study of the thousands of photographs taken by underwater cameras could not ascertain the reasons for her loss, but two possible causes were eliminated. First, she did not hit a sea mount; second, her loss was not due to the nuclear power plant. Human error also seems unlikely, since the crews of nuclear submarines are well trained. To this day, the cause is a mystery.

The 20-year-old *Scamp* and her sisters are still employed as front-line submarines *(US Navy)*

Type: Submarines (nuclear-powered) (SSN) — *Number/Class:* 4 *Skate*

Name	Number	Laid down	Launched	Commissioned	Status
Skate	SSN-578	21 July 1955	16 May 1957	23 Dec 1957	PA
Swordfish	SSN-579	25 Jan 1956	27 Aug 1957	15 Sept 1958	PA
Sargo	SSN-583	21 Feb 1956	10 Oct 1957	1 Oct 1958	PA
Seadragon	SSN-584	20 June 1956	16 Aug 1958	5 Dec 1959	PA

Builders General Dynamics Corp, Groton, Conn (SSN-578). Portsmouth Naval Shipyard, Kittery, Me (SSN-579, -584). Mare Island Naval Shipyard (SSN-583)
Displacement Surface, 2,360 tons (SSN-578); 2,547 tons (SSN-583, -584); 2,550 tons (SSN-579). Submerged, 2,861 tons
Length overall 267.7ft (81.5m)
Maximum beam 25ft (7.6m)
Maximum draught 22ft (6.7m)
Main machinery One pressurised water-cooled Westinghouse reactor (S3W, SSN-578, -583; S4W, SSN-579, -584)
Screws/s.h.p. 2/6,600
Maximum speed surface, 20 knots+; submerged, 25 knots+
Armament Eight 21in torpedo tubes (6 bow and 2 stern (short))
Complement 9/13 officers and 83/85 enlisted men

This class represents the first production design (SCB-121) SSNs. They have a modified *Guppy*-type hull design somewhat similar to, but smaller than, that of *Nautilus* (SSN-571) and *Seawolf* (SSN-575). The *Skates* have bow-mounted diving planes. They were authorised in construction programme FY-1955 (SSN-578, -579) and FY-1956 (SSN-583, -584). *Sargo* was first authorised as a diesel powered submarine, but was changed to nuclear propulsion in August 1955. *Seadragon* is scheduled to be decommissioned in September 1983 and laid up in reserve.

The propulsion system is an improved but simplified *Nautilus* type. Reactor arrangements differ within the class, but both power plants (S3W and S4W) have proved satisfactory. *Skate* steamed 120,862 miles before her first refuelling, in January 1961.

All are fitted with the Mark 101, Mod 19 torpedo fire-control system and BQS-4 sonar system.

Sargo (SSN-583) in the mid-1960s. The *Skate* class was the first SSN production series and the last to employ the old Fleet Boat/Guppy hull. Succeeding classes incorporated results from tests conducted by *Albacore* (AGSS-569)

Type: Submarine (nuclear-powered) (SSN) — *Number/Class:* 1 *Seawolf*

Name	Number	Laid down	Launched	Commissioned	Status
Seawolf	SSN-575	15 Sept 1953	21 July 1955	30 Mar 1957	PA

Builder General Dynamics Corp, Groton, Conn
Displacement surface, 3,765 tons; submerged, 4,399 tons
Length overall 337.5ft (102.9m)
Maximum beam 27.67ft (8.4m)
Maximum draught 23.17ft (7.1m)
Main machinery One pressurised water-cooled reactor, S2Wa (Westinghouse). Two General Electric geared turbines
Screws/s.h.p. 2/15,000
Maximum speed surface, 20 knots+; submerged, 20 knots+
Armament Six 21in bow torpedo tubes
Complement 11 officers and 90 enlisted men

A modified *Nautilus* design (SCB-64A), *Seawolf* was authorised in the FY-1952 construction programme. She was built with a competitive design reactor for testing against the *Nautilus* power plant. The original reactor was a General Electric liquid metal (sodium) SIR Mark II (later S2G) unit. After two years of operations on reduced power the plant was shut down when it was determined that it was impossible to prevent a sodium/potassium alloy from the reactor from entering the superheater steam piping. *Seawolf* was decommissioned on 12 December, 1958, while a water-cooled reactor (S2Wa), similar

to that in *Nautilus*, was installed. The ship was recommissioned on 30 September, 1960. The original reactor, replaced under the FY-1959 programme (SCB-648A), was cut up in 1960 and sunk in 6,000ft of water off the New England coast. *Seawolf* has mainly been assigned to research work since 1968. She is fitted with a BQS-4 sonar system and the Mark 101, Mod 8 torpedo fire-control system.

Seawolf (SSN-575) and *Nautilus* (SSN-571) in Groton, Conn, harbour together in the late 1950s. *Seawolf* has been used mainly as a research submarine since 1968 *(US Navy)*

Type: Submarine (nuclear-powered) (SSN) *Number/Class:* 1 Nautilus

Name	*Number*	*Laid down*	*Launched*	*Commissioned*	*Status*
Nautilus	SSN-571	14 June 1952	21 Jan 1954	30 Sept 1954	PR

Builder General Dynamics Corp, Groton, Conn
Displacement surface, 3,764 tons; submerged, 4,040 tons
Length overall 319.42ft (97.4m)
Maximum beam 27.67ft (8.43m)
Maximum draught 25.42ft (7.75m)
Main machinery One pressurised water-cooled reactor, S2W (Westinghouse). Two Westinghouse geared turbines (all inactivated)
Screws/s.h.p. 2/15,000
Maximum speed surface, 20 knots+; submerged, 23 knots+
Armament Six 21in bow torpedo tubes
Complement 2 officers and 24 enlisted men

The world's first nuclear powered vessel, *Nautilus* was authorised in the FY-1952 construction programme and was built to the SCB-64 design. She has a *Guppy*-type hull configuration. As an active unit she was fitted with a BQS-4 sonar system and Mark 106, Mod 13 torpedo fire control system.

In June 1948 Westinghouse began a reactor design under a Navy contract. Construction of *Nautilus*' prototype reactor was begun in Idaho in August 1950. It used pressurised water for heat transfer, which was to become the standard method in future ships. The original reactor was designated STR, but was later redesignated S2W.

It should be appreciated that no previous knowledge existed as far as the work with metals and the development of liquid metals were concerned. New techniques for welding were developed. The solving of the many technical problems which arose resulted in the world's first nuclear powered vessel, marking a revolution in undersea warfare.

Before the commissioning of *Nautilus*, submarines were really surface ships which could submerge for limited periods. The snorkel device was not needed on the new design, since oxygen for the crews was provided by a machine which extracted it from sea water while the ship was submerged. *Nautilus* was the Navy's first true submersible with virtually unlimited underwater endurance at high, sustained speed.

The later years of her useful life were spent as a research vessel. During the 1972/1974 overhaul period at Groton, *Nautilus* was modified for submarine communications research. After a successful career spanning more than 25 years, she was decommissioned at Mare Island on 3 March, 1980.

It was originally planned to preserve her as a memorial at the US Naval Academy. But when her scheduled decommissioning was announced, the Submarine Memorial Association of Groton, Connecticut, asked that they be granted custody of *Nautilus* for preservation at "her birthplace", alongside *Croaker* (SS-246). To settle the matter, the Secretary of the Navy announced on 30 October, 1979, that the Washington Navy Yard would be her final berthing place. However, in a blatantly political move, former President Carter overrode the Secretary and consigned *Nautilus* to the Submarine Association. *Nautilus* is being prepared for exhibition under the FY-1981 budget at a cost of $1.9 million. She will be towed to Groton in late 1984 or early 1985. Annual maintenance cost is estimated at $600,000. Official status of *Nautilus* as a memorial has not yet been determined.

Nautilus pictured at the beginning of her career (*General Dynamics*)

Type: Submarines (SS) *Number/Class:* 3 *Barbel*

Name	Number	Laid down	Launched	Commissioned	Status
Barbel	SS-580	18 May 1956	19 July 1958	17 Jan 1959	PA
Blueback	SS-581	15 Apr 1957	16 May 1959	15 Oct 1959	PA
Bonefish	SS-582	3 June 1957	22 Nov 1958	9 July 1959	PA

Builders Portsmouth Naval Shipyard, Kittery, Me (SS-580); Ingalls Shipbuilding Corp, Pascagoula, Miss (SS-581); New York Shipbuilding Corp, Camden, N.J. (SS-582)
Displacement surface, 1,744 tons; submerged, 2,146/2,320 tons
Length overall 219.17ft (66.8m)
Maximum beam 29ft (8.83m)
Maximum draught 27.92ft (8.51m)
Main machinery Three Fairbanks-Morse diesel engines, 1,600 s.h.p. each (surface). Two General Electric electric motors, 1,575 s.h.p. each (submerged)
Screws/s.h.p. surface, 1/4,800; submerged, 1/3,150
Maximum speed surface, 15 knots; submerged, 20.7 knots
Armament Six 21in bow torpedo tubes (Mark 58)
Complement 8 officers and 69 enlisted men

Authorised in the FY-1956 construction programme, these were the last diesel-powered attack submarines built for the US Navy. *Bonefish* and *Blueback* were the first submarines built by their respective shipyards. The *Barbel*s (SCB-150) have the highly manoeuvrable teardrop hull design proved so successfully by *Albacore* (AGSS-569). The diving planes, originally located on the bow, were later relocated to the sail structure. The BQS-4 sonar system and Mark 101, Mod 20 torpedo fire-control system are fitted.

Barbel (SS-580) and her sisters were intended to be the last diesel-powered submarines to be built for the US Navy. As a result of the increasingly high cost of SSNs, however, the Navy is now under pressure to resume construction of conventional boats. The German TR-2000 design has been suggested as a valuable basis for such a programme ▶

580
580
580

Type: Submarine (SS) — *Number/Class:* 1 *Darter*

Name	Number	Laid down	Launched	Commissioned	Status
Darter	SS-576	10 Nov 1954	28 May 1956	20 Oct 1956	PA

Builder Electric Boat Company, Groton, Conn
Displacement surface, 1,720 tons; submerged, 2,388 tons
Length overall 284.5ft (86.7m)
Maximum beam 27.25ft (8.3m)
Maximum draught 19ft (15.79m)
Main machinery Three Fairbanks-Morse diesel engines, 1,500 s.h.p. each (surface). Two Elliott electric motors, 1,600 s.h.p. each engine (submerged)
Screws/s.h.p. surface, 2/4,500; submerged, 2/3,200
Maximum speed surface, 19.5 knots; submerged, 14.3 knots
Armament Eight 21in torpedo tubes (6 bow and 2 stern)
Complement 8 officers and 75 enlisted men

Authorised in the FY-1954 construction programme, *Darter* was designed (SCB-116) to be an exceptionally quiet submarine with high submerged speed. Basically, she is an improved *Tang* with console controls, sound-proof engine room, and other material improvements. *Darter* was origianlly intended to be a unit of the *Grayback* class (SS-574), but *Grayback* and *Growler* (SS-577) of this class were re-ordered as SSGs. At Charleston Naval Shipyard in FY-1965, *Darter* was cut in half and a 16.5ft (5.02m) section was inserted. At the same time, her original diesel engines were replaced by an improved model. Although the design was considered successful, no other ships were built owing to the advent of nuclear propulsion and the teardrop hull configuration.

Darter is fitted with a BQG-4 sonar system and a Mark 106, Mod 11 torpedo fire-control system, and has been home-ported at Sasebo, Japan, since March 1979.

Darter (SS-576), showing her distinctive trio of sonar domes. The "E" above her hull number indicates that she has won a battle efficiency award. She is currently homeported at Sasebo, Japan

Type: Submarine (SS) — *Number/Class:* 1 *Grayback*

Name	Number	Laid down	Launched	Commissioned	Status
Grayback	SS-574	1 July 1954	2 July 1957	7 Mar 1958	PA

Builder Mare Island Naval Shipyard, Vallejo, Cal
Displacement surface, 2,670 tons; submerged, 3,650 tons
Length overall 334ft (101.8m)
Maximum beam 27.25ft (8.31m)
Maximum draught 19ft (5.79m)
Main machinery Three Fairbanks-Morse diesel engines for surface propulsion. Two Elliott electric motors for submerged propulsion
Screws/s.h.p. surface, 2/4,500; submerged, 2/5,500
Maximum speed surface, 20 knots; submerged, 16.7 knots
Armament Eight 21in torpedo tubes (6 bow, Mark 52, 2 stern)
Complement 12 officers and 77 enlisted men
Troops 7 officers and 60 enlisted men

Grayback and her sister *Growler* (SSG-577), were the first guided missile submarines to carry Regulus I and II surface-to-surface missiles. Authorised in the FY-1956 programme as *Darter* class units, they were reordered as SSGs under the SCB-161 design. Both ships were reclassified from SS and SSG on 24 July, 1956, the redesign increasing their length and displacement. The configuration was altered radically to accommodate the missile system, the ships being cut in two and lengthened by 50ft (15.24m). Two cylindrical hangars, each 11ft (3.35m) high and 70ft (21.3m) long, were built on the bows. A missile launcher was installed between the hangars and superstructure. When the Regulus missile system was made obsolete by the Polaris, *Grayback* and *Growler* were decommissioned at Mare Island on 25 May, 1964, and laid up.

Grayback was converted to an LPSS (originally APSS) under the FY-1965 programme (SCB-350). Conversion began on 7 November, 1967, and was completed on 21 August, 1969, after many delays resulting from her low priority. On 30 August, 1968, she was reclassified from SSG to LPSS. The missile hangars were divided into "wet" and "dry" compartments, separated by a pressure bulkhead, the hull was lengthened by 12ft (3.65m), and the sail structure was made higher. The boat can carry four swimmer delivery vehicles (SDV). Berthing and support equipment were incorporated, enabling the submarine to accommodate additional troops. As an LPSS, this ship carried USMC personnel (7 officers and 60 enlisted men), and attack submarine capabilities were retained. *Grayback* was recommissioned on 9 May, 1969. Conversion of sister ship *Growler* to LPSS was cancelled owing to the cost of converting *Grayback*.

On 30 June, 1975, *Grayback* was reclassified SS. This was an administrative change owing to funding support, and there were no changes in her configuration, capabilities, or mission. She is fitted with BQS-2 and 4 (PUFFS) sonar systems, and the Mark 106, Mod. 12 fire control system.

Growler (SSG-577) was stricken from the Navy List on 1 August, 1980, and is to be sunk as a target.

Grayback (SS-574) seen in June 1969 during sea trials after her transport submarine conversion. Along with *Darter* and *Growler*, she was initially designed as a conventional attack submarine before being rearranged for Regulus missile duties. The large compartment on the bow, which originally housed the missiles, now accommodates the swimmer gear, delivery vehicles and other equipment associated with Seal diving teams *(US Navy)*

Type: Submarines (SS/SSAG) *Number/Class:* 3 *Tang*

Name	Number	Laid down	Launched	Commissioned	Status
Wahoo	SS-565	24 Oct 1949	16 Oct 1951	30 May 1952	AR
(Trout)	SS-566	1 Dec 1949	21 Aug 1951	27 June 1952	(see notes)
Gudgeon	SSAG-567	20 May 1950	11 June 1952	21 Nov 1952	PA

Builders Portsmouth Naval Shipyard, Kittery, Me (SS-565 and SSAG-567); Electric Boat Co, Groton, Conn (SS-566)
Displacement surface, 2,050 tons; submerged, 2,700 tons
Length overall 283ft (86.25m) (SSAG-567); 277ft (84.42m) (remainder)
Maximum beam 27.25ft (8.31m)
Maximum draught 19ft (5.79m)
Main machinery Three Fairbanks-Morse diesel engines, 1,500 s.h.p. each (surface). Two electric motors for submerged propulsion, 1,600 s.h.p. each (General Electric, SS-565, -566; Westinghouse, SSAG-567)
Screws/s.h.p. surface, 2/4,500; submerged, 2/3,200
Maximum speed surface, 15.5 knots; submerged, 18.3 knots
Armament Eight 21in torpedo tubes (6 bow, 2 stern)
Complement 8 officers and 75 enlisted men

The *Tang*s were originally built as a class of six (SS-563-568). SS-565 was authorised under the FY-1948 programme and SS-566 and SSAG-567 under FY-1949. They were built to an SCB-2A design as a *Guppy*-type fast attack submarine. These craft incorporated numerous improvements learned from trials with captured Second World War German U-boats. They were faster and more dependable, had greater endurance, manoeuvrability and flexibility, and were fitted with a better fire-control system than Second World War submarines. They were the first post-war submarines to be constructed.

The original overall length of these ships was 269.17ft (82.4m). Over the years, *Wahoo* and *Trout* have been lengthened to 277.2ft (84.4m), and *Gudgeon* to 283ft (82.3m). In FY-1957, *Trout* was lengthened by 9ft. And under the FRAM II programme, *Wahoo* and *Trout* were cut in two, a section removed, and a 15ft (4.6m) section was installed to accommodate new equipment. Their original engines, which had proved unsatisfactory, were replaced with the same units as in *Gudgeon*.

Gudgeon was reclassified to AGSS on 1 April, 1978, replacing *Tang* (AGSS-563) as an acoustic and research test ship. She was reclassified SSAG on 1 November, 1979. The difference between the SSAG and the AGSS is that the SSAG retains combat capability, while the AGSS does not. *Gudgeon* is to be stricken from the Naval Vessel Register in September 1983.

Trigger (SS-564) was stricken from the NVR on 10 July, 1973, and sold on the same date to Italy as *Livio Piomarta* (S-515), while *Harder* (SS-568) was struck on 20 February, 1974, and sold to Italy the same day as *Romeo Romei* (S-516).

Trout was struck from the NVR on 19 December, 1978, and sold on that date to Iran as *Kousseh* (S-101). She lay at New London in early 1979, with her Iranian crew undergoing training. One evening in March 1979, *Kousseh* lowered the flag at evening colours and posted the evening watch. Next morning, when guests arrived aboard, the quarterdeck and ultimately the whole boat was found to be abandoned. The entire crew had disappeared, taking their flag, bag and baggage with them. They simply melted into the American population, undoubtedly because they were afraid to return home. The submarine lay at New London until late 1979, when she was towed to Philadelphia and laid up. The US has been trying to find another customer. Inspection of the boat by one of the authors at Philadelphia in May 1981, showed that ex-*Trout* had a 6° list as a result of continuously taking on water. She was being kept afloat by the ship's pumps.

Wahoo was halfway through a two-year overhaul when her pending sale to Iran was cancelled on 31 March, 1979. The overhaul was stopped and she was decommissioned on 27 June, 1980, being laid up at Philadelphia in a somewhat dismantled state.

Tang (AGSS-563), the third submarine scheduled to be sold to Iran, had her sale cancelled on 3 February, 1979. She was then leased to Turkey on 8 February, 1980, as *Piri Reis* (S-343).

Gudgeon (SSAG-567) in 1977. Serving as an acoustic research vessel, she is the last active unit of her class. The notch in the after edge of her sail is for a yet to be installed snorkel, and the box on the deck aft of the sail is used in sound experiments. Her SSAG classification indicates that she retains full combat capability

Auxiliary Submarines (AGSS)

Dolphin (AGSS-555) is the only ship of this type in service. In 1970/1971, there were 24 auxiliary submarines. That number can be deceptive, for 18 were immobile hulks assigned to the Naval Reserve as dockside trainers. Of the six remaining, four were active in research projects and two were in reserve with diminished combat capability.

Type: Auxiliary, Research Submarine (AGSS) — *Number/Class:* 1 *Dolphin*

Name	*Number*	*Laid down*	*Launched*	*Commissioned*	*Status*
Dolphin	AGSS-555	9 Nov 1962	8 June 1968	17 Aug 1968	PA

Builder Portsmouth Naval Shipyard, Kittery, Maine
Displacement surface, 796 tons; submerged, 930 tons
Length overall 152ft (46.3m)
Maximum beam 19.3ft (5.9m)
Maximum draught 18ft (5.5m)
Main machinery Surface, two Detroit Model 12V7 diesel electric engines, 825 s.h.p. each. Submerged, one Ellicott Machine Corp. electric motor
Screws/s.h.p. surface, 1/1,650; submerged, 1/1,150
Maximum speed surface, 12 knots; submerged, 15 knots+
Armament None
Complement 7 officers and 15 enlisted men

Dolphin was authorised in the FY-1961 programme (SCB-207). She was designed as a deep-diving, molecular-powered research submarine to help develop larger, deep-diving combat submarines. Construction was not of the highest priority, hence the long construction time. Delays were also caused by changes in mission and equipment. Her hull number was taken from a block of hull numbers (SS-551/562) which had been authorised on 14 June, 1940, but cancelled on 26 March, 1945.

Dolphin has a constant-diameter cylindrical pressure hull fabricated from HY-80 steel and closed at both ends with hemispherical heads. Weight reductions in secondary structures were achieved by using aluminium and glassfibre. Improved rudder design is one of the features incorporated to provide manoeuvring control and hovering capability. No conventional diving planes are fitted. When submerged this ship is powered by silver-zinc batteries giving limited underwater endurance.

Dolphin is used for acoustic and oceanographic research as well as advanced weapons evaluation. She was originally armed with one experimental 21in torpedo tube for testing weapons at extreme depths. This was removed in 1970.

Albacore (AGSS-569), struck from the Navy List on 1 May, 1980, is to be preserved at Groton, Conn, with *Croaker* and *Nautilus*. *Albacore* was the prototype test vehicle for the optimum fully-submerged hull, while *Dolphin* was the analogous deep-diving boat.

AIRCRAFT CARRIERS

In 1975 there were 16 active carriers in the US Navy (including a training carrier rated as an Auxiliary), five in reserve and two under construction. Three of these ships have since been struck from the Naval Vessel Register. In 1982, there were 15 active carriers (including the training carrier) and five in reserve. One CVN was under construction, with two more projected in the FY-1983 budget request.

The aircraft carrier active force level has dropped from a high of 26 in 1962 to a low of 13 in 1982. However, of the currently active 14 ships, one unit (*Midway* and *Nimitz* classes not included) will always be undergoing a SLEP overhaul and a second will be undergoing a regular overhaul. Thus only 11 will be available at any one time. Current plans are to increase the current force level to 15 as soon as possible, and ultimately to 17. To achieve this, *Coral Sea* (CV-43) was being retained in the active fleet when *Carl Vinson* (CVN-70) commissioned, rather than being decommissioned, and *Lexington* (AVT-16) will continue in her role of training carrier until at least FY-1989.

As fleet carriers go, only two that are now in reserve are even marginally capable of operation as part of a carrier battle group. With sufficient funding (current estimate is $503 million for each hull, for reactivation alone), the Navy could modernise and activate either or both of these ships. This would give them another 10–15 years of useful life. Considering the condition of each, it seems that the *Bon Homme Richard* would be the first choice for reactivation, having had an overhaul and new flight deck a year before being laid up. For some reason, however, the Reagan Administration advocated reactivation of *Oriskany* in the FY-1981 supplemental budget. This was rejected by Congress because of unreliable cost estimates. It was reintroduced in the FY-1982 amended budget, but again rejected by Congress for the same reasons. It was planned to reintroduce the programme for a third time in the FY-1983 budget, but when that budget was submitted, in January 1982, there was no mention of this project.

Coral Sea (CV-43), *Mattaponi* (AO-41) (since stricken) and *Rowan* (DD-782) (since stricken) conducting underway replenishment operations in January 1965. Among the aircraft types visible on the *Coral Sea*'s deck are the F-4 Phantom, A-4 Skyhawk, A-3 Skywarrior, F-8 Crusader and A-1 Skyraider *(US Navy)*

Type: Multi-purpose Aircraft Carriers (nuclear-powered) (CVN) *Number/Class:* 3 + 3 *Nimitz*

Name	Number	Laid down	Launched	Commissioned	Status
Nimitz	CVN-68	22 June 1968	13 May 1972	3 May 1975	AA
Dwight D. Eisenhower	CVN-69	15 Aug 1970	11 Oct 1975	18 Oct 1977	AA
Carl Vinson	CVN-70	11 Oct 1975	15 Mar 1980	13 Mar 1982	PA
Theodore Roosevelt	CVN-71	31 Oct 1981			BLDG
	CVN-72				ORD
	CVN-73				ORD

Carl Vinson (CVN-70), latest of the *Nimitz* class to join the fleet. She is seen here in January 1982 during sea trials off Virginia. Note the Phalanx CIWS mounts on the sponsons just forward of the angled deck and at the stern *(US Navy)*

Builder Newport News SB and DD Co, Newport News, Va
Displacement standard, 81,600 tons; full load, 91,487 tons
Length overall 1,092ft (332m)
Maximum width hull, 134ft (40.8m); flight deck, 252ft (76.8m), 257ft (78.4m (CVN-71))
Maximum draught 37ft (11.3m)
Main machinery 2 pressurised water-cooled nuclear reactors, A4W/A1G (General Electric). 4 General Electric steam turbines
Screws/s.h.p. 4/280,000
Maximum speed 30 knots+
Aircraft 90+
Catapults 4 steam (C13-1)
Armament 3 BPDMS (Mark 25) Sea Sparrow missile launchers. (2) 40mm saluting guns
Complement Including the Air Wing assigned, 569 officers and 5,718 enlisted men

CVN-71 replaces two (later reduced to one) medium aircraft carriers (CVV) in the Carter Administration's construction programme. Long-lead items were originally requested under FY-1977, but when CVN-71 was originally cancelled the parts already bought were used as spares for CVN-68/70. Long-lead items for CVN-72/73 were included in the FY-1982 budget amendment, with funds approved for construction in FY-1983 at a total cost of $6,559.5 million. CVN-72 and -73 are scheduled to be completed in FY-1989 and 1991 respectively.

The *Nimitz*s resemble the *Kitty Hawk* class minus the stack. Their smaller superstructure is a result of the lack of fossil fuel stacks. These ships have four deck-edge elevators, arranged one to port and three to starboard, two of which are forward of the island.

CVN-69 was originally named *Eisenhower*, but was renamed on 25 May, 1970 to suit President Nixon, who named her *Eisenhower* in the first place. CVN-68 and -69 were reclassified from CVAN on 30 June, 1975. Like all active carriers, they are fitted to handle ASW aircraft for their role as multi-mission carriers. CVN-70 is the first USN warship to be named after a living person since the early 19th century, and honours the Honorable Carl Vinson, who ultimately died in June 1981.

These ships have only two nuclear reactors, instead of eight as in *Enterprise*. They are fitted with the following radars: SPS-48 3-D air search, SPS-43A air search, SPS-10F surface search and LN-66 navigation. Also fitted with NTDS (Naval Tactical Data System). It is planned to add three 20mm Mark 15 CIWS (Close-In Weapon Systems) in CVN-68 and -69, and four in CVN-70 and -71. CVN-68 and -69 carry the Mark 115 missile fire-control system, while CVN-70-73 have the Mark 91 system.

Nimitz (CVN-68) en route to Norway for a NATO exercise. Seen atop the island, to starboard, is the rectangle of the SPS-43 radar antenna and, just to port and in front of the mast, the SPS-48 unit *(US Navy)*

Type: Multi-purpose Aircraft Carrier (CV) *Number/Class:* 1 *John F. Kennedy*

Name	*Number*	*Laid down*	*Launched*	*Commissioned*	*Status*
John F. Kennedy	CV-67	22 Oct 1964	27 May 1967	7 Sept 1968	AA

Builder Newport News SB and DD Co, Newport News, Va.
Displacement standard, 61,000 tons; full load, 82,000 tons
Length overall 1,052ft (320.7m)
Maximum width hull, 130ft (39.6m). Flight deck, 252ft (76.8m)
Maximum draught 35.9ft (10.9m)
Main machinery 8 Foster-Wheeler boilers. 4 General Electric geared turbines
Screws/s.h.p. 4/280,000
Maximum speed 30 knots+
Aircraft 80+
Catapults 4 steam
Armament 3 BPDMS (Mark 25) launchers with Sea Sparrow missiles. (1) 40mm saluting gun
Complement 150 officers, 2,645 enlisted men, plus 2,150 officers and men in the Air Wing assigned.

Reclassified from CVA to CV on 1 December, 1974, this ship is frequently listed with the *Kitty Hawk* class, but officially belongs in a separate class. *JKF* was the last conventionally powered carrier built. She is a modified *Kitty Hawk* with a unique stack angled to starboard, and has the same deck arrangement as *Nimitz* and *Kitty Hawk* classes. She is equipped with NTDS. Current plans call for the installation of three 20mm (Mark 15) CIWS. A Mark 28, Mod. 5 CHAFF rocket launching system is installed on board. *John F. Kennedy* is scheduled to undergo a SLEP overhaul.

January 1979 photograph of *John F. Kennedy* (CV-67). She carries the same type of air group as *Eisenhower*, and her stack is angled to starboard so that the exhaust cannot blow directly astern and blind approaching pilots *(US Navy)*

Type: Multi-purpose Aircraft Carrier (nuclear-powered) (CVN) — *Number/Class:* 1 *Enterprise*

Name	Number	Laid down	Launched	Commissioned	Status
Enterprise	CVN-65	4 Feb 1958	24 Sept 1960	25 Nov 1961	PA

Builder Newport News SB and DD Co, Newport News, Va
Displacement Standard, 75,700 tons; full load, 89,600 tons
Length overall 1,102ft (335.9m)
Maximum width Hull, 133ft (40.5m). Flight deck, 252ft (76.8m)
Maximum draught 35.8ft (10.9m)
Main machinery 8 pressurised water-cooled nuclear reactors, A2W (Westinghouse). 4 Westinghouse steam turbines
Screws/s.h.p. 4/280,000
Maximum speed 35 knots+
Aircraft 84+
Catapults 4 steam (C-13)
Armament 2 BPDMS (Mark 25) launchers with Sea Sparrow missiles. (3) single (Mark 68) 20mm guns. (2) 40mm saluting guns
Complement 162 officers and 2,940 enlisted men, plus 2,400 officers and men in the Air Wing assigned

Enterprise was reclassified from CVAN to CVN on 30 June, 1975. "Big E" is a modification of the *Forrestal* design, but with an elevator arrangement like that of the *Kitty Hawk* class. The unique dome on the superstructure was removed during a three-year overhaul at Puget Sound Naval Shipyard (4-79/3-82), when the "wedding cake" atop the bridge, with 360° antenna array, was removed and replaced with a superstructure similar to that of the *Nimitz* class. *Enterprise* was refuelled at Newport News during 1964/1965 and 1969/1971. There are two nuclear reactors for each shaft. Even with the commissioning of the *Nimitz* class, *Enterprise* is still the world's largest warship. Unlike the *Nimitz* ships, she was built in 31 months.

Originally, *Enterprise* had no armament. Sea Sparrow BPDMS launchers were installed in 1967, and will be upgraded with three 20mm (Mark 15) CIWS.

Enterprise is fitted with the following radars: SPS-48C, -49 and -65 air search and SPS-10 and -58 surface search. She also has NTDS, Tacan and three Mark 92 missile fire-control systems (replacing two Mark 117s).

Enterprise (CVN-65) in her new configuration. Taken in February 1982, this photograph shows "Big E" returning to San Francisco, her home port. Note the Sea Sparrow launcher on the after port sponson *(US Navy)*

Enterprise entering San Francisco Bay. A Phalanx CIWS mount can be seen to port of the transom

Type: Multi-purpose Aircraft Carriers (CV) — *Number/Class:* 3 *Kitty Hawk*

Name	*Number*	*Laid down*	*Launched*	*Commissioned*	*Status*
Kitty Hawk	CV-63	27 Dec 1956	21 May 1960	29 Apr 1961	PA
Constellation	CV-64	14 Sept 1957	8 Oct 1960	27 Oct 1961	PA
America	CV-66	9 Jan 1961	1 Feb 1964	23 Jan 1965	AA

Constellation (CV-64) carries AN/SPS-37A and SPS-48C air search radars and an SPS-10 surface search system *(US Navy)*

Builders New York SB Corp, Camden, N.J. (CV-63). New York Naval Shipyard, Brooklyn, N.Y. (CV-64). Newport News SB and DD Co, Newport News, Va (CV-66)
Displacement Standard, 60,300 tons (CV-66); 60,100 tons (CV-63, -64). Full load, 78,500 tons (CV-66); 80,800 tons (CV-63, -64)
Length overall 1,047.5ft (319.3m (CV-66)); 1,046ft (318.8m (CV-63, -64))
Maximum width Hull, 130ft (39.6m). Flight deck, 252ft (76.9m)
Maximum draught 37ft (11.3m)
Main machinery 8 Foster-Wheeler boilers. 4 General Electric geared turbines
Screws/s.h.p. 4/280,000
Maximum speed 33 knots+
Aircraft 70+
Catapults 4 steam
Armament Two twin Terrier surface-to-air missile launchers (CV-64, -66). Three Mark 29 BPDMS launchers with Sea Sparrow missiles (CV-63). Four 40mm saluting guns (CV-66). Two 40mm saluting guns (CV-63)
Complement 145 officers and 2,645 enlisted men, plus 2,150 officers and men in the Air Wing assigned

The *Kitty Hawks* are the follow-on class to the *Forrestals*, with improvements. They were completed with missile systems as armament instead of conventional guns. The smaller island is located further aft, and the elevator arrangement differs, with one to port and three to starboard (two of which are forward of the island). Th angled part of the flight deck is 40ft longer than that of the *Forrestals*. *America* has a stem and stern anchor because of the bow-mounted AN/SQS-23 sonar (she is the only carrier with sonar). Originally designed as a CVAN, *America* was ordered as a conventional carrier to keep down construction costs. With today's very high fuel costs and the dependence upon foreign oil, this was not a wise decision. *Kitty Hawk* was the first carrier to be armed with missiles. It is currently planned to add three 20mm Mark 10, Mod 3 CIWS on each ship. Note the small radar mast abaft the island. *Constellation* was delivered a year late owing to a ravaging fire which caused severe damage when she was about 85 per cent complete. CVA-63 was reclassified as a CV on 29 April, 1973, CVA-64 and -66 on 30 June, 1979.

The following radars are fitted: AN/SPS-52 3-D air search, SPS-43 air search, and SPS-30 and -49 search. There are also two/three Mark 91 fire-control systems for the Sea Sparrow BPDMS (Terrier in CV-64).

Type: Multi-purpose Aircraft Carriers (CV) — *Number/Class:* 4 *Forrestal*

Name	*Number*	*Laid down*	*Launched*	*Commissioned*	*Status*
Forrestal	CV-59	14 July 1952	11 Dec 1954	1 Oct 1955	AA
Saratoga	CV-60	16 Dec 1952	8 Oct 1955	14 Apr 1956	AA
Ranger	CV-61	2 Aug 1954	29 Sept 1956	10 Aug 1957	PA
Independence	CV-62	1 July 1955	6 June 1958	10 Jan 1959	AA

Forrestal's island, photographed in July 1976. The dome contains NTDS and satellite communications antennae. The two small dishes aft of the dome are AN/SPN-42 antennae, associated with the automatic Carrier Landing System (ACLS). Also visible, just to starboard of the mast, are the AN/SPS-43A air search "bedstead" and, further forward, the SPS-30 air search/heightfinding dish. The SPS-58 low-angle air search antenna is mounted halfway up the mast, directly above the dome ▶

◀ *Saratoga* (CV-60), photographed before her SLEP conversion

Builders Newport News SB and DD Co, Newport News, Va (CV-59, -61). New York SB Corp, Camden, N.J. (CV-60, -62)
Displacement Standard, 59,060 tons (CV-59, -60); 60,000 tons (CV-61, -62). Full load, 75,900 tons (CV-59, -60), 79,300 tons (CV-61, -62)
Length overall 1,066ft (331m (CV-59, -60)); 1,071ft (326.4m (CV-61, -62))
Maximum width Hull, 129.5ft (39.5m). Flight deck, 252ft (76.8m)
Maximum draught 35.4ft (10.79m)
Main machinery 8 Babcock and Wilcox boilers. 4 Westinghouse geared turbines (CV-59); 4 General Electric geared turbines (others)
Screws/s.h.p. 4/260,000 (CV-59); 4/280,000 (others)
Maximum speed 33 knots (CV-59); 34 knots (others)
Aircraft 70+
Catapults 4 steam (two C-7 and two C-11 in CV-59, -60). 4 steam (C-7 in CV-61, -62)
Armament Two BPDMS with launchers for Sea Sparrow missiles (Mark 29 in CV-61; Mark 25 in the others). Four 40mm saluting guns
Complement 150 officers and 2,465 enlisted men, plus 2,150 officers and men in the Air Wing assigned

Originally CVB-59 *Forrestal* was reclassified CVA on 1 October, 1952. Along with CVA-61, it was reclassified CV on 30 June, 1975. CVA-60 became CV on 30 June, 1972, and CVA-62 became CV on 28 February, 1973. These ships are distinguished by their midship island. They have four elevators, one to port and forward, and three to starboard, two of which are abaft the island. The *Forrestals* were the first carriers built to handle jet aircraft. The original design called for a retractable bridge and a flush deck, much like the cancelled *United States* design. As a matter of interest, the *United States* (CVA-58) was laid down on 18 April, 1949, but was cancelled on 23 April and the keel taken up.

There is one distinguishing identification feature within the class. CV-59 and -60 have open fantails while those of CV-61 and -62 are enclosed. There were originally eight 5in gun mounts arranged in sponsons located two on each quarter. These were gradually reduced in number over the years until the last mounts were removed in the late Sixties.

The angle of *Ranger*'s flight deck was increased, adding to her overall width. *Forrestal* was overhauled extensively in mid-1972. A 120ft extension was built into the side of the flight deck, increasing the landing area.

Saratoga was decommissioned at the Philadelphia Naval Shipyard on 1 October, 1980, to undergo an extensive Service Life Extension Programme (SLEP) overhaul, but was administratively recommissioned on 1 October, 1981. She was completed in February 1983. The purpose of the programme is to extend the useful life of this class by 15 years. CV-59 SLEP was approved under FY-1983 at a cost of $699.5 million, with CV-61 to follow under FY-1985, and CV-62 under FY-1987. The *Kitty Hawk* and *John F. Kennedy* classes will also undergo the SLEP modernisation. The *Forrestal* and *Saratoga* were modernised at Philadelphia Naval Shipyard.

SLEP modernisation schedule

Name	*Number*	*FY/SCB*	*Assigned*	*Started*	*Completed*	*Recommissioned*
Forrestal	CV-59	83/60	21 Jan 1983	21 Jan 1983	20 May 1985	
Saratoga	CV-60	79/60	25 May 1979	1 Oct 1980	1 Feb 1983	1 Oct 1981
Ranger	CV-61	85/60		1 July 1987*	2 Nov 1989*	(see page 234)
Independence	CV-62	87/60		1 Apr 1985*	1 Aug 1987*	

* Estimate

146702
NAVY
EAGLE I
FT. LAUDERDALE

Type: Multi-purpose Aircraft Carriers (CV) — *Number/Class:* 2 *Midway*

Name	Number	Laid down	Launched	Commissioned	Status
Midway	CV-41	23 Oct 1943	20 March 1945	10 September 1945	PA
Coral Sea	CV-43	10 July 1944	2 Apr 1946	1 Oct 1947	AA

Builder Newport News SB and DD Co, Newport News, Va
Length overall 972ft (296.27m)
Maximum width Hull, 121ft (36.9m). Flight deck, 238ft (72.5m)
Maximum draught 35.3ft (10.8m)
Main machinery 12 Babcock and Wilcox boilers. 4 Westinghouse geared turbines
Screws/s.h.p. 4/212,000
Maximum speed 30 knots+
Aircraft 70+
Catapults Two C-13 steam (CV-41); three C-11 steam (CV-43)
Armament Three 20mm CIWS (Mark 16). Two 40mm saluting guns
Complement 140/165 officers and 2,475/2,545 enlisted men, plus, 1,800 officers and men in the Air Wing assigned

Originally ordered as a class of six ships, CVB-56 and -57 were cancelled on 28 March, 1945, and CV-44 on 11 January, 1943, without construction beginning on any of the ships. *Franklin D. Roosevelt* (CV-42), a sister ship, was commissioned 27 October, 1945. Though she was modernised to some degree during 1954/1956, her useful life came to an end on 30 September, 1977, when she was decommissioned and struck from the Naval Vessel Register. CV-42 was sold for scrap on 11 April, 1978.

The original classification of CV-41 and -43 was changed to CVB on 15 July, 1943. They were reclassified CVA on 1 October, 1952, and reverted to CV on 30 June, 1975.

This class was built with flight decks of 3½in solid steel. This innovation resulted from lessons learned during the Second World War, when Japanese Kamikaze aircraft wreaked havoc upon the wooden flight decks of American carriers, but bounced off the metal decks of British carriers.

Originally fitted with 14 single 5in/54 gun mounts, 20 twin 3in/50s and 21 quad 40mm mounts, their armament was reduced at various times until the last 5in mounts were removed in 1978. Both ships are to be fitted with three 20mm (Mark 15) CIWS. *Midway* is to be armed with two Mark 25 *Sea Sparrow* missile launchers (BPDMS).

Midway was first modernised 1955/1957, and again, in 1966/1970, when the craft was virtually rebuilt. The angled deck was greatly enlarged and the angle increased, improved steam catapults were installed, three enlarged and relocated deck-edge elevators were fitted, and larger weapons elevators were provided.

Coral Sea's modernisation, in 1957/1960, was more extensive than her sisters' first modification. *Coral Sea* was scheduled to be replaced by *Carl Vinson* (CVN-70) as a front-line carrier when the latter was commissioned, but she will now be retained in active service as a front-line carrier to increase aircraft carrier force level and provide carrier mobility.

Radar suite is as follows: AN/SPS-48C long-range air search (on *Midway*), SPS-58 and -65V low-angle air search, AN/SPS-30 and SPS-43 air search, and SPS-10 surface search.

Midway in the South Pacific in October 1979. Rebuilt twice, she is now scheduled to see service into the 1990s, when she will be nearly 50 years old. *Midway* carries the AN/SPS-30, SPS-37A and SPS-65 air search radars and the SPS-10 surface search system. Her less modernised sister ship, *Coral Sea* (CV-43), was the first carrier to be fitted with the Phalanx close-in weapon system

Midway-class modernisations

Number	Naval Shipyard	FY/SCB	Decommissioned	Start	Recommissioned
CV-41	Puget Sound	55/110	14 Oct 1955	1 Sept 1955	30 Sept 1957
CV-41	San Francisco	66/101.66	15 Feb 1966	15 Feb 1966	31 Jan 1970
CV-43	Puget Sound	57/110A	24 May 1957	16 Apr 1957	25 Jan 1960

SCB-110 modernisation included moving the centreline elevator to the deck edge, the angled deck, fitting improved catapults, modifying the island structure, and enclosing the bow.

Type: Aircraft Carriers (CV/CVA/AVT) — *Number/Class:* 3 *Hancock*

Name	*Number*	*Laid down*	*Launched*	*Commissioned*	*Status*
Lexington	AVT-16	15 July 1941	26 Sept 1942	17 Feb 1943	AA
Bon Homme Richard	CVA-31	1 Feb 1943	29 Apr 1944	26 Nov 1944	PR
Oriskany	CV-34	1 May 1944	13 Oct 1945	25 Sept 1950	PR

Builders Bethlehem Steel Corp, Quincy, Mass (AVT-16). New York Navy Yard, Brooklyn, N.Y. (CVA-31, CV-34).
Displacement Light, 29,780 tons (AVT-16), 30,945 tons (CVA-31), 32,520 tons (CV-34) Full load, 42,110 tons (AVT-16), 43,110 tons (CVA-31), 45,110 tons (CV-34)
Length overall 910ft (277.37m (AVT-16, CV-34)); 892ft (271.88m (CVA-31));
Maximum width Hull; 106.5ft (32.5m (CV-34)), 103ft (31.4m (others)). Flight deck; 192ft (58.5m)
Maximum draught 31ft (9.5m)
Main machinery 8 Babcock and Wilcox boilers. 4 Westinghouse geared turbines
Screws/s.h.p. 4/150,000
Maximum speed 30 knots+
Aircraft 70/80 (CV/CVA), none (AVT)
Catapults 2 steam
Armament 4 single 5in/38 gun mounts (CVA-31), 2 single 5in/38 gun mounts (CV-34), two 40mm saluting guns (CV-34), none (AVT-16)
Accommodation 378 officers and 2,412 enlisted men (AVT-16). 329 officers and 3,247 enlisted men (CVA-31). 349 officers and 3,257 enlisted men (CV-34). This includes the Air Wing (CV/CVA) assigned. None assigned to AVT-16

Three survivors of the *Essex*-class carriers, these ships formed the backbone of the American Second World War carrier task forces. They are survivors of the greatest number of aircraft carriers of one class to be built, 24 of the 32 ordered having been completed. Although divided into two groups – short hull and long hull – the *Essex* carriers were officially of one class. All were completed as axial-deck carriers with the exception of *Oriskany*, which was suspended after the war and later completed with an angled deck and enclosed bow.

Modernisation and conversions, which changed their designations, divided these ships into several different types. Modernisation programmes split the ships into two different classes of carriers, basically, due to the fitting of hydraulic or steam catapult. All of the above were reclassified from CV to CVA on 1 October, 1952. CVA-16 became CVS on 1 October, 1962. CVA-34 reclassified to CV on 30 June, 1975. *Lexington* was reclassified from CVS to CVT-16 on 16 January, 1969, and was re-rated an auxiliary on 23 September, 1970. She was reclassified AVT-16 on 1 July, 1978.

Lexington was originally named *Cabot*, but was renamed on 16 June, 1942. She was assigned as a training carrier at Pensacola, Florida, on 29 December, 1962, replacing *Antietam* (CVS-36). *Lexington* was overhauled at Philadelphia in 1980, and will continue in service until FY-1989, with another overhaul scheduled for FY-1985. *Bonne Homme Richard* was decommissioned on 2 July, 1971, *Oriskany* on 30 September, 1976. *Hancock* (CV-19) was struck off on 31 January, 1976. *Intrepid* (CVS-11) decommissioned on 15 March, 1974, was struck from the Naval Vessel Register (NVR) on 23 February, 1982, and transferred on the same date to the *Intrepid* Memorial Museum Foundation, Pier 82, West 46th Street, Manhattan, New York, to serve as a museum. *Shangri-La* was stricken for scrapping on 15 July, 1981.

Oriskany (CVA-34) as she was just before being laid up. Plans to reactivate this ship have now been dropped.

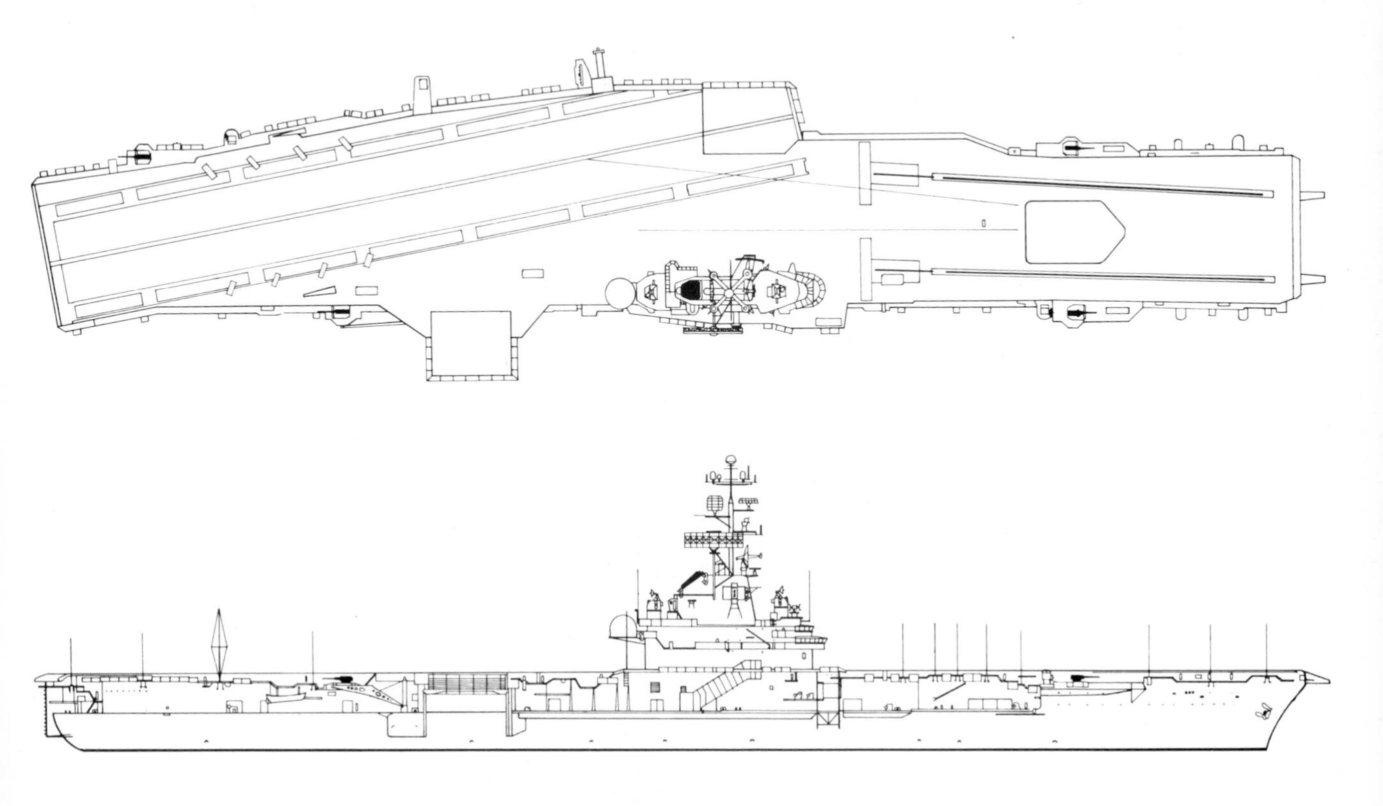

U.S.S. ORISKANY ~ CVA 34

Essex/Hancock-class modernisations

The five remaining Second World War-built carriers were converted and modernised to the SCB-27c and SCB-125 design, and one (*Oriskany*) was completed to the same basic design under SCB-125A. She was also fitted with an aluminium flight deck. Modernisation included the fitting of steam catapults, heavier arresting gear, and a streamlined superstructure, strengthening of the flight deck, moving the centreline deck elevator to the starboard side deck edge, fitting a hurricane bow, and widening the hull blisters.

The SCB-27A was similar to the SCB-27C. The hydraulic catapults were upgraded to the latest type and the hull blisters were widened, but are 1ft narrower than those of the *Hancock*. Both ships received a FRAM II modernisation. The electronics were upgraded, the CIC was enlarged, and ASW capabilities were improved. Other minor features were incorporated to prolong the ships' useful life.

Bon Homme Richard (CVA-31) in the South China Sea in May 1970 ▶

An October 1968 view of the training carrier *Lexington* (AVT-16) in the Gulf of Mexico. She has changed little since, except for the ravages of time and the removal of the fire-control systems on top of the island and the remaining 5in gun mounts. She was given an 18-month overhaul beginning in 1980, and another is scheduled for FY 1985 *(US Navy)*

NF
94 NAVY

Type: Anti-submarine Warfare Aircraft Carriers (CVS) — *Number/Class:* 2 Essex

Name	*Number*	*Laid down*	*Launched*	*Commissioned*	*Status*
Hornet	CVS-12	3 Aug 1942	30 Aug 1943	29 Nov 1943	PR
Bennington	CVS-20	15 Dec 1942	26 Feb 1944	6 Aug 1944	PR

Builders Newport News SB and DD Co, Newport News, Va (CVS-12); New York Navy Yard, Brooklyn, N.Y. (CVS-20)
Displacement Light, 28,200 tons; full load, 40,600 tons
Length overall 890ft (271.27m)
Maximum width Hull, 101ft (30.7m)
Maximum draught 31ft (9.5m)
Main machinery 8 Babcock and Wilcox boilers. 4 Westinghouse geared turbines
Screws/s.h.p. 4/150,000
Maximum speed 30 knots+
Aircraft 45, including helicopters
Catapults 2 hydraulic (H-8)
Armament 4 single 5in/38 gun mounts, (2) 40mm saluting guns (CVS-20)
Complement 115 officers and 1,500 enlisted men, plus an Air Group of 800

These are two of five survivors of the *Essex* class (see previous class for other three). *Hornet* was originally named *Kearsarge*, but was renamed 24 January, 1943. Both ships were originally classified CVs, and reclassified CVA on 1 October, 1952. CVA-12 was reclassified CVS on 27 June, 1958 and CVA-20 to CVS on 30 June, 1959. *Hornet* and *Bennington* were modernised during the Fifties.

On 26 May, 1954, *Bennington* was conducting flight operations off Newport, Rhode Island, when the port catapult accumulator burst, releasing hydraulic fluid under high pressure in the form of a mist. Somehow the vapour was ignited, and set off a series of violent explosions, causing extensive damage to the forward part of the ship. 103 men were killed and 201 were injured.

Hornet was decommissioned on 27 June, 1970. *Bennington* was decommissioned on 15 January, 1970. Both are laid up at Puget Sound Naval Shipyard, Bremerton, Washington.

Hornet in 1968. She and *Bennington* are the only US carriers still fitted with hydraulic catapults *(US Navy)*

Essex/Hancock class modernisations

CV	*Naval Shipyard*	*FY/SCB*	*Date Assigned*	*Date Started*	*Date Completed*	*FRAM II*
-12	New York	52/27A	14 June 1951	16 July 1951	1 Oct 1953	FY-1965
-12	Puget Sound	56/125	24 Aug 1955	15 Jan 1956	15 Aug 1956	—
-20	New York	51/27A	26 Oct 1950	1 Dec 1950	30 Nov 1952	FY-1963
-20	New York	55/125	31 July 1954	9 Sept 1954	15 Apr 1955	—

CV	*Naval Shipyard*	*FY/SCB*	*Date Assigned*	*Date Started*	*Date Completed*
-16	Puget Sound	53/27c	21 July 1952	1 Sept 1953	1 Sept 1955
-31	San Francisco	53/27c	21 July 1952	1 May 1953	1 Nov 1955
-34	San Francisco	57/125A	8 Apr 1957	2 Jan 1957	29 May 1959

BATTLESHIPS (BB)

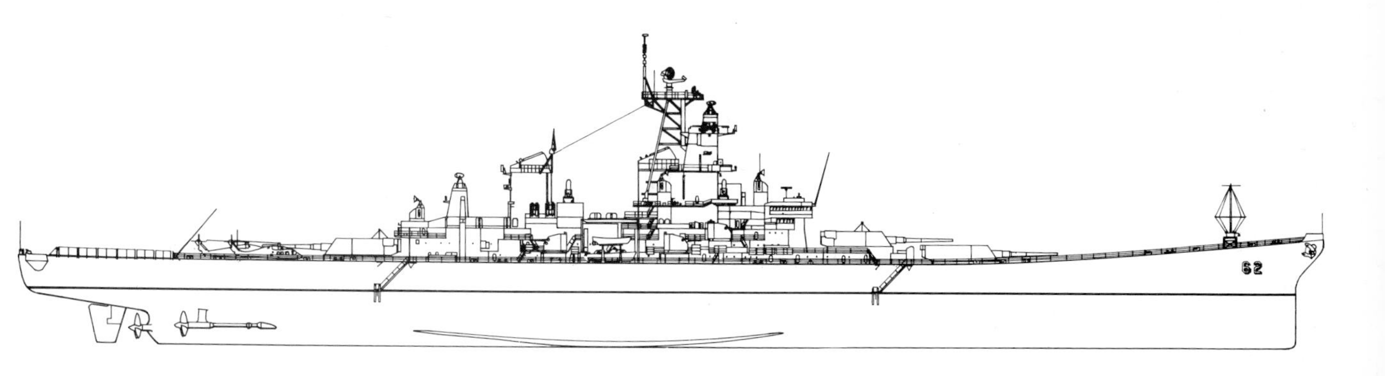

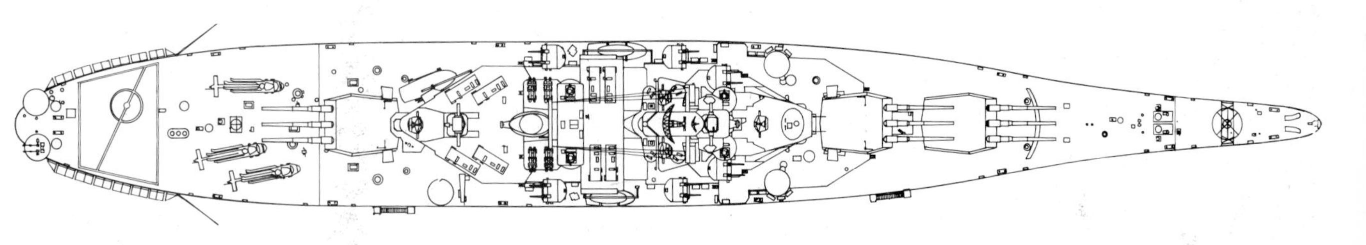

When Alfred Lord Tennyson, in his poem *The Brook*, wrote "... men may come and men may go, but I go on forever", he could have been referring to the American battleship. The coming of age of the aircraft carrier during the Second World War sounded the death knell of the battleship as a major weapon. One by one they disappeared from Naval Service until, in June 1962, the *Iowa* class were the only examples left. It should be noted that of ten Second World War-built American battleships, three survive as memorials in the state after which they were named. When *New Jersey* was recommissioned on 6 April, 1968, many said that it was "the 'last' dreadnought making her 'last' voyage". When she was decommissioned on 17 December, 1969, it appeared that the "ghost" was finally laid. On 6 June, 1973, an INSURV precept (the first step towards declaring a ship unfit and striking it from the Naval Vessel Register for scrapping) was issued on *Iowa* (BB-61) and *Wisconsin* (BB-64). Surely, *New Jersey* (BB-62) and *Missouri* (BB-63) would be next. But on 9 November, 1973, all planned disposal actions taken in regard to the *Iowas* were cancelled, and the ships remained mothballed.

The mystique of the battleship is difficult to define. There is much emotion tied to it, and emotions are not easily explained. What of the practical side? Why, in times of war, military crisis, etc., do Defence and Navy Department officials keep one eye on the battleship for possible use? As Capt J. Edward Snyder, USN, *New Jersey*'s first commanding officer during her third tour, said: "... we still had those guns, ... those 16in guns". Of the few common denominators in this world, power is one of them. Nothing, be it a nuclear-powered cruiser or carrier, better illustrates power than a battleship, and being on the receiving end of its 16in guns. First impressions are lasting. Many of those who declare the battleship obsolete do so because they look upon it only as a platform for large guns. Today, in 1983, Navy planners and other defence officials are regarding the battleship as an entity capable of carrying other weapons systems and capable of survival in any form of warfare.

Whatever happens to the battleship reactivation project, it will be interesting to see how Soviet planners cope with the additional dimensions that these ships will bring to our forces.

The reactivated *New Jersey* (BB-62). The most significant changes from the 1968 (Vietnam service) standard are the removal of the after mast, crane and four of the twin 5in mounts (two each side) and the addition of the large platform between the stacks for the Harpoon/Tomahawk missile launchers. *New Jersey* also carries the AN/SPS-49 air search and SPS-10 surface search radars *(A. D. Baker III)*

Type: Battleship (BB) *Number/Class:* 4 Iowa

Name	Number	Laid down	Launched	Commissioned	Status
Iowa	BB-61	27 June 1940	27 Aug 1942	22 Feb 1943	CONV
New Jersey	BB-62	16 Sept 1940	7 Dec 1942	23 May 1943	PA
Missouri	BB-63	6 Jan 1941	29 Jan 1944	11 June 1944	PR
Wisconsin	BB-64	25 Jan 1941	7 Dec 1943	16 Apr 1944	AR

Builders New York Navy Yard, Brooklyn, N.Y. (BB-61 and -63); Philadelphia Navy Yard, Philia, Pa (BB-62 and -64)
Displacement Standard, 45,000 tons; full load, 57,216 tons (BB-64), 57,450 tons (BB-61, -63), 59,000 tons (BB-62)
Length overall 887.3ft (270.4m), except BB-62; 887.5ft (270.5m)
Maximum beam 108.3ft (33m)
Maximum draught 37.8ft (11.5m) (BB-61, -63); 38ft (11.6m) (BB-62, -64)
Main machinery Four geared steam turbines (General Electric, BB-61, -63), (Westinghouse, BB-62, -64), reduction gear drive. Eight Babcock and Wilcox boilers
Screws/s.h.p. 4/212,000
Maximum speed 32.5 knots (except BB-63, 27.5 knots) – see notes
Missile armament Eight quadruple *Tomahawk* cruise missile launchers (32 missiles); four quadruple *Harpoon* surface to surface missile launch canisters (16 missiles) (BB-61, -62 only)
Gun armament Three triple 16in/50 gun turrets, ten twin 5in/38 gun mounts (six on BB-61, -62) two 40mm saluting guns (BB-61, -62), four 20mm CIWS (Mark 16)
Complement 67 officers and 1,460 enlisted men, plus a US Marine detachment of 2 officers and 42 enlisted men (BB-61, -62); 95 officers and 2,270 enlisted men (BB-63, -64)

The *Iowa*s represent the ultimate in US battleship design. The succeeding cancelled *Montana* class (BB-67/71) were simply four-turret versions of the *Iowa*s. Two further *Iowa*s were cancelled, *Illinois* (BB-65) on 11 August, 1945, and *Kentucky* (BB-66) on 20 January, 1950. With the exception of nuclear-powered warships, these ships have the greatest endurance of any surface combat vessels extant. They are considered to be quite stable platforms with excellent fire-control/electronic facilities. In addition, they are the most well protected ships ever built. The maximum side belt thickness runs to 12.1in, while control tower thickness is a uniform 17.5in. Protective deck thickness runs from 1.5in to 6in thickness over three decks. Turret armour ranges from 7.2in to 19.5in. The ships are so well protected that reports indicate that it would take six Soviet Styx (the SS-N-2C versions), hitting together or in echelon, even to begin to slow down an *Iowa* or marginally reduce its firepower capabilities.

The original armament of the class, besides the 16in/50 cal. turrets and 5in/38 cal. mounts, included the following: 20 quadruple 40mm mounts (except *Iowa*: 19), 41 single 20mm mounts (BB-62), 47 single 20mm mounts (BB-64), 49 single 20mm mounts (BB-63), 52 single 20mm mounts (BB-61), two twin 20mm mounts (BB-64), four twin 20mm mounts (BB-62) (except BB-61 and -63: none). These

New Jersey entering Pearl Harbor in September 1968 during a stopover en route to Vietnam. ECM/ECCM antennae can be seen projecting from the top of the ship's control tower *(US Navy)*

mounts were gradually reduced over the years, and today only *Missouri* retains a complete secondary battery.

Before *New Jersey*'s Vietnam tour, the last decommissioning dates of the *Iowa*s were as follows: *Iowa* on 24 February, 1958, at Philadelphia; *New Jersey* on 21 August, 1957, at New York (later towed to Philadelphia for berthing); *Missouri* on 26 February, 1955, at Puget Sound Naval Shipyard, Bremerton (where she is still berthed); and *Wisconsin* on 8 March, 1958, at Bayonne (later towed to Philadelphia for berthing).

The excellent endurance, speed, and capabilities of the *Iowa* design led to several ideas to exploit these attributes. Some of the proposals included converting the four completed *Iowa*'s to guided missile ships. Conversion would have included the removal of all three 16in turrets and their replacement by two twin Talos missile launchers at each position, the addition of ASROC and our first cruise missile, the *Regulus* II, and, finally, the inclusion of two twin *Tartar* missile launchers. Another proposal included the conversion of these ships to Fast Combat Support Ships (AOE), and a third suggested converting the ships to Amphibious Assault/Fire-Support ships for the Marines. This would have included removal of the aft turret and its replacement by a hangar and flight deck that would occupy the aft third of the ship, for the operation of troop-carrying helicopters (shades of the Phase II modifications of the current reactivation programme!). See later notes.

When it became evident that American land operations in Vietnam required more heavy fire support ships, it was decided to reactivate an *Iowa* class battleship instead of the two decommissioned *Des Moines* class heavy cruisers (CA). *New Jersey* was chosen because she was the most up to date, had undergone a major overhaul about a year before inactivation, and was on the East Coast

Iowa (BB-61) in dry dock at Philadelphia Naval Shipyard in May 1982. During this time her twin 5in mounts were removed and sent to the ordnance plant at Louisville, Ky, for complete renovation. She was towed to Avondale, La, in September 1982, and the industrial phase of the reactivation work began on 1 October 1982. *Iowa* will be one of the first two ships in the fleet to receive the new AN/SPS-67 surface search radar, the projected replacement for AN/SPS-10 *(Jim Murray)*

(thus keeping the West Coast yards free for Vietnam support). Her "austere" reactivation included removal of all 40mm guns, 20mm guns and associated equipment; improvement of medical facilities and habitability; the addition of ECM/ECCM systems, which necessitated the remodelling of the fire control tower and gave it a box-like appearance at the top; the addition of SPS-6 and SPS-10 radars; and the installation of two Mark 38 fire control towers to supplement the Mark 40 and 51 directors previously installed.

Reactivation took one year and cost $21.5 million dollars (FY 1968), nearly 10 per cent under budget, $25 million having been allotted for the project. *New Jersey* recommissioned on 6 April, 1968, and made one deployment to Vietnam (30 September, 1968, to March 1969) before coming home to prepare for a second deployment. It was then, while anchored at Long Beach, that a Government "economy" overtook her, and she was ordered to Puget Sound Naval Shipyard for inactivation, decommissioning there on 17 December, 1969.

Congressional complaints of the poor state of US national defence had been rising to a crescendo during the Carter Administration. Congress had added money for a fifth nuclear powered aircraft carrier to the FY-1979 Shipbuilding Programme only to have President Carter veto the entire defence bill. In the FY-1980 Programme, when the Carter Administration submitted plans to construct a "white elephant" known as the Medium Aircraft Carrier (CVV), Congress substituted money for another CVN, and won.

Flush from victory in the FY-1980 budget battles, pro-defence members of Congress added monies to reactivate *Oriskany* (CV-34) and *New Jersey* (BB-62). The monies passed the appropriation stage, but after much squabbling and hassling among the pro-defence members, anti-defence members and other opposition in Congress, the project was killed at the last moment. However, like the proverbial bad penny, the battleship kept coming back. With the replacement of the Carter Administration by the Reagan Administration, and the virtual control of Congress by the right wing of the Republican Party, it was here to stay.

In the FY-1981 Supplemental Programme, the Reagan Administration, not Congress, announced plans to reactivate all four *Iowa* class units. The Supplemental Programme requested $89 million to begin reactivation of *New Jersey*, $3 million for research and development, and $1 million to begin planning the reactivation of *Iowa*. The Reagan Administration's amendment to the Carter Administration's FY-1982 budget included $237 million to complete the refit and modernisation of *New Jersey*. In the same Amendment, $91 million was requested to begin reactivation of *Iowa*, along with another $2 million for research and development. An additional $300.8 million was approved in the FY-1983 budget to complete the reactivation of *Iowa*. *Missouri* is to follow in FY-1984, and *Wisconsin* in FY-1985. A summary follows:

Tentative Iowa-class reactivation schedule

Name/Number	*FY*	*Reactivation yard*	*Commencement*	*Completion*
Iowa (BB-61)	1983	Avondale/Ingalls	1 Oct 1982	30 June 1984
New Jersey (BB-62)	1982	Long Beach Naval Shipyard	1 Oct 1981	28 Dec 1982
Missouri (BB-63)	1985	Long Beach Naval Shipyard	Jan 1984	Spring 1987
Wisconsin (BB-64)	1986	Commercial shipyard	Jan 1985	Spring 1988

*Estimate

Because Puget Sound Naval Shipyard's industrial capacity was already stretched to the limit, it was decided to reactivate and refit *New Jersey* at Long Beach. On 27 July, 1981, she left Bremerton under the tow of *Takelma* (ATF-113), *Moctobi* (ATF-105) and *Quapaw* (ATF-110), with USNS *Narragansett* (T-ATF-167) serving as backup. Her arrival at Long Beach on 7 September was watched by an audience of thousands. The Navy intended to open the main deck to visitors only during the weekend of 8/9 August, but there were so many people that it was necessary to open the ship again the following weekend.

The first jobs were to off load all spares for cataloguing and temporary storage, and to drain the tanks of some 600,000gal of fuel so that they could be cleaned. This was started during the week of 10 August. The industrial phase of the reactivation began on 1 October. Across the country at Philadelphia Naval Shipyard, using the $91 million already appropriated, *Iowa* began off-loading spares on 1 October, 1981. The remaining funds were included in the FY-1963 Programme with the industrial phase of *Iowa*'s reactivation having begun on 1 October, 1982. *New Jersey*'s 1968/1969 configuration is being used as the "base line" for each unit.

Because the other units of the class have been out of service longer than *New Jersey*, especially *Missouri*, their reactivation will cost more than the $329 million allotted for *New Jersey*. However, a *Virginia* class CGN would cost between $1.2 and $1.6 billion and would take six years to construct, so on these figures alone it is obvious that the reactivation of the *Iowas* is a bargain.

Reactivation and Phase I modernisation will include upgrading habitability, extensive modernisation of all communications and electronic systems, convertion to Navy Distillate fuel, the upgrading of each ship's air-search capabilities by the installation of the LN-66, AN/SPS-10 and AN/SPS-49 radar systems, installing four Phalanx Close-In Weapons Systems (CIWS) (one either side of the bridge on the 01 level, and one either side of the aft Mark 37 director), installation of the new AN/SLQ-32 electronic counter measures system, fitting eight quadruple Tomahawk cruise missile launchers (32 missiles), installing four quadruple Harpoon surface-to-surface missile launch canisters (16 missiles), and, finally, fitting the fantail to land and/or park two LAMPS III (SH-60) helicopters.

A contract for the reactivation/modernisation of *Iowa* was awarded to Avondale Shipyard Inc, Westwego, La, and Ingalls Shipbuilding Corp, Pascagoula, Miss, on 13 January, 1982. Ingalls will do most of the work, with Avondale handling the underwater portion of the hull. *Iowa* arrived at Avondale under tow from Philadelphia Naval Shipyard on 15 September, 1982, and was transferred to Ingalls early in January 1983.

The accompanying drawing indicates how the refitted and Phase I modernised *New Jersey* appeared when recommissioned on 28 December, 1982.

The modernisation and refit will permit each ship to perform satisfactorily in modern warfare until Phase II modernisation occurs.

Phase II modernisation, which is still in the planning stage and very much unsettled, will be undertaken during the ship's first overhaul. This occurs some 36 to 48 months after recommissioning. For *Missouri* and *Wisconsin* it may occur during initial reactivation and modernisation overhaul. If approved, Phase II will include the removal of the aft turret and the addition of a hangar and flight deck on the rear third of the ship. The aircraft facilities will have the full capability to support and fly up to 25 VTOL aircraft (presumably Harriers). In addition, all or most of the remaining 5in mounts will be removed and replaced by vertical launch systems for Tomahawk cruise missiles, of which up to 130 will be carried. It has been suggested that a large VLS system would be added aft, using number three barbette as a base, but it would go up through the flight deck, and naval aviators dislike the prospect of flying from the flight deck with the missile launcher going off. Upon completion of Phase II the extensive modernisation undertaken on the *Iowas* will allow the to battleships serve a useful role into the 21st century, long after they were officially "buried".

Finally, the authors wish to put to rest, once and for all, the rumours concerning the material condition of *Iowa, Wisconsin*, and *Missouri*. The alleged mass stripping of *Iowa* to speed *New Jersey*'s 1967-68 reactivation did not occur. Some parts were taken, but they were easily replaceable. Furthermore, when one command "cannibalises" another it has to replace the part taken. Cannibalisation does nothing but cut the Navy Supply Corps red tape when a part is needed quickly. As to the fire damage on *Wisconsin*, it was greatly exaggerated. There *was* a fire and there *was* damage to overhead cabling and wiring, but it was not extensive. It was not repaired because *Wisconsin* was undergoing inactivation. As for the infamous grounding of *Missouri* on 17 January, 1950, evidence indicates that the damage caused a speed loss of a *maximum* of five knots. The grounding damaged the starboard keelson and the major starboard strength beam, which caused misalignment of the engine foundations over the damaged area. The damage was repaired at Norfolk by February 1950. However, once a keelson is bent and causes the engines to misalign, it is virtually impossible to fully repair the damage, hence there will always be some misalignment. The 5 knot speed loss, if there is in fact any loss at all, is insignificant when compared with speeds at which today's naval task forces travel.

That the Navy should be faced with a shortfall of fighting capabilities necessitating reactivation of the *Iowas* and possibly of two *Essex*-class carriers is due to the Carter Administration's initial failure to look after all aspects of four seaborne forces, personnel and platforms alike.

CRUISERS (CGN/CG/CA)

In 1975, the year that South Vietnam fell, there were 40 cruisers on the NVR; ten CGN, 25 CG and five CA. Of these, five CGN and 23 CG were active; two CG and five CA were in reserve, and five CGNs were building. In 1981/1982 there were 31 cruisers on the NVR. Eighteen CG and nine CGN were active, while two CG and two CA were in reserve. In addition, seven were under construction and 23 more are projected. The reduction in force level is more than compensated for by the quality of succeeding cruiser classes being added to the force. However, quality does not match the Soviet Navy's quantity, so the Navy needs to increase its fighting capability today, not ten years from now, by using readily available assets such as the two *Des Moines*-class gun cruisers.

Unlike the cruisers of olden days, their modern counterparts are far from helpless against submarines. Nuclear power has given the Navy cruisers unlimited endurance at flank speed. Highly sophisticated electronics, combined with anti-aircraft and anti-submarine weapons systems, have given the cruiser a new dimension in the Navy, and the ships of the future will even be better suited to modern warfare, whatever the challenge. All active CGN/CG are to be fitted with one or more quadruple Tomahawk cruise missile launchers in the immediate future.

With regards to the reactivation of *Missouri* (BB-63) and *Wisconsin* (BB-64), an alternative plan in Congressional circles is to reactivation of the two *Des Moines*-class gun cruisers (CA) as a substitute for one or both. It is also possible that one of the CAs might be reactivated for duty as Sixth Fleet flagship.

Type: Guided Missile Cruisers (CG) — *Number/Class:* 1+9+(20) *Ticonderoga*

Name	*Number*	*Laid down*	*Launched*	*Commissioned*	*Status*
Ticonderoga	CG-47	21 Jan 1980	25 Apr 1981	22 Jan 1983	AA
Yorktown	CG-48	19 Oct 1981	17 Jan 1983	est. July 1984	BLDG
	CG-49	19 Oct 1983		est. 1985	BLDG
	CG-50			est. 1985	ORD
	CG-51			est. 1986	ORD
	CG-52			est. 1986	ORD
	CG-53				ORD
	CG-54/56				ORD
	CG-57/60				PROJ
	CG-61/63				PROJ
	CG-64/67				PROJ
	CG-68/71				PROJ
	CG-72/77				PROJ

Builder Ingalls SB Corp, Pascagoula, Miss (except CG-51; Bath Iron Wks, Bath, Me)
Displacement 9,200 tons full load
Length overall 568.3ft (173.2m)
Maximum beam 55ft (16.8m)
Maximum draught 31ft (9.4m)
Main machinery Four General Electric LM-2500 gas turbines
Screws/s.h.p. 2/80,000
Maximum speed 30 knots+
Armament Two 8-tubed launch canisters for Harpoon surface-to-surface missiles (16 missiles), two twin Mark 26 launchers for Asroc/Standard MR missiles (CG-47 only), Mark 32 ASW torpedo tubes, two single Mark 45 5in/54 gun mounts, two 20mm Phalanx (six-barrelled Mark 15 CIWS), two 40mm saluting guns
Complement 346 total (23 officers, 323 enlisted men)

These ships were originally designated Guided Missile Destroyers (DDG), being rerated as CGs on 1 January, 1980, when DDG-47 was reclassified CG-47. CG-47 was authorised in FY-1978 ($930 million), CG-48 in FY-1980 ($820 million), CG-49 and -50 in FY-1981 ($1,613.7 million total). CG-51/53 followed in FY-1982 ($2,929.3 million) and CG-54/56 in FY-1983 ($2,901.7 million), with CG-57/60 proposed for FY-1984, CG-61/63 in FY-1985, CG-64/67 in FY-1986, CG-69/71 in FY-1987 and CG-72/77 in future programmes.

The *Ticonderoga*s are a modification of the *Spruance* class destroyers, having the same basic hull, gas turbine propulsion plant, and other similarities. They are to have the full Aegis system (SPY-1A), AN/SPS-49 search radar, QE-82 satellite communication antenna, one Mark 86 gunfire control system, one Mark 116 ASW fire control system, the AN/SQS-23 (bow-mounted) sonar, and TACTAS-19 towed array.

With the conventionally powered *Ticonderoga*-class guided missile cruisers, the Reagan FY-1981 Supplement retains the same number of platforms requested, but increases the funds requested by $149 million. On the other hand, the Reagan FY-1982 Amendment increases the number of platforms requested from two to three, and the funds requested by another $810.1 million. The Carter Administration's five-year shipbuilding programme called for the construction of two units each year, and set the ultimate force level of the class at 28 units. The Defense Department, with the Reagan Administration's approval, calls for the construction of three units per year, to an ultimate force level of 30 units, but reduces the ultimate class force level to 19 units *if* construction of the CGN-42 class and the plans to convert the CGN-38 class to Aegis platforms proceed. The reduction of the *Ticonderoga*-class force level to 19 units under this approach is made because the Radio Corporation of America (RCA), the prime contractor for the Aegis system, can reportedly only produce a maximum of five units of the system per year.

From CG-48 onwards two VLS units (one forward, one aft) will be fitted in place of the Mark 26 launchers. Each VLS will have a capacity of 12 missiles.

Ticonderoga (CG-47), first of the Aegis cruisers, on sea trials in the Gulf of Mexico in April 1982. The massive structure below the bridge houses the forward element of the AN/SPY-1A Aegis air-defence system, the octagonal plate visible above the Mark 26 launcher being the antenna. There is another antenna on the starboard side of the housing, while the after structure has antennae facing aft and to port *(US Navy)*

Type: Guided Missile Cruisers (nuclear-powered) (CGN) *Number/Class:* (5) "Modified" *Virginia*

Name	Number	Laid down	Launched	Commissioned	Status
	CGN-42			est. 1992	None
	CGN-43			est. 1993	None
	CGN-44			est. 1993	None
	CGN-45			est. 1994	None
	CGN-46			est. 1995	None

Artist's impression of the CGN-42 class. Being built to a modified *Virginia* design, the class was conceived as a replacement for the Strike Cruiser (CGSN) project. The Mark 26 missile launchers of the Aegis air-defence system will ultimately be replaced by vertical-launch units. The first of class should be authorised in FY 1986 and will commission in 1992

Builder Newport News SB and DD Co, Newport News, Va
Displacement not available
Length overall 560ft (172.2m)
Maximum beam 63ft (19.2m)
Maximum draught 24ft (7.3m)
Main machinery Two pressurised water-cooled reactors (General Electric D2G); two General Electric steam turbines
Screws/s.h.p. 2/100,000
Maximum speed 30 knots+
Armament Two twin Mark 26 launchers for Tartar/Asroc/Harpoon/Standard-ER (SM-2) missiles, two single 5in/54 (Mark 45) gun mounts, Mark 32 ASW torpedo tubes, two 40mm saluting guns
Complement 27 officers, 283 enlisted men

The Modified *Virginia* class was first conceived as a replacement for the eight nuclear strike cruisers (CSGN) proposed by the Ford Administration. Long-lead items for the construction of this Aegis-equipped class were approved in the FY-1978 budget and awarded to Newport News in November 1977. However, construction of this class was cancelled in January 1979 "because there wasn't any support within the Administration or within the Department of Defense for nuclear power – primarily on the basis of funding and affordability". In plain language, the Carter Administration lost interest in the construction of this class, as it did with so many other defence projects the four years it was in power. With the assumption of power by the Reagan Administration, the class seems to have been reborn. Funds for the construction of the first unit of the class are projected for the FY-1986 programme with two units to follow in FY-1987 and FY-1988. Current cost per unit is about $1.7 billion dollars (FY-1981). Had it been built when originally planned, the initial unit would have cost about $1 billion dollars, some 40 per cent less (see page 234).

The design of this class duplicates that of the *Virginia* class, expanded to accommodate the Aegis (SPY-1A) system. Newport News will probably be the sole contractor for this class, as it is the only yard capable of building nuclear-powered surface warships.

Electronics will consist of the AN/SQS-53 bow mounted sonar, the digital Mark 116 ASW fire control system, the Mark 74 missile fire control directors, and, as mentioned, the SPY-1A (Aegis) system with UKY-7 computers to control the radar. It is planned to replace the Mark 26 guided missile launchers by the Vertical Launch Missile System (VLS) during construction.

Type: Guided Missile Cruisers, (nuclear-powered) (CGN) — *Number/Class:* 4 *Virginia*

Name	Number	Laid down	Launched	Commissioned	Status
Virginia	CGN-38	19 Aug 1972	14 Dec 1974	11 Sept 1976	AA
Texas	CGN-39	18 Aug 1973	9 Aug 1975	10 Sept 1977	PA
Mississippi	CGN-40	22 Feb 1975	31 July 1976	5 Aug 1978	AA
Arkansas	CGN-41	17 Jan 1977	21 Oct 1978	18 Oct 1980	PA

Builders Newport News SB and DD Co, Newport News, Va
Displacement standard, 8,625 tons; full load, 10,420 tons
Length overall 585ft (178.3m)
Maximum beam 63ft (19.2m)
Maximum draught 31ft (9.5m)
Main machinery Two pressurised water-cooled reactors (General Electric D2G). Two General Electric steam turbines
Screws/s.h.p. 2/100,000
Maximum speed 30 knots+
Armament Two twin Mark 26 launchers for Harpoon/Tartar/Standard-MR/Asroc, two single Mark 45 5in/54 gun mounts, two 40mm saluting guns, two triple Mark 32 ASW torpedo tubes
Complement 27 officers and 445 enlisted men

The first three units were begun as Guided Missile Frigates (DLGN), but all were reclassified as CGNs on 30 June, 1975. CGN-38 was authorised FY-1970, CGN-39 in FY-1971, CGN-40 in FY-1972, and CGN-41 in FY-1975. CGN-42 was proposed in the FY-1976 Programme, but it was not funded by Congress. The Navy originally cancelled CGN-41 and -42 on 9 May, 1971; however, the two were kept alive by Congress and CGN-41 was ultimately built. Design and construction was originally awarded under the Total Package Procurement concept, which was the procurement method under trial at the time. This system for design and awarding was later abandoned, and the various ships being constructed under the process were assigned SCB numbers.

Improved *California*s, these ships are ten feet (3.05m) shorter because the Mark 26 combined Harpoon/Standard/Asroc launchers eliminated the need for an Asroc launcher. This class may be fitted with the Aegis system. Each ship is to be fitted with 20mm Mark 15 CIWS. Besides a helicopter landing area, these ships have a hangar with a telescoping hatch cover located beneath the fantail flight deck. A lift is provided for transporting the helicopters between the hangar and main deck.

Better AAW capabilities, electronic warfare equipment, and an anti-submarine fire control system are the main improvements over the *California* class. These ships are fitted with bow-mounted AN/SQS-53A sonar, NTDS, AN/SPS-48A three-dimensional radar, AN/SPS-40B and AN/SPS-55 radar antennas, QE-82 Satellite Communication antenna, and the Mark 86 fire control system. In addition there is the digital Mark 116 ASW fire control system, two AN/SPG-55 fire control systems, one AN/SPG-60 and one AN/SPQ-9 fire control system. The *Tomahawk* cruise missiles are to be fitted in a four-tube launcher. The Mark 36 Super Roboc chaff system is fitted.

June 1977 view of *Texas* (CGN-39). She is carrying the AN/SPS-40B and SPS-48C air search radars, the AN/UPX-23 IFF system and the SPS-55 surface search radar *(US Navy)*

California (CGN-36) in Britain during June 1977. Visible are the AN/SPS-40D and 48C air search and AN/SOS-10F surface search radar antennae. Two Mark 13 missile launchers and four AN/SPG-51 radar antennae (two aft, two forward and above the bridge) can also be seen *(C. & S. Taylor)*

Type: Guided Missile Cruisers (nuclear-powered) (CGN) *Number/Class:* 2 *California*

Name	*Number*	*Laid down*	*Launched*	*Commissioned*	*Status*
California	CGN-36	23 Jan 1970	22 Sept 1971	16 Feb 1974	AA
South Carolina	CGN-37	1 Dec 1970	1 July 1972	25 Jan 1975	AA

Builder Newport News SB and DD Co, Newport News, Va
Displacement standard, 9,561 tons; full load, 11,100 tons
Length overall 596ft (181.7m)
Maximum beam 61ft (18.6m)
Maximum draught 31.5ft (9.6m)
Main machinery Two pressurised water-cooled reactors (General Electric D2G). Two General Electric geared turbines
Screws/s.h.p. 2/60,000
Maximum speed 30 knots+
Armament Two single Mark 13 Standard-MR/Tartar D launchers, one Asroc eight-tube launcher, two single Mark 45 5in/54 gun mounts, two twin Mark 32 ASW torpedo tubes, two 40mm saluting guns
Complement 28 officers, 512 enlisted men

Completed as Guided Missile Frigates (DLGN), these ships were reclassified as CGNs on 30 June, 1975. *California* was authorised in FY-1967 ($200 million), and *South Carolina* in FY-1968 ($180 million). These large, multi-purpose warships were designed (SCB-241.66) to operate with fast carrier task forces. An improved *Truxtun* design, they have dual-purpose launchers and mixed Standard/Asroc magazines. Unlike *Truxtun*, they have tall enclosed towers instead of lattice masts. No helicopter facilities are provided, although a landing area is provided.

Originally a five-ship class, three *California* units were deferred in favour of the *Virginia* class.

Each ship is fitted with the AN/SPS-10 and AN/SPG-40 surface search radars, four AN/SPG-51 fire control radars, AN/SPG-60 and AN/SPQ-9 fire control systems, the Mark 116 ASW fire control system, and the digital Mark 86 gunfire control system for AAW/anti-surface/gunfire support, NTDS. The radar systems also include the AN/SPS-48 three-dimensional air-search plannar array for missiles and interceptor control.

Two Phalanx 20mm Mark 15 CIWS and the Mark 36 Super Roboc chaff system are to be fitted (the Mark 36 replaces the Mark 28 system).

The improved reactor core design provides these ships with a range of about 700,000 miles. Independent operations at high sustained speed and long endurance has become a reality with the advent of these ships.

Type: Guided Missile Cruiser (nuclear-powered) (CGN) *Number/Class:* 1 *Truxtun*

Name	Number	Laid down	Launched	Commissioned	Status
Truxtun	CGN-35	17 June 1963	19 Dec 1964	27 May 1967	PA

Builder New York SB Corp, Camden, N.J.
Displacement Standard, 8,200 tons; full load, 9,127 tons
Length overall 564ft (171.9m)
Maximum beam 58ft (17.7m)
Maximum draught 31ft (9.5m)
Main machinery Two pressurised water-cooled reactors (General Electric D2G). Two General Electric geared turbines
Screws/s.h.p. 2/60,000
Maximum speed 30 knots+
Armament One twin Mark 10 guided missile launcher for Standard-ER/Terrier/Asroc, two quadruple canister launchers for Harpoon surface-to-surface missiles (16 missiles), one single 5in/54 Mark 42 gun mount, two twin Mark 32 fixed ASW torpedo tubes, two 40mm saluting guns
Complement 36 officers, 492 enlisted men

Truxtun was completed as a Guided Missile Frigate (nuclear powered) (DLGN) and reclassified CGN-35 on 30 June, 1975. Authorised in the FY-1962 programme, she is an improved *Bainbridge* design (SCB-222). Her engineering plant duplicates that of CGN-25.

Although *Truxtun* was originally requested as a unit of the *Belknap* class, Congress directed that one of the seven requested DLGs in the FY-1962 Programme be nuclear powered. As such, she became the fourth surface "nukie" warship in the USN. The weapons and electronics nearly duplicate those of the *Belknap* class. She has two heavy lattice masts, but no "macks", and is distinguishable from the *Belknaps* by her reversed armament arrangement. The twin missile launcher has been modified to fire Standard-ER missiles and Asroc. Two Phalanx 20mm CIWS are to be fitted, along with the Mark 36 Super Roboc system, replacing the Mark 28 Chaffroc system.

Truxtun has the AN/SPS-48 planar air search array for missiles and interceptor control, AN/SPS-10 surface search radar on the forward mast, and AN/SPS-40 air search radar on the aft mast. She also has NTDS, a QE-82 satellite communications antenna, AN/SQS-26 bow-mounted sonar, two Mark 76 missile fire control systems, one Mark 68 fire control system, one Mark 114 ASW fire control system, four AN/SPG-51 gunfire control systems, one AN/SPG-60 gun fire control system, and one AN/SPQ-9 fire control system.

A DLGN armed with the ill-fated Typhon missile system was requested in the FY-1963 Programme, but was cancelled when the missile system proved too expensive and too big to install on a ship. The craft was to be over 9,000 tons at full load displacement, more than 600ft (182.9m) long, have one twin Typhon launcher for long range and two single short-range launchers, and mount two single 5in/54 gun mounts and NTDS.

Truxtun (CGN-35) off Hawaii in July 1970 *(US Navy)*

Type: Guided Missile Cruisers (CG) *Number/Class:* 9 *Belknap*

Name	Number	Laid down	Launched	Commissioned	Status
Belknap	CG-26	5 Feb 1962	20 July 1963	7 Nov 1964	AA
Josephus Daniels	CG-27	23 Apr 1962	2 Dec 1963	8 May 1965	AA
Wainwright	CG-28	2 July 1962	25 Apr 1964	8 Jan 1966	PA
Jouett	CG-29	25 Sept 1962	30 June 1964	3 Dec 1966	PA
Horne	CG-30	12 Dec 1962	30 Oct 1964	15 Apr 1967	PA
Sterett	CG-31	25 Sept 1962	30 June 1964	8 Apr 1967	PA
William H. Standley	CG-32	29 July 1963	19 Dec 1964	9 July 1966	PA
Fox	CG-33	15 Jan 1963	21 Nov 1964	28 May 1966	PA
Biddle	CG-34	9 Dec 1963	2 July 1965	21 Jan 1967	AA

Builders Bath Iron Works, Bath, Maine (CG-26/28, -32, -34); Puget Sound Naval Shipyard, Bremerton, Wash (CG-29, -31); San Francisco Naval Shipyard, San Francisco, Cal (CG-30); Todd SY Corp, San Pedro, Cal (CG-33)
Displacement Standard, 6,570 tons. Full load, 8,200 tons (CG-27/29); 8,065 tons (remainder)
Length overall 547ft (166.7m)
Maximum beam 54.8ft (16.7m)
Maximum draught 28.8ft (8.8m)
Main machinery Four boilers (Babcock and Wilcox, CG-26/28, -32, -34; Combustion Engineering, remainder). Two geared turbines (General Electric, CG-26/28, -32; DeLaval, remainder)
Screws/s.h.p. 2/85,000
Maximum speed 32.5 knots
Armament One twin Mark 10 launcher for Terrier/Standard ER/Asroc, two quadruple launch canisters for Harpoon surface-to-surface missiles (8 missiles, except CG-29, -30: none), one single 5in/54 Mark 42 gun mount, two single 3in/50 Mark 34 gun mounts (CG-30 only), two Mark 32 ASW torpedo tubes, two 40mm saluting guns
Complement 47 officers and 464 enlisted men (CG-26, includes flag accommodation); 38 officers and 387 enlisted men (remainder)
Flag accommodation 6 officers and 12 enlisted men

The *Belknaps* were completed as Guided Missile Frigates (DLG) and reclassified as CG-26/34 on 30 June, 1975 retaining the same hull numbers. They were authorised in FY-1961 (CG-26/28) and FY-1962 (CG-29/34). An enlarged *Leahy*, this successful design

William H. Standley (CG-32) in February 1976. This ship and her sisters, minus the rebuilt *Belknap* (CG-26), are essentially the same as the *Leahy* class. This unit carries the AN/SPS-40C air search radar, the AIMS (Mark 12) IFF system and the AN/SPS-10F surface search radar *(US Navy)*

(SCB-212), is considered excellent for anti-submarine/anti-aircraft warfare, and is the only conventionally powered cruiser with full helicopter capability. The LAMPS system was installed under the FY-1974 Programme.

Electronics included NTDS, AN/SPS-48 three dimensional plannar array for missiles or interceptor control (replacing AN/SPS-39 or -52), AN/SPS-10 surface search radar, and SQS-26 bow-mounted sonar. In addition, SPS-37 and SPS-40 air search radars are installed on the after "mack" and the remainder on the forward "mack". All ships were fitted with the Mark 68 fire-control system, Mark 114 ASW fire-control system (except CG-26, which has Mark 116), and AN/SPG-53 and -55 gunfire-control systems. In this class the missile/Asroc launcher is installed forward, enabling the missiles and rockets to be stored in the larger bow area. The original 12in ASW torpedo tubes, which were located forward of the 5in mount, have been removed. The class is to be fitted with two 20mm Mark 16 CIWS (already on CG-26, -29 and -34) and one Mark 36 Super Roboc chaffroc system. *Fox* served as a sea-testing ship for the Tomahawk cruise missile during 1977, with successful results.

Aircraft carriers, while pleased to have excellent escorts to protect them, sometimes damage the smaller ships. On 22 November, 1975, *Belknap* was engaged in night air operations in the Ionian Sea with the USS *John F. Kennedy* (CV-67). When *Kennedy* began a turn to port to recover aircraft, *Belknap* became confused by the many lights aboard the bigger ship and began to slow turn to starboard. The two ships collided, and *Belknap*'s port side hit the carrier's port side beneath the angled deck, smashing *Belknap*'s aluminium superstructure. On *Kennedy* fuel tanks ruptured, and fuel poured down upon the cruiser and ignited, causing her superstructure to melt in the flames. Eight men died on the cruiser and 25 more were injured as a result of the collision. The Officer of the Deck on *Belknap* at the time of the collision was court martialled and the Commanding Officer was reprimanded.

Belknap was towed across the Atlantic to the Philadelphia Naval Shipyard, where she was placed out of commission, special, on 20 December, 1975. She was repaired and modernised at an estimated cost of $213 million, the work beginning on 9 January, 1978. She was stripped to the bare hull and virtually rebuilt to a new design, which sets her apart from her sisters. The work was completed on 30 April, 1980, and she was placed in full commission on 10 May, that year.

Type: Guided Missile Cruiser (nuclear-powered) (CGN)				*Number/Class:* 1 *Bainbridge*	
Name	*Number*	*Laid down*	*Launched*	*Commissioned*	*Status*
Bainbridge	CGN-25	15 May 1959	15 Apr 1961	6 Oct 1962	PA

Builder Bethlehem Steel Corp, Quincy, Mass
Displacement standard, 7,804 tons; full load, 8,592 tons
Length overall 565ft (172.2m)
Maximum beam 57.8ft (17.6m)
Maximum draught 25.42ft (7.7m)
Main machinery Two pressurised water-cooled reactors (General Electric D2G). Two General Electric geared turbines
Screws/s.h.p. 2/60,000
Maximum speed 30 knots+
Armament Two twin Mark 10 Terrier/Standard-ER launchers (80 missiles), two quadruple launch canisters for Harpoon surface-to-surface missiles (8 missiles), one Asroc launcher, two twin 20mm Mark 67 guns, two Mark 32 ASW torpedo tubes, two 40mm saluting guns
Complement 34 officers, 436 enlisted men
Flag accommodation 6 officers and 12 enlisted men

Bainbridge was completed as a Guided Missile Frigate, nuclear powered (DLGN). Reclassified CGN-25 on 30 June, 1975, she retained her original hull number. Authorised in FY-1959 (SCB-189) and built at a cost of $163.6 million, *Bainbridge* is similar to the *Leahy* class, but has two heavy lattice masts instead of "macks". She is highly manoeuvrable and has proved to be a good seaboat, while nuclear power gives her virtually unlimited endurance at flank speed. Designed to screen fast carriers and to defend them against air attacks, she can perform equally well in the ASW mode.

ASW and AAW capabilities were upgraded considerably. Funding was authorised in FY-1974 (SCB-189.74), and *Bainbridge* was assigned to Puget Sound Naval Shipyard on 5 November, 1973. The work began on 30 June, 1974, and was completed 24 September, 1976, at a cost of $103 million.

During the modernisation the two twin 3in mounts were removed. NTDS and on improved missile guidance system was installed, along with AN/SPS-52 three-dimensional search radar and AN/SPS-10 and AN/SPS-37 search radars on either mast. *Bainbridge* is equipped with the Mark 76 missile fire-control system, Mark 111 ASW fire-control system, AN/SPG-55 gunfire-control system, AN/SQS-23 bow-mounted sonar, and QE-82 satellite communications antenna. She has the LAMPS I system.

Bainbridge (CGN-25) off San Diego, Calif, in April 1979. She was fully modernised between June 1974 and September 1976. She carries the AN/SPS-48 air search and SPS-10 surface search radars *(US Navy)*

Type: Guided Missile Cruisers (CG) — *Number/Class:* 9 *Leahy*

Name	Number	Laid down	Launched	Commissioned	Status
Leahy	CG-16	3 Dec 1959	1 July 1961	4 Aug 1962	PA
Harry E. Yarnell	CG-17	31 May 1960	9 Dec 1961	2 Feb 1963	AA
Worden	CG-18	19 Sept 1960	2 June 1962	3 Aug 1963	PA
Dale	CG-19	6 Sept 1960	28 July 1962	23 Nov 1963	AA
Richmond K. Turner	CG-20	9 Jan 1961	6 Apr 1963	13 June 1964	AA
Gridley	CG-21	15 July 1960	31 July 1961	25 May 1963	PA
England	CG-22	4 Oct 1960	6 March 1962	7 Dec 1963	PA
Halsey	CG-23	26 Aug 1960	15 Jan 1962	20 July 1963	PA
Reeves	CG-24	1 July 1960	12 May 1962	15 May 1964	PA

Builders Bath Iron Works, Bath, Me (CG-16/18); New York SB Corp, Camden, N.J. (CG-19, -20); Puget Sound Bridge and DD Co, Seattle, Wash (CG-21); Todd SY Corp, San Pedro, Cal (CG-22); San Francisco Naval Shipyard, San Francisco, Cal (CG-23); Puget Sound Naval Shipyard, Bremerton, Wash (CG-24)
Displacement standard, 5,670 tons; full load, 8,200 tons
Length overall 533ft (162.5m)
Maximum beam 54.83ft (16.7m)
Maximum draught 25.83ft (7.9m)
Main machinery Four boilers (Babcock and Wilcox, CG-16/20); Foster-Wheeler, remainder). Two geared turbines (General Electric, CG-16/18; DeLaval, CG-19/22; Allis-Chalmers, CG-23, -24
Screws/s.h.p. 2/85,000
Maximum speed 32.7 knots
Armament Two twin Mark 10 launchers for Terrier/Standard-ER missiles, two quadruple Harpoon launch canisters (8 missiles; all except CG-16, 18 and 19), one Asroc launcher, two triple ASW torpedo tubes, two 40mm saluting guns
Complement 18/32 officers; 359/381 enlisted men
Flag accommodation 6 officers and 12 enlisted men

The first purpose-built double-ended missile ships, the *Leahys* were designed (SCB-172) mainly to provide anti-aircraft defence for fast carriers. They also carry a fine ASW battery. Authorised in FY-1958 (CG-16/18) and FY-1959 (CG-19/24), these ships were completed as Guided Missile Frigates (DLG), being re-rated and reclassified as CGs with the same hull numbers on 30 June, 1975. All DL/DLG/DLGN were officially listed as destroyer types. By the mid-1970s the designations did not properly identify and reflect the multi-mission capabilities of these ships by the standards of the world's navies.

Resembling the *Belknap* class, these craft can be quickly distinguished by the missile launchers forward and aft. *Belknaps* have a missile launcher forward and a 5in gun mount aft, while *Leahys* are fitted with NTDS and bow-mounted sonar. They also carry AN/SPS-10 and AN/SPS-48 search radars, and an AN/SPS-37 search radar on the aft 'mack''. Much of this equipment was installed during the class AAW modernisation programme. They are also fitted with AN/SPG-55 fire control radar and the Mark 114 ASW fire control system. Modernised between 1967 and 1972, their AAW capabilities were upgraded. In addition to the above, AN/SPS-52 air search radar, an improved Terrier fire control system and large turbo generators were fitted, and certain electronic improvements were made.

Reeves (CG-24), representative of the *Leahy* class, in August 1975. This class was designed primarily for anti-air warfare (AAW) missions *(US Navy)*

Anti-air warfare modernisations (SCB-244)

Number	Programme	Decommissioned	Started	Completed	Recommissioned
CG-16	FY-1966	18 Feb 1967	15 Feb 1967	17 Aug 1968	4 May 1968
CG-17	FY-1967	9 Feb 1968	9 Feb 1968	27 June 1969	12 July 1969
CG-18	FY-1967	10 Nov 1969	10 Nov 1969	8 Jan 1971	16 Jan 1971
CG-19	FY-1971	10 Nov 1970	10 Nov 1970	22 Nov 1971	11 Dec 1971
CG-20	FY-1971	5 May 1971	5 May 1971	19 May 1972	27 May 1972
CG-21	FY-1967	10 Sept 1968	10 Sept 1968	9 Jan 1970	17 Jan 1970
CG-22	FY-1967	10 Apr 1970	10 Apr 1970	16 June 1971	26 June 1971
CG-23	FY-1971	4 Nov 1971	4 Nov 1971	8 Dec 1972	16 Dec 1972
CG-24	FY-1967	10 Apr 1969	10 Apr 1969	14 Aug 1970	29 Aug 1970

Leahy received the prototype mod at Philadelphia Naval Shipyard. All of the others were done by Bath Iron Works. *Dale* was originally in the FY-1968 Programme, but was deferred until FY-1971.

These ships have a helicopter landing area with limited support facilities, but no hangar. Two Phalanx 20mm CIWS (Mark 15) (already in CG-22) and the Mark 36 Super Roboc chaff system (already in CG-17, -21, -22 and -24) are to be fitted.

Even friendly missiles can be dangerous. While patrolling off the North Vietnam coast on 16 April, 1972, *Worden* was hit by at least two missiles fired by friendly aircraft. Her superstructure was damaged, one man was killed, and nine were wounded.

Type: Guided Missile Cruisers (CG) — *Number/Class:* 2 Albany

Name	Number	Laid down	Launched	Commissioned	Status
Albany	CG-10	6 Mar 1944	30 June 1946	15 June 1946	AR
Chicago	CG-11	28 July 1943	20 Aug 1944	10 Jan 1945	PR

Chicago (CG-11). Converted from a *Baltimore*-class heavy cruiser (CA), *Chicago* is the other half of the two-ship *Albany* class *(US Navy)*

Builders Bethlehem Steel Corp, Fore River, Mass (CG-10); Philadelphia Navy Yard, Philadelphia, Pa (CG-11)
Displacement standard, 14,600 tons (CG-10); 13,200 tons (CG-11). Full load, 19,000 tons (CG-10), 17,700 tons (CG-11)
Length overall 674ft (205.4m)
Maximum beam 71ft (21.6m)
Maximum draught 30ft (9.1m)
Main machinery Four Babcock and Wilcox boilers. Four General Electric geared turbines
Screws/s.h.p. 4/120,000
Maximum speed 32 knots
Armament Two twin Tartar Mark 11 missile launchers, one Asroc 8-tube launcher, two single 5in/38 gun mounts, two triple Mark 32 ASW torpedo tubes, two 40mm saluting guns
Complement 1,248 total (79 officers and 1,169 enlisted men – CG-10); 1,302 total (86 officers and 1,216 enlisted men – CG-11)
Flag accommodation 10 officers and 58 enlisted men

This class represented the first of the double-ended cruiser designs. A third ship, *Columbus* (CG-12), was struck from the NVR on 9 August, 1976, and sold for scrapping on 3 October, 1977. *Albany* was originally a heavy cruiser of the *Oregon City* class. She was decommissioned 30 June, 1958, for converson to a missile cruiser and reclassified from CA-123 to CG-10 on 1 November the same year. *Chicago* (CA-136) was decommissioned at Bremerton on 6 June, 1947. She was reclassified to CG-11 on 1 November, 1958.

Conversion of the *Oregon City* class ship and the two *Baltimores* was compatable, since *Albany* was basically a one-stack *Baltimore* and dimensions, armament, and propulsion systems were quite similar. All three ships were converted to the same design (SCB-173) to form a new class of a new type. They were stripped down to the main hull and rebuilt. All guns and turrets were removed, though 5in gun mounts were later added for low-level and close-in defence. To keep weight down and increase stability, aluminium was used wherever possible. They were fitted with "macks", a means of combining the stack and mast in one structure. A plan to install eight *Polaris* missile tubes amidships was cancelled.

Missile conversion

Name	*Programme*	*Naval shipyard*	*Assigned*	*Started*	*Completed*
Albany	FY-1958	Boston	26 Nov 1957	2 Jan 1959	2 Nov 1962
Chicago	FY-1958	San Francisco	23 Sept 1958	1 July 1959	1 Dec 1963

Albany recommissioned on 3 November, 1962; *Chicago* on 2 May, 1964. The Talos systems were declared unsupportable and removed early on FY-1979.

Albany was decommissioned at Boston for an update of AAW capabilities on 1 February, 1967. Authorised in the FY-1966 Programme (SCB-002), modernisation began 1 February, 1967, and was completed 30 June, 1969. The ship recommissioned on 9 November, 1968. Since the useful life of the *Albany*s was so brief, it was decided not to upgrade her sister ships. Among the major installations made during modernisation was the fitting of a digital computer for target detection and guidance control, and much improved radar equipment, including NTDS.

It was originally planned to strike and dispose of both of these ships, but because of rising world tensions *Chicago* was decommissioned at Bremerton on 1 March, 1980, and laid up. *Albany* was decommissioned on 29 August, 1980, and laid up partially mothballed (75 per cent) at Norfolk. Both of these ships are to be retained in this status for 3/5 years. *Albany* was Sixth Fleet flagship throughout the 1970s.

Disposal notes *Boston* (CAG-1) and *Canberra* (CAG-2), the world's first missile cruisers, were struck from the Navy List on 4 January, 1974, and 31 July, 1978, respectively. The last *Baltimore* class all-gun heavy cruiser (CA), *Saint Paul* (CA-73), was struck from the Navy List on 31 July, 1978. She was sold for scrapping on 10 January, 1980.

Type: Guided Missile Cruiser (nuclear-powered) (CGN) — *Number/Class:* 1 *Long Beach*

Name	*Number*	*Laid down*	*Launched*	*Commissioned*	*Status*
Long Beach	CGN-9	2 Dec 1957	14 July 1959	9 Sept 1961	PA

Builder Bethlehem Steel Co, Quincy, Mass
Displacement standard, 15,540 tons; full load, 17,525 tons
Length overall 721.25ft (219.8m)
Maximum beam 73.25ft (22.3m)
Maximum draught 31ft (9.5m)
Main machinery Two pressurised water-cooled reactors (Westinghouse C1W). Two General Electric geared turbines
Screws/s.h.p. 2/80,000
Maximum speed 32 knots+
Armament Two twin Terrier/Standard-ER Mark 10 launchers (120 missiles), two quadruple Harpoon launchers (8 missiles), one Asroc launcher, two single 5in/38 mounts, two triple Mark 32 ASW torpedo tubes, two 40mm saluting guns
Complement 79 officers and 1,081 enlisted men
Flag accommodation 10 officers and 58 enlisted men

The world's first nuclear powered combatant, *Long Beach* is the first USN cruiser built since the Second World War. The original design was for a DLGN of 7,800 tons, but it was recast in 1956 and displacement eventually grew to 14,000 tons, largely owing to the addition of Talos Terrier missile systems). Authorised in the FY-1957 (SCB-169), she was ordered as CLGN-160 and changed to CGN-9 on 1 July, 1957.

The original plan to install a Regulus II missile system gave way to a plan for eight tubes for launching Polaris missiles, but this idea was dropped to hold down construction costs. *Long Beach* cost an estimated $332.85 million. She was completed without conventional armament, but two single 5in/38 gun mounts were installed amidships for low-level and close-in defence at the Philadelphia Naval Shipyard soon after completion.

Having steamed 167,700 miles on her initial core, *Long Beach* was refuelled from August 1965 to February 1966 at Newport News.

Long-lead funding of the installation of the Aegis system on *Long Beach* was authorised in FY-1977. Conversion would have taken place between October 1978 and October 1981, but was cancelled in December 1976 and the funds rescinded. Instead a mid-life modernisation was authorised under FY-1980 at a total cost of $175.2 million. Besides updating the missile system, the modernisation will include replacement of the AN/SPS-32 and 33 air-search radars by AN/SPS-48 and -49 systems, replacement of the ship's computer systems, and complete modernisation of her communications system. The work was begun at Puget Sound Naval Shipyard, on 6 October, 1980, and completed on 26 January 1983.

Long Beach is fitted with AN/SQS-23 sonar (bow-mounted), one AN/SPS-48 three-dimensional search radar, AN/SPS-10 air search radar and four AN/SPG-55B fire control radar, two AN/SPG-49 fire control radars, one Mark 111 ASW fire control radar, and four Mark 76 missile fire control systems. The

Tomahawk cruise missile system, one Mark 36 Super RBOC Chaffroc launcher and two twin Mark 16 CIWS gun systems are fitted.

▲ *Long Beach* in June 1976, before modernisation *(US Navy)*

▼ Artist's impression of *Long Beach* (CGN-9) after a modernisation which included removal of the AN/SPS-32 and 33 radar antennae fixed to the sides of the bridge, and addition of Harpoon launchers in place of the aft Mark 10 launcher

Type: Gun Cruisers (CA) *Number/Class:* 2 Des Moines

Name	Number	Laid down	Launched	Commissioned	Status
Des Moines	CA-134	28 May 1945	27 Sept 1946	16 Nov 1948	AR
Salem	CA-139	4 July 1945	25 Mar 1947	14 May 1949	AR

Builder Bethlehem Steel Corp, Fore River, Mass
Displacement standard, 17,000 tons; full load, 21,470 tons
Length overall 716.43ft (218.4m)
Maximum beam 76.3ft (23.3m)
Maximum draught 25.5ft (7.8m)
Main machinery Four Babcock and Wilcox boilers. Four General Electric geared turbines
Screws/s.h.p. 4/120,000
Maximum speed 33 knots
Armament Three triple 8in/55 gun turrets, six twin 5in/38 mounts, ten twin 3in/50 mounts (CA-134), eleven twin 3in/50 mounts (CA-139)
Complement 1,803 total (116 officers, 1,687 enlisted men – CA-134); 1,738 total (115 officers, 1,623 enlisted men – CA-139)

The largest and most powerful heavy cruisers ever built, these ships were designed as fast, mobile, steady platforms equipped with the latest rapid-fire 8in gun. Formerly designated heavy cruisers (CA), the *Des Moines* class were redesignated gun cruisers (CA). Twelve units of this class were planned. A third completed ship, *Newport News* (CA-148), was decommissioned after 26 years of continuous service on 27 June, 1975, and was struck from the Navy List on 31 July, 1978.

Des Moines was completed with two stern catapults and carried four floatplanes. These were later removed. Encased ammunition and fast automatic handling equipment give these ships' guns a rate of fire four times faster than that of earlier Mark 8in guns.

Des Moines was decommissioned on 14 July, 1961, and *Salem* on 30 January, 1959. Both ships were decommissioned at Boston Naval Shipyard, and both are currently laid up at Philadelphia.

Currently under consideration is a plan to reactivate one of these ships as Sixth Fleet flagship in place of *Puget Sound* (AD-38), which is in need of an extended overhaul.

Salem (CA-139) and her sister, *Des Moines* (CA-134), are the largest heavy cruisers ever built. It has been proposed to reactivate one or both of these ships as an alternative to *Missouri* (BB-63) and *Wisconsin* (BB-64) of the *Iowa* class *(US Navy)*

Destroyers (DDG/DD)

At the end of FY-1975, 106 destroyer types were on the Naval Vessel Register, not including 28 destroyers under construction. Of 39 DDGs, all were active. Of 67 destroyers, 34 were active, one was laid up in reserve, and 32 were serving as Naval Reserve Training ships.

At the end of FY-1982 79 destroyer types were on the Register, not including one DD under construction. All 40 DDGS were active. 46 destroyers were active and another four were serving as NRT ships.

This decrease is misleading. Although the USN has fewer destroyer types than six years ago, the present force level is far better for dealing with an adversary because the majority of the ships are modern, with advanced improvements and capabilities. Also, the large class of *Ticonderogas*, then classified DDGs, were reclassified Guided Missile Cruisers (CGN), as they should have been in the first place.

The planned successor to the CG-16, CG-26. and DDG-37 classes in the Programme is the DDGX, now the *Arleigh Burke* (DDG-51) class. At least 60 are to be built. Long-lead items will be requested in FY-1984, and construction funds in FY-1985 for the prototype (DDG-51). Long-lead items for DDG-52/54 are planned to be requested in the FY-1986 budget, followed by construction funding in FY-1987.

Type: Guided Missile Destroyers (DDG) — *Number/Class:* 4 *Kidd*

Name	*Number*	*Laid down*	*Launched*	*Commissioned*	*Status*
Kidd	DDG-993	26 June 1978	11 Aug 1979	27 June 1981	AA
Callaghan	DDG-994	23 Oct 1978	1 Dec 1979	29 Aug 1981	AA
Scott	DDG-995	12 Feb 1979	1 Mar 1980	24 Oct 1981	AA
Chandler	DDG-996	7 May 1979	24 May 1980	13 Mar 1982	AA

Scott (DDG-995) and her three sisters would have been the pride of the Imperial Iranian Navy had the Shah not been overthrown. Each ship of this class carries the AN/SPS-48C air search radar, the AIMS IFF system, the SPS-55 surface search radar and the AN/SPG-51 and 60 fire-control system *(US Navy)*

Builder Ingalls Shipbuilding Corp, Pascagoula, Miss
Displacement light, 6,210 tons; full load, 8,300 tons
Length overall 563.2ft (171.7m)
Maximum beam 55ft (16.8m)
Maximum draught 30ft (9.1m)
Main machinery Four General Electric LM2500 gas turbines
Screws/s.h.p. 2/80,000
Maximum speed 30 knots+
Armament Two twin Mark 32 launchers for Standard-ER missiles/Asroc, two twin Harpoon launch canisters (4 missiles), two single 5in/54 lightweight gun mounts, two 20mm Mark 16 CIWS, two triple Mark 32 ASW torpedo tubes
Complement 20 officers, 318 enlisted men

The world's most powerful general-purpose destroyers, these ships are missile versions of the *Spruance* class. The same modular concept that was so successful with the *Spruances* was used to construct these ships. This concept is intended to facilitate construction and modernisation. The engineering plant duplicates that in the *Ticonderoga* (CG-47) and *Spruance* (DD-963) classes.

This class, as originally ordered by the Government of Iran, comprised six ships, which were assigned hull numbers (DD-993/998) for accounting purposes. In June 1976 DD-995 and -997 were cancelled. On 23 April, 1978, DD-996 and -998 were reclassified DD-995 and -996. Then, when the US Navy took over the ships, DD-993/996 were reclassified to DDG-993/996 on 8 August, 1979. Despite repeated attempts, including letters to the Secretary of the Navy and the Commander, Naval Sea Systems Command, the editors have been unable to determine why the ships were not reclassified DDG-48/51, which would have been the logical numbers. DDG-993 is ex-Iranian *Kouroosh* (11); DDG-934 is ex-Iranian *Daryush* (12); DDG-995 is ex-Iranian *Andushiruan* (13); and DDG-996 is ex-Iranian *Nader* (14).

Under the FY-1979 Supplemental budget request, the Navy took over the contracts of the four remaining Iranian destroyers (they rated them as cruisers) still on order, which had been ordered originally on 23 April, 1978, but were cancelled on 3 February, 1979 (DD-995 and -996), and 31 March, 1979 (DD-993 and -994). The four ships were finally officially acquired on 25 July, 1979.

Two 20mm Mark 16 CIWS (one starboard forward and one port aft) and a Mark 36 Super Chaffroc system are installed.

Electronics comprise a navigational/surface search radar AN/SPS-55 and air search radar AN/SPS-48, TACTAS SQR-19, two Mark 74 missile fire control systems, two Mark 86 gunfire control systems with AN/SPG-51 radar, one Mark 117 underwater fire control system, an AN/SLQ-32 electronic countermeasures set, and SQS-53 bow-mounted sonar.

Type: Guided Missile Destroyers (DDG) — *Number/Class:* 0+(60) *Arleigh Burke*

Name	Number	Laid down	Launched	Commissioned	Status
Arleigh Burke	DDG-51				PROJ
	DDG-52/54				PROJ
	DDG-55/59				PROJ

Displacement full load 8,500 tons
Length overall 466ft (139.8m)
Maximum beam 60ft (18.3m)
Maximum draught 25ft (7.5m)
Main machinery Four Gas turbines (General Electric LM-2500)
Screws/s.h.p. 2/100,000
Maximum speed 30 knots +
Endurance 5,000nm at 20kt
Armament SSM: two quadruple Harpoon launch canisters; Tomahawk cruise missiles; SAM/ASW: Standard-ER (SM-2) missiles in two vertical launch systems (VLS) (90 missiles each); two triple Mark 32 ASW torpedo tubes; one single 5in/54 (Mark 45) gun mount; two 20mm CIWS Phalanx (Mark 16) gun mounts
Complement 21 officers and 286 enlisted men

This class is designed to replace the *Coontz* class Guided Missile Destroyers (DDG) and the *Leahy* and *Belknap* Guided Missile Cruisers (CG), starting in the early 1990s. Long-term lead items for the prototype are to be requested in the FY-1984 budget, with construction funds following in the FY-1985 budget. Three more units are to be requested in the FY-1987 budget, and five more units in the FY-1988 programme.

These ships will be less capable than the *Ticonderoga* class CGs, and are intended to supplement them. Their primary mission will be anti-air warfare, but they will also have a surface-to-surface capability.

The entire ship, except for the aluminium funnels, is made of steel. It is planned to construct all future non-aviation surface ships from steel, which is more resistant to the elements and to fire. It is also being done to avoid a recurrence of what happened to *Belknap* when it collided with *John F. Kennedy*. Some 130 tons of Kevlar armour is fitted to protect vital spaces.

This is the first US Navy ship class designed with a "collective protection system for defence against the fallout associated with NBC Warfare. The ship's crew will be protected by double air-locked hatches, fewer accesses to the weatherdecks, and positive pressurisation of the interior of the ship to keep out contaminants. All incoming air will be filtered and more reliance placed on recirculating air inside the ship . . ." Until the advent of this class, the *Herbert J. Thomas* (DD-833) of the *Gearing* class (FRAM I), since sold to Taiwan, was the only US Navy ship fully equipped for NBC warfare.

Electronics comprise the AN/SPY-1D version of Aegis, an AN/SLQ-32 electronic countermeasures suit, three Mark 99 fire-control systems, three SPG-62 illuminating radars, the Seafire fire control system with laser capabilities, and an AN/SPS-10 surface-to-surface radar. These vessels will be equipped with the Mark 36 Super RBOC Chaffroc system, the AN/SQS-53C sonar, and the Tactass (AN/SQR-19) towed-array sonar. The Mark 32 tubes will be the first to employ the Advanced Light Weight Torpedo (ALWT).

April 1982 artist's impression of the new DDG-51 class (formerly DDGX). This design marks a return by the US Navy to the practice of building surface combatants entirely of steel rather than with steel hulls and aluminium superstructures

Type: Guided Missile Destroyers (DDG) *Number/Class:* 10 Coontz

Name	Number	Laid down	Launched	Commissioned	Status
Farragut	DDG-37	3 June 1957	18 July 1958	10 Dec 1960	AA
Luce (ex-**Dewey**)	DDG-38	1 Oct 1957	11 Dec 1958	20 May 1961	AA
MacDonough	DDG-39	15 Apr 1958	9 July 1959	4 Nov 1961	AA
Coontz	DDG-40	1 Mar 1957	6 Dec 1958	15 July 1960	AA
King	DDG-41	1 Mar 1957	6 Dec 1958	17 Nov 1960	AA
Mahan	DDG-42	31 July 1957	7 Oct 1959	25 Aug 1960	AA
Dahlgren	DDG-43	1 Mar 1958	16 Mar 1960	8 Apr 1961	AA
William V. Pratt	DDG-44	1 Mar 1958	16 Mar 1960	4 Nov 1961	AA
Dewey	DDG-45	10 Aug 1957	30 Nov 1958	7 Dec 1959	AA
Preble	DDG-46	16 Dec 1957	23 May 1959	9 May 1960	AA

Builders Bethlehem Steel Corp, Quincy, Mass (DDG-37/39); Puget Sound Naval Shipyard, Bremerton, Wash (DDG-40, -41); San Francisco Naval Shipyard, San Francisco, Cal (DDG-42); Philadelphia Naval Shipyard, Pa (DDG-43, -44); Bath Iron Works, Bath, Me (DDG-45, -46)
Displacement standard, 4,150–4,580 tons; full load, 5,709–5,907 tons
Length overall 512.5ft (156.2m)
Maximum beam 52.5ft (16m)
Maximum draught 25ft (7.62m)
Main machinery Four boilers, (Foster-Wheeler, DDG-37/39); (Babcock and Wilcox, DDG-40/46). Two geared turbines. (DeLaval, DDG-37/39, -45, -46); (Allis-Chalmers, DDG-40/44)
Screws/s.h.p. 2/85,000
Maximum speed 35 knots
Armament One twin Terrier Mark 10 missile launcher, two twin Harpoon missile launch canisters (4 missiles, except DDG-38 and -41, none) one single 5in/54 gun mount, one 8-tube Asroc launcher, two Mark 32 triple ASW torpedo tubes, two 40mm saluting guns
Complement 21 officers and 356 enlisted men
Flag accommodation 7 officers and 12 enlisted men

These ships were built for anti-air warfare and to screen carrier task forces. They are also very capable in the ASW role. Completed as Guided Missile Frigates (DLG), they were the only DLG class with separate masts and stacks. They were authorised under the FY-1956 Programme (DDG-37/42) and FY-1957 (DDG-43/46).

Having an aluminium superstructure to reduce topside weight and improve stability, the original design called for two 5in mounts, but the "B" position mount was replaced by the then new Asroc rocket launcher. These ships resemble those of the *Charles F. Adams* class, but have salient differences. The *Coontz*-class ships have two masts, compared with one in the DDG-2 ships, one 5in gun mount instead of two, and the Asroc is forward rather than amidships.

The stern helicopter landing area in this class has no hangar, and the support capabilities are limited.

DDG-37/39 were originally ordered as DL-6/8 of a modified *Mitscher*-class frigate design, but were reordered to the *Coontz* DLG design (SCB-142) before being laid down. They were reclassified from DL-6/8 to DLG-6/8 on 14 November, 1956. DLG-6/15 were reclassified DDG-37/46 on 30 June, 1975, rather than to CGs, because of their size and capability. *Luce* (DDG-38) was originally named *Dewey*, but was renamed on 12 February, 1957.

DDG-41 and -42, along with *Oriskany* (CV-34), were the first warships to receive the Naval Tactical Data System (NTDS) (later removed from all three).

These ships have been modernised to improve their AAW capabilities (SCB-243). The superstructure was enlarged to provide space for additional electronic equipment, including the installation of NTDS (already fitted in DDG-41 and -42). An improved Tacan was installed, plus an improved guidance system for Standard missiles (SPG-55 fire control radar), and larger ship's service turbo-generators were also fitted. *Farragut* had an improved Asroc reload system installed abaft the launcher, below the bridge, and the two twin 3in/50 mounts were removed and the after deckhouse was enlarged. DDG-37 modernisation was authorised under the FY-1966 Programme, DDG-46 in FY-1968, DDG-45 in FY-1969, DDG-38 in FY-1970, DDG-40 in FY-1971, DDG-43 and -44 in FY-1972, DDG-39 in FY-1973, and DDG-41 and -42 in FY-1974. Modernisation cost per ship was $39 million in FY-1970 dollars. DDG-41 was modernised by the Boland Machine Co of Louisiana; DDG-42 by Bath Iron Works, Bath, Maine, and the remainder by Philadelphia Naval Shipyard, Philadelphia, Pennsylvania.

Farragut (DDG-37) off St Croix, Virgin Islands. This is the only unit of the class to carry an Asroc reload system. Note that the Mark 32 ASW torpedo tubes, just below the foremast, are trained out *(US Navy)*

Anti-air warfare modernisations

DDG	Assigned/Awarded	Conversion begun	Conversion completed	Recommissioned
-37	13 Oct 1966	1 May 1968	10 Mar 1969	13 Sept 1969
-38	1 Nov 1969	28 Feb 1970	9 July 1971	22 May 1971
-39	15 Nov 1972	9 Apr 1973	26 Apr 1974	4 May 1974
-40	24 July 1970	28 Feb 1971	27 Apr 1972	18 Mar 1972
-41	19 Apr 1974	1 July 1974	8 Mar 1977	17 Sept 1977
-42	20 June 1973	31 Aug 1973	22 Mar 1975	1 Apr 1975
-43	30 Sept 1971	28 Feb 1972	29 Mar 1973	17 Mar 1973
-44	12 Jan 1970	10 Oct 1972	18 Oct 1973	6 Oct 1973
-45	22 Aug 1968	24 Nov 1969	23 Apr 1971	13 Mar 1971
-46	29 Feb 1968	31 Jan 1969	1 July 1970	23 May 1970

These ships will eventually be fitted with the Mark 36 Super Chaffroc system.

Electronics comprise the AN/SPS-48 three dimensional search radar (SPS-52 in DDG-41, -44), AN/SPS-10 and -37 navigation and search radars, NTDS and SQS-23 hull-mounted sonar, two Mark 76 missile fire control systems, one Mark 68 gunfire control system, one SPG-53A and two AN/SPG-55B fire control radars, Mark 11 WDS, and one Mark 111 ASW fire control system.

Type: Guided Missile Destroyers (DDG) *Number/Class:* 4 *Decatur*

Name	Number	Laid down	Launched	Commissioned	Status
Decatur	DDG-31	13 Sept 1954	15 Dec 1955	7 Dec 1956	PR
John Paul Jones	DDG-32	18 Jan 1954	7 May 1955	5 Apr 1956	PR
Parsons	DDG-33	17 June 1957	19 Aug 1958	29 Oct 1959	DPR
Somers	DDG-34	4 Mar 1957	30 May 1958	3 Apr 1959	PR

Builders Bethlehem Steel Corp, Quincy, Mass (DDG-31); Bath Iron Works, Bath, Me (DDG-32, -34); Ingalls SB Corp, Pascagoula, Miss (DDG-33)
Displacement light, 2,863–3,075 tons; full load, 4,049–4,200 tons
Length overall DDG-31 and -32, 418.4ft (127.5m); DDG-33 and -34, 418ft (127.4m)
Maximum beam 45ft (13.7m)
Maximum draught 22ft (6.71m)
Main machinery Four boilers (Foster-Wheeler, DDG-31, -33), (Babcock and Wilcox, DDG-32, -34). Two geared turbines (General Electric, DDG-33, -34); (Westinghouse, DDG-31, -32)
Screws/s.h.p. 2/70,000
Maximum speed 31 knots
Armament One single Tartar Mark 13 missile launcher, one single 5in/54 gun mount, one 8-tube Asroc launcher, two Mark 32 triple ASW torpedo tubes
Complement 22–25 officers and 315–339 enlisted men

Mounting engineering problems resulted in a decision to decommission this class and the *Forrest Sherman/Hull* DD's. *Parsons* and *Somers* were decommissioned on 19 November, 1982, followed by *John Paul Jones* on 15 December, 1982, and *Decatur* on 30 June, 1983. Parsons is to be stricken and disposed of, while the remaining units will be retained in the reserve fleet at Puget Sound Naval Shipyard, Bremerton.

It was originally planned to convert all *Forrest Sherman* (11) and *Hull* (7) class ships to DDG-31/48. However, because of the programme costs this was reduced to four ships. *Turner Joy* (DD-951) was to have become DDG-35. *John Paul Jones* was chosen for conversion because she was due for an extensive overhaul. *Decatur* was selected because she had been badly damaged in a collision. Most of the superstructure had been torn away as a result of the collision with *Lake Champlain* (CVS-39) on 5 May, 1964. As DDGs, the enormous amount of electronics and superstructure added topside tended to make these ships somewhat top-heavy.

DD-936 was reclassified DDG-31 on 15 September, 1966, followed by DD-932, -949 and -947 to DDG-32/34 on 15 March, 1967. The conversion (SCB-240) was funded in the FY-1964 Programme. The work was performed at Naval Shipyards as follows: Boston (DDG-31), Philadelphia (DDG-32), Long Beach (DDG-33), and San Francisco (DDG-34). Conversions were assigned to each Shipyard on 22 December, 1964.

John Paul Jones (DDG-32) in August 1977. Originally built as a conventional destroyer of the *Forrest Sherman* class, she carries AN/SPS-48 and SPS-29E air search radars, AN/UPX-1A IFF and SPS-10B surface search radar. The dish behind and above the gun mount is an OE-82 satellite communications antenna *(US Navy)*

DDG conversions

DDG	*Decommissioned*	*Conversion begun*	*Recommissioned*	*Conversion completed*
-31	June 1965	15 June 1965	29 Apr 1967	28 Apr 1967
-32	20 Dec 1965	2 Dec 1965	23 Sept 1967	13 Dec 1967
-33	19 Jan 1966	30 June 1965	3 Nov 1967	30 Nov 1967
-34	11 Apr 1966	30 Mar 1966	10 Feb 1968	27 Mar 1968

During the conversion all existing armament, except the forward 5in gun mount, was removed. To accommodate the extensive communication and electronic suite, two heavy lattice masts were installed. An Asroc launcher was fitted, replacing the DASH deck originally planned; a single Mark 13 missile launcher was installed aft on the 01 level; and two triple banks on Mark 32 torpedo tubes were installed, one each side of the superstructure.

Electronics comprise three-dimensional AN/SPS-48, AN/SPS-10 and -37 (AN/SPS-40 in *Somers*) navigational and search radars; AN/SQS-23 hull-mounted sonar; one Mark 74 missile fire-control system; one Mark 68 gunfire-control system; one AN/SPG-51C and one AN/SPG-53B fire-control radars; and one Mark 114 ASW fire control system.

Disposals: *Mitscher* (DDG-35) and *John S. McCain* (DDG-36) of the *Mitscher* class were originally classified DL-2 and DL-3 respectively. They were struck from the Navy List, because of major engineering material problems, on 1 June, 1978, and 29 April, 1978, respectively, and sold for scrapping.

Type: Guided Missile Destroyers (DDG) — *Number/Class:* 23 *Charles F. Adams*

Name	*Number*	*Laid down*	*Launched*	*Commissioned*	*Status*
Charles F. Adams	DDG-2	16 June 1958	8 Sept 1959	10 Sept 1960	AA
John King	DDG-3	25 Aug 1958	30 Jan 1960	4 Feb 1961	AA
Lawrence	DDG-4	27 Oct 1958	27 Feb 1960	6 Jan 1962	AA
Claude V. Ricketts	DDG-5	18 May 1959	4 June 1960	5 May 1962	AA
Barney	DDG-6	10 Aug 1959	10 Dec 1960	11 Aug 1962	AA
Henry B. Wilson	DDG-7	28 Feb 1958	22 Apr 1959	17 Dec 1960	PA
Lynde McCormick	DDG-8	4 Apr 1958	28 July 1959	3 June 1961	PA
Towers	DDG-9	1 Apr 1958	23 Apr 1959	6 June 1961	PA
Sampson	DDG-10	2 Mar 1959	21 May 1960	24 June 1961	AA
Sellers	DDG-11	3 Aug 1959	9 Sept 1960	28 Oct 1961	AA
Robison	DDG-12	28 Apr 1959	27 Apr 1960	9 Dec 1961	PA
Hoel	DDG-13	3 Aug 1959	4 Aug 1960	16 June 1962	PA
Buchanan	DDG-14	23 Apr 1959	11 May 1960	7 Feb 1962	PA
Berkeley	DDG-15	29 Aug 1960	29 July 1961	15 Dec 1962	PA
Joseph Strauss	DDG-16	27 Dec 1960	9 Dec 1961	20 Apr 1963	PA
Conyngham	DDG-17	1 May 1961	19 May 1962	13 July 1963	AA
Semmes	DDG-18	15 Aug 1960	20 May 1961	10 Dec 1962	AA
Tattnall	DDG-19	14 Nov 1960	26 Aug 1961	13 Apr 1963	AA
Goldsborough	DDG-20	3 Jan 1961	15 Dec 1961	9 Nov 1963	PA
Cochrane	DDG-21	31 July 1961	18 July 1962	21 Mar 1964	PA
Benjamin Stoddert	DDG-22	11 June 1962	8 Jan 1963	12 Sept 1964	PA
Richard E. Byrd	DDG-23	12 April 1961	6 Feb 1962	7 March 1964	AA
Waddell	DDG-24	6 Feb 1962	26 Feb 1963	28 Aug 1964	PA

Builders Bath Iron Works, Bath, Me (DDG-2, -3, -10, -11); New York SB Corp, Camden, N.J. (DDG-4/6, 15/17); Defoe SB Co, Bay City, Mich (DDG-7, -8, -12, -13); Todd Shipyards, Inc, Seattle, Wash (DDG-9, -14, -23, -24); Avondale Marine Ways Inc, Westwego, La (DDG-18, -19); Puget Sound Bridge and Dredging Co, Seattle, Wash (DDG-20/22)
Displacement light, 3,103–4,104 tons; full load, 4,500–4,900 tons
Length overall DDG-2/19, 437ft (133.2m); DDG-20/24, 440ft (134.1m)
Maximum beam 47ft (14.3m)
Maximum draught 21–25ft (6.4–7.62m)
Main machinery Four boilers, (Babcock and Wilcox, DDG-2, -3, -7, -8, -10/13, -20/22); (Foster-Wheeler, DDG-4/6, -9, -14, -23, -24); (Combustion Engineering, DDG-15/19). Two geared turbines, (General Electric, DDG-2, -3, -7, -8, -10/13, -15/22); (Westinghouse, DDG-4/6, -9, -14, -23, -24)
Screws/s.h.p. 2/70,000
Maximum speed 30 knots
Armament One twin Tartar Mark 11 missile launcher (DDG-2/14), one single Tartar Mark 13 missile launcher (DDG-15/24), two single 5in/54 gun mounts, one 8-tube Asroc rocket launcher, two triple Mark 32 ASW torpedo tubes
Complement 24 officers and 330 enlisted men

These ships are of modified *Forrest Sherman/Hull* class design (SCB-155). They are excellent sea boats, and are also considered to be excellent multi-purpose ships. DDG-20/24 have stem anchors owing to their bow-mounted sonars.

DDG-2/9 were originally classified DD-952/959 of an improved *Hull* class design, being reclassified to DDG-952/959 on 16 August, 1956, and to DDG-2/9 on 26 June, 1957. DDG-2/9 were authorised under the FY-1957 Programme. DDG-10/14 were authorised in FY-1958, DDG-15/19 in FY-1959, DDG-20/22 in FY-1960, and DDG-23 and -24 in FY-1961.

All 23 ships were to receive a mid-life modernisation, but the programme was reduced to ten (DDG-3, -10, 16/22, -24) under the FY-1980/1983 programmes. Although Congress rejected the whole plan, the Navy still intended to carry out this work on DDG-15/24, doing it over two overhaul periods and using Fleet Maintenance funds. However, the programme has been further reduced to DDG-17, -19, -20, -22, -23 and -24. The remaining 17 ships are to be deleted, beginning in the late 1980s. Each modernisation will cost between $125.7 to 178.5 million in FY-1979 dollars and take 20/24 months. It will include the installation of Harpoon missiles; the upgrading of various electronic systems, including the Anti-Ship Missile Defence System (ASMD); installation of AN/SPS-48 radar; installation of an integrated automatic detection and tracking system (SYS-1); the fitting of the Mark 86 fire control system for the Standard Arm missiles and gun armament; and the fitting of AN/SQS-23 sonar domes with control units. The following table gives the provisional modernization schedule:

Hull No	FY	Yard	From	To
DDG-17	83	Philadelphia Naval Shipyard	15 Jul 1984	15 Oct 1985
	89	—	—	—
DDG-19	82	Philadelphia Naval Shipyard	31 Aug 1981	29 Nov 1982
	86	Philadelphia Naval Shipyard	1 Feb 1987	1 Apr 1988
DDG-20	82	Pearl Harbor Naval Shipyard	11 Mar 1983	28 July 1984
	86	Pearl Harbor Naval Shipyard	15 June 1987	15 Apr 1988
DDG-22	83	Pearl Harbor Naval Shipyard	9 Apr 1984	2 Aug 1985
	87	Pearl Harbor Naval Shipyard	11 July 1988	11 May 1989
DDG-23	84	Philadelphia Naval Shipyard	1 Aug 1985	1 July 1986
	89	—	—	—
DDG-24	83	Long Beach Naval Shipyard	3 Oct 1983	11 Jan 1985
	87	Long Beach Naval Shipyard	15 Feb 1988	16 Dec 1988

Charles F. Adams (DDG-2) in 1978. The class can be divided into two sub-groups distinguished by the fact that DDG-2 to 14 have the twin Mark 11 SAM missile launcher while the remainder have the single Mark 13 launcher *(US Navy)*

Electronics comprise AN/SPS-39 three-dimensional search radar (AN/SPS-52 being fitted), AN/SPS-10 and 37 navigation and search radars (DDG-15/24, AN/SPS-40 on remainder), AN/SQS-23 bow-mounted (DDG-20/24) and AN/SQS-23 hull-mounted sonar, two Mark 74 missile fire-control systems, one Mark 68 gunfire-control system (to be replaced with Mark 86), one Mark 4 Weapon Detection System (to be replaced with Mark 13, already on DDG-9, -12, -15, -21), one AN/SPG-51C and one AN/SPG-53A weapon-control radars, and one Mark 114 (DDG-16/24) or Mark 111 (remainder) ASW fire-control system. Mark 36 Super Chaffroc (already on DDG-14 and -22) is also to be fitted (see page 234 for more data).

Gyatt (DD-712) was reclassified DDG-712, then DDG-1, and then reverted to DD-712.

DDG-25/27 were *Charles F. Adams* class ships built for Australia and completed during 1965/1967. DDG-28/30 were built for West Germany, being completed in 1969/1970.

Benjamin Stoddert (DDG-22). The *Charles F. Adams* class are regarded by many as the finest destroyers built by the US since the Second World War *(US Navy)*

Type: Destroyers (DD) — *Number/Class:* 31 + (1) *Spruance*

Name	Number	Laid down	Launched	Commissioned	Status
Spruance	DD-963	27 Nov 1972	10 Nov 1973	20 Sept 1975	AA
Paul F. Foster	DD-964	6 Feb 1973	22 Feb 1974	21 Feb 1976	PA
Kincaid	DD-965	19 Apr 1973	25 May 1974	10 July 1976	PA
Hewitt	DD-966	23 July 1973	24 Aug 1974	25 Sept 1976	PA
Elliot	DD-967	15 Oct 1973	19 Dec 1974	22 Jan 1977	PA
Arthur W. Radford	DD-968	31 Jan 1974	27 Mar 1975	16 Apr 1977	AA
Peterson	DD-969	29 Apr 1974	21 June 1975	9 July 1977	AA
Caron	DD-970	1 July 1974	23 June 1975	1 Oct 1977	AA
David R. Ray	DD-971	23 Sept 1974	24 Aug 1975	19 Nov 1977	PA
Oldendorf	DD-972	17 Dec 1974	21 Oct 1975	4 Mar 1978	PA
John Young	DD-973	17 Feb 1975	6 Jan 1976	20 May 1978	PA
Comte de Grasse	DD-974	4 Apr 1975	26 Mar 1976	5 Aug 1978	AA
O'Brien	DD-975	9 May 1975	8 July 1976	3 Dec 1977	PA
Merrill	DD-976	16 June 1975	1 Sept 1976	11 Mar 1978	PA
Briscoe	DD-977	21 July 1975	28 Dec 1976	3 June 1978	AA
Stump	DD-978	22 Aug 1975	21 Mar 1977	19 Aug 1978	AA
Conolly	DD-979	29 Sep 1975	3 June 1977	14 Oct 1978	AA
Moosbrugger	DD-980	3 Nov 1975	23 July 1977	16 Dec 1978	AA
John Hancock	DD-981	16 Jan 1976	28 Sept 1977	10 Mar 1979	AA
Nicholson	DD-982	20 Feb 1976	29 Nov 1977	12 May 1979	AA
John Rodgers	DD-983	12 Aug 1976	25 Feb 1978	14 July 1979	AA
Leftwich	DD-984	12 Nov 1976	8 Apr 1978	25 Aug 1979	PA
Cushing	DD-985	2 Feb 1977	17 June 1978	4 Sept 1979	PA
Harry W. Hill	DD-986	1 Apr 1977	10 Aug 1978	11 Nov 1979	PA
O'Bannon	DD-987	24 June 1977	25 Sept 1978	15 Dec 1979	AA
Thorn	DD-988	29 Aug 1977	14 Nov 1979	16 Feb 1980	AA
Deyo	DD-989	14 Oct 1977	20 Jan 1979	22 Mar 1980	AA
Ingersoll	DD-990	16 Dec 1977	10 Mar 1979	12 Apr 1980	PA
Fife	DD-991	6 Mar 1978	1 May 1979	31 Apr 1980	PA
Fletcher	DD-992	24 Apr 1978	16 June 1979	12 July 1980	PA
Hayler	DD-997	20 Oct 1980	2 Mar 1982	5 March 1983	AA

Builder Ingalls Shipbuilding Corp, Pascagoula, Miss
Displacement standard, 5,830 tons; full load, 7,800 tons
Length overall 563.2ft (171.7m)
Maximum beam 55.1ft (16.8m)
Maximum draught 29ft (8.8m)
Main machinery Four General Electric LM2500 gas turbines
Screws/s.h.p. 2/80,000
Maximum speed 33 knots
Armament Two single 5in/54 gun mounts, one 8-tube Asroc rocket launcher, one Nato Sea Sparrow Mark 29 missile launcher, two quad Harpoon launch canisters (4 missiles each) two triple Mark 32 ASW torpedo tubes
Complement 24 officers and 272 enlisted men

These ships were built as replacements for the *Gearing*-class (FRAM I) destroyers. They were procured under the Total Package Procurement concept, in which the design and construction was awarded to one builder. This idea was later abandoned, and an SCB number was assigned (SCB-224.71). As it transpired, Ingalls did an excellent job on the project, and in good time (see the construction table dates). Unfortunately, the same cannot be said for succeeding projects.

John Rodgers (DD-983) in 1979, shortly after commissioning. The Mark 29 Nato Sea Sparrow launcher, to be installed amidships aft, is still in its crate on the after port corner of the deck *(Ingalls Shipbuilding)*

These ships were built under the modular assembly technique. Large sections of the hull were constructed in various sections of the shipyard and ultimately welded together to form a ship. The keel-laying dates mark the start of erection of the first module. The aim is to facilitate initial construction and later modernisation. The high level of automation in these ships results in a 20 per cent reduction in personnel compared with a similar ship having conventional systems. The *Spruance*s were built primarily as ASW platforms, and are the first large US warships to employ gas turbine propulsion.

Authorisations were as follows: DD-963/965 under the FY-1970 Programme, DD-966/971 under FY-1971, DD-972/978 under FY-1972, DD-979/985 under FY-1974, DD-986/992 under FY-1975, and DD-997 under FY-1978. The Navy plans to resume construction of this class, with three units projected for the FY-1986 programme, as replacement for the *Forrest Sherman/Hull* classes. DD-997 was originally to be an air-capable *Spruance*, having a large flight deck aft and an enlarged hangar to accommodate up to four LAMPS III ASW helicopters or two Harrier VTOL aircraft. Two of these ships were added by the Senate, but the House of Representatives failed to provide the funds. In the Conference Committee it was later agreed to provide a maximum of $310 million for one ship, with the caveat that if the ship exceeded that limit the air-capable features of the design would have to be deleted. They were, and the ship became another *Spruance* (see page 234).

Electronics comprise an AN/SQS-53 bow-mounted sonar, AN/SLQ-32 (V) electronic countermeasures suite, AN/SPS-40 and AN/SPS-55 search radars, AN/SPG-60 and AN/SPQ-9 fire-control radars, one Mark 116 digital ASW fire-control system, one Mark 86 gunfire-control system, and one Mark 91 missile fire control system. These ships carry on SH-2D (LAMPS I) helicopter, to be replaced by the SH-3 Sea King.

Elliot (DD-967) of the *Spruance* class. Because of the increasing "gun gap" resulting from the wholesale scrapping of surface combatants after the Vietnam War, it was planned to arm this class and succeeding designs with a lightweight 8in gun. This plan was however dropped in 1980, after the gun had been successfully tested at sea and was about to enter production *(US Navy)*

The Tomahawk cruise missile system is scheduled to be installed on DD-964, -969, -973, -979, -984, -985, -988, -989, and -992. Space and weight are allowed for the installation of two Mark 16 CIWS (already on DD-965). The Mark 36 Super RBOC Chaffroc system will replace the Mark 33 system currently installed.

DD-934 and -935 were Second World War German destroyers taken as war prizes, while DD-939 was a Japanese war prize. After use in tests, all three were scrapped. DD-960 and -961 were built as Japanese *Moon*-class destroyers. DD-962 was HMS *Charity*, purchased from the Royal Navy for transfer to Pakistan.

Type: Destroyers (DD) *Number/Class:* 5 Hull

Name	Number	Laid down	Launched	Commissioned	Status
Hull	DD-945	12 Sept 1956	10 Aug 1957	3 July 1958	DPR
Edson	DD-946	3 Dec 1956	4 Jan 1958	7 Nov 1958	NRF
Morton	DD-948	4 Mar 1957	23 May 1958	26 May 1959	PR
Richard S. Edwards	DD-950	20 Dec 1956	24 Sept 1957	5 Feb 1959	PR
Turner Joy	DD-951	30 Sept 1957	5 May 1958	3 Aug 1959	PR

Builders Bath Iron Works, Bath, Me (DD-945, -946); Ingalls SB Corp, Pascagoula, Miss (DD-948); Puget Sound Bridge and Drydock Co, Seattle, Wash (DD-950, -951)
Displacement standard, 2,863–3,000 tons; full load, 4,049–4,200 tons
Length overall 418ft (127.4m)
Maximum beam 45ft (13.7m)
Maximum draught 20ft (6.1m)
Main machinery Four Babcock and Wilcox boilers. Two General Electric geared turbines
Screws/s.h.p. 2/70,000
Maximum speed 33 knots
Armament Three single 5in/54 gun mounts (DD-945, -946, -951); two single 5in/54 gun mounts (DD-948, -950); one Asroc 8-tube rocket launcher (DD-948, -950); two triple Mark 32 ASW torpedo tubes
Complement 17 officers and 275 enlisted men (except ASW-modified units: 17 officers and 287 enlisted men)

This class represents a modified *Forrest Sherman* class. There are only minor differences between the two classes, the major one being the bow design. Originally there were seven ships in the class. Two, DD-947 and -949, were converted to guided missile destroyers (see *Decatur*, DDG-31 class). All of these ships were authorised in the FY-1956 Programme, and were built at a cost of $26 million each. The design, SCB-85A, included an aluminium superstructure for maximum stability and minimum displacement.

Turner Joy was originally named *Joy*, and was renamed on 26 July, 1957. *Edson* was assigned as a Naval Reserve Training ship on 1 April, 1977, for employment as schoolship for engine-room training and reservist training. Stationed at Newport, Rhode Island, she is the only active unit, the others having been decommissioned as follows: *Morton* and *Turner Joy* on 22 November, 1982; *Richard S. Edwards* on 15 December, 1982; and *Hull* scheduled for 10 July, 1983. *Edson* and *Turner Joy* will be retained in reserve at Puget Sound Naval Shipyard, Bremerton, and *Morton* and *Richard S. Edwards* at Pearl Harbor; *Hull* will be stricken and scrapped.

Both the *Forrest Sherman* and *Hull* classes were originally armed with three single 5in/54 gun mounts, two twin 3in/50 mounts, four fixed 21in ASW torpedo tubes amidships, two ASW Hedgehogs and two depth charge racks.

Morton (DD-948) (illustrated) and *Richard S. Edwards* (DD-950) received major ASW modernisations in 1970–1971. The remainder of the class underwent only minor modifications and retain the basic configuration with which they were commissioned. *(US Navy)*

The following applies to both the *Hull* and *Forrest Sherman*-class ASW modernisation projects. Two units of the *Hull* class and six *Forrest Shermans* were modified. DD-933 (SCB-251) were authorised in the FY-1964 Programme. The remaining ships (SCB-222) were authorised as follows: DD-941 and -943 in FY-1967; DD-937, -938, -940, -948 and -950 in FY-1968. DD-933, -937 and -941 were converted by the Boston Naval Shipyard, DD-938, -940 and -943 by Philadelphia Naval Shipyard, and DD-948 and -950 by Long Beach Naval Shipyard.

Primary changes included the addition of Asroc, relocation of the triple Mark 32 tubes from midships to forward, deletion of one 5in and two 3in gun mounts, and modification and improvement of the fire control systems. The Combat Information Center (CIC) area was increased, improved radars and communications were installed, and underway replenishment capabilities were improved. Habitability was enhanced by enlarging the pilot house and electronic spaces, and relocating various living and stores areas. The conversion schedule was as follows:

Forrest Sherman/Hull-class ASW modernisations

DD	*Date assigned*	*Conversion started*	*Conversion completed*	*Recommissioned*
-933	22 Dec 1964	5 Jan 1967	20 May 1968	19 Apr 1968
-937	2 May 1969	3 Nov 1969	4 Dec 1970	17 Oct 1970
-938	17 May 1968	30 Apr 1969	14 Sept 1970	1 Aug 1970
-940	17 May 1968	1 Feb 1970	27 May 1971	17 Apr 1971
-941	27 Mar 1969	26 May 1969	23 June 1970	9 May 1970
-943	17 May 1968	18 Jan 1969	16 June 1970	2 May 1970
-948	2 May 1969	30 Sept 1969	2 Oct 1970	17 Aug 1970
-950	2 May 1969	2 Mar 1970	2 Mar 1971	15 Jan 1971

DD-942, authorised for conversion in FY-1968, was assigned to Philadelphia on 17 May, 1968, but her conversion was cancelled in April 1969. *Hull* (DD-945), authorised for conversion in FY-1968, was assigned to the Philadelphia Naval Shipyard on 17 May, 1968, but was cancelled in September 1968 and replaced in the programme by *Richard S. Edwards* (DD-950).

Current electronics comprise AN/SPS-10, 37, or 40 search radars; SQS-23 sonar (bow-mounted in *Barry*); AN/SQS-35 VDS in ASW ships; one Mark 56 and one Mark 68 gunfire control systems, one Mark 114 ASW fire control system (except DD-931, -942, -945, -946 and -951, which have no ASW fire control system); one AN/SPG-53A and 35 fire control radars; and one Mark 5 target designation system.

During 1974/1975, when the "gun gap" became a major concern to Navy planners, *Hull* was fitted with a prototype 8in/55 Mark 71 lightweight gun mount in place of mount "51", for testing. The projectile was laser guided and stabilised in flight by tail fins controlled by a seeker device. The gun was removed in 1980 after tests were successfully completed, but there was insufficient priority to continue the project.

Due to increasing costs, further ships of both classes had their modernisations cancelled. These ships, DD-931, -944/946, and -951, received minor improvements to increase their capabilities. The improvements included the removal of the forward 3in twin mount and the fitting of a deckhouse in its place. The superstructure between the stacks was built up to house the extra ECM and electronic gear.

Hull numbers DD-952/959 were originally allotted for a modified *Hull* class design. On 16 August, 1956, they were reclassified DDG-952/959, and on 26 June, 1957, to DDG-2/9.

Type: Destroyers (DD)

Number/Class: 9 *Forrest Sherman*

Name	*Number*	*Laid down*	*Launched*	*Commissioned*	*Status*
Forrest Sherman	DD-931	27 Oct 1953	5 Feb 1955	9 Nov 1955	AR
Barry	DD-933	15 Mar 1954	1 Oct 1955	31 Aug 1956	MUSEUM
Davis	DD-937	1 Feb 1955	28 Mar 1956	28 Feb 1957	AR
Jonas Ingram	DD-938	15 June 1955	7 Aug 1956	19 July 1957	DAR
Manley	DD-940	10 Feb 1955	12 Apr 1956	1 Feb 1957	AR
Du Pont	DD-941	11 May 1955	8 Sept 1956	1 July 1957	AR
Bigelow	DD-942	6 July 1955	2 Feb 1957	8 Nov 1957	AR
Blandy	DD-943	29 Dec 1955	19 Dec 1956	26 Nov 1957	AR
Mullinnix	DD-944	5 Apr 1956	18 Mar 1957	7 Mar 1958	AR

Builders Bath Iron Works, Bath, Me (DD-931, -933, -940/942); Bethlehem Steel Corp, Quincy, Mass (DD-937, -938, -943, -944)
Displacement standard, 2,800–3,000 tons; full load, 3,960–4,080 tons
Length overall 418ft (127.4m)
Maximum beam 45ft (13.7m)
Maximum draught 20ft (6.1m)
Main machinery Four boilers, (Babcock and Wilcox, DD-931, -933, -940/942); (Foster-Wheeler, DD-937, -938, -943, -944). Two geared turbines, (Westinghouse, DD-931, -933, -937, -938); (General Electric, DD-940/944)
Screws/s.h.p. 2/70,000
Maximum speed 33 knots
Armament Three single 5in/54 gun mounts (DD-931, -942, -944), two single 5in/54 gun mounts (remainder), one Asroc 8-tube launcher (DD-933, -937, -938, -940, -941, -943). Two triple Mark 32 ASW torpedo tubes
Complement 17 officers and 287 enlisted men (except -931, -942 and -944: 17 officers and 275 enlisted men)

Barry (DD-933) is the only one of the ASW-modernised units of this and the *Hull* classes to have the sonar dome mounted in the bow *(US Navy)*

These ships (SCB-85) were the first US Navy destroyers built after the Second World War. Originally, there were 11 ships in the class, but two were converted to guided missile destroyers (see *Decatur* class, DDG-31). DD-931 and -933 were authorised in FY-1953, and the remaining ships in FY-1954. Each ship cost $26 million.

Ships from DD-937 onwards have higher bows. *Barry*'s sonar dome was moved forward in 1959 and a stem anchor was fitted.

ASW modernisations and minor upgrading of some ships in this class is detailed in the *Hull* class section to avoid duplication of the data. Electronics and other common features are also recorded in the *Hull* (DD-945) section.

Because of major problems with their powerplants this class and the *Hull* and *Decatur* classes have been decommissioned. The *Forrest Sherman*-class ships were decommissioned as follows: *Forrest Sherman, Barry, Bigelow* and *Blandy* on 5 November, 1982; *Davis* on 20 December, 1982; *Jonas Ingram*, *Manley* and *Du Pont* were scheduled for 4 March, 1983; and *Mullinnix* for 11 August, 1983. All but two will be retained in reserve at Philadelphia Naval Shipyard. *Jonas Ingram* will be scrapped, while *Barry* will be rerated as "floating equipment" and berthed at Washington DC Naval Yard as a museum ship under operational control of the Naval District Washington.

Type: Destroyers (DD)

Number/Class: 2 *Gearing* (FRAM I)

Name	Number	Laid down	Launched	Commissioned	Status
William C. Lawe	DD-763	12 Mar 1944	21 May 1945	18 Dec 1946	NRF
Harold J. Ellison	DD-864	3 Oct 1944	14 Mar 1945	23 June 1945	NRF

Builders Bethlehem Steel Co, San Francisco, Cal (DD-763); Bethlehem Steel Co, Staten Island, N.Y. (DD-864)
Displacement standard, 2,425 tons; full load, 3,498–3,528 tons
Length overall 390.5ft (119m)
Maximum beam 41.2ft (12.6m)
Maximum draught 19ft (5.8m)
Main machinery Four Babcock and Wilcox boilers. Two General Electric geared turbines
Screws/s.h.p. 2/60,000
Maximum speed 32.5 knots
Armament Two twin 5in/38 gun mounts, one Asroc 8-tube rocket launcher, two triple Mark 32 ASW torpedo tube mounts
Complement 12 officers and 176 enlisted men (active duty), 7 officers and 112 enlisted men (NRF)

Sole survivors of America's once mighty Second World War destroyer force. A total of 152 units of this class was projected; 98 were completed, five were launched and laid up as incomplete hulls (DD-720 and -721, which were struck in 1954, DD-766 and -767, struck in 1958, and DD-791, struck in 1961), and 49 were cancelled during or at the end of the war. *William C. Lawe* and *Harold J. Ellison* are scheduled for disposal by foreign transfer on 1 October 1983.

The original armament for the *Gearing*s was three twin 5in/38 mounts, two quad and two twin 40mm mounts, 11 single 20mm mounts, two quintuple 21in torpedo tube mounts, and two depth charge racks. Armament varied over the years as modernisation and changes of the basic configuration took place, and secondary armaments were slowly eliminated. In addition, the original pole masts were replaced by a tripod mast to support the heavier radar antenna.

Many *Gearing*s were extensively modernised under the FRAM I and II Programmes. During this work they were fitted with the Dash hangar and flight deck. Although Dash (Drone Anti-Submarine Helicopter) was sound in principal, it was plagued with problems, such as disappearing over the horizon after launch. The "Down At Sea Helicopter" concept was ultimately abandoned.

Current electronics comprise an AN/SPS-10 navigation radar, AN/SPS-37 or 40 search radar, AN/SQS-23 hull-mounted sonar, one Mark 37 gunfire-control system, one Mark 114 ASW fire-control system in DD-864 and on Mark 111 in DD-763, and one Mark 5 target designator system.

William C. Lawe (DD-763), one of two remaining *Gearing*-class (FRAM I) destroyers in the US Navy. These ships are the sole survivors of the Second World War destroyer building programme and of the planned 152 units of this class. The FRAM (Fleet Rehabilitation and Modernisation) overhauls, carried out in the early 1960s, were designed to extend ship life by eight years. Eighteen years later, the FRAM I *Gearings* looked set for at least two more years of service *(US Navy)*

Gearing-class (FRAM I) disposals since 1 January, 1976

Name	DD	Date stricken	Comments
William R. Rush	-714	1 July 1978	Sold 1 July, 1978, to South Korea as **Kang Won** (DD-922)
William M. Wood	-715	1 Dec 1976	Sunk as target May 1983 by seven Harpoon hits
Wiltsie	-716	23 Jan 1976	Sold 29 April, 1977, to Pakistan as **Tariq** (D-165)
Hamner	-718	1 Oct 1979	Sold 17 December, 1980, to Taiwan as **Chao Yang** (912)
Epperson	-719	1 Dec 1975	Sold 29 April, 1977, to Pakistan as **Talmur** (D-166)
Southerland	-743	19 Feb 1981	Disposition by foreign transfer pending
Rowan	-782	18 Dec 1975	Sold 10 June, 1977, to Taiwan as **Chao Yang** (912). Grounded on 22 August, 1977, while under tow to Taiwan. Total loss
Gurke	-783	30 Jan 1976	Sold 17 March, 1977, to Greece as **Tombasiz** (D-215)
McKean	-784	1 Oct 1981	Sold as spare parts to Turkey 25 November, 1982
Henderson	-785	1 Oct 1980	Sold 30 September, 1980, to Pakistan as **Turghil** (D-167)
Richard B. Anderson	-786	20 Dec 1975	Sold 10 June, 1977, to Taiwan as **Kai Yang** (915)
Hollister	-788	1 Oct 1979	Sold 3 March, 1983, to Taiwan for service
Higbee	-806	31 Aug 1979	Hulk used as target in tests
Corry	-817	1 Oct 1980	Sold 8 July, 1981, to Greece
New	-818	1 July 1976	Sold 23 February, 1977, to South Korea as **Taejon** (DD-99)
Holder	-819	1 Oct 1976	Sold 1 September, 1978, to Ecuador as **Presidente Eloy Alfaro** (DD-01)
Johnston	-821	27 Feb 1981	Sold 27 February, 1981, to Taiwan
Robert H. McCard	-822		Leased 5 June, 1980, to Turkey as **Kalic Ali Pasa** (D-349)
Basilone	-824	1 Nov 1977	Hulk to be used as target in tests
Agerholm	-826	1 Dec 1978	Sunk as test target 18 July, 1982
Myles C. Fox	-829	1 Oct 1979	Sold 2 August, 1980, to Greece as **Kriesis** (D-217)
Charles P. Cecil	-835	1 Oct 1979	Sold 2 August, 1980, to Greece as **Apostolis** (D-216)
George K. MacKenzie	-836	1 Oct 1976	Sunk as target 17 October, 1976
Sarsfield	-837	1 Oct 1977	Sold 1 October, 1977, to Taiwan as **Te Yang** (925)
Power	-839	1 Oct 1977	Sold 1 October, 1977, to Taiwan as **Shen Yang** (932)
Glennon	-840	1 Oct 1976	Sunk as target, 26 February, 1981
Fiske	-842		Leased 5 June, 1980, to Turkey as **Piyale Pasa** (D-348)
Bausell	-845	30 May 1978	Sunk as target
Richard E. Kraus	-849	1 July 1976	Sold 23 February, 1977, to South Korea as **Kwang Ju** (DD-90)
Leonard F. Mason	-852	2 November 1976	Sold 10 March, 1978, to Taiwan as **Lai Yang** (981)
Vogelgesang	-862	23 Feb 1982	Sold 24 February, 1982, to Mexico as **Quetzalcoatl** (E-03)
Steinaker	-863	23 Feb 1982	Sold 24 February, 1982, to Mexico as **Netzahualcoyoti** (E-04)
Cone	-866	1 Oct 1982	Sold 1 October, 1982, to Pakistan as **Alamgir** (D-160)
Stribling	-867	1 July 1976	Sunk as target, 27 July, 1980
Brownson	-868	30 Sept 1976	Sold 10 June, 1977, for scrapping
Damato	-871	30 Sept 1980	Sold 30 September, 1980, to Pakistan as **Tippu Sultan** (D-168)
Hawkins	-873	1 Oct 1979	Sold 19 March, 1983, to Taiwan for service
Rodgers	-876	1 Oct 1980	Sold 25 July, 1981, to South Korea as **Jeon Ju** (DD-925)
Vesole	-878	1 Dec 1976	Sunk as target in mid-1983
Dyess	-880	27 Feb 1981	Sold 8 July, 1981, to Greece
Bordelon	-881	1 Feb 1977	Sold July 1977 to Iran for cannibalisation and scrapping after being severely damaged in a collision with **John F. Kennedy** (CV-67) on 22 November, 1975
Newman K. Perry	-883	27 Feb 1981	Sold 27 February, 1981, to South Korea as **Kyong Ki** (DD-923)
John R. Craig	-885	27 July 1979	Disposition pending
Orleck	-886		Leased 1 October, 1982, to Turkey as **Yucetepe** (D-345)
Meredith	-890	29 June 1979	Sold 7 December, 1979, to Turkey for cannibalisation and scrapping. However, she was recommissioned as **Savas Tepe** (D-348) instead
Carpenter-class disposals			
Carpenter	-825	20 Feb 1981	Sold 20 February, 1981, to Turkey as **Anittepe** (D-347). Renamed **Gemlik** in March 1981
Robert A. Owens	-827	—	Leased to Turkey 22 February, 1982, as **Alciptepe** (D-346)

Frigates (FFG/FF)

At the end of FY-1975 there were 68 frigates on the Navy List; 6 FFG and 58 FF were active, four FFG were under construction, and 26 more FFG were projected. By the end of FY-1982, 82 frigates were on the NVR, of which 27 were FFG and 55 FF. All were active except for four FF, which were assigned to the NRF. In addition, 27 FFG were under construction and at least ten more projected.

A cheaper version of the *Oliver Hazard Perry* class FFGs was being planned. As in the *Knox* class frigates, this design was being criticised by the "doomsayers" before it was off the drawing boards, as being too slow and under-armed. Called the FFGX it was intended primarily for the Naval Reserves and would have been capable of low-threat-area missions, thus relieving the more costly frigates of these lesser, but still important, tasks. This programme was to replace the ill-fated FFX class programme, and would have saved the Navy about $150 million, as opposed to the Carter Administration's FFX proposals. However, the FFGX has now been cancelled. As in many other areas, it will take the Navy many years, and many more dollars, just to get back to where they were before the Carter Administration.

Fitting out at Bath Iron Works in May 1980 are, from left to right, *Clark* (FFG-11), *Estocin* (FFG-15) and *Samuel Eliot Morison* (FFG-13) *(Bath Iron Works)*

Type: Guided Missile Frigates (FFG) *Number/Class:* 29+21+(0) *Oliver Hazard Perry*

Name	Number	Laid down	Launched	Commissioned	Status
Oliver Hazard Perry	FFG-7	12 June 1975	25 Sept 1976	17 Dec 1977	AA
McInerney	FFG-8	16 Jan 1978	4 Nov 1978	15 Dec 1979	AA
Wadsworth	FFG-9	13 July 1977	29 July 1978	2 Apr 1980	PA
Duncan	FFG-10	29 Apr 1977	1 Mar 1978	24 May 1980	PA
Clark	FFG-11	17 July 1978	24 Mar 1979	17 May 1980	AA
George Philip	FFG-12	14 Dec 1977	16 Dec 1978	15 Nov 1980	PA
Samuel Eliot Morison	FFG-13	4 Dec 1978	14 July 1979	11 Oct 1980	AA
Sides	FFG-14	7 Aug 1978	19 May 1979	30 May 1981	PA
Estocin	FFG-15	2 Apr 1979	3 Nov 1979	10 Jan 1981	AA
Clifton Sprague	FFG-16	30 July 1979	16 Feb 1980	21 Mar 1981	AA
John A. Moore	FFG-19	19 Dec 1978	20 Oct 1979	14 Nov 1981	PA
Antrim	FFG-20	21 June 1978	27 Mar 1979	26 Sept 1981	PA
Flatley	FFG-21	13 Nov 1979	15 May 1980	20 June 1981	AA
Fahrion	FFG-22	1 Dec 1978	24 Aug 1979	16 Jan 1982	PA
Lewis B. Puller	FFG-23	23 May 1979	15 Mar 1980	17 Apr 1982	AA
Jack Williams	FFG-24	25 Feb 1980	30 Aug 1980	19 Sept 1981	AA
Copeland	FFG-25	24 Oct 1979	26 July 1980	7 Aug 1982	PA
Gallery	FFG-26	17 May 1980	20 Dec 1980	5 Dec 1981	AA
Mahlon S. Tisdale	FFG-27	19 Mar 1980	7 Feb 1981	13 Nov 1982	PA
Boone	FFG-28	27 Mar 1979	16 Jan 1980	15 May 1982	AA
Stephen W. Groves	FFG-29	16 Sept 1980	4 Apr 1981	17 Apr 1982	AA
Reid	FFG-30	8 Oct 1980	27 June 1981	19 Feb 1983	PA
Stark	FFG-31	24 Aug 1979	30 May 1980	23 Oct 1982	AA
John L. Hall	FFG-32	5 Jan 1981	24 July 1981	26 June 1982	PA
Jarrett	FFG-33	11 Feb 1981	17 Oct 1981	2 July 1983	PA
Aubrey Fitch	FFG-34	10 Apr 1981	17 Oct 1981	9 Oct 1982	AA
Underwood	FFG-36	30 July 1981	6 Feb 1982	29 Jan 1983	AA
Crommelin	FFG-37	30 May 1980	1 July 1981	18 June 1983	PA
Curts	FFG-38	1 July 1981	6 Mar 1982	21 May 1983	BLDG
Doyle	FFG-39	23 Oct 1981	23 May 1982		PA
Halyburton	FFG-40	26 Sept 1980	13 Oct 1981		BLDG
McClusky	FFG-41	21 Oct 1981	18 Sept 1982		BLDG
Klakring	FFG-42	19 Feb 1982	18 Sept 1982		BLDG
Thach	FFG-43	6 Mar 1982	18 Dec 1982		BLDG
De Wert	FFG-45	14 June 1982	18 Dec 1982		BLDG
Rentz	FFG-46	18 Sept 1982	16 July 1983		BLDG
Nicholas	FFG-47	27 Sept 1982	23 April 1983		BLDG
Vandergrift	FFG-48	13 Oct 1981	15 Oct 1982		BLDG
Robert G. Bradley	FFG-49	28 Dec 1982			BLDG
Taylor	FFG-50	2 May 1983			BLDG
Gary	FFG-51	18 Dec 1982			BLDG
Carr	FFG-52	26 Mar 1982	26 Feb 1983		BLDG
Hawes	FFG-53	16 July 1983			ORD
Ford	FFG-54				BLDG
	FFG-55				ORD
	FFG-56				ORD
	FFG-57				ORD
	FFG-58				ORD
	FFG-59				ORD
	FFG-60				ORD

Builders Bath Iron Works, Bath, Me (FFG-7, -8, -11, -13, -15, -16, -21, -24, -26, -29, -32, -34, -36, -39, -42, -45, -47, -49, -50, -53, -55, -56, -58, -59); Todd Shipyards Inc, San Pedro, Cal (FFG-9, -12, -14, -19, -23, -25, -27, -30, -33, -38, -41, -43, -46, -51, -54, -57, -60); Todd Shipyards Inc, Seattle, Wash (FFG-10, -20, -22, -28, -31, -37, -40, -48, -52)
Displacement standard, 2,750 tons; full load, 3,605 tons
Length overall 445ft (135.6m)
Maximum beam 47ft (14.3m)
Maximum draught 24.5ft (5.7m)
Main machinery Two General Electric model LM2500 gas turbines
Screws/s.h.p. 1/40,000
Maximum speed 29 knots
Armament One single Mark 13 missile launcher (40 Harpoon/Standard-MR missiles carried); one 76mm/62 Mark 75 OTO Melara Compact gun mount; two triple Mark 32 ASW torpedo tubes
Complement 11 officers and 153 enlisted men, plus 146 air crewmen

These ships were designed (SCB-261) with anti-ship/anti-aircraft/anti-missile capabilities. They were built in modular fashion, and are longer but lighter than the *Knox* class frigates. FFG-7 was authorised in the FY-1973 Programme, FFG-8/10 in FY-1975, FFG-11/16 in FY-1976, FFG-19/26 in FY-1977, FFG-27/34 in FY-1978, FFG-36/43 in FY-1979, FFG-45/49 in FY-1980, FFG-50/55 in FY-1981, FFG-56/58 in FY-1982 and FFG-59/60 in FY-1983. The estimated cost per ship has risen from $45.7 million in 1973 to $340.6 million in 1983, mainly because of inflation and design-cost estimate changes.

FFG-7 was originally classified PF-109 but was reclassified FFG-7 on 30 June, 1975. FFG-13, originally named *Samuel E. Morison*, was renamed on 17 August, 1979. It cost $6,600 to change the ship's transom lettering. FFG-45, originally named *Dewert*, was renamed on 2 December, 1982. FFG-17, -18, -35 and -44 were/are built for Australia as *Adelaide, Canberra, Sydney*, and *Darwin*, respectively. Three other units, with no USN hull numbers assigned, are being built for Spain.

The OTO-Melara 76mm Compact gun can fire 90 rounds per minute. Space and weight has been reserved for the installation of the Phalanx 20mm CIWS (Mark 16), atop the after end of the hangar. The Mark 36 Super Chaffroc RBOC launcher is installed on these ships.

Originally a single helicopter hangar was provided, but this has been modified to two side-by-side hangars, each housing one LAMPS I (FFG-7/16, 19/34) or LAMPS III (remainder) ASW helicopter. FFG-8 is serving as an operational test and evaluation ship for the LAMPS III and RAST systems. This modification added 8ft (2.4m) to the ship's overall length.

Electronics comprise an AN/SPS-49 long-range search radar, AN/SPS-55 search and navigation radar, STIR weapons control (modified AN/SPG-60), one Mark 92 weapons control system (note dome antenna atop the bridge), one Mark 13 weapons direction system, and AN/SQS-56 hull-mounted sonar fitted with AN/SQR-19 Tactass towed army. OE-82 satellite communications antennas are also fitted.

These ships have two auxiliary retractable pods installed abaft the sonar dome to provide emergency propulsion in case of engine

or propeller shaft failures. Each pod has a 325bhp diesel engine which gives the ship a maximum speed of 10 knots.

As part of the effort to modernise the NRF a total of 16 units of this class will be reassigned, beginning in May 1984. The proposed schedule is as follows: FFG-7 May 1984, FFG-9 June 1985, FFG-10 January 1984, FFG-11 September 1985, FFG-12 January 1986, FFG-13 June 1986, FFG-14 August 1986, FFG-15 September 1986, FFG-16 August 1986, FFG-19 January 1987, FFG-20 January 1987, FFG-21 November 1987, FFG-22 January 1988, FFG-23 June 1987, FFG-25 and -27 January 1988.

Samuel Eliot Morison (FFG-13) during sea trials off the coast of Maine in mid-1980. FFG-7, 9-16, 19-23 and FFG-25 will be assigned to the Naval Reserve Force (NRF), replacing the *Knox* class and the since deleted *Gearing*s

Estocin on sea trials in September 1980 *(Bath Iron Works)*

McInerney (FFG-8) after modification as the operational evaluation ship for the LAMPS III ASW helicopter (seen on deck) and the Rapid Hauldown and Traversing System (RAST)

Type: Guided Missile Frigates (FFG)

Number/Class: 6 Brook

Name	Number	Laid down	Launched	Commissioned	Status
Brooke	FFG-1	19 Dec 1962	19 July 1963	12 Mar 1966	PA
Ramsey	FFG-2	4 Feb 1963	15 Oct 1963	3 June 1967	PA
Schofield	FFG-3	15 Apr 1963	7 Dec 1963	11 May 1968	PA
Talbot	FFG-4	4 May 1964	6 Jan 1966	22 Apr 1967	AA
Richard L. Page	FFG-5	4 Jan 1965	4 Apr 1966	5 Aug 1967	AA
Julius A. Furer	FFG-6	12 July 1965	22 July 1966	11 Nov 1967	AA

Builders Lockheed SB and Const Co, Seattle, Wash (FFG-1/3); Bath Iron Works, Bath, Me (FFG-4/6)
Displacement standard, 2,643 tons (2,800 tons FFG-3); full load 3,426–3,596 tons
Length overall 414.5ft (126.3m)
Maximum beam 44.2ft (13.5m)
Maximum draught (24.2ft (7.4m)
Main machinery One geared turbine (Westinghouse, FFG-1/3; General Electric, FFG-4/6). Two Foster-Wheeler boilers
Screws/s.h.p. 1/35,000
Maximum speed 27.2 knots
Armament One single Tartar/Standard-MR Mark 22 launcher (16 missiles carried); one single 5in/38 Mark 30 gun mount; one Asroc 8-tube launcher; two triple Mark 32 ASW torpedo tubes
Complement 17 officers, 231 enlisted men

These were the first FF (DE) types to be armed with missiles. Except for the missile system, they are identical to the *Garcia*-class design. A total of 19 ships of this class was planned. However, construction was limited to six ships because of the excessive costs over conventional FFs (DEs), plus other considerations.

Although *Brookes* are destroyer size, their single screw propulsion, and hence their limited speed, rates them as frigates.

This class (SCB-199B) was authorised in FY-1962 (FFG-1/3) and FY-1963 (FFG-4/6). An additional ten ships in the FY-1964 Programme were cancelled. Commissioned as DEG-1/6, they were reclassified FFG-1/6 on 30 June, 1975. DEG-7/11 were missile versions of the *Knox* class design, built in Spain for that country. FFG-6 was originally named *Furer*, but was renamed on 5 April, 1966, because "the *Furer* sounded too much like *Der Fuhrer*."

To hold down construction costs, existing in-house 5in/38 gun mounts were installed, rather than the planned 5in/54s. Though it is a reliable weapon, the 5in/38 gun has less range and a slower rate of fire. The Tartar launcher replaces the No 2 5in gun mount of the *Garcia* class design. These ships were fitted during 1972/1975 to operate an SH-2D (LAMPS) helicopter. FFG-4/6 have automatic Asroc loading systems.

Electronics fitted are one AN/SPS-10 and one AN/SPS-52 search radar, AN/SPG-51C missile control radar, one AN/SQS-26 AX bow-mounted sonar, one AN/SPG-51 and on AN/SPG-35 fire-control radars, one Mark 7 missile fire-control system, one Mark 5 gunfire-control system, and one Mark 11 ASW fire-control system.

These ships have the Mark 33 Super RBOC Chaffroc system (Mark 36 replaces the Mark 33 in FFG-1/3). OE-82 satellite communications antennae and the AN/SLQ-32 ECM suite are also fitted.

Talbot (FFG-4) in the Kiel Canal, West Germany, during 1979. Except for the missile armament, these ships are the same as the *Garcia*-class FFs. In the mid-1970s *Talbot* was reconfigured to serve as a testbed for the systems to be used on the new FFG-7 and *Pegasus* classes, returning to her original configuration in 1976-77

Type: Frigates (FF) — *Number/Class:* 46 Knox

Name	Number	Laid down	Launched	Commissioned	Status
Knox	FF-1052	5 Oct 1965	19 Nov 1966	12 Apr 1969	PA
Roark	FF-1053	2 Feb 1966	24 Apr 1967	22 Nov 1969	PA
Gray	FF-1054	19 Nov 1966	3 Nov 1967	4 Apr 1970	NRF
Hepburn	FF-1055	1 June 1966	25 Mar 1967	3 July 1969	PA
Connole	FF-1056	23 Mar 1967	20 July 1968	30 Aug 1969	AA
Rathburne	FF-1057	8 Jan 1968	2 May 1969	16 May 1970	PA
Meyerkord	FF-1058	1 Sept 1966	15 July 1967	28 Nov 1969	PA
W. S. Sims	FF-1059	10 Apr 1967	4 Jan 1969	3 Jan 1970	AA
Lang	FF-1060	25 Mar 1967	17 Feb 1968	28 Mar 1970	NRF
Patterson	FF-1061	12 Oct 1967	3 May 1969	14 Mar 1970	NRF
Whipple	FF-1062	24 Apr 1967	12 Apr 1968	22 Aug 1970	PA
Reasoner	FF-1063	6 Jan 1969	1 Aug 1970	31 July 1971	PA
Lockwood	FF-1064	3 Nov 1967	5 Sept 1968	5 Dec 1970	PA
Stein	FF-1065	1 June 1970	19 Dec 1970	8 Jan 1972	PA
Marvin Shields	FF-1066	12 Apr 1968	23 Oct 1969	10 Apr 1971	PA
Francis Hammond	FF-1067	15 July 1967	11 May 1968	25 July 1970	PA
Vreeland	FF-1068	20 Mar 1968	14 June 1969	13 June 1970	AA
Bagley	FF-1069	22 Sept 1970	24 Apr 1971	6 May 1972	PA
Downes	FF-1070	5 Sept 1968	13 Dec 1969	28 Aug 1971	PA
Badger	FF-1071	17 Feb 1968	7 Dec 1968	1 Dec 1970	PA
Blakely	FF-1072	3 June 1968	23 Aug 1969	18 July 1970	NRF
Robert E. Peary	FF-1073	20 Dec 1970	23 June 1971	23 Sept 1972	PA
Harold E. Holt	FF-1074	11 May 1968	3 May 1969	26 Mar 1971	PA
Trippe	FF-1075	29 July 1968	1 Nov 1969	19 Sept 1970	AA
Fanning	FF-1076	7 Dec 1968	24 Jan 1970	23 July 1971	PA
Ouellet	FF-1077	15 Jan 1969	17 Jan 1970	12 Dec 1970	PA
Joseph Hewes	FF-1078	15 May 1969	7 Mar 1970	24 Apr 1971	AA
Bowen	FF-1079	11 July 1969	2 May 1970	22 May 1971	AA
Paul	FF-1080	12 Sept 1969	20 June 1970	14 Aug 1971	AA
Aylwin	FF-1081	13 Nov 1969	29 Aug 1970	18 Sept 1971	AA
Elmer Montgomery	FF-1082	23 Jan 1970	21 Nov 1970	30 Oct 1971	AA
Cook	FF-1083	20 Mar 1970	23 Jan 1971	18 Dec 1971	PA
McCandless	FF-1084	4 June 1970	20 Mar 1971	18 Mar 1972	AA
Donald B. Beary	FF-1085	24 July 1970	22 May 1971	22 July 1972	AA
Brewton	FF-1086	2 Oct 1970	24 July 1971	8 July 1972	PA
Kirk	FF-1087	4 Dec 1970	25 Sept 1971	9 Sept 1972	PA
Barbey	FF-1088	5 Feb 1971	4 Dec 1971	11 Nov 1972	PA
Jesse L. Brown	FF-1089	8 Apr 1971	18 Mar 1972	17 Feb 1973	AA
Ainsworth	FF-1090	11 June 1971	15 Apr 1972	31 Mar 1973	AA
Miller	FF-1091	6 Aug 1971	3 June 1972	30 June 1973	NRF
Thomas C. Hart	FF-1092	8 Oct 1971	12 Aug 1972	28 July 1973	AA
Capodanno	FF-1093	12 Oct 1971	21 Oct 1972	17 Nov 1973	AA
Pharris	FF-1094	11 Feb 1972	16 Dec 1972	26 Jan 1974	AA
Truett	FF-1095	27 Apr 1972	3 Feb 1973	1 June 1974	AA
Valdez	FF-1096	30 June 1972	24 Mar 1973	27 July 1974	NRF
Moinster	FF-1097	25 Aug 1972	12 May 1973	2 Nov 1974	AA

Builders Todd Shipyards, Seattle, Wash (FF-1052/1054, -1062, -1064, -1066, -1070, -1071); Todd Shipyards, San Pedro, Cal (FF-1055, -1058, -1060, -1067, -1074, -1076); Avondale Shipyards, New Orleans, La (FF-1056, -1059, -1061, -1068, -1072, -1075, -1077/1097); Lockheed SB and Cons Co, Seattle, Wash (FF-1057, -1063, -1065, -1069, -1073)
Displacement standard, 3,011 tons; full load, 3,877 tons (FF-1052/1077), 4,200 tons
Length overall 438ft (133.5m)
Maximum beam 46.8ft (14.3m)
Maximum draught 24.8ft (7.8m)
Main machinery One Westinghouse steam turbine. Two boilers (Combustion Engineering, FF-1052/1055, -1058, -1060, -1062, -1064, -1066/1071, -1074, -1076, -1078/1097; Babcock and Wilcox, FF-1056, -1057, -1059, -1061, -1063, -1065, -1072, -1073, -1075, -1077)
Screws/s.h.p. 1/35,000
Maximum speed 27 knots
Armament One Mark 25 Sea Sparrow BPDMS launcher (FF-1052/1069, -1071/1083); one Nato Sea Sparrow launcher (Mark 29) (FF-1070); two quad Harpoon launch canisters (total 8 missiles) in FF-1053, -1062, -1064, -1066, -1067, -1069/1077 and -1080/1097; one single 5in/54 gun mount (Mark 42); one Asroc 8-tube launcher; four fixed Mark 32 ASW torpedo tubes
Complement 17 officers and 228 enlisted men (22 officers and 261 enlisted men on ships with BPDMS and LAMPS)

Commissioned as Ocean Escorts (DE), this class was re-rated Frigates (FF) and reclassified FF-1052/1097 on 30 June, 1975. FF-1073 was originally named *Connolly*, but was renamed on 12 May, 1971. The largest post-World War Two escort vessels, these craft were authorised as follows: FY-1964, FF-1052/1061 (SCB-199C); FY-1965, FF-1062/1077 (SCB-200.65); FY-1966, FF-1078/1087, and FY-1967, FF-1088/1097 (SCB-200.66). The average cost per ship was $31 million. The programme was plagued by cost over-runs.

FF-1060 and -1091 were assigned to the NRF on 15 January, 1982, FF-1054 on 15 July, 1982, and FF-1096 on 14 August, 1982. FF-1054 and -1061 are based at Long Beach, California, and FF-1091 and -1096 at Newport, Rhode Island, FF-1072 followed them to the NRF in June 1983, as will FF-1055 and -1058 in June 1985, and FF-1057 in June 1986.

A total of 50 units of this class was planned and authorised as DEs. Ten were cancelled as priorities shifted to faster and more versatile

▲ *Bowen* (FF-1079), illustrating the current standard configuration of the *Knox* class. It is planned to replace the BPDMS launcher on the stern with the Phalanx CIWS

▼ *Downes* (FF-1070) of the *Knox* class. She is fitted with an AN/SPS-65 threat-detection radar and an Improved Point Defence/target Acquisition System. She is the only ship of the class so fitted *(US Navy)*

Vreeland (FF-1068), showing the new *Knox*-class bow configuration. This retrofit programme began in FY 1979 in response to complaints of these ships being too wet forward. The fit adds 9.1 tons to displacement and 3.5ft to length

ships. DE-1098/1100 were cancelled on 24 February, 1969, and their appropriated funds used to help reduce cost over-runs on attack submarine construction. DE-1101, planned to have gas turbine propulsion, was cancelled on 9 April, 1969. FF-1102/1107 were cancelled in 1968. FF-1078/1097 were originally rated as a separate class because the electronic suite differs slightly from that of FF-1052/1077. This idea was dropped, however, and the two groups combined into one class.

FF-1078 onwards were awarded to one builder to reduce construction costs. An interesting technique was employed by Avondale Shipyards. The hulls were assembled upside down, and when that phase was completed, four huge turning rings were slid under and around the hull and locked. The rings were then rotated until the hull was upright, at which time the rings were unlocked and withdrawn. The ship was then moved sideways for the next assembly phase while another hull was begun in the place vacated.

Beginning in 1979, each ship, during its next overhaul, is to be fitted with 3.5ft (1.1m) bow bulwarks and spray strakes (also adding 9.1 tons to the displacement). By August 1982, FF-1052, -1053, -1059, -1062/1065, -1067, -1069, -1071, -1072, -1075, -1077/1079, -1081, -1086, -1090, -1095 and -1097 had been so fitted. Electronics comprise one AN/SPS-10 surface search and one SPS-40 search radars (FF-1070 has AN/SPS-48 threat detection radar), one Mark 68 gunfire-control with AN/SPG-53A radar, one Mark 115 missile fire-control system, one Mark 114 ASW fire-control system and one target designation system, one bow-mounted AN/SQS-26 CX, one AN/SQS-35 (IVDS) except in FF-1053/1055, -1057/1062, -1072 and -1077 (19 more ships will be so fitted). In addition, all except FF-1053/1055, -1057/1062, -1072 and -1077 will receive the AN/SQR-18A Tactass sonar. Each ship has an OE-82 satellite communications antenna, SSR-1 receiver and WSL-3 transceiver.

The Harpoon missile system has been fitted in FF-1090 and -1092, and will be fitted in all other ships of this class. One Sea Sparrow BPDMS (Mark 25) was installed in 31 ships during 1971/1975 (FF-1052/1069, 1071/1083) at a cost of $400,000 per ship, with a modified Mark 29 version on FF-1070. Two of the eight-tube Asroc launcher tubes have been modified to fire Standard missiles. This, plus other modifications to give the class a standard missile capability, cost $750,000 per ship.

All of these ships are to be fitted with the 20mm Phalanx CIWS (Mark 16) on the fantail, replacing the Sea Sparrow BPDMS launcher on those ships that have it. The Mark 36 Super Chaffroc RBOC system will replace the Mark 33 system in FF-1052, -1055, -1061, -1065, -1068, -1072, -1074/1076, -1078/1085 and -1087. The Mark 36 system is already installed on the remaining ships.

The Light Airborne Multi-Purpose Systems (LAMPS) modification programme was authorised as follows: FY-1972 (FF-1063, -1066, -1074, -1078/1080), FY-1973 (FF-1055, -1059, -1065, -1069, -1071/1073, -1075, -1081, -1083/1088), FY-1974 (FF-1053, -1054, -1056/1058, -1060, -1076, -1089/1097), FY-1975 (FF-1062, -1064, -1067, -1077, -1082), FY-1976 (FF-1052, -1061, -1068, -1070). Communications were improved, electronics and control gear added, and the existing Dash hanger and flight deck were enlarged to handle the SH-2D (LAMPS II) ASW helicopter. Cost of these modifications were about $1 million per ship.

Type: Frigate (FF)

Number/Class: 1 *Glover*

Name	Number	Laid down	Launched	Commissioned	Status
Glover	FF-1098	29 July 1963	17 Apr 1965	13 Nov 1965	AA

Builders Bath Iron Works, Bath, Me
Displacement standard, 2,643 tons; full load, 3,584 tons
Length overall 416ft (126.8m)
Maximum beam 44.2ft (13.5m)
Maximum draught 24ft (7.3m)
Main machinery One Westinghouse steam turbine. Two Foster-Wheeler boilers
Screws/s.h.p. 1/35,000
Maximum speed 27 knots
Armament One single 5in/38 Mark 30 gun mount, one Asroc 8-tube launcher, two triple Mark 32 ASW torpedo tubes
Complement 50 officers, 231 enlisted men (flagship)

Authorised in the FY-1961 Programme as AG-163, this ship was later reclassified AGDE-1. *Glover* was built (SCB-198) to test advanced hull design and propulsion systems. She also served as a test ship for sonar theories and systems, while retaining full combat capabilities. *Glover* was reclassified to AGFF-1 on 30 June, 1975, and to FF-1098 on 1 October, 1979. She can easily be mistaken for a *Garcia* class frigate, but her distinguishing feature is the raised stern.

Electronics consist of one AN/SPS-10 and one AN/SPS-40 search radars, one Mark 56 gunfire control system (associated with the AN/SPG-35 fire control radar), one Mark 114 ASW fire control system and one Mark 1 target designation system.

Glover has one AN/SQS-26 bow-mounted sonar, the hull-mounted AN/SQR-13 Passive/Active Detection and Location (PADLOC) sonar, and one AN/SQS-35 Independent Variable Depth Sonar (IVDS), which is lowered from the stern. In addition, the OE-82 satellite communication antenna is fitted.

Glover (FF-1098) in April 1972, while still classified AGDE-1. Her external configuration has not changed since *(US Navy)*

Type: Frigates (FF)

Number/Class: 10 *Garcia*

Name	Number	Laid down	Launched	Commissioned	Status
Garcia	FF-1040	16 Oct 1962	31 Oct 1963	21 Dec 1964	AA
Bradley	FF-1041	17 Jan 1963	26 Mar 1964	15 May 1965	PA
Edward McDonnell	FF-1043	1 Apr 1963	15 Feb 1964	15 Feb 1965	AA
Brumby	FF-1044	1 Aug 1963	6 June 1964	5 Aug 1965	AA
Davidson	FF-1045	20 Sept 1963	2 Oct 1964	7 Dec 1965	PA
Voge	FF-1047	21 Nov 1963	4 Feb 1965	25 Nov 1966	AA
Sample	FF-1048	19 July 1963	28 Apr 1964	23 Mar 1968	PA
Koelsch	FF-1049	19 Feb 1964	8 June 1965	10 June 1967	AA
Albert David	FF-1050	29 Apr 1964	19 Dec 1964	19 Oct 1968	PA
O'Callahan	FF-1051	19 Feb 1964	20 Oct 1965	13 July 1968	PA

Builders Bethlehem Steel Corp, San Francisco, Cal (FF-1040, -1041); Avondale Shipyards Inc, New Orleans, La (FF-1043/1045); Defoe SB Co, Defoe, Mich (FF-1047, -1049, -1051); Lockheed SB and Cons Co, Seattle, Wash (FF-1048, -1050)
Displacement standard, 2,620 tons; full load, 3,403 tons
Length overall 414.5ft (126.3m)
Maximum beam 44.2ft (13.5m)
Maximum draught 25ft (7.6m)
Main machinery One Westinghouse geared turbine, except in FF-1047/1051 (General Electric). Two Foster-Wheeler boilers
Screws/s.h.p. 1/35,000
Maximum speed 29 knots
Armament Two single 5in/38 Mark 30 gun mounts, one Asroc 8-tube launcher, two triple Mark 32 ASW torpedo tubes
Complement 13 officers and 226 enlisted men (FF-1040, -1041, -1043 and -1044), 16 officers and 231 enlisted men (remainder)

A modified version of the *Bronstein*-class design (SCB-199A). the *Garcia*s are larger than many of the world's destroyers, but are rated frigates because of their single screw propulsion and limited speed. They were authorised in the following Programmes: FY-1961 (FF-1040, -1041), FY-1962 (FF-1943/1045), FY-1963 (FF-1047/1051). Originally designated DEs, they were rerated as Frigates and reclassified FFs on 30 June, 1975. DE-1042 and -1046 were built for Portugal under the Off-Shore Programme.

Electronics: FF-1047 and -1049 are fitted with a specialised ASW NTDS. This class has one AN/SPS-10 and AN/SPS-40 search radars, one AN/SPG-35 fire-control radar, one Mark 56 gunfire-control system, one Mark 114 ASW fire-control system, and one Mark 1 target designation system. One AN/SQS-26 AXR bow-mounted sonar is fitted in FF-1040, -1041, -1043, -1045, and one AN/SQS-26 BR bow-mounted sonar in FF-1047/1051. All units have OE-82 satellite communications antennae.

Most of these ships were completed with two Mark 25 torpedo tubes built into the transom, for launching wire-guided ASW torpedoes. These were subsequently removed from those ships and were not fitted on the later units. The Sea Sparrow BPDMS was installed in FF-1041 during 1967/1968, but it was later removed and installed aboard *Forrestal* (CV-59).

In all but FF-1048 and -1050 the Dash hangar and flight decks were modified in the early 1970s to handle the LAMPS II helicopter. The LAMPS modifications were authorised in the following programmes: FY-1972 (FF-1040, -1041, -1044, -1051), FY-1973 (FF-1043, -1045), FY-1974 (FF-1049), FY-1975 (FF-1047). Reportedly, FF-1041 actually operated with the Dash system.

Davidson (FF-1045) pictured in March 1978. The diagonal line on the fantail of approach for helicopters coming aboard *(US Navy)*

Type: Frigates (FF) — *Number/Class:* 2 *Bronstein*

Name	*Number*	*Laid down*	*Launched*	*Commissioned*	*Status*
Bronstein	FF-1037	16 May 1961	31 Mar 1962	16 June 1963	PA
McCloy	FF-1038	15 Sept 1961	9 June 1962	21 Oct 1963	AA

Builder Avondale Shipyards Inc, New Orleans, La
Displacement Standard, 2,480 tons (FF-1037); 1,975 tons (FF-1038). Full load, 2,650 tons
Length overall 371.5ft (113.2m)
Maximum beam 40.5ft (12.3m)
Maximum draught 24ft (7.32m)
Main machinery One De Laval geared turbine. Two Foster-Wheeler boilers
Screws/s.h.p. 1/20,000
Maximum speed 26 knots
Armament Two twin (Mark 33) 3in/50 gun mounts, one Asroc 8-tube launcher, two triple Mark 32 ASW torpedo tubes
Accommodation 16 officers, 184 enlisted men (FF-1037); 193 enlisted men (FF-1038)

Authorised in the FY-1960 construction programme, these are the first escort-type ships to be fitted with "macks". The *Bronstein*s are the lead class of the second generation of post Second World War frigates. Comparable in size and ASW capabilities with contemporary destroyers, they were rated as FFs on 30 June, 1975, having originally been designated DEs. DE-1039 was built for Portugal under the Off-Shore Programme.

Several successful features in this design (SCB-199) were incorporated into the follow-on classes of FF/FFGs.

Electronics comprise one AN/SPS-10 and one AN/SPS-40 search radars, one Mark 56 gunfire-control system, one Mark 114 ASW fire-control system, one AN/SPG-35 fire-control radar, one Mark 1 Target Designation System, and one AN/SQS-26 bow mounted sonar. The Towed Array Surveillance System (Tactass) was installed during the mid-1970s. The cable reel is located on the quarterdeck, necessitating the removal of a single 3in gun mount abaft the helicopter deck to accommodate this installation.

McCloy, one of the first of the USN's second generation of frigates. The cable reel of the TASS variable-depth sonar is located in the position originally occupied by the aft 3in gun mount *(US Navy)*

Naval Reserve Force training destroyers/frigates

Name/Hull Number	*NRF Homeport*	*Assignment Date*	*Remarks*
William C. Lawe (DD-763)	New Orleans, LA	31 Aug 1973	Replaced **Putnam** (DD-757)
Harold J. Ellison (DD-864)	Philadelphia, Pa	30 Nov 1974	Replaced **Robert L. Wilson** (DD-847)
Edson (DD-946)	Newport, R.I.	1 Apr 1977	Replaced **Holder** (DD-819)
Gray (FF-1054)	Long Beach, Calif	15 July 1982	
Lang (FF-1060)	Long Beach, Calif	15 Jan 1982	
Patterson (FF-1061)	Newport, R.I.	15 June 1983	
Blakely (FF-1072)	Newport, R.I.	15 June 1983	
Miller (FF-1091)	Newport, R.I.	15 Jan 1982	
Valdez (FF-1096)	Newport, R.I.	14 Aug 1982	

PATROL COMBATANTS

Mk III PBs cruising in formation in Chesapeake Bay. Note that the pilot house is offset to starboard. Commercial name for this class is Sea Specter

Beginning in FY-1976, there were 14 PGs and six PHMs on the Navy List. Four PGs and one PHM were active, eight PGs were in the Naval Reserve Force, one had been reclassified as a "boat", and one was in reserve. In addition, five PHMs were under construction, with 23 more projected. By the end of 1982 six PHMs were in commission. Six PGs are in reserve.

The successful use of riverine craft during the Vietnam War (1963/1973) induced the Navy to retain a small force in the NRF to sustain the art. In FY-1982 one PCH, classified as a "boat", remains active, along with 93 riverine craft for training purposes.

Type: Patrol Combatants, Missile (Hydrofoils) (PHM) — *Number/Class: 6 Pegasus*

Name	*Number*	*Builder*	*Commissioned*	*Status*
Pegasus (ex-**Delphinus**)	PHM-1	Boeing Co, Seattle, Wash	9 July 1977	AA
Hercules	PHM-2	Boeing Co, Seattle, Wash	15 Jan 1983	AA
Taurus	PHM-3	Boeing Co, Seattle, Wash	10 Oct 1981	AA
Aquila	PHM-4	Boeing Co, Seattle, Wash	19 Dec 1981	AA
Aries	PHM-5	Boeing Co, Seattle, Wash	11 Sept 1982	AA
Gemini	PHM-6	Boeing Co, Seattle, Wash	13 Nov 1982	AA

Displacement 239.6 tons full load
Length overall Foils extended, 132.9ft (40.5m); foils retracted, 145.3ft (44.3m)
Maximum beam 28.2ft (8.6m)
Maximum draught Foils extended, 23.2ft (7.1m); foils retracted, 6.2ft (1.9m)
Main machinery Hull-borne, two MTU 8V 331 TC81 diesel engines (1,600 b.h.p.); foil-borne, one General Electric LM-2500 gas turbine (18,000 s.h.p.)
Maximum speed Hull-borne, 12 knots (two water jet propulsion units); foil-borne, 48 knots+ (water jet propulsion units)
Armament Two quadruple Harpoon launch canisters (8 missiles total), one single 76mm OTO Melara mount (US Mark 75)
Complement 4 officers, 17 enlisted men

The *Pegasus* design (SCB-602.73) was developed in conjunction with Italy and the Federal Republic of Germany. *Pegasus*, authorised in FY-1973, was laid down on 10 May that year and launched on 9 November, 1974. *Hercules*, originally laid down on 30 May, 1974, was authorised FY-1973. She was suspended in August 1974 when 40.9 per cent complete, and all funds were diverted to the completion of *Pegasus*. PHM-2 hull was scrapped. Funds to construct PHM-3/6 were authorised in the FY-1975 Programme and in FY-1976 funding was provided to build another PHM-2. However, the Secretary of Defense impounded the funds. In August 1977, after considerable Congressional pressure, the Secretary released the appropriated $272.7 million to complete the six-ship programme, and a contract was awarded to Boeing on 20 October, 1977. At this time the original PHM-2 hull was scrapped. A second PHM-2 hull was laid down on 12 September, 1980, PHM-3 on 30 January, 1979, PHM-4 on 10 July, 1979, PHM-5 on 7 January, 1980, and PHM-6 on 13 May, 1980. All are assigned to the Atlantic Fleet and based at Key West, Florida.

Originally classified Patrol Hydrofoil, Missile, these craft were reclassified Patrol Combatant, Missile (Hydrofoil) on 30 June, 1975. PHM-1 was originally named *Delphinus*, but was renamed on 26 April, 1974. The Mark 92 fire control system (except PHM-1, which has the Mark 94 system) and the Mark 34 Chaffroc system are fitted. Radar is the commercial SMA 3TM20H2.

Taurus (PHM-3) on trials in the summer of 1981 in Puget Sound, Washington State. Note the single Harpoon launch canisters aft; it was originally planned to fit two sets of quad launchers. PHM-2-6 resemble PHM-1 externally but vary widely internally *(US Navy)*

Type: Patrol Combatants (PG) — *Number/Class:* 6 *Asheville*

Name	Number	Builder	Commissioned	Status
Gallup	PG-85	Tacoma Boatbuilding Co	22 Oct 1966	PR
Canon	PG-90	Tacoma Boatbuilding Co	26 July 1968	PR
Tacoma	PG-92	Tacoma Boatbuilding Co	14 July 1969	AR
Welch	PG-93	Peterson Builders	8 Sept 1969	AR
Beacon	PG-99	Peterson Builders	21 Nov 1969	AR
Green Bay	PG-101	Peterson Builders	5 Dec 1969	AR

Displacement Standard 225 tons; full load 235 tons
Length overall 164.5ft (50.1m)
Maximum beam 23.8ft (7.3m)
Maximum draught 9.5ft (2.9m)
Main machinery One General Electric LM-1500 gas turbine engine; two Cummins diesel engines
Screws/s.h.p. 2/13,330 (gas turbine); 2/1,450 (diesels)
Maximum speed 40 knots + (gas turbine); 16 knots (diesels)
Armament One single 76 cal/50mm (Mark 34) gun mount, one single 40mm mount
Complement 3 officers and 21 enlisted men

Originally in a 17-ship class, these were first classified as PGMs. They were reclassified as PGs on 1 April, 1967, and re-rated Patrol Combatants on 30 June, 1975.

Designed purely to perform patrol and surveillance missions, and incorporating lessons learned from the 1963 Cuban Blockade, they have an aluminium hull and aluminium glassfibre superstructure. Using gas turbine propulsion, they can accelerate from stationary to 40 knots in one minute, and are highly manoeuvrable. When they were originally tested, problems were experienced with the air intakes for the turbines, which kept ingesting salt water, causing the engines to stop. Intake modifications provided the solution. They are fitted with the AN/SPG-50 fire control radar and the Mark 63 gunfire control system.

Beacon and *Green Bay* were decommissioned on 1 April, 1977, at Little Creek, Virginia, followed by *Tacoma* and *Welch* on 30 September, 1981. *Tacoma* and *Welch* had been employed in training Saudi Arabian Naval crews for the PCG and PGG types which they were acquiring from the USA. *Gallup* and *Canon* were originally stricken from the Naval Vessel Register on 31 January, 1977, but were reinstated on 17 July, 1981.

Defiance (PG-95) and *Surprise* (PG-97) were leased to Turkey on 11 June, 1973, and

28 February, 1973, respectively. *Benicia* (PG-96) was leased to South Korea on 15 October, 1971.

Asheville (PG-84), *Crockett* (PG-88) and *Marathon* (PG-89) were struck off on 31 January, 1977. *Antelope* (PG-86), *Ready* (PG-87), and *Douglas* (PG-100) were struck from the Navy List on 1 October, 1977.

The current disposition of each ship is as follows. *Chehalis* (PG-94), which was reclassified a "boat" on 21 August, 1975, after being struck off on 1 August that year, has been disarmed and now serves as an experimental boat, M/V *Athena I*, at the Naval Scientific Research and Development Center (NSRDC), Annapolis, Md. *Grand Rapids* (PG-98) was reclassified a "boat" on 1 October, 1977, and transferred to NSRDC for service as M/V *Athena II*. *Asheville* (PG-84) and *Marathon* (PG-89) were transferred to the Massachusetts Maritime Academy as training ships on 11 April, 1977, and 18 April, 1977, respectively. *Antelope* (PG-86) and *Crockett* (PG-88) were transferred to the Environmental Protection Agency on 17 January, 1978, and 18 April, 1977, respectively for use as research ships, their gas turbines having been removed. *Crockett* may be transferred to the Egyptian Government for use as a civilian AGOR. The surviving six units on the NVR units are awaiting transfer to foreign countries.

▲ *Green Bay* (PG-101) in Washington Navy Yard in May 1976. The small boat aft of the superstructure is used for boarding ships at sea *(Samuel Loring Morison)*

▼ *Welch* (PG-93) (illustrated) and *Tacoma* (PG-92) spent the last of their active years training Saudi Arabian crews for service on that nation's new patrol vessels

A 1981 view of *Antelope* (ex-PG-86) in her current role as a research ship for the Environmental Protection Agency. A sister ship, *Crockett* (ex-PG-88) serves in the same role on the Great Lakes

Type: Patrol Craft (Hydrofoil) (PCH) *Number/Class:* 1 *High Point*

Name	Number	Builder	In Service	Status
High Point	PCH-1	Boeing Co, Seattle, Wash	15 Aug 1963	PSA

Displacement Full load 110 tons
Length overall 115ft (35m)
Maximum beam 31ft (9.4m)
Maximum draught foils retracted, 6ft (1.8m); foils extended, 17ft (5.2m)
Main machinery Hull-borne, one Packard diesel engine (one screw/600 b.h.p.); foil-borne, two Bristol Siddeley Marine Proteus gas turbines (two screws/6,200 s.h.p.)
Maximum speed Hull-borne, 12 knots; foil-borne, 48 knots
Armament Removed
Accommodation 22 total (1 officer, 21 enlisted men)

High Point was authorised under the FY-1960 Programme (SCB-202). Rated as "floating equipment", she has served as an experimental vehicle, and is built entirely of aluminium except for the steel foils and struts. *High Point* served as an experimental at-sea platform for the *Harpoon* system, and was also evaluated by the Coast Guard early 1975.

Foil-borne, this vessel has two paired counter-rotating propellers. The single 40mm mount forward has been removed. *High Point* was scheduled to be deleted in September 1978, but Congress provided additional funds (unrequested by the Navy) in FY-1979 for her continued service, and have since continued to do so.

The last Fast Patrol Craft owned by the Navy, PTF-25, was deleted in July 1981 for disposal.

Type: Patrol Boats (PB) *Number/Design:* 19 Mark I (2) and Mark III (17)

Displacement Mk.I, 26.9 tons (light); 36.3 tons (full load). Mk.III, 31.5 tons (light); 41.25 tons (full load)
Length overall 65ft (19.8m)
Maximum beam Mk.I, 16ft (4.9m); Mk.III, 18ft (5.5m)
Maximum draught Mk.I, 4.9ft (1.5m); Mk.III, 5.9ft (1.8m)
Machinery Three General Motors type 8V71T1 diesel engines
Screws/b.h.p. 3/1,950
Maximum speed 30 knots
Armament One twin and four single 20mm mounts, or five machine guns

These PBs were built to replace the ageing PCF *Swift* boats. Their mission is inshore patrol duties. Mark I was built by Sewart Seacraft, Berwick, Lousiana. Mark III was built by Peterson Builders, Sturgeon Bay, Wisconsin.

The first two Mark I boats were built in 1972 and delivered to the Navy in 1973 for evaluation. They were subsequently assigned to the Naval Reserve Force. The Mark II boats were never built. The Mark III design provides additional weapons space on the port side by offsetting the pilothouse to starboard.

August 1978 view of a Mk III patrol boat. Location of the pilot house offset to starboard provides for any type of weapon fit, up to the Norwegian Penguin missile *(US Navy)*

Type: Inshore Patrol Craft (PCF) *Number/Design:* 5 Mark I (3) and Mark II (2)

Displacement Full load, 22.5 tons (Mk.I); 24.5 tons (Mk.II)
Length overall 50.1ft (15.3m) (Mk.I); 51.3ft (15.6m) (Mk.II)
Maximum beam 13ft (4m) (Mk.I); 15ft (4.6m) (Mk.II)
Maximum draught 3.5ft (1.1m) (Mk.I); 4.8ft (1.5m) (Mk.II)
Main machinery Two General Motors type 12V71N diesel engines
Screws/b.h.p. 2/850
Maximum speed 28 knots (Mk.II); 24.4 knots (Mk.I)
Armament One 81mm mortar, 3/5 machine guns (one twin machine gun mount atop pilot house and one single machine gun mount "piggyback" over mortar)
Complement One officer, five enlisted men

Developed by Sewart Seacraft, the PCF design was adapted from an all-metal crew boat used by the crews of off-shore oil drilling rigs in the Gulf of Mexico. About 125 customised units were built for the Navy, commencing in 1965. Numerous PCFs were transferred to South East Asian navies, in addition to those units built specifically for them. These boats gained fame in the Vietnam War as "Swift" boats.

The first 104 were built to the Mark I design; the rest as Mark IIs. The characteristics are basically the same between the two groups, but configuration differs slightly.

PCF-51, a Mk I PCF, running trials in Subic Bay, Philippines, after the completion of an overhaul *(US Navy)*

Type: River Patrol Boats (PBR) *Number/Design:* 37 Mark I (2); Mark II (35)

Displacement 8.9 tons
Length overall 32ft (9.8m)
Maximum beam 11.8ft (3.6m)
Maximum draught 2.6ft (0.8m)
Main machinery Two General Motors 6V53N diesels, water jet propulsion
b.h.p. 430
Maximum speed 23.9 knots
Armament Three to five machine guns (one twin mount forward, one single mount aft), one 40mm grenade launcher, (one 60mm mortar in some craft)
Complement Five or more enlisted men

These glassfibre-hulled river patrol boats, designed for shallow-water missions, were the first jet-propelled craft to be used in combat. At full speed they have a draught of only 9in (0.23m). The water jet pumps are linked directly to the steering system, thereby eliminating the need for propellers and rudders.

During 1967/1973 about 500 PBRs were built, most of which were transferred to South Vietnam. The first 160 boats were Mark Is; the rest were Mark IIs. The first group were built by United Boat Builders, Bellingham, Washington. As with the *Swift* class PCFs, the PBRs were adapted from a commercial design. Characteristics of both Marks vary somewhat.

Type: "Mini" Armoured Troop Carriers (ATC) *Number:* 22

Displacement Full load, 14.8 tons
Length overall 36ft (11m)
Maximum beam 12.7ft (3.9m)
Maximum draught 3.5ft (1.1m)
Main machinery Two General Motors type 8V53N diesel engines, water jet propulsion; 566 b.h.p.
Accommodation Crew, 2; troops, 15–20

The ATC is employed as a small troop carrier for riverine and swimmer delivery operations. All were built with aluminium hulls and ceramic armour. The LCM (6) conversions, first version of the ATC, have been disposed of.

Note Thirteen submarine-chasers (SC) lent to the Soviet Union in 1945 under Lend-Lease but never accounted for or returned (SC-500, -538, -643, -647, -660, -661, -675, -774, -1007, -1031, -1295, -1324 and -1364) were stricken from the Navy List on 1 January, 1983.

56ft Mk I ATC in action on a South Vietnamese river. No longer in the US naval inventory, the Mk I ATC is typical of the hundreds of riverine craft used during the Vietnam War

MINE WARFARE SHIPS AND CRAFT

RH-53D Sea Stallion helicopter receives a Mk 103 mechanical minesweeping sled from *Illusive* (MSO-448) *(US Navy)*

Beginning in FY-1976, 46 minesweepers were on the Navy List. Of these, three MSOs were active, 22 in the Naval Reserve Force and 12 held in reserve. In addition, nine Coastal Minesweepers (MSC) were in the NRF. No new construction was contemplated.

It is embarrassing to report that, at the beginning of FY-1982, only 25 MSOs remained on the Navy List. Of these, three were active and the rest served in the NRF. The prototype of a new class (MCM) is under construction, with at least 13 more planned. If it was not such a serious matter, it would be amusing to compare the force level in this category with that of the Russians, who have more than 270 mine warfare vessels and employ technology equal to ours.

From the First World War to the Vietnamese conflict, the Americans have never had enough mine warfare ships when they were needed. When the shooting started, this force would be the first to be increased. Yet, when the shooting stopped, it was the first to suffer severe post-war cutbacks and shrink to virtually a token force until the next time. Then frantic efforts would be made, including a lot of makeshift conversions, to meet the requirements of the forward commands.

Mines are a relatively cheap weapon to deploy. Less advanced nations can lay crude, but effective, minefields, causing untold problems for assault and/or patrol ships. Neutralising these minefields, however, is a precise science, and an art at which Americans excel providing they have the tools to do the job.

The Americans have no dedicated mine laying ships. Attack submarines, carrier-based aircraft, and the land-based B-52D bomber can lay mines, but not to the extent of a purpose-designed minelaying ship. Furthermore, all of the B-52D bombers are to be laid up.

To reinforce the MSOs in sweeping mines in shallow waters, the US Navy has but seven Minesweeping Boats (MSB), hardly enough in a time of need. Despite the insufficient funds, technology has not been idle. The RH-53D Sea Stallion helicopter is fitted for minesweeping. It can tow minesweeping sleds and is readily deployable by carriers and certain amphibious ships to critical areas. One towed device, the Mark 103, is used to sweep moored mines. The Mark 105 is a hydrofoil sled fitted with a turbogenerated and/or magnetic cable. This sled has an acoustic device called the Mark 104, which sets off mines.

Helicopters have two distinct disadvantages. They cannot remain on station like surface ships, and they have no capability against deep water mines. In short, the minesweeping helicopter is the aerial counterpart of the Inshore and Coastal Minesweeper (MSI and MSC).

However, a light can now be seen at the end of the tunnel, and some positive steps have been taken. At last, a programme for a new class of Mine Countermeasures Ships for deep water operations is under way. A comparison of the planned Carter Administration five-year programme with the one envisioned by the Reagan Administration reveals the following figures:

Carter/Reagan

FY-1982	1/1	**FY-1985**	4/5
FY-1983	-/4	**FY-1986**	4/-
FY-1984	4/4	**FY-1987**	-/-
Total	13/14		

Obtaining money in the budget for these much-needed vessels has not been easy. The Reagan Administration wants at least 14 MCMs to replace the ageing MSOs. Depending on the status of the MSH design (see below), they might want to build even more. The Carter Administration wanted only nine MCMs. Their approach to the Mine Force in particular, and to the Navy in general, was to delay, defer, and hope for the best, without the least idea of the American Navy's serious shortcomings in this area.

Type: Mine Countermeasures Ships (MCM) *Number/Class:* 0+1 + (20)

Name	*Number*	*Laid down*	*Launched*	*Commissioned*	*Status*
Avenger	MCM-1	6 May 1983		est. 1985	BLDG
	MCM-2				PROJ
	MCM-3				PROJ
	MCM-4				PROJ
	MCM-5				PROJ
	MCM-6/14				PROJ

Builder Peterson Builders Inc, Sturgeon Bay, Wisc (Contract awarded 28 June, 1982)
Displacement Full load, 1,040 tons
Length overall 210ft (64m)
Maximum beam 44.3ft (13.5m)
Maximum draught 10.5ft (3.2m)
Main machinery Four Waukesha diesel engines
Screws/b.h.p. 2/6,800
Maximum speed 14 knots
Armament Two .50 cal gun mounts
Complement Five officers and 57 enlisted men

1981 artist's impression of the new *Avenger*-class Mine Countermeasures Ship (MCM). To be built by Peterson Builders Inc, this class and the new Minesweeper/Hunter (MSH) are to replace the remaining MSOs. Twenty-one MCMs and 17 MSHs are currently projected

These ships are to replace the ageing MSOs. At least 21 units are planned over the next 10–15 years. Current delays in the Programme are due to constant improvements being made to the original design. The construction programme is as follows: FY-1982 MCM-1, FY-1983 MCM-2, FY-1984 MCM-3/6, FY-1985 MCM-7/10 and FY-1986 MCM-11/14. Unit construction cost in 1983 dollars is $100 million.

Electronic fit includes the AN/SPS-55 surface search radar and AN/SQQ minehunting sonar. Hulls will be made of fir and oak, resulting in a low magnetic signature.

Type: Mine Hunter (MSH) — *Number/Class:* 0+0+(17)/'MSH-1'

Name	Number	Laid down	Launched	Commissioned	Status
	MSH-1				PROJ
	MSH-2/6				PROJ
	MSH-7/11				PROJ

Builder
Displacement 450 tons full load
Length overall 140–150ft (42.7–45.7m)
Maximum beam 20–25ft (6.1–7.6m)
Maximum draught 9–12ft (2.7–3.7m)
Main machinery Not available
Screws/b.h.p. Not available
Maximum speed 12 knots
Armament Not available
Complement 40 total

All characteristics are approximate. This class is designed to supplement the new *Avenger* class of MCMs, and with them will form the US mine warfare force of the future. It combines features of the mine hunter and the minesweeper. Construction funds for the prototype are to be requested in the FY-1984 programme, with five more units to follow in each of the FY-1986 and 1987 budgets. Six more units, for a total of 17, will follow in future programmes.

The class will be equipped with the following minesweeping equipment: size 1 mechanical; Mk 5 magnetic and AMk-4V and AMk-6G acoustic. It will also carry the AN/SQQ-56 minesweeping sonar. Details of the radar type are not available.

Type: Ocean Minesweepers (MSO) — *Number/Class:* 2 *Acme*

Name	Number	Laid down	Launched	Commissioned	Status
Adroit	MSO-509	18 Nov 1954	20 Aug 1955	4 Mar 1957	NRF
Affray	MSO-511	24 Aug 1955	18 Dec 1956	8 Dec 1958	NRF

Builder Frank L. Sample, Jr Inc Boothbay Harbor, Maine
Displacement Light, 750 tons (MSO-509); 633 tons (MSO-511). Full load, 900 tons (MSO-509); 924 tons (MSO-511)
Length overall 173ft (52.7m)
Maximum beam 35ft (10.7m)
Maximum draught 14ft (4.3m)
Main machinery Two Packard diesel engines
Screws/s.h.p. 2 (controllable-pitch)/2,280
Maximum speed 15 knots
Armament Two twin 20mm mounts
Complement Active duty: 7 officers and 37 enlisted men; NRF: 4 officers and 33 enlisted men

These ships, which are fitted as flagships, have plywood hulls and stainless steel engines. They were authorised in the FY-1954 Programme (SCB-45A), and ships have not been modernised. It was originally a four-ship class, but *Acme* (MSO-508) and *Advance* (MSO-510) were struck off the Navy List on 15 May, 1976, and sold for scrap.

The three *Ability* class ships were stricken from the Navy List, *Ability* (MSO-519) on 1 February, 1971, and *Alacrity* (MSO-520) and *Assurance* (MSO-521) on 30 September, 1977, having served some four years as AG-520 and -521, respectively.

The four ships of the *Dash* class – *Dash* (MSO-428), *Detector* (MSO-429), *Direct* (MSO-430) and *Dominant* (MSO-431) – were decommissioned and stricken for disposal on 1 October, 1982.

Type: Ocean Minesweepers (MSO) — *Number/Class:* 19 *Aggressive*

Name	Number	Laid down	Launched	Commissioned	Status
Constant	MSO-427	16 Aug 1951	14 Feb 1953	8 Sept 1954	NRF
Engage	MSO-433	7 Nov 1951	18 June 1963	29 June 1954	NRF
Enhance	MSO-437	12 July 1952	11 Oct 1952	16 Apr 1955	NRF
Esteem	MSO-438	1 Sept 1952	20 Dec 1952	10 Sept 1955	NRF
Excel	MSO-439	9 Feb 1953	25 Sept 1953	24 Feb 1955	NRF
Exploit	MSO-440	28 Dec 1951	10 Apr 1953	31 Mar 1954	NRF
Exultant	MSO-441	22 May 1951	6 June 1953	22 June 1954	NRF
Fearless	MSO-442	23 July 1952	17 July 1953	22 Sept 1954	NRF
Fidelity	MSO-443	15 Dec 1952	21 Aug 1953	19 Jan 1955	AA
Fortify	MSO-446	30 Nov 1951	14 Feb 1953	16 July 1954	NRF
Illusive	MSO-448	23 Oct 1951	12 July 1952	14 Nov 1953	AA
Impervious	MSO-449	18 Nov 1951	29 Aug 1952	15 July 1954	NRF
Implicit	MSO-455	29 Oct 1951	1 Aug 1953	10 Mar 1954	NRF
Inflict	MSO-456	29 Oct 1951	16 Oct 1953	11 May 1954	NRF
Pluck	MSO-464	31 Mar 1952	6 Feb 1954	11 Aug 1954	NRF
Conquest	MSO-488	26 Mar 1953	20 May 1954	20 July 1955	NRF
Gallant	MSO-489	21 May 1953	4 June 1954	14 Sept 1955	NRF
Leader	MSO-490	22 Sept 1953	15 Sept 1954	16 Nov 1955	AA
Pledge	MSO-492	24 June 1954	20 July 1955	20 Apr 1956	NRF

Fidelity (MSO-443) (illustrated) and the other two fully active MSOs serve as tenders for research establishments; in *Fidelity*'s case it is the Mine Warfare Centre in Panama City, Fla. The structure before the bridge is the prototype AN/SQQ-30 sonar, being tested for the new *Avenger*-class MCMs *(US Navy)*

Builders Fulton Shipyard, Antioch, Cal (MSO-427); Colberg Boat Works, Stockton, Cal (MSO-433); Martinolich SB Co, San Diego, Cal (MSO-437, -438, -448, -449); Higgins Inc, New Orleans, La (MSO-439/443); Seattle SB and DD Corp, Seattle, Wash (MSO-446); Wilmington Boat Works Inc, Wilmington, Cal (MSO-455, -456, -464); J. M. Martinac SB Corp, Tacoma, Wash (MSO-488/490, -492)
Displacement Light, 620–829 tons; full load, 729–924 tons
Length overall 173ft (52.7m)
Maximum beam 36ft (11m)
Maximum draught 16.6ft (4.2m)
Main machinery Two Packard diesel engines (MSO-440); Four Packard diesel engines (MSO-439, -455, -464, -489, -492); Four Waukesha diesel engines (remainder)
Screws/s.h.p. 2/2,150 (MSO-448, -449); 2/2,280 (MSO-438, -439, -455, -489, -492); 2/2,400 (remainder)
Maximum speed 15 knots
Armament One single 20mm (Mark 68) mount (MSO-438, -440, -455, -464, -489, -492)
Complement 5–10 officers and 66–72 enlisted men

Authorised under the following construction programmes: FY-1951 (MSO-427, -433, -437/443, -446, -448, -449); FY-1952 (MSO-455, -456, -464); FY-1953 (MSO-488/490, -492). These vessels (SCB-45A) resulted from lessons learned in the Korean War. They have wooden hulls, non-magnetic fittings wherever possible, and stainless steel alloy engines. A total of 58 were built for US Navy service, plus another 35 ships for NATO navies (MSO-497 was never built). The class seems to be prone to fires. Six ships have caught fire, four of which were total losses. Another unit was scrapped after grounding.

MSO-433 was originally named *Elusive*, but was renamed 6 March, 1953, to avoid confusion with MSO-448. MSO-438 and -488 were originally assigned to the Naval Reserve Force in 1972. They were placed in full commission 27 January, 1973, and deployed overseas to clear mines from North Vietnam waters, returning to the NRF upon completion of the task. The three active MSOs serve as tenders to various research facilities.

All MSOs in commission in the mid-1960s were to be modernised (SCB-502). Nineteen MSOs were taken in hand, but only 13 were actually completed. Modernisation of six had begun but was cancelled before completion on 16 October, 1970. One, *Avenge* (MSO-423), caught fire while in dry dock and was badly damaged. Considered a total loss, she was struck off the Navy List on 1 February, 1970, and disposed of. The other five MSOs were also deleted and disposed of. Further modernisation was cancelled when the emphasis switched to minesweeping helicopters. Modernisation authorisations for the surviving units were as follows: FY-1968 (MSO-433, -441/443, -446, -449, -456); FY-1969 (MSO-437, -448, -488, -490).

MSO modernisation programme

Name	Number	Modernisation yard	Modernisation begun	Modernisation completed
Engage	MSO-433	Dillingham Shipyard Div, Honolulu, Hawaii	31 Oct 1968	14 Aug 1970
Enhance	MSO-437	Harbor Boat Bldg, Terminal Island, Cal	30 Oct 1970	22 Nov 1971
Esteem	MSO-438	Harbor Boat Bldg, Terminal Island, Cal	30 Sept 1970	13 Aug 1971
Exultant	MSO-441	Bethlehem Steel Corp, Baltimore, Md	31 Aug 1968	8 June 1970
Fearless	MSO-442	Bethlehem Steel Corp, Baltimore, Md	30 Sept 1968	19 Oct 1970
Fidelity	MSO-443	Bethlehem Steel Corp, Baltimore, Md	30 Sept 1968	9 Dec 1970
Fortify	MSO-446	Dillingham Shipyard Div, Honolulu, Hawaii	31 Oct 1968	28 Sept 1970
Illusive	MSO-448	Harbor Boat Bldg, Terminal Island, Cal	30 Nov 1970	14 Feb 1972
Impervious	MSO-449	Dillingham Shipyard Div, Honolulu, Hawaii	30 Nov 1968	4 Dec 1970
Inflict	MSO-456	Dillingham Shipyard Div, Honolulu, Hawaii	30 Nov 1968	10 Feb 1970
Conquest	MSO-488	Harbor Boat Bldg, Terminal Island, Cal	30 Oct 1970	30 Sept 1971
Leader	MSO-490	Harbor Boat Bldg, Terminal Island, Cal	30 Nov 1970	31 Jan 1972

The modernised *Force* (MSO-445) caught fire at sea (proven to be due to negligence) on 24 April, 1973, and sunk.

The estimated cost per ship for modernisation was $5 million, with a yard period of ten months. In fact the costs were much higher, and yard periods stretched to about two years for each ship. The work involved replacing the original Packard engines by Waukeshas, extending the bridge structure around the mast and aft to the funnel, replacing the original AN/UQS-1 with AN/SQQ-14 sonar, replacing the single 40mm mount with one twin 20mm mount (in some ships), updating communications and improving hability.

The following ships have been struck from the Navy List – *Embattle* (MSO-434) and *Lucid* (MSO-458) on 15 May, 1976; *Nimble* (MSO-459) on 1 November, 1976; *Energy* (MSO-436) and *Firm* (MSO-444) on 1 July, 1977; and *Agile* (MSO-421), of the *Agile* class, *Observer* (MSO-461), *Pinnacle* (MSO-462), *Skill* (MSO-471), *Vital* (MSO-474), *Sturdy* (MSO-494), *Swerve* (MSO-495), and *Venture* (MSO-496), all on 1 November, 1977.

Type: ex-Inshore Minesweepers (MSI) — *Number/Class:* 2 Cove

Name	Number	Builder	In service	Status
Cove	ex-MSI-1	Bellingham Shipyard Co, Bellingham, Wash	20 Nov 1958	Active
Cape	ex-MSI-2	Bellingham Shipyard Co, Bellingham, Wash	27 Feb 1959	Active

Displacement Light, 120 tons; full load, 240 tons
Length overall 105ft (32m)
Maximum beam 22ft (6.7m)
Maximum draught 10ft (3m)
Main machinery Two General Motors diesel engines
Screws/b.h.p. 1/650
Maximum speed 12 knots
Complement 21 total

The *Coves* were designed as smaller versions of the Coastal Minesweeper (MSC) design, a type phased out of US Naval service. They were authorised in the FY-1956 Programme (SCB-136). The MSI design proved to be a failure, and *Cove* was transferred to Johns Hopkins University Applied Physics Labortory, Silver Springs, Maryland, on 31 July, 1970. *Cape* was transferred to the Naval Underseas Development Center, San Diego, California, on 25 September, 1970. Both ships serve as research vessels and are civilian-manned. Neither is on the Navy List and both are rated as "floating equipment".

Originally, MSI-1/54 were to be built for USN service and MSI-55/101 for foreign transfer. However, the USN programme ended with the first two ships, and MSI-3/54 were added to the foreign transfer list.

The foreign distribution of the MSIs was as follows: MSI-3/10 to the Netherlands, MSI-11 and -12 to Denmark, MSI-13 and -14 to Iran, MSI-15/18 to Turkey, MSI-55/74 to Italy, MSI-75/89 to France, MSI-90/92 to Belgium, MSI-93 to South Korea, and MSI-98/101 to Yugoslavia.

Cove (ex-MSI-1) operating as a commissioned naval ship. It was originally planned to build 54 ships of this class to supplement the MSO/MSC force, but the design proved to be unworkable and only *Cove* and her sister ship *Cape* (ex-MSI-2) were retained by the Navy. Both have served as non-commissioned tenders for research establishments since the early 1970s and are civilian-manned

Type: Minesweeping Boats (MSB) — *Number:* 7

6 "MSB-6" Class
Displacement Light, 37 tons; full load, 44 tons
Length overall 57.2ft (17.4m)
Maximum beam 15.7ft (4.8m)
Maximum draught 5.1ft (1.6m)
Main machinery Two Packard diesel engines
Screws/b.h.p. 2/600
Maximum speed 10 knots
Armament Several machine guns
Complement 6-8 enlisted men

1 MSB-29 Class
Displacement Light, 63 tons; full load, 80 tons
Length overall 82ft (25m)
Maximum beam 19.3ft (5.9m)
Maximum draught 5.5ft (1.7m)
Main machinery Two Packard diesel engines
Screws/b.h.p. 2/600
Maximum speed 9.5 knots
Armament Several machine guns
Complement 8–10 enlisted men

Designed as harbour and channel minesweeping boats, these craft were originally intended to be carried to assault areas on parent ships. However, the design grew until they became too heavy for boom handling. They are transportable, but only by heavy-lift ships or in the well decks of LPD/LSDs, as they were in *Unitas XXII*, and must be loaded and off-loaded by heavy cranes.

The "MSB-6" class originally consisted of 46 units (three more were never built). All saw extensive service during the Vietnam War, in which four boats were lost: MSB-14, -22, -49 and -54. Six units remain active: MSB-15, -16, -25, -28, -41, and -51. The first two were authorised in the FY-1951 Programme (SCB-62) and the other four in FY-1952.

MSB-29 is a one-boat class, authorised in the FY-1952 Programme (SCB-62). It was built some 25ft (7.6m) longer to improve seagoing qualities.

MSBs were rated a service craft until 14 August, 1968, when they were re-rated as combatant craft. All surviving units are based at Charleston, South Carolina, assigned to the Naval Reserve Force. They are the only small mine warfare types left on the Naval Vessel Register.

An MSB-6 unit, MSB-21 (since deleted), in the Long Tau River, South Vietnam. The MSB's primary mission was to keep the major South Vietnamese waterways free of mines and other obstacles *(US Navy)*

AMPHIBIOUS WARFARE

As FY-1976 began, there were 101 amphibious ships on the Navy List, not including five LHAs then under construction. Active: two LCC, five LKA, 14 LPD, seven LPH, one LPSS, 13 LSD, and 20 LST. Assigned to the Naval Reserve Training Force (NRF): one LKA and two LPA. Assigned to the Military Sealift Command: 14 LST. In Navy Reserve there were two LPR, one LPSS, one LSD and four LST. In the Maritime Reserve Fleet were one LCC, six LKA, one LPA, three LSD and three LST.

At the beginning of FY-1983 only 68 amphibious ships were on the Navy List, with the first two units of the *Whidbey Island* class LSDs under construction. Active were two LCC, five LHA, seven LPH, one LKA, 13 LPD, 13 LSD, and 18 LST. Assigned to NRF: four LKA and two LST. All of the NRF-assigned LKA are scheduled to return to the active fleet in FY-1983. In the Maritime Reserve were three LSTs, all of the *De Soto County* class. In addition, two stricken LST-511-class units (LST-566 and -715) and six stricken MSC-configured LSTs of the *Terrebonne Parish* class (LST-1158, -1160, 1162/65) are in the Maritime Reserve.

The Navy's amphibious force lost 33 ships between the two aforementioned fiscal years, one-third the Navy's lift capability. While it is true that most of these ships would be of little value to meet the Navy's present requirements, because of age and obsolescence, the Carter Administration did nothing to initiate any programmes to replace any of these ships. Conversely, it tried to kill every programme, the LSD-41 class included.

The Reagan Administration plans to accelerate programmes designed to increase the sealift capability of troops and their support from the current 51,900 men to twice that number by the 1990s, namely two Marine Amphibious Forces (MAFs). According to the Secretary of the Navy, the Navy must build at least five amphibious ships per year to accomplish this.

This began with the LSD-41 Class, but the replacement design for the *Thomaston* (LSD-28) Class is not encouraging since it is somewhat outmoded technologically. The Carter Administration, unqualified, from the top down, in Military affairs, delayed requesting the LSD-41 prototype because it needed to "assess the change in future amphibious lift requirements". It took considerable Congressional pressure to reinstate the project as a three-ship class. This explains why the upgrading and orderly replacement of the American amphibious force is so far behind schedule and in a state of confusion.

The Reagan Administration also intends to proceed with new types of amphibious assault ships, such as the LHD-1 and LPD-16 Classes. Furthermore, with the approval of the FY-1982 funds the Navy began mass production of the Amphibious Air Cushion Vehicles (LCAC).

Amphibious Warfare Ships

Type: Amphibious Command Ships (LCC)

Number/Class: 2 *Blue Ridge*

Name	*Number*	*Laid down*	*Launched*	*Commissioned*	*Status*
Blue Ridge	LCC-19	27 Feb 1967	4 Jan 1969	14 Nov 1970	PA
Mount Whitney	LCC-20	8 Jan 1969	8 Jan 1970	16 Jan 1971	AA

Builders Philadelphia Naval Shipyard, Phil, Pa (LCC-19); Newport News SB and DD Co, Newport News, Va (LCC-20)
Displacement Light, 16,790 tons (LCC-19); 11,600 tons (LCC-20). Full load, 19,100 tons
Length overall 620ft (189m)
Maximum beam hull; 620ft (189m). Deck; 108ft (32.9m) (LCC-19), 102ft (31.1m) (LCC-20)
Maximum draught 30ft (9.1m)
Main machinery One General Electric steam turbine. Two Foster-Wheeler boilers
Screws/s.h.p. 1/22,000
Maximum speed 23 knots
Armament Two Sea Sparrow BPDMS (Mark 25) launchers, two twin 3in/50 (Mark 33) mounts
Complement 40 officers and 680 enlisted men.
Accommodation 272 officers and 1,242 enlisted men

The first post Second World War amphibious force command ships (SCB-400.65, formerly SCB-248), these craft provide integrated command and facilities for sea, air and land commanders in amphibious operations. Originally classified AGC-19 and 20, they were reclassified LCC-19 and -20 on 1 January, 1969. A third unit of this class, AGC-21, was cancelled in 1969. *Blue Ridge* currently serves as flagship, Commander Seventh Fleet, and is homeported at Yokosuka, Japan. *Mount Whitney* currently serves as the flagship of the Commander Second Fleet and is homeported at Norfolk, Va.

Designed from the keel up as amphibious force flagships, they represent a marked departure from the converted or modified mercantile hulls. The flight deck provides more antenna space, but the antenna and their supports severely restrict the firing arcs of guns. It was this restriction that eliminated two twin 3in/50 gun mounts in the final design stages. In addition to the armament listed, these ships carry two 40mm saluting guns, and it is intended to fit two 20mm CIWS (Mark 15). The machinery arrangement and hull are similar to those of the *Iwo Jima* (LPH-2) class. The *Blue Ridges* can carry one utility helicopter.

These ships are equipped with Tacan, NTDS (supported by three computer systems), Amphibious Command Information System (ACIS), and the Naval Intelligence Processing System (NIPS). One Mark 36 Super Chaffroc (RBOC) system is carried on *Blue Ridge*, and is to be fitted on *Mount Whitney*.

Radars comprise AN/SPS-48 three-dimensional search radar, AN/SPS-10 surface search radar, AN/SPS-40 search radar, and two Mark 115 missile fire-control systems. Also fitted with OE-82 satellite communications antenna, SSR-1 receiver and WSC-3 transceiver.

Disposals: *Mount McKinley* (LCC-7) and *Estes* (LCC-12), of the *Mount McKinley* class, were struck from the Navy List on 30 July, 1976. *Pocono* (LCC-16) and *Taconic* (LCC-17), of the *Adirondack* class, were struck off on 1 December, 1976. All have been sold for scrapping.

Mount Whitney (LCC-20) (illustrated) and her sister ship, *Blue Ridge* (LCC-19), are the first Amphibious Command Ships to be built for the purpose. Note the similarity of the hull to that of the *Iwo Jima*-class LPHs *(US Navy)*

Type: Amphibious Assault Ships (LHA) *Number/Class:* 5 Tarawa

Name	Number	Laid down	Launched	Commissioned	Status
Tarawa	LHA-1	15 Nov 1971	1 Dec 1973	29 May 1976	PA
Saipan	LHA-2	21 July 1972	18 July 1974	15 Oct 1977	AA
Belleau Wood	LHA-3	5 Mar 1973	11 Apr 1977	23 Sept 1978	PA
Nassau	LHA-4	13 Aug 1973	21 Jan 1978	28 July 1979	AA
Pelileu (ex-**Da Nang**)	LHA-5	12 Nov 1976	25 Nov 1978	3 May 1980	PA

Builder Ingalls SB Corp, Pascagoula, Miss
Displacement light, 25,330 tons; full, 39,900 tons (LHA-1, -2) and 38,900 tons (LHA-3/5)
Length overall 820ft (250m)
Maximum beam hull, 106ft (32.3m); flight deck, 198.1ft (36m)
Maximum draught 26ft (7.9m)
Main machinery Two Westinghouse geared turbines; two Combustion Engineering boilers
Screws/s.h.p. 2/140,000
Maximum speed 24 knots
Armament Two Sea Sparrow BPDMS (Mark 25) launchers, three single 5in/54 Mark 45 gun mounts, six single 20mm (Mark 67) mounts
Complement 90 officers, 812 enlisted men
Troops 172 officers, 1,731 enlisted men

Tarawa (LHA-1) in the Gulf of Mexico in July 1976. The opening just inboard and one deck below the BPDMS launcher marks the beginning of a steep ramp that leads below decks and enables tracked vehicles to come on to the flight deck *(US Navy)*

This class represents a new type of amphibious ship that can carry out missions assigned to the LPH/LPD/LSD types. LHA-1 was authorised in the FY-1969 Programme (SCB-410.68), LHA-2 and -3 in FY-1970, and LHA-4 and -5 in FY-1971. Four additional sister ships were cancelled on 20 January, 1971. LHA-5 was renamed on 15 February, 1978. The estimated average cost per ship, in FY-1974 dollars, is $229 million.

This multi-capability ship has large-vehicle storage and maintenance facilities for tanks and trucks. Cargo is moved automatically by conveyors, with nine elevators provided for moving helicopters, personnel, cargo, and equipment. There is a floodable docking well beneath the after elevator, measuring 268ft (81.7m) by 78ft (23.8m), and capable of accommodating four LCU-1610 type landing craft or two LACVs or six LCM (6) or LCM (8)s. In addition, these ships have extensive medical facilities, including operating rooms. Cargo capacity is 33,730ft² for vehicles and 116,900ft² for cargo.

The *Tarawas* can operate nine CH-53 *Sea Stallion* or 12 CH-46 *Sea Knight* helicopters. The hangar deck can accommodate 19 *Sea Stallions* or 30 *Sea Knights*. The AV-8A *Harrier* can also be embarked.

A fixed bow thruster (900 h.p.) is provided to hold the position of the ship while it is unloading landing craft.

Electronics comprise the Integrated Tactical Amphibious Warfare Data System (ITAWDS), and navigational equipment for computerised support in control of helicopters and aircraft, shipboard weapons and sensors, navigation, landing craft control, and electronics warfare.

Radars comprise three-dimensional air search, AN/SPS-52, AN/SPS-10 surface search, AN/SPS-40 air search, and the AN/SPN-35 navigation radar. There is also one Mark 86 gunfire-control system, two Mark 115 missile fire-control systems, one AN/SPG-80, and one AN/SPQ-9A weapon-control radar on each ship.

Two 20mm CIWS (Mark 16) and one Mark 36 Super Chaffroc (RBOC) systems are to be fitted. Each ship is fitted with two 40mm saluting guns.

From 13 April to 29 May, 1981, *Nassau* (LHA-4) deployed to the Mediterranean with an air wing of 20 Marine Corps Harrier (AV-8A) aircraft. The object was to demonstrate the ability of the LHAs to serve as Amphibious Assault Ships carrying helicopters and Marines, or as "Harrier Carriers", with a minimum of change.

Type: Amphibious Assault Docks (LHD) — *Number/Class:* 12 (Projected)

Name	*Number*	*Status*
—	LHD-1	Proposed FY-1984 programme
—	LHD-2	Proposed FY-1986 programme
—	LHD-3	Proposed FY-1987 programme
—	LHD-4/12	Future programmes

Builder Ingalls SB Corp, Pascagoula, Miss
39,384 tons full load
Dimensions 840ft × 106ft (flight deck) × 26.1ft (256.0m × 32.3m × 8.0m)
Aircraft see Aircraft notes
Missiles Two Sea Sparrow NSSMS launchers (8 cells)
Guns Three 20mm Phalanx CIWS (Mark 16) mounts
Main engines Gas turbines, total 140,000 shp
Boilers Two (600 psi each)
Speed 24+ knots
Complement 98 officers and 982 enlisted men
Troops 1,873 total

All characteristics are provisional and subject to change. Slightly larger than the *Tarawa*-class LHAs, this class will help bring the Navy's current amphibious-lift capacity up to the newly required level. Originally only seven of this class were to have been built, as one-for-one replacements for the *Iwo Jima*-class LPHs. However, the force level has since been raised to 12 units. The first five or six units will be used to augment the Navy's existing capabilities, while the remainder will replace the *Iwo Jimas* beginning in the 1990s. Long-lead item funds totalling $55.0 million, for the prototype were approved in the FY-1983 programme. Construction funds are being requested in the FY-1984 programme, with delivery scheduled for FY-1989.

Each unit can carry 42 CH-46 Sea Knight helicopters, though a typical aircraft complement would be a mix of 30 helicopters and 6–8 AV-8B Harriers. In their secondary role of sea control ship these vessels would carry 20 Harriers and 4–6 SH-60B Seahawk helicopters. The following types of aircraft can be supported: CH-53E Super Stallion, CH-53D Sea Stallion, CH-46E Sea Knight, UH-1N, AH-1T Sea Cobra, SH-60B Seahawk AV-8B Harrier II V/Stol aircraft.

Each ship has two elevators: one to starboard and aft of the island and one to port amidships. The well deck is 50ft (15.2m) wide and can accommodate up to three Amphibious Air-cushion Vehicles (LCAC). The flight deck will have nine helicopter landing spots. Cargo capacity is 100,900ft³ with an additional 22,000ft² to accommodate vehicles. The bridge is two decks lower than that of an LHA; command, control and communications spaces having been moved inside the hull to avoid "cheap kill" damage.

A 600-bed hospital and six operating rooms will be standard.

The following radars will be fitted; AN/SPS-67 (SPS-10 replacement) surface search; AN/SPS-52C three-dimensional and AN/SPS-49 two-dimensional air search; Mark 23 target-acquisition. Also fitted will be the OE-82 satellite communications antenna, SSR-1 receiver and WSC-3 transceiver. Electronic countermeasures include the AN/SLQ-32 suite and the AN/SLQ-25 Nixie acoustic torpedo decoy.

Of the three 20mm mounts, one will be fitted on each quarter and one forward of the NSSMS launcher on the island.

One NSSMS (Nato Sea Sparrow Missile System) launcher will be located aft, on a specially built transom overhanging the stern, and the second on a raised deck forward of the superstructure.

Artist's impression of the new Amphibious Assault Dock (LHD), projected as the replacement for the *Iwo Jima*-class LPHs. The LHD is similar to but slightly smaller than the *Tarawa*-class LHAs, and is designed to be convertible into a V/STOL carrier in 24 hours

Type: Amphibious Assault Ships (LPH) *Number/Class:* 7 *Iwo Jima*

Name	*Number*	*Laid down*	*Launched*	*Commissioned*	*Status*
Iwo Jima	LPH-2	2 Apr 1959	17 Sept 1960	26 Aug 1961	AA
Okinawa	LPH-3	1 Apr 1960	14 Aug 1961	14 Apr 1962	PA
Guadalcanal	LPH-7	1 Sept 1961	16 Mar 1963	20 July 1963	AA
Guam	LPH-9	15 Nov 1962	22 Aug 1964	16 Jan 1965	AA
Tripoli	LPH-10	15 June 1964	31 July 1965	6 Aug 1966	PA
New Orleans	LPH-11	1 Mar 1966	3 Feb 1968	16 Nov 1968	PA
Inchon	LPH-12	8 Apr 1968	24 May 1969	20 June 1970	AA

Builders Puget Sound Naval Shipyard, Bremerton, Wash (LPH-2); Philadelphia Naval Shipyard, Phil, Pa (LPH-3, -7, -9, -11); Ingalls SB Corp, Pascagoula, Miss (LPH-10, -12)
Displacement light, 10,722/11,877 tons; full load, 17,515/18,825 tons

Iwo Jima with part of her CH-46 Sea Knight and CH-53 Sea Stallion helicopter complement on deck and *Trenton* (LPD-14) in the background. A BPDMS launcher can be seen on the starboard side of *Iwo Jima*, forward of the bridge *(US Navy)*

Length overall 602.3ft (183.7m) (LPH-2); 592ft (180.4m) (LPH-10, -11); 598ft (182.3m) (remainder)
Maximum beam hull, 84ft (25.6m); flight deck, 104ft (31.7m)
Maximum draught 28/31ft (8.53/9.45m)
Main machinery One geared turbine (DeLaval, LPH-10); (General Electric, LPH-12); (Westinghouse, rest). Two boilers: Babcock and Wilcox (LPH-9); Combustion Engineering (remainder)
Screws/s.h.p. 1/22,000
Maximum speed 23 knots
Armament Two Sea Sparrow BPDMS (Mark 25) launchers, two twin 3in/50 (Mark 33) gun mounts
Complement 47 officers and 562 enlisted men
Troops 144 officers and 1,602 enlisted men

These are the first ships designed specifically to operate helicopters. They can carry a Marine battalion with associated gear and transport helicopters. They also have extensive medical facilities.

LPH-2 was authorised in the FY-1958 Programme, LPH-3 in FY-1959, LPH-7 in 1960, and LPH-9 in FY-1962 (all SCB-157). LPH-10 was authorised in FY-1963 (SCB-157A), LPH-11 in FY-1965, and LPH-12 in FY-1966 (both SCB-401.65). The estimated construction costs of *Iwo Jima*, in FY-1958 dollars, was $40 million. From January 1972 to 1974 *Guam* served as an Interim Sea Control Ship, carrying AV-8A Harriers and SH-3 Sea King ASW helicopters and acting as a trials ship for the Sea Control Ship concept.

The flight deck arrangement of the *Iwo Jima*s permits simultaneous operation of seven CH-46 Sea Knight or four CH-53 Sea Stallion helicopters. The hangar deck accommodates 20 CH-46 or 11 CH-53 helicopters. Cargo capacity is 4,300ft² for vehicles and 37,400ft³ for cargo. Two deck-edge elevators are fitted, one each side of the ship, but these ships have no catapults or arresting gear.

As completed, this class has four twin 3in gun mounts; two forward of the island and two on the stern. Two BPDMS launchers, one on the port quarter and one forward of the bridge, replaced two of these mounts. Two 40mm saluting guns are fitted. Two 20mm CIWS (Mark 16) and one Mark 36 Super Chaffroc (RBOC) are to be fitted (already on LPH-7). All units are fitted with the OE-82 satellite communications antenna, SSR-1 receiver and WSC-3 transceiver.

Advanced electronic warfare equipment is fitted. Radars comprise one AN/SPS-10 surface search, one AN/SPS-40 air search, and one AN/SPN-10 navigational radars. Two Mark 115 missile fire-control systems are carried.

Disposals: LPH-1 was originally assigned to the *Commencement Bay* class unit *Block Island* (CVE-106), but her conversion to LPH was cancelled in 1955. LPH-6 was *Thetis Bay* (CVE-90) of the *Casablanca* class escort carriers. She was commissioned as CVHA-1 on 20 July, 1956, and struck from the Navy List as LPH-6 on 1 March, 1964, and sold for scrapping. LPH-4, -5 and -8 were originally *Boxer* (CV-21), *Princeton* (CV-37), and *Valley Forge* (CV-45) of the *Essex* class carriers. They were struck from the NVR on 1 December, 1969, 30 January, 1970 and 15 January, 1970, respectively, and sold for scrapping.

Type: Amphibious Transport Docks (LPD) — *Number/Class:* 5+ (Projected)

Name	*Number*	*Laid down*	*Launched*	*Commissioned*	*Status*
	LPD-17				PROJ
	LPD-18				PROJ
	LPD-19				PROJ

Provisional characteristics
Displacement 17,700 tons
Length overall 608ft (185.3m)
Maximum beam 88ft (26.8m)
Aircraft Four CH-46 helicopters
Boats 12 LCM-6 or two LCAC
Complement Not available
Troops 600

Designed as replacements for the ageing *Raleigh/Austin* class. Funding for long-lead items for the prototype are planned for the FY-1987 budget, with plans for construction funding in FY-1988. It is very possible that this programme will be accelerated by the Reagan Administration, ahead of the plan already mentioned. The prototype, LPD-17, is scheduled for launching in the early 1990's.

Type: Amphibious Transport Docks (LPD) — *Number/Class:* 11 *Austin*

Name	*Number*	*Laid down*	*Launched*	*Commissioned*	*Status*
Austin	LPD-4	4 Feb 1963	27 June 1964	6 Feb 1965	AA
Ogden	LPD-5	4 Feb 1963	27 June 1964	19 June 1965	PA
Duluth	LPD-6	18 Dec 1963	14 Aug 1965	18 Dec 1965	PA
Cleveland	LPD-7	30 Nov 1964	7 May 1966	21 Apr 1967	PA
Dubuque	LPD-8	25 Jan 1965	6 Aug 1966	1 Sept 1967	PA
Denver	LPD-9	7 Feb 1964	23 Jan 1965	26 Oct 1968	PA
Juneau	LPD-10	23 Jan 1965	12 Feb 1966	12 July 1969	PA
Shreveport	LPD-12	27 Dec 1965	22 Oct 1966	12 Dec 1970	AA
Nashville	LPD-13	14 Mar 1966	7 Oct 1967	14 Feb 1970	AA
Trenton	LPD-14	3 Aug 1966	3 Aug 1968	6 Mar 1971	AA
Ponce	LPD-15	31 Oct 1966	20 May 1970	10 July 1971	AA

Builders New York Naval Shipyard, Brooklyn, N.Y. (LPD-4/6); Ingalls SB Corp, Pascagoula, Miss (LPD-7, -8); Lockheed SB and Const Co, Seattle, Wash (LPD-9, -10, -12/15)
Displacement Light, 10,000 tons. Full load, 15,900 tons (LPD-4/6); 16,550 tons (LPD-7/10); 16,900 tons (LPD-12, -13); 17,000 tons (LPD-14, -15)

Juneau (LPD-10) on sea trials. Starting in the mid-1980s, all of this class will receive a Service Life Extension Programme (SLEP) overhaul to carry them over until the new LPD-17 class is introduced *(Lockheed Shipbuilding)*

Length overall 570ft (173.3m)
Maximum beam 100ft (30.5m)
Maximum draught 23ft (7m)
Main machinery Two steam turbines: General Electric (LPD-9, -10); DeLaval (remainder). Two boilers: Babcock and Wilcox (LPD-4/6); Foster-Wheeler (remainder)
Screws/s.h.p. 2/24,000
Maximum speed 21 knots
Armament Two twin 3in/50 (Mark 33) gun mounts
Complement 27 officers, 446 enlisted men
Troops 840 (LPD-7/13), 930 (remainder)
Flag personnel 90 (LPD-7/10, -12, -13)

Designed as enlarged versions of the *Raleigh* (LPD-1) class, these were authorised as follows: FY-1962 (LPD-4/6) an FY-1963 (LPD-7/10), all under SCB-187B; LPD-12 and -13 in FY-1965 (SCB-187C); LPD-14 and -15 in FY-1965 (SCB-402.65). A sixteenth unit, LPD-16, was authorised in the FY-1966 Programme, but was cancelled on 24 February, 1969, and the funds were diverted to the Vietnam War. The twelfth unit in the class, *Coronado* (LPD-11), was reclassified AGF-11 on 1 October, 1980. She serves as temporary relief ship for *La Salle* (AGF-3), while that ship is in overhaul. At the time of writing, *Coronado* is scheduled to be reclassified back to LPD-11 when *La Salle* resumes her duties.

Construction of *Duluth* was begun by New York Naval Shipyard, but after launch was re-assigned to Philadelphia on 24 November,

1965, when New York Navy Yard was closed down. These ships are fitted with telescopic hangars for helicopter storage and maintenance. The well deck measures 168ft (51.2m) by 50ft (15.2m). Cargo is loaded/unloaded on landing craft by overhead monorails, and handled by six cranes. Docking well capacity is one LCU and three LCM-6s, four LCM-8s, or 20 LVTs (amphibious tractors). In addition, two LCM-6s or four LCPLs are carried on the boat deck, being handled by crane. Vehicles can be driven between the helicopter deck, parking area, and docking well by means of connecting ramps. Side ports provide roll-on/roll-off capability when docks are available.

Two 20mm Mark 16 CIWS and one Mark 36 RBOC (Super Chaffroc) are to be fitted (already on AGF/LPD-11 and LPD-13), replacing the Mark 28 installation on LPD-13. Starting in the mid-1980s, all of this class will receive the SLEP (Service Life Extension Program) overhaul.

Electronics comprise an OE-82 Satellite Communication Antenna, SSR-1 Receiver, and WSC-3 transceiver.

Nashville (LPD-13) on sea trials. The stern gate covers almost the entire transom. On the Soviet Navy's comparable *Ivan Rogov* class it covers only the middle third, and there have been reports that this is too narrow to permit undocking of the air-cushion vehicles carried on the well deck *(Lockheed Shipbuilding)*

Type: Amphibious Transport Docks (LPD) — *Number/Class:* 2 *Raleigh*

Name	Number	Laid down	Launched	Commissioned	Status
Raleigh	LPD-1	23 June 1960	17 Mar 1962	8 Sept 1962	AA
Vancouver	LPD-2	19 Nov 1960	15 Sept 1962	11 May 1963	PA

Builder New York Naval Shipyard, Brooklyn, N.Y.
Displacement Light; 8,000 tons (LPD-1), 8,276 tons (LPD-2). Full load; 13,600 tons
Length overall 521.8ft (158.4m)
Maximum beam 100ft (30.5m)
Maximum draught 22ft (6.7m)
Main machinery Two DeLaval steam turbines. Two Babcock and Wilcox boilers
Screws/s.h.p. 2/24,000
Maximum speed 21 knots
Armament Three twin 3in/50 (Mark 33) gun mounts
Complement 30 officers and 460 enlisted men
Troops 143 officers and 996 enlisted men

This design (SCB-187) resembles the LSD types somewhat, but has a fully enclosed docking well, the roof of which provides a permanent helicopter landing deck. Furthermore, the Amphibious Transport Docks are more versatile and were originally designed to replace the Dock Landing Ship (LSD). Amphibious Transport (LPA) and Amphibious Cargo Ship (LKA) by combining the best features of all three. However, because of the Vietnam War, they supplemented the aforementioned vessels instead. The estimated cost of each ship was $29 million. LPD-1 was authorised in the FY-1959 Programme; LPD-2 in FY-1960.

Features and capabilities of this class are similar to those of the *Austin* (LPD-4) class, and are given in that section. In addition, two 20mm (Mark 16) CIWS and one Mark 36 Super Chaffroc (RBOC) are to be fitted. The docking well can hold one LCU and three LCM-6s or four LCM-8s or 20 LVTs. Two LCM-6s or four LCPLs can be carried on the boat deck.

Originally a three-ship class, the third unit, *La Salle* (LPD-3), was reclassified as a Miscellaneous Flagship (AGF-3) on 1 July, 1972 (see Auxiliary Section).

Electronics: OE-82 satellite communications antenna, SSR-1 receiver, and WSC-3 transceiver.

Raleigh (LPD-1) and the rest of her class combine the functions of Dock Landing Ships (LSD), Amphibious Transport (LPA) and Amphibious Cargo Ship (LKA), which they were originally intended to replace. The demands of the Vietnam War meant that the LPDs supplemented the three earlier types instead *(US Navy)*

Type: Dock Landing Ships (LSD) — *Number/Class:* 0+3+(9) *Whidbey Island*

Name	Number	Laid down	Launched	Commissioned	Status
Whidbey Island	LSD-41	4 Aug 1981	10 June 1983	Est. 1985	BLDG
	LSD-42	5 Aug 1982			BLDG
	LSD-43	11 June 1983			BLDG
	LSD-44				PROJ
	LSD-45/52				PROJ

Artist's impression of the new *Whidbey Island*-class LSDs, designed to replace the *Thomaston*-class LSDs and to increase the Navy's lift capability from 1.0 Marine amphibious force to double that by the 1990s

Builder Lockheed SB and Const Co, Seattle, Wash (LSD-41/43)
Displacement Light, 11,125 tons; full load, 15,726 tons
Length overall 609ft (185.6m)
Maximum beam 84ft (25.6m)
Maximum draught 19.7ft (6m)
Main machinery Four Colt-Pielstick type 16PC2V diesels
Screws/s.h.p. 2/34,000
Maximum speed 23 knots
Armament Two 20mm (Mark 16) CIWS
Complement 19 officers and 337 enlisted men
Troops 25 officers and 313 enlisted men

Designed to replace the *Thomaston* (LSD-28) class, this class had a colourful history even before the prototype was authorised. Six ships were originally planned, but this was later reduced to three because the then Secretary of Defence considered the LSD-41 design outmoded. There was a measure of truth in his thinking, since the design was based on that of the 11-year-old *Anchorage* (LSD-36) class. Under extremely heavy Congressional pressure, the Secretary of Defence approved the construction of LSD-41 through -43. The Reagan Administration later increased the programme to ten units. However, the Secretary's refusal at the time, to approve modifications made by the Navy, indicated that there was more to the original disapproval than design considerations. In short, it was an overzealous determination to put economy before strategic requirements.

LSD-41 was authorised in the FY-1981 programme, with LSD-42 approved in FY-1982 and LSD-43 in FY-1983, LSD-44 projected in FY-1984, and LSD-45/52 following through each fiscal year from 1985 to 1988 at the rate of two a year. The prototype is to cost $417.7 million dollars, while LSD-43 will cost $373.1 million. These ships will be able to handle the CH-53 helicopters and/or AV-8A Harrier V/Stol aircraft, as well as air-cushion landing craft vehicles. The docking well will be 440ft (134.1m) long by 50ft (15.2m) wide. One Mark 36 Super Chaffroc (RBOC) will be fitted. The first ship of this class is expected to be completed in early 1985. They are to be fitted with AN/SPS-49 and AN/SPS-67V radars as well as AN/SLQ-32V ECM systems and LN-66 navigation radar.

Cargo capacity is 12,000ft² for vehicles and 5,000ft³ for freight. The well deck can accommodate four LCACs or 21 LCM-6s.

Type: Dock Landing Ships (LSD) — **Number/Class:** 5 Anchorage

Name	Number	Laid down	Launched	Commissioned	Status
Anchorage	LSD-36	13 Mar 1967	5 May 1968	15 Mar 1969	PA
Portland	LSD-37	21 Sept 1967	20 Dec 1969	3 Oct 1970	AA
Pensacola	LSD-38	12 Mar 1969	11 July 1970	27 Mar 1971	AA
Mount Vernon	LSD-39	29 Jan 1970	17 Apr 1971	13 May 1972	PA
Fort Fisher	LSD-40	15 July 1970	22 Apr 1972	9 Dec 1972	PA

Builders Ingalls SB Corp, Pascagoula, Miss (LSD-36); General Dynamics Corp, Quincy, Mass (remainder)
Displacement Light; 8,600 tons (LSD-36, 8,100 tons
Length overall 562ft (171.3m) (LSD-36); 553.3ft (168.6m) (LSD-37); 561ft (171m) (LSD-38/40)
Maximum beam 84ft (25.6m)
Maximum draught 20ft (6m)
Main machinery Two DeLaval steam turbines. Two Combustion Engineering boilers (LSD-36); Foster-Wheeler (remainder)
Screws/s.h.p. 2/24,000
Maximum speed 22 knots
Armament Three twin 3in/50 (Mark 33) gun mounts
Complement 21 officers and 376 enlisted men
Troops 28 officers and 348 enlisted men

Similar to the *Thomaston* (LSD-28) class, these craft have a tripod mast and enclosed 3in gun mounts forward of the bridge. LSD-36 was authorised in the FY-1965 Programme (SCB-404.65); LSD-37/39 in FY-1966, and LSD-40 in FY-1967 (all SCB-404.66). A conservative estimate of construction cost is $11.5 million per ship.

The *Anchorages* have a removable helicopter platform aft with the docking well partially open. The well is 430ft (131.1m) long by 50ft (15.2m) wide, and can accommodate three LCU-type landing craft. One LCM can be carried on deck, and davits are provided for one LCPL and one LCVP. The class is to be fitted with two 20mm (Mark 16) CIWS and one Mark 36 Super Chaffroc (RBOC) system.

Electronics comprise AN/SPS-10 surface search and AN/SPS-49 air search radar; an OE-82 satellite communications antenna, an SSR-1 receiver and a WSC-3 transceiver.

Anchorage (LSD-36) departing San Diego. The helicopter platform aft is removable

Mount Vernon seen in 1980. Her stern gate is down and two LCMs can be seen in the well deck

Type: Dock Landing Ships (LSD)

Number/Class: 8 *Thomaston*

Name	*Number*	*Laid down*	*Launched*	*Commissioned*	*Status*
Thomaston	LSD-28	3 Mar 1953	9 Feb 1954	17 Sept 1954	PR
Plymouth Rock	LSD-29	5 May 1953	7 May 1954	29 Nov 1954	AR
Fort Snelling	LSD-30	17 Aug 1953	16 July 1954	24 Jan 1955	AR
Point Defiance	LSD-31	23 Nov 1953	28 Sept 1954	31 Mar 1955	PR
Spiegel Grove	LSD-32	7 Sept 1954	10 Nov 1955	8 June 1956	AA
Alamo	LSD-33	11 Nov 1954	20 Jan 1956	24 Aug 1956	PA
Hermitage	LSD-34	11 Apr 1955	12 June 1956	14 Dec 1956	AA
Montecello	LSD-35	6 June 1955	10 Aug 1956	29 Mar 1957	PR

Builder Ingalls SB Corp, Pascagoula, Miss
Displacement Light, 6,880 tons; full load, 12,000 tons
Length overall 510ft (155.5m)
Maximum beam 84ft (25.6m)
Maximum draught 19ft (5.8m)
Main machinery Two General Electric geared turbines. Two Babcock and Wilcox boilers
Screws/s.h.p. 2/24,000
Maximum speed 22.5 knots
Armament Three twin 3in/50 Mark 33 gun mounts
Complement 400 total
Troops 340 total

The first post-war LSD class, to be replaced by the *Whidbey Island* class LSDs. In the face of Marine Corps objections, all of this class – except *Spiegel Grove, Alamo* and *Hermitage* – are to be laid up in FY-1983. *Spiegel Grove* and *Hermitage* are scheduled to be decommissioned in FY-1987 and *Alamo* no earlier than FY-1989. They have a well deck measuring 391ft (119.2m) by 48ft (14.6m). A helicopter is accommodated over the docking well. The *Thomastons* can carry 21 LCM-6 or 3 LCU landing craft, or about 50 Amphibious Tractors (LVT) in the docking well, plus 30 more on the mezzanine and super decks (see page 234).

In the SCB-75 design, the following authorisations were made: LSD-28/31 in the FY-1952 Programme, LSD-32 and -33 in FY-1954, and LSD-34 and -35 in FY-1955.

The *Thomastons* were completed with eight twin 3in gun mounts, but two mounts have since been removed.

Electronics fitted are one OE-82 satellite communication antenna, an SSR-1 receiver and a WSC-3 transceiver.

Hermitage (LSD-34) in October 1980. Her pole mast contrasts with the lattice stanchions of *Mount Vernon* and *Anchorage (Skyfotos)*

Type: Amphibious Cargo Ships (LKA) — *Number/Class:* 5 *Charleston*

Name	Number	Laid down	Launched	Commissioned	Status
Charleston	LKA-113	5 Dec 1966	2 Dec 1967	14 Dec 1968	AA
Durham	LKA-114	10 July 1967	29 Mar 1968	24 May 1969	PA
Mobile	LKA-115	15 Jan 1968	19 Oct 1968	29 Sept 1969	PA
St Louis	LKA-116	3 Mar 1968	4 Jan 1969	22 Nov 1969	PA
El Paso	LKA-117	22 Oct 1968	17 May 1969	17 Jan 1970	AA

Builder Newport News SB and DD Co, Newport News, Va
Displacement Light; 10,000/13,727 tons. Full load; 18,241/18,648 tons
Length overall 575.5ft (175.4m)
Maximum beam 82ft (24.99m)
Maximum draught 28ft (8.5m)
Main machinery One Westinghouse steam turbine. Two Combustion Engineering boilers
Screws/s.h.p. 1/22,000
Maximum speed 22 knots
Armament Three twin 3in/50 (Mark 33) gun mounts
Complement 24 officers and 310 enlisted men
Troops 15 officers and 211 enlisted men

This class was the first to be specially designed (SCB-403.65) as Amphibious Cargo Ships (originally Attack Cargo Ships). they can carry up to nine LCM landing craft and supplies for amphibious operations. LKA-113/116 were authorised in the FY-1965 Programme, and LKA-117 in FY-1966. Originally designated AKA, these ships were reclassified LKA (*Charleston* on 14 December, 1968, and the remainder on 1 January, 1969). Estimated cost of construction for each ship is $21 million.

The *Charlestons* have a fully automated main propulsion plant with the control console located on the bridge. This allows for a reduced crew complement. They are fitted with two heavy-lift cranes of 78.4 tons capacity, plus two 40-ton and eight 15-ton capacity booms. A helicopter platform is fitted aft. Two 20mm (Mark 16) CIWS and one Mark 36 Super Chaffroc (RBOC) system are to be fitted on these ships (already on LKA-117).

Durham was transferred to the Naval Reserve Force on 1 October, 1979, and was based at San Diego, California. *Charleston* was transferred to the NRF on 21 November, 1979, and was based at Norfolk, Virginia. It was followed by *Mobile* on 1 September, 1980, and *El Paso* on 1 March, 1981, these two having been based at Long Beach, California, and Norfolk, Virginia, respectively. *Durham* and *El Paso* were returned to the active fleet

Durham (LKA-114). Note the battle-efficiency "E" on the funnel, awarded for engineering excellence *(US Navy)*

Charleston (LKA-113) (illustrated) and her four sisters are the only LKAs to be built as such from the keel up, the previous 112 units being converted mercantile hulls *(Skyfotos)*

on 1 October, 1982, followed by *Charleston* on 18 February, 1983. *Mobile*, the last unit, is scheduled to return to the active fleet on 30 September, 1983.

Disposals of old Amphibious Cargo Ships are as follows: *Winston* (LKA-94), *Merrick* (LKA-97), *Seminole* (LKA-104), and *Union* (LKA-106) were struck off the Naval Vessel Register on 1 September, 1976. *Algol* (LKA-54), *Capricornus* (LKA-57), *Yancey* (LKA-93), *Rankin* (LKA-103), and *Vermilion* (LKA-107) were struck off the NVR on 1 January, 1977. *Tulare* (LKA-112) was decommissioned on 15 February, 1980, and struck off the NVR on 1 August, 1981.

Disposals of Amphibious Transports are as follows: *Magoffin* (LPA-199), *Navarro* (LPA-215), *Pickaway* (LPA-222), *Renville* (LPA-227), and *Bexar* (LPA-237) were struck off the NVR in 1 September, 1976. *Paul Revere* (LPA-248) was sold to Spain on 17 January, 1980, and *Francis Marion* (LPA-249) on 11 July, 1980; after both had been struck off on 1 January, that year.

Type: Tank Landing Ships (LST) — *Number/Class:* 20 *Newport*

Name	Number	Laid down	Launched	Commissioned	Status
Newport	LST-1179	1 Nov 1966	3 Feb 1968	7 June 1969	AA
Manitowoc	LST-1180	1 Feb 1967	4 June 1969	24 Jan 1970	AA
Sumter	LST-1181	14 Nov 1967	13 Dec 1969	20 June 1970	AA
Fresno	LST-1182	16 Dec 1967	28 Sep 1968	22 Nov 1969	PA
Peoria	LST-1183	22 Feb 1968	23 Nov 1968	21 Feb 1970	PA
Frederick	LST-1184	13 Apr 1968	8 Mar 1969	11 Apr 1970	PA
Schenectady	LST-1185	2 Aug 1968	24 May 1969	13 June 1970	PA
Cayuga	LST-1186	28 Sept 1968	12 July 1969	8 Aug 1970	PA
Tuscaloosa	LST-1187	23 Nov 1968	6 Sept 1969	24 Oct 1970	PA
Saginaw	LST-1188	24 May 1969	7 Feb 1970	23 Jan 1971	AA
San Bernardino	LST-1189	12 July 1969	28 Mar 1970	27 Mar 1971	PA
Boulder	LST-1190	6 Sept 1969	22 May 1970	4 June 1971	NRF
Racine	LST-1191	13 Dec 1969	15 Aug 1970	9 July 1971	NRF
Spartanburg County	LST-1192	7 Feb 1970	11 Nov 1970	1 Sept 1971	AA
Fairfax County	LST-1193	28 Mar 1970	19 Dec 1970	16 Oct 1971	AA
La Moure County	LST-1194	22 May 1970	13 Feb 1971	18 Dec 1971	AA
Barbour County	LST-1195	15 Aug 1970	15 May 1971	12 Feb 1972	PA
Harlan County	LST-1196	7 Nov 1970	24 July 1971	8 Apr 1972	AA
Barnstable County	LST-1197	19 Dec 1970	2 Oct 1971	27 May 1972	AA
Bristol County	LST-1198	13 Feb 1971	4 Dec 1971	5 Aug 1972	PA

Builders Philadelphia Naval Shipyard, Phil, Pa (LST-1179/1181); National Steel and SB Co, San Diego, Cal (LST-1182/1198)
Displacement Light; 4,750/4,973 tons. Full load; 8,450/8,516 tons
Length overall 522.3ft (159.2m)
Maximum beam 69.5ft (21.2m)
Maximum draught 17.5ft (5.9m)
Main machinery Six Alco diesel engines (General Motors, LST-1179/1181), geared reduction drive
Screws/b.h.p. 2/16,000
Maximum speed 22 knots
Armament Two twin 3in/50 (Mark 33) gun mounts
Complement 14 officers and 211 enlisted men
Troops 20 officers and 400 enlisted men

LST-1179 was authorised in the FY-1965 Programme, LST-1180/1187 in FY-1966, and LST-1188/1198 in FY-1967. Seven additional units of this class planned for the FY-1971 Programme were deferred.

To achieve the objective of a 20-knot amphibious force, it was necessary to build a faster and larger LST. US designers indicated that the bow door design had to be discarded

Cayuga (LST-1186) off Guam in 1979 *(US Navy)*

Fresno (LST-1182). In operation the tank landing ramp is run forward, the top part of the bow folds back and the ramp is then lowered to a previously installed pontoon causeway *(US Navy)*

in favour of the clipper bow if the objective was to be reached, so a unique method of offloading vehicles from the bow was devised. Interestingly, Soviet ship designers, reportedly years behind the USA in technology, designed and built the LPD *Ivan Rogov*, the first of a new class of Soviet amphibious ships. This has a maximum speed of 24 knots and has a bow door of the same type as our old bow-door-equipped LSTs. In addition, our "unique" method of offloading on the *Newport* class has a documented history of track jamming.

The *Newport* class design, SCB-405, incorporates two large derrick arms which swing a 40-ton, 112ft (34.1m) long aluminium ramp forward and on to the beach. At the same time, the upper part of the bow folds back on the hinges. This configuration causes the class to resemble Netlayers (ANL).

The traditional name category for Tank Landing Ships in all previous cases had been *County* names. In keeping with the "new" tradition of being inconsistent, this was temporarily abandoned. However, the Navy returned to the "*County*" category in time to name the last seven ships of this class in the proper manner.

The *Newport* class is unique in many ways, having superior features over previous LST classes, but also some inferior features. Ramps just ahead of the box-like superstructure provide access to and from the tank deck below. On deck, vehicles can drive from one end of the ship to the other through a tunnel in the superstructure. A 30ft (9.1m) diameter turntable at each end of the deck can turn the vehicles round without them having to reverse. The stern gate to the tank deck permits loading/unloading of amphibious tractors into the water. An 800 b.h.p. bow thruster is fitted to hold the ship's position offshore while it is unloading LVTs.

These ships have twin side-by-side stacks, a large one to port and a much smaller one to starboard, arranged in echelon. They also have a helicopter deck, but no storage facilities. One Mark 36 Super Chaffroc (RBOC) (already on LST-1182) and two 20mm (Mark 16) CIWS are to be fitted.

LST-1190 was assigned to the Naval Reserve Force on 1 December, 1980, and is based at Little Creek, Virginia. LST-1191 was assigned to the NRF on 15 January, 1981, and is based at Long Beach, California.

Electronics comprise an OE-82 Satellite Communication Antenna and a WSC-3 transceiver.

Type: Tank Landing Ships (LST) — *Number/Class:* 3 *De Soto County*

Name	*Number*	*Builder*	*Commissioned*	*Status*
Suffolk County	LST-1173	Boston Naval Shipyard, Boston, Mass	15 Aug 1957	MAR
Loraine County	LST-1177	American SB Co, Lorain, Ohio	3 Oct 1959	MAR
Wood County	LST-1178	American SB Co, Lorain, Ohio	5 Aug 1959	MAR

Displacement Light 4,164 tons; full load 7,100 tons
Length overall 445ft (135.6m)
Maximum beam 62ft (18.9m)
Maximum draught 17.5ft (5.3m)
Main machinery Six Cooper-Bessemer diesel engines (Fairbanks-Morse on LST-1173); geared reduction
Screws/b.h.p. 2/13,700
Maximum speed 16.5 knots
Armament Three twin 3in/50 (Mark 33) gun mounts
Complement 15 officers and 173 enlisted men
Troops 30 officers and 604 enlisted men

This class represents the ultimate in traditional bow-door designed (SCB-119) Tank Landing Ships (LST). LST-1171 was authorised in the FY-1954 Programme, and LST-1173/1178 in FY-1955. LST-1172 was never built. These ships were faster and could carry more troops than preceding classes, and their 288ft (87.8m) long tank decks can carry 23 medium tanks or other vehicles up to 75 tons. Four davits carry one LCVP landing craft each. The *De Soto County* class can carry 170,000gal of various fuels and by reducing troop accommodation this can be increased by a further 250,000gal.

LST-1173 was decommissioned 25 August, 1972; LST-1177 on 1 September, 1972, and LST-1178 on 1 May, 1972. LST-1177 and -1178 were transferred to the temporary custody of the Maritime Administration Reserve Fleet, James River, on 31 January, 1973, and 15 August, 1972, respectively. All three ships are awaiting Congressional approval for sale to foreign navies.

Originally a seven-ship class, four sisters have been disposed of by transfer to foreign countries. *De Soto County* (LST-1171) and *York County* (LST-1175) were leased to Italy on 17 July, 1972. *Grant County* (LST-1174) was leased to Brazil, 15 January, 1973, and sold to that country outright on 11 February, 1980. *Graham County* (LST-1176) was reclassified AGP-1176 and has since been struck off the Navy List. A sister ship, LST-1172, was never built.

Wood County (LST-1178), one of three remaining bow-door LSTs still on the Naval Vessel Register. She and her sisters, *Loraine County* (LST-1177) and *Suffolk County* (LST-1173), are scheduled to be transferred to foreign countries *(US Navy)*

Amphibious Warfare Craft

Type: Landing Craft Air Cushion (LCAC) — *Number/Class:* 0+9+(99)

Number	*Builder*	*Completed*	*Status*
LCAC-1/6	Bell Aerospace Textron Co, New Orleans, La	est March 1985	BLDG

Displacement 149.2 tons gross; 87.2 tons empty
Length overall Hard structure: 81ft (24.7m); On cushion: 88ft (26.8m)
Maximum beam On cushion: 47.0ft (13.1m); hard structure: 43.0ft (8.2m)
Maximum draught Off cushion: 2.11ft (0.6m)
Main propulsion machinery Four Avco-Lycoming TF40B gas turbines
Propellers/b.h.p. Two shrouded reversible-pitch/12,280; four double-entry fans, centrifugal or mixed-flow
Maximum speed 50 knots
Range 300 nautical miles at 35 knots
Complement 5 total (5 enlisted men)

The design of this class contains the best features of the Jeff A and Jeff B designs, with emphasis on the Jeff B design. The first three craft under the FY-1982 Programme at a total cost of $98.4 million (FY-1982). Another three units were approved in the FY-1983 budget at a cost of $65.3 million. The contract for the long-term lead items for the first six units of the class was awarded to Bell Aerospace on 5 June, 1981. A construction contract for LCAC-1/3 was awarded to Bell on 22 February, 1981, followed by LCAC-4/6 on 15 October, 1982. These craft will be capable of being carried by the LHA/LHD/LPD/LSD types, and able to land on 70 per cent of the world's beaches. A total of 108 units is planned. The first six will be assigned to the Pacific Fleet. Maximum cargo capacity is 75 tons.

Artist's impression of the production LCAC, construction of which began in September 1982. This design is intended to incorporate the best features of the Jeff A and Jeff B trials craft during sustained operations in heavy seas *(Bell Aerospace Textron)*

Type: Amphibious Assault Landing Craft (AALC)

1 Bell Design Jeff B Type

Displacement Normal, 60 tons; gross, 160 tons
Length overall On air cushion, 86.75ft (26.4m); at rest, 80ft (24.4m)
Maximum beam On air cushion, 47ft (14.3m); at rest, 23.5ft (7.2m)
Maximum draught On air cushion, 23.5ft (7.2m); at rest, 19ft (5.8m)
Main machinery Six Avco-Lycoming T-40 gas turbine engines, generating 2,800 h.p. each
Propellers/h.p. 2/16,000
Cruising speed 50 knots+, air cushion mode
Armament None
Complement Six (total)

Built by Bell Aerospace Textron Co, New Orleans, La, Jeff B was completed in 1976. It is a competing design with Jeff A to decide the characteristics of the projected 109-unit LCAC Class. Both are experimental vessels constructed from aluminium. This vessel has both bow and stern ramps to handle vehicles or cargo up to 75 tons capacity. Jeff B differs from Jeff A craft by having only two propellers in rotating shrouds for thrust and steering instead of four. Unlike all Soviet amphibious air-cushion vehicles, the cargo deck is uncovered, as it will be in the LCAC design. Four fans provide cushion lift. The six engines are housed three on each side of the superstructure, with a raised pilot house on the starboard side. As a result of the experiments with Jeff A and Jeff B, it is planned that air cushion vehicles will eventually replace such landing craft as the LCUs and some smaller craft now on the Navy inventory.

The Jeff B has a cargo capacity of 1,738ft², and is based at Panama City, Fla.

Jeff B trials ACV *(US Navy)*

Type: Amphibious Assault Landing Craft (AALC)

1 Aerojet Design Jeff A Type

Weight Gross, 167 tons; normal, 90 tons
Length overall On air cushion, 96.1ft (29.3m); at rest, 92ft (28m)
Maximum beam On air cushion, 48ft (14.6m), at rest, 44ft (13.4m)
Maximum draught On air cushion, 23.2ft (7.1m); at rest, 18.75ft (5.7m)
Main machinery Propulsion: Four Avco-Lycoming T-40 gas turbine engines, generating 3,750 h.p. each. Lift engines: Two Avco-Lycoming T-40 gas turbine engines, generating 3,750 h.p. each
Propellers/h.p. 4/15,000 (propulsion)
Cruising speed 50 knots+, air cushion mode
Armament None
Complement Six (total)

In 1971 Bell Aerospace and Aerojet-General of Todd Shipyards, Seattle, Wash, were awarded contracts for competing designs. The best features of the Jeff A and Jeff B are to be incorporated into a design for mass production. Some general notes given under Jeff B apply to this vehicle as well. Jeff A is based at Panama City, Fla.

Air-cushion vehicles (ACV) are supported above land and water surfaces on a continuously generated air cushion contained by flexible skirts surrounding the vehicle's base. The Surface Effect Ship (SES) has rigid sidewalls that penetrate the water's surface to help contain the air cushion.

Type: Utility Landing Craft (LCU) — *Number/Class:* 51 "LCU-1610"

LCU	LCU	LCU	LCU	LCU	LCU
-1616	-1630	-1645	-1655	-1663	-1672
-1617	-1631	-1646	-1656	-1664	-1673
-1619	-1632	-1648	-1657	-1665	-1674
-1621	-1633	-1649	-1658	-1666	-1675
-1623	-1634	-1650	-1659	-1667	-1676
-1624	-1635	-1651	-1660	-1668	-1677
-1627	-1643	-1652	-1661	-1669	-1678
-1628	-1644	-1653	-1662	-1670	-1679
-1629		-1654		-1671	

Builders Gunderson Bros. Engineering Corp, Portland, Oregon (LCU-1616, -1617, -1619, -1623, -1624); Southern SB Corp, Sidell, La (LCU-1621, -1629, -1630); General Ship and Engine Works, East Boston, Mass (LCU-1627, -1628, -1631/1635, -1667/1670); Marinette Marine Corp, Marinette, Wisc (LCU-1643/1645, -1671/1679); Defoe SB Co, Bay City, Mich (LCU-1646, -1648/1666)
Displacement Light, 200 tons; full load, 375 tons
Length overall 134.9ft (41.1m)
Maximum beam 29ft (8.8m)
Maximum draught 6.1ft (1.9m)
Main engines Four Detroit diesels, geared reduction (except LCU-1621, see notes)
Screws/b.h.p. 2/1,000 (Kort nozzles)
Maximum speed 11 knots
Armament Two .50 calibre machine guns
Complement 12/14 enlisted men

Many versions of this handy utility craft serve in other capacities within the Navy and with many foreign navies as well. This design is the outgrowth of the LCT(5) and LCT(6) landing craft of the Second World War. A total of 1,670 of this type landing craft was authorised, and most were built. They are used to land tanks and heavy gear and to carry cargo from point to point. LCU-1667/1679 are under the operational control of the Army.

Truly utility craft, many have been converted to YFUs, IXs, and Salvage Craft. Originally all LCUs were on the Naval Vessel Register (NVR) and, as a result, carried hull numbers. In February 1955 all existing LCUs were reclassified "floating equipment" and removed from the NVR, but retained their hull numbers.

This LCU class is an improved and larger version of the LCU-1466 class. They can carry three M-103 and M-48 tanks (estimated 112 tons) or a cargo of 170 tons. LCU-1679, the last unit built, was completed in 1976.

LCU-1636 and -1638/1640 were reclassified as YFB-88/91 in October 1969, and LCU-1620 and -1625 to YFU-92 and -93 in April 1971, followed by LCU-1611, -1615 and -1622 to YFU-97/99 in February 1972, and LCU-1610 and -1612 to YFU-100 and 101, respectively, in August 1972.

LCU-1618 was reclassified IX-508 (see Auxiliary Section). LCU-1637 was converted to an "at sea-simulator" in 1979 and re-rated as "floating equipment". She is stationed at Roosevelt Roads Naval Air Station in Puerto Rico.

Note LCU-1621 has two diesel engines and is fitted with vertical cycloidal propellers.

LCU-1651, one of 51 units in the LCU-1610 class. Capable of carrying three M-48 tanks or a cargo of 170 tons, these craft are true workhorses, having seen service under a variety of other classifications *(US Navy)*

Type: Utility Landing Craft (LCU) — *Number/Class:* 4 "LCU-1466"

LCU	LCU
-1473	-1564
-1544	-1578

Displacement Light, 180 tons; full load, 360 tons
Length overall 119ft (36.3m)
Maximum beam 34ft (10.4m)
Maximum draught 6ft (1.8m)
Machinery Three Gray Marine diesel engines
Screws/b.h.p. 3/675
Maximum speed 10 knots
Armament Two 20mm gun mounts
Complement 14 enlisted men

These craft were built in the early 1950s as successors to the Second World War LCU-501 Class. Some were reclassified as YFUs in 1966/1971. All surviving units of this class, except LCU-1473, were acquired from the Army in September 1978, whence they had originally been transferred upon completion. LCU-1473 is assigned to the Naval Reserve Force at Buffalo, New York. Though classified as LCUs, these craft are not all actually employed as such.

Type: Mechanized Landing Craft (LCM) — *Number/Class:* "LCM-8"

Displacement Full load, 115 tons (steel), 105 tons (aluminium)
Length overall 73.7ft (22.5m)
Maximum beam 21ft (6.4m)
Maximum draught 5.2ft (1.6m)
Machinery Two Detroit or General Motors diesel engines
Screws/b.h.p. 2/650
Maximum speed 9 knots
Armament None
Complement 5 enlisted men

The LCM-8 design is a further development of the LCM-6. Several hundred of these craft are used by the Army and Navy. They can be carried on LKA, LPD, and LSD-type amphibious ships. None are on the Naval Vessel Register (NVR).

The later units of this class are constructed largely from aluminium. They can carry one M-48 or M-60 tank (48 tons) or 60 tons of cargo.

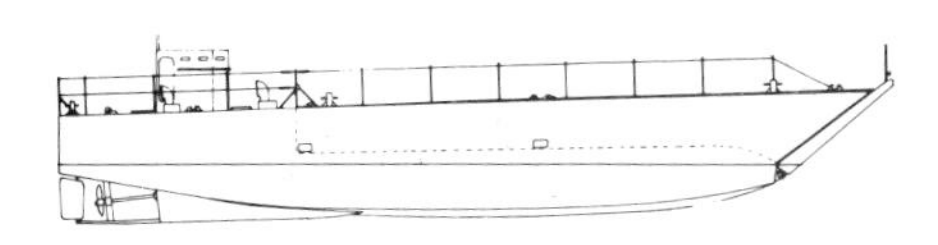

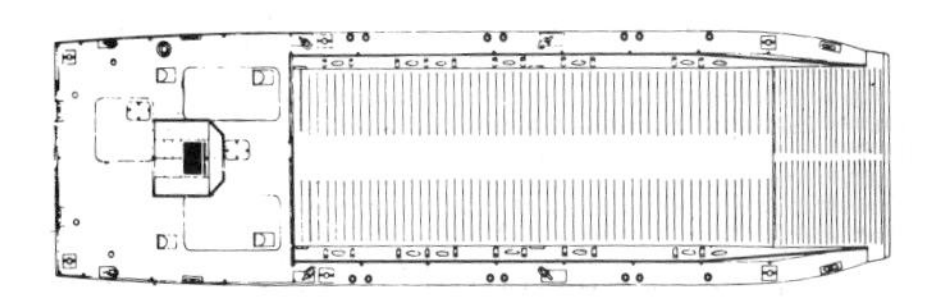

A typical LCM-8, capable of carrying one M-48 or M-60 tank or 60 tons of cargo

Type: Mechanized Landing Craft (LCM) — *Number/Class:* "LCM-6"

Displacement Full load, 61 tons
Length overall 56.2ft (17.1m)
Maximum beam 14ft (4.3m)
Maximum draught 3.9ft (1.2m)
Machinery Two diesel engines
Screws/b.h.p. 2/450
Maximum speed 9 knots
Accommodation Not available

Of welded steel construction, these craft can carry 80 troops or 34 tons of cargo. They are highly versatile and useful. The LCM-6 design was developed in World War Two and is still being built. Many LCMs were converted to Riverine craft during the Vietnam War. Like their big sisters, they can be transported on LKA, LPD, and LSDs. None are on the Naval Vessel Register (NVR).

Type: Landing Craft Vehicle and Personnel (LCVP)

Displacement Full load, 13.5 tons
Length 35.8ft (10.9m)
Maximum beam 10.5ft (3.2m)
Maximum draught 3.5ft (1.1m)
Machinery Diesel engine
Screws/b.h.p. 1/325
Maximum speed 9 knots
Armament One .30 cal machine gun (in combat areas only)
Complement Not available

The LCVP is one of the most successful landing craft still being built to the original Second World War design, but with minor modifications. Basically, it is a small davit-launched vehicle carried on certain amphibious ships for the purpose of landing troops. Originally constructed of plywood, it is now reinforced with plastic. It has a cargo capacity of 3.5 tons. None are on the Naval Vessel Register (NVR).

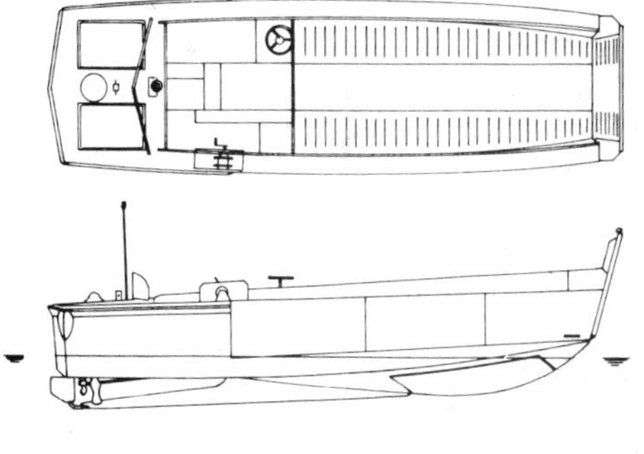

Typical 36ft (11m) Mk 1 LCVP

Type: Warping Tugs (LWT) — *Number/Class:* Several, unnumbered; 2 LWT-1

Characteristics	Unnumbered	LWT-1
Displacement	about 120 tons	61 tons (hoisting weight)
Length overall	92.9ft (28.3m)	85ft (25.9m)
Maximum beam	23ft (7m)	22ft (6.7m)
Maximum draught	6.5ft (2m)	6.8ft (2.1m)
Machinery	Two outboard propulsion units	Two Harbourmaster diesel engines
Screws/b.h.p.		Two steerable shafts/420
Maximum speed	6.5 knots	9 knots
Armament	None	None
Complement	max 6 enlisted men	Six enlisted men

Designed to serve as small tug boats in amphibious landings, these handy craft can salvage stranded landing craft and handle pontoon causeways and anchors. They are another outgrowth of Second World War amphibious vessels. The unnumbered types are fabricated from pontoon sections and are assembled by the major amphibious commands as required. The early LWTs were pontoon craft fitted with a powerful winch and A-frame. They can be transported by various amphibious ships.

A two-craft class (LWT-1 and -2) was built by the Campbell Machine Company of San Diego, California, being completed in 1970. They are LWT prototypes constructed from aluminium, and can be side-loaded on the main deck of the *Newport* (LST-1179) class or carried on LPD and LSD type ships. The need for rudders has been eliminated by the propulsion units, which are similar to outboard motors and provide both steering and thrust.

AUXILIARIES

At the beginning of FY-1976 there were 240 auxiliaries on the Navy List and 15 ships under construction. 122 were active, 20 in reserve, 19 in temporary custody of the Maritime Administration (Marad), 65 in Military Sealift Command (MSC) service, and 14 were on loan to other Government and non-Government agencies.

By FY-1982 223 auxiliaries were on the Navy List and 22 ships were under construction and/or proposed. Of the former, 78 were active, three were laid up in reserve, 27 were in Marad custody, eight were in Naval Reserve Force Training, six were on loan to other Government and non-Government agencies, and 82 were in MSC service, In addition, two Unclassified Vessels (IX) are listed here, as well as 12 ships under bareboat charter to MSC (the latter are not on the Navy List).

In the past 20 years, the Fleet has seen newly constructed vessels replace most Second World War Auxilaries. These new ships are far more advanced and sophisticated than the ships they replace. This is neccessitated by more advanced and sophisticated warships. Fortunately, planners pressed for, and were able to obtain, the funds needed for modern auxiliary ships.

Auxiliaries can be placed in three broad categories. First, underway replenishment. Designers have kept abreast of the new-ship requirement for fast underway replenishment with fuel and a wide variety of supplies and stores. In addition to fast methods of transferring supplies while underway and alongside, the concept of vertical replenishment was born. Helicopters, operating from the replenishment ships, have landing decks from which to load and off-load supplies, and most auxiliaries operate their own. The second category is Fleet Support Ships, which include tenders, repair ships, tugs and salvage vessels. The third category includes research and operational test ships.

Of late, replenishment and fleet support ships which were previously all-Navy manned are increasingly being transferred to, and operated by, the Military Sealift Command. Although they are still used for fleet support, they are civilian manned, and are unarmed. The prefix "T" is used before their designations. Except for Oilers (AO), they do not wear their hull numbers, nor are they in commission. Most MSC ships are painted Navy grey, and all bear the distinctive black, blue and yellow stack band.

Type: Destroyer Tenders (AD) — *Number/Class:* 4+(1) *Yellowstone*

Name	*Number*	*Laid down*	*Launched*	*Commissioned*	*Status*
Yellowstone	AD-41	27 June 1977	27 July 1979	28 June 1980	AA
Acadia	AD-42	14 Feb 1978	28 July 1979	6 June 1981	PA
Cape Cod	AD-43	27 Jan 1979	2 Aug 1980	17 Apr 1982	PA
Shenandoah	AD-44	2 Aug 1980	6 Feb 1982	20 Sept 1983	AA

Builder National Steel and SB Co, San Diego, Cal
Displacement Light, 13,280 tons; full load, 20,224 tons
Length overall 642ft (192.6m)
Maximum beam 85ft (25.5m)
Maximum draught 24ft (7.3m)
Main machinery One De Laval steam turbine. Two Combustion Engineering boilers
Screws/s.h.p. 1/20,000
Maximum speed 20 knots
Armament One Nato Sea Sparrow missile system, four 20 mounts (Mark 67)
Complement 400 officers and 1,784 enlisted personnel (includes 4 officers and 96 enlisted women)

This class design (SCB-700) is a slightly improved version of the *Samuel Gompers* class, to which it is quite similar. Notes appearing under the AD-37 class apply to these ships as well. They were authorised under the following Programmes: FY-1975 (AD-41), FY-1976 (AD-42), FY-1977 (AD-43), and FY-1979 (AD-44). A fifth unit (AD-45) is proposed for the FY-1987 Programme.

The new Destroyer Tender (AD) *Yellowstone* (AD-41) conducting sea trials

Type: Destroyer Tenders (AD) — *Number/Class:* 2 *Samuel Gompers*

Name	*Number*	*Laid down*	*Launched*	*Commissioned*	*Status*
Samuel Gompers	AD-37	9 July 1964	14 May 1966	1 July 1967	PA
Puget Sound	AD-38	15 Feb 1965	16 Sept 1966	27 Apr 1968	AA

Builder Puget Sound Naval Shipyard, Bremerton, Wash
Displacement Light, 13,600 tons; full load, 20,500 tons
Length overall 645ft (196.5m)
Maximum beam 85ft (25.9m)
Maximum draught 30ft (9.1m)
Main machinery One De Laval steam turbine. Two Combusion Engineering boilers
Screws/s.h.p. 1/20,000
Maximum speed 18 knots
Armament One single 5in/38 mount (Mark 30) (AD-38), four 20mm mounts (Mark 67)
Complement 40 officers and 1,784 enlisted personnel (includes 4 officers and 96 enlisted women)

The first post-Second World War design of destroyer tender, these ships are fully capable of servicing modern cruisers, destroyers, and frigates. They also have the means to service nuclear powerplants. The design virtually duplicates that of the *L. Y. Spear* and *Simon Lake*-class of submarine tenders. Each ship has two 7,000lb capacity cranes, and a helicopter platform and hangar to maintain LAMPS helicopters. AD-37 was authorised in the FY-1964 Programme (SCB-244), and AD-38 in FY-1965 (SCB-700.65). Two further units, AD-39 and -40, were authorised, but were cancelled on 11 December, 1965, and in April 1974, respectively, owing to the cost overruns of their sisters. These ships are fitted with two 40mm saluting guns. Electronics comprise an AN/SPS-10 surface search radar, an OE-82 satellite communications antenna, and a WSC-3 receiver.

Puget Sound (AD-38). After an extensive conversion she replaced *Albany* (CG-10) as Sixth Fleet flagship and is now based at Gaeta, Italy *(C.N. Dragonette)*

Type: Destroyer Tenders (AD) — *Number/Class:* 4 *Dixie*

Name	*Number*	*Builder*	*Commissioned*	*Status*
Dixie	AD-14	New York SB Corp, Camden, N.J.	25 Apr 1940	MPR
Prairie	AD-15	New York SB Corp, Camden, N.J.	5 Aug 1940	PA
Sierra	AD-18	Tampa SB Co Inc, Tampa, Fla	20 Mar 1944	AA
Yosemite	AD-19	Tampa SB Co Inc, Tampa, Fla	25 Mar 1944	AA

Displacement Light, 8,986/9,876 tons; full load, 17,345/18,400 tons
Length overall 530.5ft (161.7m)
Maximum beam 73.3ft (22.3m)
Maximum draught 25.5ft (7.8m)
Main machinery Turbine reduction engines (New York SB Corp, AD-14, -15; Allis-Chalmers, AD-17 and -19). Four Babcock and Wilcox boilers
Screws/s.h.p. 2/12,000
Maximum speed 20 knots
Armament Four single 20mm mounts (Mark 67)
Complement 46/70 officers; 915/979 enlisted men

These ships have the same general appearance as the *Vulcan* (AR) and *Fulton* (AS) tenders. The *Dixies*, under the FRAM II Programme, were given the capability of servicing destroyers equipped with Asroc, improved electronic suits, helicopters, etc. Two 40mm saluting guns are carried. All 5in/38 gun mounts and eight 40mm gun mounts were removed during modernisations and in subsequent years.

Electronics comprise an AN/SPS-10 surface search radar, an OE-82 Satellite Communication Antenna, and an SSR-1 receiver.

Dixie, the oldest active ship in the Navy, was decommissioned on 15 June, 1982. She was transferred for disposal to the Maritime Administration Reserve fleet at Suisun Bay, Calif, on 14 October, 1982. *Piedmont* was decommissioned on 30 September, 1982, and was leased to Turkey as *Derya* (A-576) on 2 October, 1982. *Everglades* (AD-24), the last of the four *Klondike* class tenders, currently serves as Depot Ship for the Philadelphia Inactive Maintenance Facility, having replaced ex-*Chandeleur* (AV-10) in that capacity. The transfer of *Everglades* to Pakistan is pending.

The following *Shenandoah* class tenders have been struck from the Naval Register: *Shenandoah* (AD-24) on 1 April, 1980, *Isle Royale* (AD-29) on 15 September, 1976, *Tidewater* (AD-31) on 15 June, 1978, (already transferred to Indonesia), and the last of the class, *Bryce Canyon* (AD-36), on 30 June, 1981. All except AD-31 (sold to Indonesia on 14 March, 1980) were sold for scrap.

Prairie (AD-15), second of the *Dixie*-class Destroyer Tenders. Of all the US ships built during the Second World War, the *Vulcan*-class Ars, the *Dixie* class and the Fulton-class AS, all three built to the same basic design, lasted the longest. *Piedmont* (AD-17) was transferred to the Turkish Navy and this is likely to remain in service for another decade *(US Navy)*

Type: Ammunition Ships (AE) — *Number/Class:* (+3) Unnamed

A new class of ammunition ship is proposed. Advanced procurement of long-lead items will be requested in the FY-1984 Budget, and construction funds for the prototype in FY-1986. Two more ships are planned, one in the FY-1986 Programme, and a second in FY-1987. They will replace the two *Suribachis* and three *Nitros*. No further details are known at present.

Type: Ammunition Ships (AE) — *Number/Class:* 8 *Kilauea*

Name	Number	Laid down	Launched	Commissioned	Status
Kilauea	T-AE-26	10 Mar 1966	9 Aug 1967	10 Aug 1968	MSC
Butte	AE-27	21 July 1966	9 Aug 1967	14 Dec 1968	AA
Santa Barbara	AE-28	20 Dec 1966	23 Jan 1968	11 July 1970	AA
Mount Hood	AE-29	8 May 1967	17 July 1968	1 May 1971	PA
Flint	AE-32	4 Aug 1969	9 Nov 1970	20 Nov 1971	PA
Shasta	AE-33	10 Nov 1969	3 Apr 1971	26 Feb 1972	PA
Mount Baker	AE-34	5 Oct 1970	23 Oct 1971	22 July 1972	AA
Kiska	AE-35	8 Apr 1971	11 Mar 1972	16 Dec 1972	PA

Builders General Dynamics Corp, Quincy, Mass (AE-25, -26); Bethlehem Steel Corp, Sparrows Point, Md (AE-28, -29); Ingalls SB Corp, Pascagoula, Miss (AE-32/35)

Displacement Light, 9,369–13,688 tons; full load, 18,088 (except AE-26 and -27, 17,931 tons

Length overall 564ft (171.9m)

Maximum beam 81ft (24.7m)

Maximum draught 30ft (9.1m)

Main machinery One General Electric steam turbine. Three Foster-Wheeler boilers

Screws/s.h.p. 1/22,000
Maximum speed 21 knots
Armament Four twin 3in/50 gun mounts (Mark 33) (AE-28/33); Two twin 3in/50 gun mounts (Mark 33) (rest). *Kilauea* is unarmed
Complement 38 officers and 373 enlisted men; *Kilauea*: 121 civilians, 67 Naval detachment

This class of ammunition ships can easily be recognised by the superstructure just forward of the helicopter deck aft. In addition to Fast transfer of ammunition to ships alongside, the *Kilaueas* can use their helicopters for vertical replenishment (Vertrep) as well. These ships are fitted with fin stabilisers. The original design number, SCB-249, was later changed to SCB-703. They were authorised under the following Programmes: FY-1965 (AE-26, -27), FY-1966 (AE-28, -29), FY-1967 (AE-32, -33), FY-1968 (AE-34, -35). The missing numbers AE-30 and -31 were converted *Andromeda* class AKAs, and have since been disposed of.

The 3in/50 gun mounts forward are closed, and the two mounts aft are open. The Mark 36 Super Chaffroc (RBOC) has been fitted in AE-27, and the remaining ships (except AE-26) will also be so equipped. Two 20mm Mark 16 CIWS are to be installed on AE-32/35, but the installation of the Nato Sea Sparrow system on the entire class has been cancelled.

Electronics comprise an OE-82 Satellite Communications Antenna and SSR-1 Receiver and an AN/SPS-10 surface search radar.

Kilauea was transferred to MSC for service on 1 October, 1980. *Butte* is scheduled to be transferred to MSC in FY-1984.

Butte (AE-27). The two twin 3in mounts atop the superstructure have been removed since this photo was taken *(General Dynamics)*

Type: Ammunition Ships (AE) — *Number/Class:* 3 Nitro

Name	*Number*	*Builder*	*Commissioned*	*Status*
Nitro	AE-23	Bethlehem Steel Corp, Sparrows Point, Md	1 May 1959	AA
Pyro	AE-24	Bethlehem Steel Corp, Sparrows Point, Md	24 July 1959	PA
Haleakala	AE-25	Bethlehem Steel Corp, Sparrows Point, Md	3 Nov 1959	PA

Displacement Light, 9,907 tons (AE-23), 12,497 tons (AE-24), 10,265 tons (AE-25); full load, 17,350 tons (AE-23), 17,450 tons (remainder)
Length overall 512ft (156.1m)
Maximum beam 72ft (21.9m)
Maximum draught 29ft (8.8m)
Main machinery One Bethlehem geared turbine. Two Combustion Engineering boilers
Screws/s.h.p. 1/16,000
Maximum speed 20.6 knots
Armament Two twin 3in/50 gun mounts (Mark 33)
Complement 20 officers and 330 enlisted men

These are nearly identical in design (SCB-114A) to the *Suribachi*-class AEs, and notes appearing under that class apply to the *Nitro* class as well. They were authorised under the following Programmes: FY-1956 (AE-23, -24) and FY-1957 (AE-25). In the 1960s these ships were modernised and provided with high speed transfer equipment (Fast). The helicop-

ter deck was retrofitted. *Pyro* served with the Naval Reserve Force from 1 September, 1980, until 1 June, 1982, when she returned to the active fleet. Electronics consist of the AN/SPS-10 surface search radar, OE-82 satellite communications antenna, and SSR-1 receiver. One Mark 36 Super Chaffroc RBOC mount is to be installed on each unit.

Nitro (AE-23)

Type: Ammunition Ships (AE) *Number/Class:* 2 *Suribachi*

Name	Number	Builder	Commissioned	Status
Suribachi	AE-21	Bethlehem Steel Corp, Sparrows Point, Md	17 Nov 1956	AA
Mauna Kea	AE-22	Bethlehem Steel Corp, Sparrows Point, Md	30 Mar 1957	PA

Displacement Light, 10,160 tons (AE-21), 9,913 tons (AE-22); full load, 17,450 tons
Length overall 511ft (155.7m)
Maximum beam 72ft (21.9m)
Maximum draught 29ft (8.8m)
Main machinery One Bethlehem geared turbine. Two Combustion Engineering boilers
Screws/s.h.p. 1/16,000
Maximum speed 21 knots
Armament Two twin 3in/50 gun mounts (Mark 33)
Complement 16 officers and 370 enlisted men

Authorised in the FY-1954 Programme (SCB-114A), these ships and the *Nitro*s were designed specifically for carrying ammunition. They were modernised in the 1960s, when they were given high speed transfer equipment (Fast) that can handle the latest heavy missiles as well as conventional ammunition. The two aft 3in gun mounts differ in both classes; some are in tandem, some are side-by-side.

Electronics comprise the AN/SPS-10 surface search radar, OE-82 satellite communications antenna, and SSR-1 receiver.

Mauna Kea served with the Naval Reserve Force from 1 October, 1979, until 1 January, 1982, when she was returned to the active fleet.

A Mark 36 Super Chaffroc RBOC is to be installed in AE-21.

The following older ammunition ships have been struck off the Naval Register: *Mauna Loa* (AE-8), of the *Mount Lassen* class, on 1 October, 1976; and *Wrangell* (AE-12) and *Firedrake* (AE-14), of the *Mount Hood* class, on 1 October, 1976, and 15 July, 1976, respectively. All were sold for scrapping.

Mauna Kea (AE-22). The radar antenna atop the mast has since been replaced by an AN/SPS-10 unit

Type: Store Ship (AF) *Number/Class:* 1 *Rigel*

Name	Number	Builder	Commissioned	Status
Rigel	T-AF-58	Ingalls Shipbuilding Corp, Pascagoula, Miss	2 Sept 1955	MSC

Displacement Light, 7,956 tons; full load, 15,500 tons
Length overall 502ft (153m)
Maximum beam 72ft (22m)
Maximum draught 28ft (8.5m)
Main machinery One General Electric geared turbine. Two Combustion Engineering boilers
Screws/s.h.p. 1/16,000
Maximum speed 21 knots
Complement approx 120 civilians, 60 Navy detachment

The only store ship (AF) remaining on the Navy List, *Rigel*, and her now departed sister ship *Vega*, were the only built-for-purpose vessels of their type. Authorised under the FY-1953 Programme, *Rigel* and *Vega* were built to the Navy's specifications using a Maritime Administration R3-S-4A design. *Rigel* was laid down on 15 March, 1954, and launched exactly one year later. A helicopter platform has been added aft. She was transferred to MSC service on 23 June, 1975, when all guns were removed. *Vega* was to have been transferred to MSC also, but instead was struck off the Navy List on 30 June, 1977. *Rigel* has been operating in the Indian Ocean since May 1981.

Electronics comprise a CAS-1650/6X surface search radar.

Disposals: *Hyades* (AF-28) was struck off the Navy List on 1 October, 1976; *Zelima* (AF-49) on 1 June, 1976; *Arcturus* (AF-52) on 1 October, 1976; *Pictor* (AF-54) and *Aludra* (AF-55) on 1 June, 1976; *Denebola* (AF-56) on 30 April, 1976, and *Procyon* (AF-61) on 1 June, 1976. All were sold for commercial service. *Aludra* (AF-55) became M/V *Aleutian Monarch*, a fish processing vessel. On 12 November, 1981, she was gutted by fire beyond economical repair, and was scuttled at sea by explosives seven days later.

Rigel (T-AF-58) pictured before her transfer to Military Sealift Command. The last of her kind in the Navy, she and her stricken sister *Vega* (AF-57) were the only purpose-built ships of their type. Among other alterations, *Rigel* was disarmed when transferred to MSC

Type: Combat Store Ships (AFS) — *Number/Class:* 2 +1 *Sirius*

Name	*Number*	*Builder*	*Acquired*	*Status*
Sirius (ex RFA **Lyness**)	T-AFS-8	Swan Hunter and Wigham Richardson Ltd, Wallsend-on-Tyne	17 Jan 1981	MSC
Spica (ex RFA **Tarbatness**)	T-AFS-9	Swan Hunter and Wigham Richardson Ltd, Wallsend-on-Tyne	4 Nov 1981	MSC
Saturn (ex RFA **Stromness**)	T-AFS-10	Swan Hunter and Wigham Richardson Ltd, Wallsend-on-Tyne	1983	

Displacement Light, 9,010 tons; full load, 16,792 tons
Length overall 524ft (159.7m)
Maximum beam 72ft (22m)
Maximum draught 22ft (6.7m)
Main machinery One Wallsend-Sulzer 8-cylinder RD. 76 diesel engine
Screws/b.h.p. 1/11,520
Maximum speed 18 knots
Armament None
Complement 25 officers and 126 enlisted men (civilians), plus one officer and 17 enlisted men (Naval detachment)

These ships were acquired from Britain's Royal Navy to relieve a chronic shortage of underway replenishment ships, first on time charter, then on bare-boat charter on 17 January, 1981, (AFS-8) and 4 November, 1981, (AFS-9) respectively. Both ships were named, classified and instated on the Navy List on their time-charter dates. They were purchased on 1 March, 1982, and 30 September, 1982, respectively, under the FY-1982 Programme, at a cost of $37 million for the two. They became available when the Royal Navy laid them up owing to lack of operating funds. They were built from the keel up as support ships (AFS) with a helicopter deck and three underway replenishment stations per side. One unit, *Lyness*, was employed as an Aviation Supply Ship (AVS). The massive stack amidships quickly distinguishes them. *Sirius* was launched on 7 April, 1966, and entered service in the Royal Navy on 22 December, 1966. *Spica* was launched on 22 February, 1967, and entered service on 21 March, 1967.

The US Navy is currently negotiating the purchase of the third, and last, ship of this class, RFA *Stromness*. This was launched on 16 September, 1966, and commissioned on 10 August, 1967 (see page 234).

Each of these ships cost about $8.2 million (US) to build. *Sirius* had just completed a $5.5 million (US) overhaul at a British shipyard, but as there were no operating funds to put her back in service she was offered to the US Navy. All three were originally chartered because it would expedite their deployment to US Fleet use. *Sirius* deployed to the Sixth Fleet in March 1981, and *Spica* to the Seventh Fleet in July 1982. It would have cost some $300 million and taken six years to build an equivalent ship.

Sirius (T-AFS-8) shortly after her transfer from the Royal Fleet Auxiliary. Formerly RFA *Lyness*, she has proved welcome reinforcement to the US Navy's replenishment force, already stretched to the limit and beyond because of increased operations in the Indian Ocean

Type: Combat Store Ships (AFS) — *Number/Class:* 7 *Mars*

Name	*Number*	*Laid down*	*Launched*	*Commissioned*	*Status*
Mars	AFS-1	5 May 1962	15 June 1963	21 Dec 1963	PA
Sylvania	AFS-2	18 Aug 1962	10 Aug 1963	11 July 1964	AA
Niagara Falls	AFS-3	22 May 1965	26 Mar 1966	29 Apr 1967	PA
White Plains	AFS-4	2 Oct 1965	26 July 1966	23 Nov 1968	PA
Concord	AFS-5	26 Mar 1966	17 Dec 1966	27 Nov 1968	PA
San Diego	AFS-6	11 Mar 1967	13 Apr 1968	24 May 1969	AA
San Jose	AFS-7	8 Mar 1969	13 Dec 1969	23 Oct 1970	AA

Builder National Steel and SB Co, San Diego, Cal
Displacement Light, 9,200 tons (AFS-1/3), 9,400 tons (AFS-4/7); full load, 15,900–18,663 tons
Length overall 581ft (177.1m)
Maximum beam 79ft (24.1m)
Maximum draught 28ft (8.5m)
Main machinery One DeLaval geared turbine (Westinghouse in AFS-3 and -6). Three Babcock and Wilcox boilers
Screws/s.h.p. 1/22,000
Maximum speed 20 knots
Armament Four twin 3in/50 (Mark 33) gun mounts
Complement 45 officers and 441 enlisted men

An entirely new design (SCB-208), including the replenishment at sea system, succeeding the AF/AKS/AVS ship types. Conventional kingposts and booms are replaced by "M" frames with automatic tension devices which keep the lines taut when transferring cargo. A helicopter is located aft. Two *Sea Knight* (UH-46) helicopters are normally assigned. As in the *Sirius* class, closed circuit television monitors the movement of stores. One of the five cargo holds is refrigerated.

Authorised in the following Programmes: FY-1961 (AFS-1), FY-1962 (AFS-2), FY-1964 (AFS-3), FY-1965 (AFS-4, -5), FY-1966 (AFS-6), and FY-1967 (AFS-7).

The Mark 36 Super Chaffroc RBOC is to be installed in these ships (already in AFS-4).

Electronics comprise the OE-82 satellite communications antenna and SSR-1 receiver. Some ships are equipped with Tacan. The AN/APS-40 radar on AFS-1 and -2 has been removed. AN/SPS-10 surface search radar is fitted on each ship.

San Jose (AFS-7). Note the helicopter control booth atop the hangar. Normal aircraft complement is two UH-46 Sea Knight helicopters *(US Navy)*

Type: Miscellaneous (AG) *Number/Class:* 1 Unnamed

It is planned under the FY-1985 programme to acquire a merchant hull as a replacement for *Monob I* (YAG-61, ex-IX-309, ex-YW-87), which is used for acoustic research. The new ship will be classified AG-195.

Type: Miscellaneous (AG) *Number/Class:* 1 *Vanguard*

Name	*Number*	*Builder*	*Acquired*	*Status*
Vanguard	T-AG-194	Marine SB Corp, Sausalito, Cal	21 Oct 1947	MSC

Displacement Light, 16,844 tons; full load, 22,310 tons
Length overall 595ft (181.4m)
Maximum beam 75ft (22.9m)
Maximum draught 25ft (7.6m)
Main machinery General Electric turbine electric engine. Two Babcock and Wilcox boilers
Screws/s.h.p. 1/10,000
Maximum speed 14 knots
Complement 20 officers, 71 enlisted men, 108 technicians

Vanguard has had an interesting career. Built as a T2-SE-A2 class AO, she was laid down on 26 August, 1943, launched on 25 November, 1943, and delivered to the Maritime Commission on 29 February, 1944, as *Mission San Fernando*. Acquired by the Navy in 1947 and designated AO-122, served with the Naval Overseas Transportation Service (NOTS) until the organisation became part of the Military Sea Transportation Service (MSTS). Struck off Navy List on 4 September, 1957, she was re-acquired on 28 September, 1964, and reinstated on the Register 1 July, 1964, for conversion to a Mission Range Instrumentation Ship (AGM-19). Renamed *Muscle Shoals* on 8 April, 1965, she was again renamed, as *Vanguard*, on 1 September, 1965. She was converted at Bethlehem Steel Company, Quincy, Mass and placed in service under the Military Sealift Command (MSC) on 28 February, 1966. More data on the conversion will be found under the *Redstone* (AGM-20) (*Vanguard* class).

The Todd Shipyard Corporation of Brooklyn, New York, was awarded a contract on 12 January, 1979, to convert *Vanguard* for her new mission as replacement for *Compass Island* (AG-153). The main change to her appearance was the removal of her radar antennas and pedestals amidships. *Vanguard* was transferred to the Navy's Strategic Systems Project Office on 1 October, 1978, for operational employment. She was reclassified from AGM-19 to AG-194 on 30 September, 1980.

Vanguard in her days as AGM-19. As AG-194 *Vanguard* serves as the successor to *Compass Island* (AG-153). She now lacks the three midships radar antennae and the communications antenna forward *(US Navy)*

Type: Miscellaneous (AG) — *Number/Class:* 1

Name	*Number*	*Builder*	*Completed*	*Status*
Unnamed	AG-193	Sun SB and DD Co, Chester, Pa	July 1973	MPR

Displacement Full load, 63,300 tons
Measurements Deadweight: 39,705 tons; Gross: 27,445 tons; Net: 18,511 tons
Length overall 618.8ft (188.6m)
Maximum beam 115.7ft (35.3m)
Maximum draught 46.7ft (14.3m)
Main machinery Five Nordberg diesel engines, six General Electric electric motors (diesel electric drive). Four boilers
Screws/b.h.p. 2/13,200
Maximum speed 10.8 knots
Complement 178 total

Built for the Summa Corporation as M/V *Hughes Glomar Explorer*, this vessel was officially classified by the American Bureau of Shipping as a "survey ship". In 1975–1976, she participated secretly in the salvage of a portion of a Russian *Golf* class submarine. Following the death of Howard Hughes, *Hughes Glomar Explorer* was acquired by the Navy on 30 September, 1976, and reclassified as AG-193. She was deactivated and transferred on 17 January, 1977, to the Maritime Administration for lay-up at Suisun Bay. Leased to Global Marine Development, Inc, of Newport Beach, Cal, on 1 June, 1978, which paid for the re-activation and overhaul costs, in addition to the cocooning costs when she was laid up. She was to be used for "scientific and mineral exploration". However, the lease was abruptly terminated in early 1980 and she was returned to the Navy on 25 April, 1980 and retransferred to the Maritime Administration on the same date. AG-193 has three bow and two stern thrusters to help maintain position during exploration work.

AG-193 pictured while she was known as *Hughes Glomar Explorer*. In 1975–76, under the auspices of the CIA, she almost succeeded in salvaging the hulk of a Soviet Golf-class submarine *(US Navy)*

Type: Miscellaneous (AG) — *Number/Class:* 1 *S. P. Lee*

Name	*Number*	*Builder*	*Completed*	*Status*
S. P. Lee (ex- AGS-31)	AG-192	Defoe SB Co, Bay City, Mich	2 Dec 1968	Loan

Displacement Full load, 1,297 tons
Length overall 208.3ft (63.5m)
Maximum beam 39ft (11.9m)
Maximum draught 14.1ft (4.3m)
Main machinery Two diesel electric engines
Screws/b.h.p. 1/1,000
Maximum speed 12 knots
Complement 23 officers, 20 enlisted men, 13 technicians

Completed as AGS-31, this ship was transferred to MSC for service as T-AGS-31 upon completion. Laid up in 1969 owing to lack of operating funds, she was put back in service on 10 September, 1970, and reclassified AG-192 on 25 September, 1970. *S. P. Lee* was then transferred to operational control of the Naval Electronics Laboratory in San Diego, replacing the *Rexburg* (PCER-855) and *Marysville* (PCER-857), which had been struck from the List. She served as hydrographic research ship until taken out of service 27 February, 1974, and transferred on indefinite loan to the Geological Survey, Department of Interior, for further service.

S.P. Lee (AG-192) while classified as AGS-31. Having served on loan to the Geological Survey of the Department of the Interior for several years.

Type: Miscellaneous (AG) — *Number/Class:* 1 *Kingsport*

Name	Number	Builder	Acquired	Status
Kingsport (ex-SS **Kingsport Victory**)	T-AG-164	California SB Corp, Los Angeles, Cal	1 Mar 1950	MSC

Displacement Light, 7,190 tons; full load, 10,680 tons
Length overall 455ft (138.7m)
Maximum beam 62ft (18.9m)
Maximum draught 22ft (6.7m)
Main machinery One Westinghouse geared turbine. Two Babcock and Wilcox boilers
Screws/s.h.p. 1/8,500
Maximum speed 15.2 knots
Complement 13 officers, 42 enlisted men, 15 technicians

Built to the VC2-S-AP3 design by the California Shipbuilding Corporation of Los Angeles, California, this vessel was laid down on 4 April, 1944, launched on 29 May that year, and delivered to the Maritime Commission on 12 July, 1944, as SS *Kingston Victory*. On 1 March, 1950 the US Navy acquired her from the Maritime Commission for service as USNS *Kingsport Victory* (T-AK-239). She was renamed and reclassified *Kingsport* (AG-164) on 1 November, 1964, becoming the world's first satellite communications ship, with a 56ft (17.1m) diameter antenna sphere installed abaft the superstructure. Upon completion of "Project Advent" in 1966, the sphere was removed and the ship was modified for further service as a hydrographic vessel. A helicopter platform is located aft.

Disposals: *Sequoia* (AG-23) struck from the Naval Register on 1 October, 1968, was rerated as "floating equipment" on the same date and continued in service until early 1977, when she was sold on 23 May on the order of President Carter. *Private Jose F. Valdez* (AG-169) was struck off on 15 August, 1976 and sold for scrap. *Alacrity* (AG-520) and *Assurance* (AG-521) were both struck off on 30 September, 1977. *Private Valdez* had served as an intelligence-collecting ship (AGI); the last two ships were sold for scrapping on 14 November, 1979.

For the record, the ice-breaking tugs AG-51/65, leased to Russia in 1944–1945, are still carried on the Naval Vessel Register because the Russians stubbornly refuse to account for the ships. One found its way into the Chinese Navy and is still active.

Kingsport (T-AG-164) pictured in the mid-1960s. The spherical radome has since been removed

Type: Auxiliary Deep Submergence Support Ship (AGDS) — *Number/Class:* 1 *Point Barrow*

Name	Number	Builder	Commissioned	Status
Point Loma (ex-**Point Barrow** AKD-1)	AGDS-2	Maryland SB and DD Co, Baltimore, Md	28 Feb 1958	PA

Displacement Standard, 9,415 tons; full load, 14,000 tons
Length overall 465ft (141.6m)
Maximum beam 74ft (22.5m)
Maximum draught 20ft (6.1m)
Main machinery Westinghouse steam turbines. Two Foster-Wheeler boilers
Screws/s.h.p. 2/6,000
Maximum speed 15 knots
Armament None
Complement 160 total, including civilian technicians

Built for Arctic service under the S2-ST-23A Maritime Administration design, *Point Loma* was launched on 25 May, 1957, and commissioned date above as *Point Barrow* (AKD-1). She resembles the LSD/LPD amphibious ship types. Decommissioned on 29 May, 1958, she was transferred to the Military Sea Transportation Service (MSTS) on the same date. With a hangar fitted over the docking well, *Point Barrow* was used to transport Saturn booster rockets to Cape Kennedy Space Centre until she was placed out of service, in reserve, on 28 September, 1972, and laid up.

On 28 February, 1974, *Point Barrow* was returned to the Navy and placed in commission, special. At the same time, she was renamed and reclassified *Point Loma* (AGDS-2), and was then modified as a deep submergence vehicle support vessel for *Trieste II*, replacing *White Sands* (AGDS-1). Among other alterations, the canopy hangar over the well deck was removed, and large gasoline tanks (100,000 gal max) were installed for storage of ballast for *Trieste II*. She was placed in full commission on 30 April, 1975.

Electronics comprise AN/SPS-10 surface search radar, an OE-82 satellite communications antenna and an SSR-1 receiver.

The designation "AGDS-1" was assigned briefly to *White Sands* (ARD-20), a Floating Drydock which had also served as support vessel for *Trieste II*.

Disposal: The Hydrofoil Research Vessel *Plainview* (AGEH-1) was sold for scrapping on 21 June, 1979.

Type: Miscellaneous Command Ship (AGF) — *Number/Class:* 1 *Raleigh*

Name	Number	Builder	Commissioned	Status
La Salle (ex-LPD-3)	AGF-3	New York Naval Shipyard, Brooklyn, N.Y.	22 Feb 1964	AA

Displacement Light, 8,000 tons; full load, 15,000 tons
Length overall 521.8ft (159.1m)
Maximum beam 104ft (31.7m)
Maximum draught 21ft (6.4m)
Main machinery Two De Laval steam turbines. Two Babcock and Wilcox boilers
Screws/s.h.p. 2/24,000
Maximum speed 21 knots
Armament Four twin 3in/50 gun mounts, two 20mm (Mark 16) CIWS mounts
Complement 25 officers and 415 enlisted men
Flag accommodation 12 officers and 47 enlisted men

La Salle was authorised in the FY-1961 Programme as LPD-3 (SCB-187A) of the *Raleigh* class Amphibious Transports, and commissioned as such on the above date. She was reclassified AGF-3 on 1 July, 1972, and modified for that mission at the Philadelphia Naval Shipyard. Elaborate command and communication facilities were installed, additional air conditioning was provided, and the ship was painted white to reflect the heat of the Persian Gulf. The ship has two 40mm saluting guns. During her overhaul at Philadelphia (27 January, 1981, to 1 September, 1982), *La Salle* was fitted with two CIWS mounts and the Mark 36 Super Chaffroc RBOC.

Electronics are AN/SPS-10 surface search and AN/SPS-40 air search radars, OE-82 Satellite Communication Antenna, an SSR-1 receiver and an WSC-3 transceiver.

October 1980 view of *Coronado* (AGF-11) departing Hampton Roads, Va, en route to the Persian Gulf to relieve *La Salle* (AGF-3) as flagship of the Commander, Middle East Force *(US Navy)*

Type: Miscellaneous Command Ship (AGF) — *Number/Class:* 1 *Austin*

Name	Number	Builder	Commissioned	Status
Coronado (ex-LPD-11)	AGF-11	Lockheed SB and Cons Co, Seattle, Wash	23 May 1970	AA

Displacement Standard, 11,482 tons; full load 16,912 tons
Length overall 570ft (173.3m)
Maximum beam 108ft (32.9m)
Maximum draught 23ft (7m)
Main machinery Two De Lavel steam turbines; two Foster-Wheeler boilers
Screws/s.h.p. 2/24,000
Maximum speed 21 knots
Armament Two twin 3in/50 gun mounts (Mark 33)
Complement 106 officers and 1,247 enlisted men
Flag accommodation 12 officers and 47 enlisted men

Built and commissioned as LPD-11 of the *Austin* class Amphibious Transports, *Coronado* was authorised in the FY-1964 Programme. On 1 October, 1980, the vessel was temporarily reclassified AGF-11 to serve as relief ship for *La Salle* (AGF-3), while that ship was undergoing major overhaul. Modified for duty as Miscellaneous Command Ship, she retained some amphibious capability. The mission is to last as long as AGF-3 is in overhaul, following which *Coronado* will in turn be relieved in the Persian Gulf. It is expected that she will be reclassified back to LPD-11.

Electronics comprise and AN/SPS-10 surface search radar, and AN/SPS-40 air search radar. A Super Chaffroc RBOC mount is fitted.

The designation "AGF" has been assigned to only three ships: *Valcour* (AGF-1), which was struck from the Navy List on 15 January, 1973, and used as a test hulk until scrapped. *La Salle* is AFG-3 and *Coronado* is AGF-11. Other numbers have never been assigned.

La Salle in the Persian Gulf in August 1975. She and *Coronado* are the only US Navy ships to be painted in heat-reflecting white *(US Navy)*

Type: Missile Range Instrumentation Ship (AGM) — *Number/Class:* 1 *Observation Island*

Name	Number	Builder	Commissioned	Status
Observation Island (ex-AG-154, EAG-154, YAG-57)	T-AGM-23	New York SB Corp, Camden, N.J.	5 Dec 1958	MSC

Displacement Light 13,060 tons; full load, 17,015 tons
Length overall 564ft (171.8m)
Maximum beam 76ft (23.2m)
Maximum draught 28ft (8.5m)
Main machinery One General Electric geared turbine. Two Foster-Wheeler boilers
Screws/s.h.p. 1/19,250
Maximum speed 21 knots
Armament None
Complement 78, plus 64 technicians

This ship was laid down on 15 September, 1952, under the Maritime Administration design C4-S-1A and launched 15 August, 1953, as SS *Empire State Mariner*. Acquired from MARAD on 10 September, 1954, as YAG-57, she was reclassified EAG-154 on 19 June, 1956, and commissioned as such on the indicated date. *Observation Island* served as test ship for the Polaris and Poseidon missiles. She fired the first ship-launched Polaris missile in 1959 and the first Poseidon in 1969. She also played an important role in the development of the Ships Inertial Navigational System (Sins). On 29 September, 1972, she was decommissioned, being transferred to the MARAD Reserve Fleet, James River, on 26 January, 1973, for layup. On 1 May, 1979, *Observation Island* was reclassified AGM-23, and was reacquired from MARAD on 15 July, 1977, custody being transferred to the Military Sealift Command. Converted to Missile Range Instrumentation Ship from July 1979 to April 1981 at Maryland SS and DD Company, Baltimore, Maryland, she carries an Air Force ship-borne phased-array radar system called Cobra Judy. This enables her to monitor and collect data on Soviet ballistic missile tests. The radar "turret" measures 22.5ft (6.9m) across. Although she is under the operational control of the Air Force, the Navy retains title.

Disposal/Cancellation: Sister ship *Compass Island* (AG-153) was decommissioned at Charleston, South Carolina, on 1 May, 1980, and struck off the Naval Register on 1 October, 1981. She is laid up in the James River MARAD Reserve Fleet for use as logistics support for AGM-23. Acquisition of a third ship of this class, to have been reclassified EAG-155, was cancelled.

Observation Island (T-AGM-23), formerly employed as seagoing platform for the testing of SLBMs such as Poseidon and Polaris, now monitors Soviet SLBM tests in the Northern Pacific. The box aft of the superstructure houses the Cobra Judy phased-array radar which is used for these observations

Type: Missile Range Instrumentation Ship (AGM) — *Number/Class:* 1 *Range Sentinel*

Name	*Number*	*Builder*	*Commissioned*	*Status*
Range Sentinel (ex-**Sherburne**, APA-205)	T-AGM-22	Permanente Metals Corp, Richmond, Cal	20 Sept 1944	MSC

Displacement 11,800 tons full load
Length overall 455ft (138.7m)
Maximum beam 62ft (18.9m)
Maximum draught 23ft (7m)
Main machinery One Westinghouse geared turbine. Two Combustion Engineering boilers
Screws/s.h.p. 1/8,500
Maximum speed 17.7 knots
Complement 14 officers, 54 enlisted men, 27 technicians

Completed and commissioned as *Sherburne* (APA-205) of the *Haskell* class Attack Transports, this ship, built to the Maritime Commission VC2-S-AP5 design, was typical of American ship construction during the Second World War. Decommissioned on 3 August, 1946, and laid up, she was struck off the Naval Vessel Register on 1 October, 1958 and transferred to the Maritime Administration. *Sherburne* was reclassified AGM-22 on 16 April, 1969, re-acquired from the Maritime Administration and re-instated on the Navy List on 22 October, 1969. Authorised under the FY-1969 Conversion Programme (SCB-731) for conversion to Missile Range Instrumentation Ship to support the Fleet Ballistic Missile Programme. *Sherburne* was converted between October 1969 and October 1971 at Northwest Marine Iron Works, Portland, Oregon, being renamed *Range Sentinel* on 26 April, 1971. She completed conversion and was transferred to the Military Sealift Command on 21 October, 1971 for service.

Electronics: TM-1650/6X and TM-1660/12S radars.

Formerly Attack Transport *Sherburne* (APA-205), *Range Sentinel* (T-AGM-22) is one of only three AGMs left out of a fleet that once numbered 21

Type: Missile Range Instrumentation Ship (AGM) — *Number/Class:* 1 *Vanguard*

Name	*Number*	*Builder*	*Acquired*	*Status*
Redstone (ex **Johnstown**, ex **Mission de Pala**, ex AO-114)	T-AGM-20	Marine Ship Corp, Sausalito, Cal	22 Oct 1947	MSC

Displacement Full load, 22,310 tons
Length overall 595ft (181.2m)
Maximum beam 75ft (22.9m)
Maximum draught 25ft (7.6m)
Main machinery Westinghouse turbine electric. Two Babcock and Wilcox boilers
Screws/s.h.p. 1/10,000
Maximum speed 14 knots
Complement 20 officers, 71 enlisted men, 120 technicians

Built to the Maritime Commission T2-SE-A2 design as *Mission de Pala*, this ship was delivered to the Commission on 22 April, 1944. The Navy acquired her on the date given as *Mission de Pala* (AO-114), and she served with the Naval Overseas Transportation Service until 1 October, 1949, when it entered the Military Sea Transportation Service (MSTS). She continued in service until struck off the Naval Register on 13 March, 1958, and was reinstated on the Navy List on 1 July, 1964, and reacquired on 19 September of that year for conversion to Missile Range Instrumentation Ship (AGM). The vessel was renamed *Johnstown* on 8 April, 1965, but renamed *Redstone* on 1 September, 1965, and converted by Bethlehem Steel Co, Quincy, Mass. Major work included the installation of a 72ft (21.9m) mid-body, which increased the ship's length, and the addition of 450 tons of electronic equipment for support of lunar flight operations. A balloon hangar platform was installed aft. The mission was to support lunar flight operations, utilising the tracking and communications systems. Although she serves under the Military Sealift Command, she is operated for Nasa's Goddard Space Flight Centre.

Electronics: TM-1650/9X and TM-1660/12S radars.

The *Vanguard* class AGMs originally comprised three ships. *Mercury* (AGM-21) was transferred to the Maritime Administration on 29 October, 1969, and struck off the Navy List on 28 April, 1970. She was later acquired by the Matson Navigation Company and converted for mercantile service as a sugar carrier. Class leader *Vanguard* (AGM-19) was reclassified AG-194 q.v. on 30 September, 1980, and is in service.

Redstone (T-AGM-20) departing Cape Canaveral in May 1970. Her configuration has not changed since then *(US Air Force)*

Disposals: Both units of the *General H. H. Arnold* class have been stricken, *General H. H. Arnold* (AGM-9) on 1 March, 1982, and *General Hoyt S. Vandenberg* (AGM-10) in February 1983. *General Arnold* will be expended as a target and *General Vandenberg* was transferred to the Maritime Commission for disposal. *Wheeling* (AGM-8), the last of the five *Range Tracker* class vessels, was struck off the Naval Register on 31 October, 1980, and is to be expended as a target.

Type: Oceanographic Research Ships (AGOR) — *Number/Class:* 2 Gyre

Name	Number	Builder	Completed	Status
Gyre	AGOR-21	Halter Marine Services Inc, New Orleans, La	14 Nov 1973	Loan
Moana Wave	AGOR-22	Halter Marine Services Inc, New Orleans, La	16 Jan 1974	Loan

Displacement Full load 950 tons
Length overall 165ft (50.3m)
Maximum beam 36ft (11m)
Maximum draught 14.5ft (4.4m)
Main machinery Two Caterpillar Tractor Co. turbo-charged diesel engines
Screws/b.h.p. 2/1,700
Maximum speed 12 knots
Complement 10–15 crew, 13–19 scientists

These ships, based on a commercial design, were authorised under the FY-1971 Programme (SCB-734). Estimated cost per ship is $1.9 million. An open deck aft provides space for equipment vans. They have 150 h.p. bow thrusters for station-keeping while the main machinery is shut down. *Gyre* is assigned to Texas A & M University, and *Moana Wave* is assigned to the University of Hawaii, both ships being on loan.

Gyre (AGOR-21) on trials. These ships were built to a commercial design for an oil rig support vessel.

Gyre is now operated by Texas A&M University in support of Navy programmes

Type: Oceanographic Research Ship (AGOR) — *Number/Class:* 1 Hayes

Name	Number	Builder	Completed	Status
Hayes	T-AGOR-16	Todd Shipyards Inc, Seattle, Wash	21 July 1971	MSC

Displacement Light 2,329 tons; full load 2,876 tons
Length overall 246.5ft (75.1m)
Maximum beam 75ft (22.9m)
Maximum draught 18.7ft (6.7m)
Main machinery Two General Motors diesel engines
Screws/b.h.p. 2/5,400
Maximum speed 13 knots
Complement 11 officers, 33 enlisted men, 30 scientists

This successful catamaran-hulled ship (SCB-726) was authorised in the FY-1967 Programme and cost $15.9 million to build. It was transferred to the Military Sealift Command on 13 August, 1971, for service and operation by the Office of Naval Research.

The catamaran hull provides a large deck working area, while the centre well isolates the laboratory areas from the main propulsion machinery and equipment can be operated at great depths more readily. Each hull is 24ft (7.3m) wide, and there are three 36in (.91m) diameter wells for instruments. Bow thrusters are not needed because *Hayes* has excellent manoeuvrability. An auxiliary 165 h.p. diesel is fitted in each hull to give a "creeping" speed of 2-4 knots.

Electronics: TM-1650/6X and TM-1660/12S radars.

Hayes (T-AGOR-16), one of three catamaran-hulled ships in the Navy. She has excellent manoeuvrability but suffers severe pitch problems *(US Navy)*

Type: Oceanographic Research Ships (AGOR) — *Number/Class:* 2 Melville

Name	Number	Builder	Completed	Status
Melville	AGOR-14	Defoe SB Co, Bay City, Mich	27 Aug 1969	Loan
Knorr	AGOR-15	Defoe SB Co, Bay City, Mich	14 Jan 1970	Loan

Displacement Light, 1,520 tons; full load, 1,915 tons
Length overall 244.9ft (74.7m)
Maximum beam 46.3ft (14.1m)
Maximum draught 16ft (4.9m)
Main machinery Two De Laval diesel engines
Screws /b.h.p. 2/2,500
Maximum speed 12.5 knots
Complement 9 officers, 16 enlisted men, 25 scientists

Of improved *Robert D. Conrad* class design (SCB-710), these ships are operated by Scripps Institute of Oceanography (*Melville*) and Woods Hole Oceanography Institute (*Knorr*) for the Office of Naval Research.

They can turn 360° in their own length due to their cycloidal propellers, one of which is fitted at each end of the ship. In addition, they can move in any direction or "hover" on station, all without the need for thrusters. Internal wells are provided for lowering equipment, underwater lights, and observation ports.

Two additional units of this class, AGOR-19 and -20, were cancelled on 24 February, 1969.

Melville (T-AGOR-14) (illustrated) and *Knorr* (AGOR-15) are modified versions of the *Robert D. Conrad*-class AGORs. *Melville* is operated for the Navy by the Scripps Institute of Oceanography *(Defoe Shipbuilding)*

Type: Oceanographic Research Ships (AGOR) — *Number/Class:* 2 *Eltanin*

Name	Number	Builder	Completed	Status
Eltanin (ex **Islas de Orcades**, Q-9; **Eltanin**, AGOR-8; AK-270)	AGOR-8	Avondale Marine Ways, New Orleans, La	12 Oct 1957	AR
Mizar (ex-AK-272)	T-AGOR-11	Avondale Marine Ways, New Orleans, La	7 Mar 1958	MSC

Displacement Light, 2,022 tons (AGOR-8); 2,488 tons (AGOR-11). Full load, 3,886 tons (AGOR-8); 3,481 tons (AGOR-11)
Length overall 266ft (81m)
Maximum beam 51.5ft (15.7m)
Maximum draught 18.7ft (5.7m)
Main machinery Two Alco diesel engines
Screws/b.h.p. 2/2,700
Maximum speed 12 knots
Complement 13 officers, 26 enlisted men, 24 scientists

These were built for Arctic operations with an ice-strengthened hull (C1-ME-13A design) as cargo ships of the *Eltanin* class. The third ship of the original class, *Mirfak* (AK-271), is in reserve as an AK. *Mizar* was reclassified to AGOR-11 on 15 November, 1962, and *Eltanin* to AGOR-8 on 15 April, 1964.

They have been converted to oceanographic research ships for operation with MSC under the control of the Naval Research Laboratory. These deep sea research ships are equipped with a central well for lowering oceanographic equipment, including towed sensor platforms. Laboratories and elaborate photographic facilities are provided. *Mizar* played a big role in the searches for the sunken US nuclear submarines *Thresher* and *Scorpion* and the French submarine *Eurydice*.

Electronics: TM-1650/6X radar (AGOR-11).

Eltanin was leased to Argentina on 19 February, 1974, and commissioned as *Islas de Orcades* (Q-9). Returned to US custody on 1 August, 1979, she was laid up at Norfolk. Her foreign transfer is pending.

Mizar (AGOR-11). Originally completed as AK-272, she was converted to an AGOR in 1964 *(US Navy)*

Type: Oceanographic Research Ships (AGOR) — *Number/Class:* 7 *Robert D. Conrad*

Name	Number	Builder	Completed	Status
Robert D. Conrad	AGOR-3	Gibbs Corp, Jacksonville, Fla	29 Nov 1962	Loan
James M. Gilliss	AGOR-4	Christy Corp, Sturgeon Bay, Wisc	5 Nov 1962	None
Lynch	T-AGOR-7	Marietta Mfg Co, Point Pleasant, West Va	27 Mar 1965	MSC
Thomas G. Thompson	AGOR-9	Marinette Marine Corp, Marinette, Wisc	24 Aug 1965	Loan
Thomas Washington (ex-**Silas Bent**)	AGOR-10	Marinette Marine Corp, Marinette, Wisc	7 Sept 1965	Loan
De Steiguer	T-AGOR-12	Northwest Marine Iron Works, Portland, Ore	28 Feb 1969	MSC
Bartlett	T-AGOR-13	Northwest Marine Iron Works, Portland, Ore	31 Mar 1969	MSC

Displacement Light, 1,200 tons (AGOR-3, -4); 950 tons (rest). Full load, 1,370 tons (AGOR-3, -4); 1,362 tons (rest)
Length overall 208.9ft (63.7m)
Maximum beam 40ft (12.2m)
Maximum draught 15.3ft (4.7m)
Main machinery Two Caterpillar diesel engines (AGOR-3, -4); two Cummins diesel engines (remainder)
Screws/b.h.p. 1/1,000
Maximum speed 13 knots
Complement 9 officers (8 on AGOR-12, -13), 17 enlisted men (18 on AGOR-12, -13) and 15 scientists

This class comprised the first oceanographic research ships designed by and built for the Navy. They are fitted with elaborate research instrumentation and laboratories, and have a 10-ton boom for over-the-side equipment handling. Bow thrusters and a 620 h.p. gas turbine (housed in the funnel structure) provide "quiet" power while sensitive experiments and/or research are being carried out. Whether operated by MSC or on loan to various universities, these active ships are under the technical control of the Oceanographer of the Navy.

AGOR-7 was transferred to the Military Sealift Command on 23 July, 1965, AGOR-12 on 28 February, 1969, and AGOR-13 on 31 March, 1969. AGOR-3 is operated by the Lamont Geological Observatory (Columbia University), AGOR-9 by the University of Washington (state), and AGOR-10 by Scripps Institute of Oceanography (University of California). From 1970 to 1980 AGOR-4 was operated by the University of Miami (Florida). On 18 March, 1980, she was transferred to the Beaumont, Texas, Reserve Fleet of the Maritime Administration for layup. Her lease to Mexico is pending (see page 234).

Electronics: Radar, TM-1650/6X and TM-1660/12S (AGOR-7, -12); TM-1660/12S (AGOR-13).

Charles H. Davis (AGOR-5) of this class was leased to New Zealand on 10 August, 1970. *Sands* (AGOR-6) was leased to Brazil on 1 July, 1974.

Disposals: *Josiah Willard Gibbs* (AGOR-1), formerly *San Pablo* (AVP-51) of the *Barnegat* class small seaplane tenders (AVP), was converted to an AGOR and leased to Greece, to whom she was later sold, being struck off the Navy List on 15 February, 1977. *Chain* (AGOR-17), ex-ARS-20, a converted salvage ship of the *Diver* class, was struck off the Navy List on 30 December, 1977, and sold for scrapping on 23 October, 1979.

De Steiguer (T-AGOR-12) on trials in June 1969

Type: Ocean Surveillance Ships (AGOS) — *Number/Class:* 0+(6) *Swath*

Name	Number	Laid down	Launched	Commissioned	Status
	T-AGOS-13/18				PROJ

A new class of AGOS is planned, employing Swath technology to provide a more stable platform in high seas. The first ship is to be requested in the FY-1984 Programme, two more units follow in FY-1986, and three more in FY-1987. $24.3 million was requested in the FY-1983 Programme for advanced procurement, but this was not approved. All of this class will be Navy manned. No further data are available.

Type: Ocean Surveillance Ships (AGOS) — *Number/Class:* 0+12 *Stalwart*

Name	Number	Laid down	Launched	Commissioned	Status
Stalwart	T-AGOS-1	3 Nov 1982			BLDG
Contender	T-AGOS-2	10 Jan 1983			BLDG
Vindicator	T-AGOS-3	Apr 1983			BLDG
Triumph	T-AGOS-4	July 1983			BLDG
Assurance	T-AGOS-5				ORD
Persistent	T-AGOS-6				ORD
Indomitable	T-AGOS-7				ORD
Prevail	T-AGOS-8				ORD
Assertive	T-AGOS-9				ORD
Invincible	T-AGOS-10				ORD
Dauntless	T-AGOS-11				ORD
Vigorous	T-AGOS-12				ORD

Builder Tacoma Boat Building Co, Tacoma, Wash
Displacement Full load, 2,285 tons (approximate)
Length overall 224ft (68.3m)
Maximum beam 43ft (13.1m)
Maximum draught 15.1ft (4.6m)
Main machinery Diesel electric
Screws/b.h.p. 2/not available
Maximum speed 11 knots sustained
Complement 9 officers, 11 enlisted men, 10 technicians

Procurement of this new type of ship was authorised in the following Programmes (SCB-745.78): FY-1979 (AGOS-1/2); FY-1980 (AGOS-3); FY-1981 (AGOS-4/8), and FY-1982 (AGOS-9/12).

The mission of these ships is to tow, worldwide, a special sonar array known as Surtass (Surveillance Towed Array Sensor). The array will gather oceanographic acoustic data and transmit it ashore for display and evaluation. Surtass is a passive underwater surveillance sensing system that uses an acoustic sensor towed by the array towing-winch aft. It will be operated by civilian technicians.

There will be individual staterooms for the ships' civilian crews (MSC operated). The enclosed ship and winch control house aft, for array handling, will be a prominent recognition feature. Endurance of these ships on a mission will be about 90 days at a 3-knot towing speed, plus 3,000 nautical miles at 11 knots en route. Super-silencing measures will be built into the ships by vibration dampening, and the lack of reduction gears. Acoustical insulation for noise reduction will be added.

Construction time will be 12–14 months, and unit cost varies from $35.8 million to $40 million.

Type: Surveying Ship (AGS)

Number/Class: 1 H. H. Hess

Name	Number	Builder	Acquired	Status
H. H. Hess (ex-M/V **Canada Mail**)	T-AGS-38	National Steel and SB Co, San Diego, Cal	9 July 1976	MSC

Displacement full load 22,625 tons
Measurement 14,747 tons dead weight
Length overall 535.7ft (163.3m)
Maximum beam 76ft (23.2m)
Maximum draught 41ft (12.5m)
Main machinery General Electric geared turbines. Two Foster-Wheeler boilers
Screws/s.h.p. 1/19,250
Maximum speed 20 knots
Complement 57 total

Completed in 1965 under the Maritime Administration design C4-S-A1, this ship was acquired by the Navy for conversion to a surveying ship (AGS). Converted by the National Steel and SB Company, San Diego, California, between March 1977 and January 1978, she replaced *Michelson* (AGS-23) of the *Bowditch* class. Transferred to MSC on 16 January, 1978, for service, *H. H. Hess* is operated by the Military Sealift Command for the Oceanographer of the Navy.

Radars: RM-1650/6X and RM-1660/12S.

Disposals/cancellations: The conversion of *Twin Falls* (AGM-11) to AGS-37 (SCB-735.72) was cancelled. *Coastal Crusader* (AGS-36) was struck from the Navy List on 30 April, 1976 and sold for scrap. *Sgt. George D. Keathley* (AGS-35) was struck from the Naval Register on 15 April, 1976. She had been leased to Taiwan on 29 March, 1972.

Note It is planned to convert the ex-M/V *Pride*, *Mormacpride*, and ex-M/V *Scan* and *Mormacscan* of the "C3-S-33a" class (see under AK-284 and AK-285 for further data) to AGS-39 and AGS-40 under the FY-1985 programme replacing *Bowditch* (T-AGS-21) and *Dutton* (T-AGS-22) of the *Victory* class.

H.H. Hess (T-AGS-38), replacement for *Michaelson* (AGS-23)

Type: Surveying Ships (AGS)

Number/Class: 2 Wilkes

Name	Number	Builder	Completed	Status
Wilkes	T-AGS-33	Defoe SB Co, Bay City, Mich	28 June 1971	MSC
Wyman	T-AGS-34	Defoe SB Co, Bay City, Mich	3 Nov 1971	MSC

Displacement Standard, 1,935 tons; full load, 2,540 tons (AGS-33), 2,420 tons (AGS-34)
Length overall 283ft (86.2m)
Maximum beam 48ft (14.6m)
Maximum draught 15.1ft (4.6m)
Main machinery Two General Electric diesel engines
Screws/b.h.p. 1/3,000
Maximum speed 15 knots
Complement 12 officers, 35 enlisted men, 30 scientists

These ships were authorised in the FY-1967 Programme as an improved *Silas Bent* design (*Wyman*, SCB-728; *Wilkes*, SCB-725). Somewhat resembling the *Robert D. Conrad* (AGOR-3) class, they are fitted with a bow propulsion unit for station keeping and precise manoeuvrability, and anti-roll devices.

Wilkes was transferred to MSC for service on 16 July, 1971. *Wyman* was transferred to MSC for service on 5 November, 1971. Both ships are operated for the Oceanographer of the Navy.

Wilkes (T-AGS-33), an enlarged *Silas Bent*-class design. The hatch in the side of the hull just below the bridge permits the trolling of hydraulic devices *(Defoe Shipbuilding)*

Type: Surveying Ships (AGS) — *Number/Class:* 2 *Chauvenet*

Name	Number	Builder	Completed	Status
Chauvenet	T-AGS-29	Upper Clyde SB, Glasgow, Scotland	13 Nov 1970	MSC
Harkness	T-AGS-32	Upper Clyde SB, Glasgow, Scotland	29 Jan 1971	MSC

Displacement Light, 2,640 tons; full load, 3,670 tons
Length overall 393.2ft (119.8m)
Maximum beam 54ft (16.5m)
Maximum draught 16ft (4.9m)
Main machinery One Alco diesel engine
Screws/b.h.p. 1/3,400
Maximum speed 15 knots
Complement 13 officers, 150 enlisted men and technicians, 12 scientists

These large steel-hulled surveying ships are strengthened against ice. *Chauvenet* was authorised under the FY-1965 Programme, and *Harkness* in FY-1966, both being of SCB-723 design. They are fitted with a helicopter platform and two hangars.

Chauvenet was transferred to MSC on 13 November, 1969, and *Harkness* on 30 April, 1971. Both ships are operated by the MSC for the Oceanographer of the Navy.

Radars: TM-1650/6X (both ships); TM-1660/12S (AGS-29).

Chauvenet (T-AGS-29) (illustrated) and her sister *Harkness* are tasked with the surveying of locations likely to meet fleet and landing force requirements *(US Navy)*

Type: Surveying Ships (AGS) — *Number/Class:* 2 *Silas Bent*

Name	*Number*	*Builder*	*Completed*	*Status*
Silas Bent	T-AGS-26	American SB Co, Lorain, Ohio	24 July 1965	MSC
Kane	T-AGS-27	Christy Corp, Sturgeon Bay, Wisc	19 May 1967	MSC

Silas Bent (T-AGS-26) photographed at Boston before her first operational deployment *(US Navy)*

Displacement Light, 1,935 tons; full load, 2,580 tons (AGS-26), 2,489 tons (AGS-27)
Length overall 285.3ft (87m)
Maximum beam 48ft (14.6m)
Maximum draught 15.1ft (4.6m)
Main machinery Two diesel engines (Westinghouse, AGS-26; Alco, AGS-27)
Screws/b.h.p. 1/3,000
Maximum speed 15 knots
Accommodation 14 officers, 36 enlisted men, 24 technicians and scientists

These vessels were designed specifically as Surveying Ships (SCB-226). As in the *Wilkes* (AGS-33) class, these ships have a bow thruster propulsion unit for maintaining headway when the main engines are shut down. They are also fitted with anti-roll devices.

Silas Bent was transferred to MSC on 24 September, 1965, and *Kane* on 19 May, 1967. These ships are operated by MSC for the Oceanographer of the Navy.

Radar: RM-1650/9X and TM-1660/12S (*Silas Bent*).

Disposal: *Kellar* (AGS-25) was loaned to Portugal on 21 January, 1972, with whom she still serves.

Type: Surveying Ships (AGS) — *Number/Class:* 2 *Bowditch*

Name	*Number*	*Builder*	*Acquired*	*Status*
Bowditch	T-AGS-21	Oregon SB Co, Portland, Ore	2 Aug 1957	MSC
Dutton	T-AGS-22	Oregon SB Co, Portland, Ore	5 Nov 1957	MSC

Displacement Light, 4,918 tons; full load, 13,050 tons
Length overall 455.2ft (138.7m)
Maximum beam 62.2ft (19m)
Maximum draught 25ft (7.6m)
Main machinery One turbine (General Electric, AGS-21; Westinghouse, AGS-22). Two boilers (Combustion Engineering, AGS-21, Babcock and Wilcox, AGS-22)
Screws/s.h.p. 1/8,500
Maximum speed 17 knots
Complement 13 officers, 47 enlisted men, 40 technicians

This class was built to the VC2-S-AP3 Maritime Commission design. *Bowditch* was originally completed as SS *South Bend Victory*. She was laid down 11 May, 1945, launched on 30 June, and delivered on 27 July, the same year. *Dutton*, originally *Tuskegee Victory*, was laid down 27 March, 1945, launched 8 May, and delivered 5 June that year.

Conversion of *Bowditch* was carried out at Charleston Naval Shipyard between 10 October, 1957, and 16 November, 1958, and that of *Dutton* was made at the Philadelphia Naval Shipyard between 8 November, 1957, and 16 November, 1958. The conversion (SCB-179) was made to enable them to support the Fleet Ballistic Missile Programme, for general surveying, and to record magnetic fields and gravity. These ships are operated by the Military Sealift Command for the Oceanographer of the Navy. Both are to be disposed of in the mid-1980s, having been replaced by two units of the C3-S-33a class (see AK-284 class).

Disposal: *Michelson* (AGS-23), the third ship of this class, was struck off the Naval Vessel Register (NVR) on 15 April, 1975.

▲ *Mormacscan* in commercial operation. She and *Mormalake* are to be converted into AGS as replacements for the two *Bowditch*-class units

▼ *Dutton* (T-AGS-22) (illustrated) and her sister *Bowditch* (T-AGS-21) support SSBN operations. Both will be replaced in the mid to late 1980s

Type: Hospital Ships (AH) — *Number/Class:* 1+(1) "AH-19"

Name	*Number*	*Builder/converter*	*Acquired*	*Status*
(ex-tanker **Worth**)	T-AH-19	National Steel & SB Co, San Diego, Calif	June 1983	CONV
(ex-tanker **Rose City**)	T-AH-20	National Steel & SB Co, San Diego, Calif		PROJ

Measurements Deadweight 93,323 tons
Length overall 894ft (272.5m)
Maximum beam 144ft (43.9m) (approximate)
Maximum draught 49.2ft (15m)
Main machinery Two turbines (General Electric)
Screws/s.h.p. 1/24,500
Maximum speed 16.5 knots
Complement 3,500 total (crew plus medical contingent, approximate), plus 21-man Navy communications team.

It is proposed to acquire two of these ships, one each in the FY-1983 and FY-1984 Programmes, for conversion to hospital ships. The characteristics listed above represent their approximate size and shape. Each vessel will be designed to hold a total of 1,000 beds, and will have 12 operating rooms. Upon completion of the conversion, each ship will be assigned to the Rapid Deployment Force (RDF). Both ships will be civilian-manned and operated under the administrations control of Military Sealift Command. They will be stationed in a continental US port on 15 days notice, ready for operational deployment. The conversion of T-AH-19 at a cost of $300 million was authorised in FY-1983. Characteristics given are before conversion. Contract for the conversion of T-AH-19 was awarded to National Steel and SB Co, San Diego, California, with an option for T-AH-20, on 28 June 1983.

Type: Hospital Ship (AH) *Number/Class:* 1 *Haven*

Name	Number	Builder	Commissioned	Status
Sanctuary (ex-SS-**Marine Owl**)	AH-17	Sun Ship Building and DD Co, Chester, Pa	20 June 1945	MAR

Displacement Standard, 11,141 tons; full load, 15,500 tons
Length overall 520ft (158.5m)
Maximum beam 71.5ft (21.8m)
Maximum draught 22ft (6.7m)
Main machinery One General Electric geared turbine. Two Babcock and Wilcox boilers
Screws/s.h.p. 1/9,000
Maximum speed 18.3 knots
Accommodation 487 (67 officers, 420 enlisted men); medical contingent, 165 (45 officers, 120 enlisted men)

Built to the C4-S-B2 Maritime Commission hull design and survivor of a six-ship class, this ship was laid down for mercantile service on 22 November, 1943, launched on 15 August, 1944, and delivered incomplete on 30 September, 1944, to the Navy for conversion to hospital ship. The work was done by Todd SB Company, Hoboken, New Jersey.

Sanctuary was first commissioned on the date indicated above, and was decommissioned on 15 August, 1946. Recommissioned on 15 November, 1966, for Vietnam service, she was again decommissioned at Hunter's Point on 15 December, 1971, for conversion to a "Dependent Support Ship". Medical capabilities were upgraded and otherwise modified for the mission. The familiar red crosses on the sides of the ship were also removed, because in her new role *Sanctuary* no longer qualified as an "AH" under the terms of the Geneva Convention, despite being officially classified as such. She was recommissioned on 18 November, 1972.

The first deployment was scheduled to be to Piraeus, Greece, to support the destroyer squadron, and their dependents based there. However, *Sanctuary* was not deployed because of a change in the Greek political situation, and she was decommissioned at Philadelphia on 28 March, 1975. She was laid up there until transferred to the MARAD Reserve Fleet, James River, on 23 August, 1978.

Disposals: *Haven* (AH-12) was sold and converted to a chemical carrier. *Benevolence* (AH-13) was sunk in 1950 in a collision. *Tranquility* (AH-14) was laid up in the MARAD Reserve Fleet until she was struck from the Navy List and sold on 15 July, 1974. *Consolation* (AH-15) was chartered as a private hospital ship under the name of SS *Hope*, but was returned and struck off on 16 September, 1974. She was sold on 22 January, 1975, for scrapping. *Repose* (AH-16) was struck off on 15 March, 1974, after Vietnam service, and was sold on 18 April, 1975, for scrapping.

Note It was proposed to convert the former liner SS *United States* into a hospital ship at a cost of $301.4 million under the FY-1983 Programme. The ship was to have been fitted with 2,500 beds. This project has been cancelled.

Sanctuary (AH-17), the Navy's last Hospital Ship, leaving San Francisco for the East Coast after conversion to a Dependants Support Ship

Type: Cargo Ships (AK) — *Number/Class:* 8 Algol

Name	Number	Builder	Delivered	Status
Algol (ex **Sea-Land Exchange**)	T-AK-287	Rotterdamsche DD Maats, NV Rotterdam	1973	CONV
Bellatrix (ex **Sea-Land Trade**)	T-AK-288	Rheinstahl Nordseewerke, Emden, West Germany	4 Dec 1973	CONV
Denebola (ex **Sea-Land Resource**)	T-AK-289	Rotterdamsche DD Maats, NV Rotterdam	1973	MAR
Pollux (ex **Sea-Land Market**)	T-AK-290	A. G. Weser, Bremen, West Germany	20 Sept 1973	MAR
Altair (ex **Sea-Land Finance**)	T-AK-291	Rheinstahl Nordseewerke, Emden, West Germany	17 Sept 1973	MAR
Regulus (ex **Sea-Land Commerce**)	T-AK-292	A. G. Weser, Bremen, West Germany	30 Mar 1973	MPR
Capella (ex **Sea-Land McLean**)	T-AK-293	Rotterdamsche DD Maats, NV Rotterdam	1972	CONV
Antares (ex **Sea-Land Galloway**)	T-AK-294	A. G. Weser, Bremen, West Germany	1972	CONV

Antares (AK-294) while still in commercial service as *Sealand Galloway* in August 1980. Her conversion to a Vehicle Cargo Ship (AKR), along with seven sisters, for use in the Rapid Deployment Force (RDF) is being carried out in FY 1983–84 *(Skyfotos)*

Measurements Dead weight, 27,051–28,095 tons; Net, 25,389 tons; Gross, 41,127 tons
Length overall 946.2ft (288.4m)
Maximum beam 106ft (32.2m)
Maximum draught 34.8ft (10.6m)
Main machinery General Electric type MST-19 steam turbine
Screws/s.h.p. 2/120,000
Maximum speed 33 knots
Complement 42 total (as merchant)
(All characteristics are pre-conversion)

These eight "SL-7" class container ships were purchased from Sea-Land Services. Temporarily classified as Cargo Ships (AK), they will be converted to Vehicle Cargo Ships (AKR) and reclassified as such when conversion has been completed. The block of AKR hull numbers to be used is not known.

When Sea-Land Services decided to lay these ships up because they were uneconomical to run, using too much fuel, they were offered to the Navy, who decided to take them over to improve the Navy's sealift capability. Purchase of the first six ships was approved in the FY-1981 programme, with the final two units being purchased under the FY-1982 Programme. Acquisition and instatement dates are as follows: 13 October, 1981 (AK-287, -288), 27 October, 1981 (AK-289), 10 November, 1981 (AK-292), 16 November, 1981 (AK-290), 15 January, 1982 (AK-291), and 16 April, 1982 (AK-293, -294). The conversion of the first four ships was approved in the FY-1982 Programme, and the conversion of the second four was requested in the FY-1983 Programme but not approved. It is planned to resubmit the request in FY-1984. Conversion, which will cost about $60 million (FY-1982) per ship.

A helicopter flight deck and an upper and lower hangar will be incorporated by building up the area between the forward and after superstructures to the top of the forward structure. Proposed capacities are as follows: upper hangar, 32,986ft²; lower hangar, 32,986ft²; upper intermediate vehicles, 30,670ft²; heavy vehicles (forward), 28,823ft²; lower intermediate vehicles, 22,737ft²; small vehicles, 18,718ft²; heavy vehicles (aft), 24,251ft², and general cargo hold 1,908ft², giving a total storage capacity of 193,079ft². All decks are arranged in descending order to the keel, except for the heavy vehicles area, which is located aft. The general cargo area will be located in the bow. All decks will be joined by at least two ramps, except for the flight deck, upper hangar and lower hangar, which will be connected by two small lifts. Upon completion, all ships will be loaded with a 30-day supply of equipment, manned by the MSC and maintained in "reduced operational" status under a five-day steaming notice in a US port. Proposed conversion schedule is as follows:

Name/Hull number	FY	Yard	Start	Completion
Algol (AK-287)	82	National Steel & SB Co, San Diego	13 Oct 1982	30 June 1984
Bellatrix (AK-288)	82	National Steel & SB Co, San Diego	22 Oct 1982	30 Oct 1984
Denebola (AK-289)	84	Pennsylvania SB Co, Chester, Pa	—	28 Feb 1986
Pollux (AK-290)	84	Avondale Shipyards Inc, Westwego	—	30 June 1986
Altair (AK-291)	84	Avondale Shipyards Inc, Westwego	—	28 Feb 1986
Regulus (AK-292)	84	National Steel & SB Co, San Diego	—	28 Feb 1986
Capella (AK-293)	82	Pennsylvania SB Co, Chester, Pa	22 Oct 1982	30 June 1984
Antares (AK-294)	82	Avondale Shipyards Inc, Westwego	6 Oct 1982	30 June 1984

Value of conversion contracts for first four ships are as follows: $85,508,132 (National Steel, $48,274,600 (Avondale) and $50,294,000 (Pennsylvania SB). All conversion contracts awarded 10 September, 1982. (See page 234 for further conversion data.)

Type: Cargo Ships (AK) — *Number/Class:* +(3) *Northern Light*

Name	Number	Builder	Completed	Status
Northern Light (ex SS **Cove**; **Mormacove**)	T-AK-284	Sun SB and DD Co, Chester, Pa	14 Oct 1960	MSC
Southern Cross (ex SS **Trade**; **Mormactrade**)	T-AK-285	Sun SB and DD Co, Chester, Pa	1962	MSC
Vega (ex SS **Bay**; **Mormacbay**)	T-AK-286	Sun SB and DD Co, Chester, Pa	1960	MSC

Measurements Dead weight, 12,537 tons (AK-284), 12,519 tons (AK-285), 3,801 tons (AK-286). Gross 9,631 tons (AK-284), 9,259 tons (AK-285), 6,590 tons (AK-286)
Length overall 483.3ft (147.2m)
Maximum beam 68ft (20.7m)
Maximum draught 31ft (9.4m)
Main machinery One General Electric steam turbine. Two Combustion Engineering boilers
Screws/s.h.p. 1/12,100
Maximum speed 18 knots (**Vega**, 19 knots)
Accommodation 67 total plus 7-man naval contingent

These vessels were built to Maritime Administration C3-S-33a design. AK.284 was acquired, named, classified, and instated on the NVR on 22 April, 1980, as a replacement for USNS *Private John R. Towle* (T-AK-240); AK-285 on 30 April, 1980, as a replacement for USNS *Schuyler Otis Bland* (T-AK-277); and AK-286 was acquired on 29 April, 1980, as a replacement for USNS *Furman* (T-AK-280), being instated on the Naval Vessel Register on 15 October, 1981.

Northern Light and *Southern Cross* are employed on general cargo handling. *Vega* was approved for conversion to an AK (FBM) under the FY-1981 Programme, replacing *Victoria* (T-AK-281). Boland Marine and Manufacturing Co received the contract for conversion on 29 April, 1981, and the work began on 22 May that year being completed 18 March, 1983. *Vega* is due to deploy to the Atlantic Fleet in July 1983.

Ex-SS *Cape Mormacape* of this class is to be acquired under the FY-1985 Programme for conversion to an AK (FBM), replacing USNS *Marshfield* (T-AK-281) in June 1987. Ex-SS *Lake*, *Mormaclake* will also be acquired under a future programme for conversion to an AK (FBM).

Two additional ships of this class, ex-SS *Scan*, *Mormacscan* and ex-SS *Pride*, *Mormacpride*, are to be acquired under the FY-1985 Programme for conversion to AGS-39 and -40.

Mormactrade in commercial service before being converted to become *Southern Cross* (AK-285). She replaced *Pvt Leonard C. Brostrom* (T-AK-255) in the Military Sealift Command nucleus fleet

Type: Cargo Ship (AK) — *Number/Class:* 1 Wyandot

Name	*Number*	*Builder*	*Commissioned*	*Status*
Wyandot (ex-AKA-92)	AK-283	Moore DD Co, Inc, Oakland, Cal	30 Sept 1944	MPR

Displacement Light, 7,360 tons; full load, 11,000 tons
Length overall 459.1ft (139.8m)
Maximum beam 63ft (19.2m)
Maximum draught 26.2ft (7.98m)
Main machinery One General Electric geared turbine. Two Combustion Engineering boilers
Screws/s.h.p. 1/6,000
Maximum speed 16.5 knots
Complement 38 officers, 385 enlisted men (as AKA)

This ship, built to the Maritime Commission C2-S-B1 hull design, was laid down on 6 May, 1944, launched 28 June, 1944, and delivered to the Navy on 30 September, the same year. Commissioned as AKA-92 of the *Andromeda* class Attack Cargo Ships, she was decommissioned on 10 July, 1959, and struck off the Naval Register on 1 July, 1960, being transfered to MARAD for layup. She was reinstated on the NVR in 1961 and recommissioned in November 1961. She was transferred to the Military Sea Transportation Service on 5 August, 1962, for service as a cargo ship. *Wyandot* is winterised for service in the Arctic. Reclassified AK-283 on 1 January, 1969, *Wyandot* was transferred to MARAD Reserve Fleet, Suisun Bay, on 5 March, 1976, for layup.

Wyandot (T-AK-283) while still classified as T-AKA-92. Ice-strengthened for Antarctic operations, she was transferred to the Maritime Administration in March 1976 and is now laid up in the Suisun Bay reserve fleet *(US Navy)*

Type: Cargo Ships (AK) — *Number/Class:* 3 Norwalk

Name	*Number*	*Builder*	*Acquired*	*Status*
Furman (ex-SS **Furman Victory**)	T-AK-280	Oregon SB Corp, Portland, Ore	18 Sept 1963	MSC
Victoria (ex-SS **Ethiopia Victory**)	T-AK-281	Permanente No. 2, Permanente Metals Corp, Richmond, Cal	13 Aug 1964	MSC
Marshfield (ex-SS **Marshfield Victory**)	T-AK-282	Oregon SB Corp, Portland, Ore	22 Aug 1968	MSC

Displacement Light, 5,469 tons (AK-282); 7,000 tons (rest). Full load, 11,277 tons (AK-282), 11,100 tons (rest)
Length overall 455.25ft (138.8m)
Maximum beam 62ft (18.9m)
Maximum draught 22ft (6.7m)
Main machinery One geared turbine (Westinghouse, AK-282; General Electric, rest). Two Babcock and Wilcox boilers (AK-280) (Combustion Engineering, rest)
Screws/s.h.p. 1/4,250 (AK-282); 1/8,500 (rest)
Maximum speed 16.5 knots
Complement 14 officers (AK-282); 18 officers (remainder). 54 enlisted men (AK-282), 71 enlisted men (remainder)

These were built as "Victory" type mercantile cargo ships (VC2-S-AP3). AK-280 was laid down on 1 April, 1944, launched 15 May, 1944, and delivered on 7 June, 1944, to the Maritime Commission. She was converted to an FBM supply ship at the American SB Company, this being completed on 7 October, 1964. AK-281 was laid down on 20 January, 1944, launched on 20 April, 1944, and delivered on 17 July, 1944. Her conversion by the Philadelphia Naval Shipyard was completed on 15 October, 1965. AK-282 was laid down on 25 March, 1944, launched on 12 May, 1944, and delivered on 31 May, 1944. She was converted by Boland Machine and Mfg. Company, being completed on 28 May, 1970.

The conversions were extensive. Tankage was provided to carry 800,000gal of fuel, hold number 3 was fitted with silos to carry 16 Polaris missiles (later modified for Poseidon), and vacant spaces were modified to carry spare parts, torpedoes, and general stores. These ships carry a detachment of Navy personnel.

Radars are TM/RM-1650/6X and TM-1660/12S.

Class leader *Norwalk* (AK-279), was struck from the NVR on 1 August, 1979. *Furman* was to be struck on 30 September, 1981, but this was cancelled on 15 September, 1981, and she was reassigned to the Naval Electronics Command for service as an underwater cable-layer and transporter. Her FBM capabilities were removed.

Victoria (AK-281) is scheduled to be transferred to MARAD for layup in November, 1983.

She will be retained in ready reserve as a backup for USNS *Marshfield* (T-AK-282), until replaced by ex-SS *Cape*, *Mormacape* in FY-1985.

► *Furman* (T-AK-280). Formerly used as an AK (FBM), she is now an undersea cable transporter, probably in support of the SOSUS network and other communications systems *(US Navy)*

Victoria, one of two surviving AK (FBM)s of the *Norwalk* class used to carry SLBMs from depot to SSBN bases such as Holy Loch

Type: Cargo Ship (AK) — *Number/Class:* 1 *Ethanin*

Name	Number	Builder	In Service	Status
Mirfak	AK-271	Avondale Marine Ways, Avondale, La	30 Dec 1957	MAR

Displacement Light, 2,022 tons; full load, 3,886 tons
Length overall 262.2ft (79.9m)
Maximum beam 51.5ft (15.7m)
Maximum draught 18.7ft (5.7m)
Main machinery Two Alco diesel engines, Westinghouse electric motors
Screws/b.h.p. 2/2,700
Maximum speed 13 knots
Complement 48 total (14 officers, 34 enlisted men)

This ship is the sole unit of a three-ship class still to be employed as an AK, her two sisters having been reclassified AGORs (see *Eltanin*-class AGORs). Laid down on 5 July, 1956, she was launched 5 August, 1957, and placed in service as T-AK-271 on 30 December, 1957, under the operational control of the Military Sealift Command. This class was built to the C1-ME2-13a hull design. *Mirfak* has an ice breaking bow and is otherwise strengthened for Arctic operations. She was transferred to the Maritime Reserve Fleet, James River, on 11 December, 1979 for layup.

Disposals: USNS *Schuyler Otis Bland* (T-AK-277) was struck from the Naval Register on 15 August, 1979, and sold for scrapping on 28 November, 1979. USNS *Lt James E. Robinson* (T-AK-274) was struck from the NVR on 16 January, 1981, and sold for scrap.

Type: Cargo Ship (AK) — *Number/Class:* 1 *Marine Fiddler*

Name	Number	Builder	Acquired	Status
Marine Fiddler (ex-SS **Marine Fiddler**)	AK-267	Sun SB and DD Co., Chester, Pa	10 Dec 1952	MAR

Displacement Light, 8,250 tons; full load, 22,094 tons
Length overall 520ft (158.4m)
Maximum beam 72ft (21.9m)
Maximum draught 33ft (10.1m)
Main machinery One Westinghouse geared turbine. Two Babcock and Wilcox boilers
Screws/s.h.p. 1/9,000
Maximum speed 15.8 knots
Complement 82 total (23 officers, 59 enlisted men)

A Second World War construction based on a Maritime Commission C4-S-B5 hull design, this vessel was laid down on 15 December, 1944, launched 15 May, 1945, and delivered to the Maritime Commission on 30 August, 1945. She served with the Army from 1946 to 1952 and was acquired by the Navy on the indicated date for service with the Military Sea Transportation Service as T-AK-267. The ship's massive booms have a lift capacity of 150 tons.

Transferred to the Maritime Reserve Fleet, James River, on 14 September, 1973, *Marine Fiddler* is retained on the Naval Vessel Register because of her heavy lift capability.

Marine Eddler (T-AK-267) in a Far Eastern port. Currently in reserve, she has a 150-ton lift capacity, the heaviest in the fleet

Type: Cargo Ship (AK) — *Number/Class:* 0 *Pvt Leonard C. Brostrom*

Name	Number	Builder	Acquired	Status
Pvt Leonard C. Brostrom (ex-SS **Marine Eagle**)	AK-255	Sun SB and DD Co, Chester, Pa	31 July 1950	None

Displacement Light, 8,590 tons; full load, 12,056 tons
Length overall 520ft (158.5m)
Maximum beam 71.5ft (21.8m)
Maximum draught 33ft (10.1m)
Main machinery One General Electric geared turbine. Two Babcock and Wilcox boilers
Screws/s.h.p. 1/9,000
Maximum speed 17 knots
Complement 20 officers, 59 enlisted men

Built to the Second World War C4-S-B1 hull design, this ship was laid down on 5 December, 1942, launched on 10 May, 1943, and delivered on 18 September, 1943, being acquired by the Navy on the date above after service with the Army Transportation Service. She was transferred to the Military Sea Transportation Service on 3 August, 1950, for service. Like her near-sister *Marine Fiddler* (AK-267), this ship is fitted with 150-ton capacity booms. Both ships are capable of carrying locomotives and other heavy equipment as deck cargo. Transferred to the Maritime Reserve Fleet, Suisun Bay, on 29 May, 1980, for layup, she is kept on the NVR because of her heavy lift capability. (See page 234 for additional data.)

Type: Cargo Ships (AK) — *Number/Class:* 0 + 1 + 12 "*AKX*"

It was planned to acquire a total of 13 ships under time charter between January and March 1983. These ships will be converted to operate with the Rapid Deployment Force (RDF) and will replace the various commercial cargo ships now operating temporarily with the RDF. All will be civilian-manned and under the administrative control of Military Sealift Command (MSC). Before deployment all 13 will be converted to Vehicle Cargo Ships (AKR).

The M/V *John B. Waterman*, built to the Maritime Administration C7-S-133A hull design, was acquired on time charter on 1 November, 1982, from the Waterman Steamship Corp. Two more ships, M/V *Charles Carroll* and *Thomas Heywood*, are to be acquired in the immediate future. All are to be converted to AKRs at the National Steel and Shipbuilding Co, San Diego, Calif, at Waterman Steamship Corp's expense. The *John B. Waterman* is currently undergoing conversion. (See page 234 for additional data.)

A total of five ships, names not specified, are to be chartered from the Maersk Co, the first three being acquired under the FY-1983 programme. All will be converted to AKRs at the Bethlehem Steel Co, Sparrows Point Yard (first three acquisitions), and Beaumont, Texas (remaining acquisitions).

A total of five ships are to be built by General Dynamics Corp for the charter. All will have AKR features incorporated during construction.

All time charters are initially for five years, subject to renewal.

Disposals: *Sgt Andrew Miller* (AK-242) was transferred to the Maritime Reserve Fleet on 22 March, 1976. *Sgt Truman Kimbro* (AK-254) was transferred to MARAD on 16 March, 1976. *Greenville Victory* (AK-237) was transferred to the Maritime Administration on 23 March, 1976. All three ships were struck off the NVR on 16 January, 1981, for disposal. The last of the class, *Pvt John R. Towle* (AK-240), was stricken for disposal on 31 July, 1982. (See page 234 for additional data.)

Type: Cargo Ship (AK) — *Number/Class:* 1 *American Spitfire*

Name	*Number*	*Builder*	*Completed*	*Status*
American Spitfire (ex-SS **Idaho**)	T-AK	Avondale Shipyards Inc, Avondale, La	1969	RDF

Measurements Deadweight, 13,286 tons; net, 5,243 tons; gross, 9,493 tons
Length overall 579ft (176.5m)
Maximum beam 82.1ft (25m)
Maximum draught 30.9ft (9.4m)
Main machinery General Electric steam turbine
Screws/s.h.p. 1/24,000
Maximum speed 23 knots
Complement Not available

Built to the Maritime Administration hull design C4-S-69a, this vessel was bare-boat chartered on 1 September, 1981, and assigned to the Rapid Deployment Force (RDF), deploying to Diego Garcia in November 1981. This ship is not on the Naval Vessel Register. (See page 234.)

The bare-boat chartered Cargo Ships (AK) *American Courier* and *American Champion* were returned to the owners on 30 September, 1982. They had been assigned to the RDF since July 1980.

Type: Cargo Ships, Barge (AKB) — *Number/Class:* 2 *Lash* Type

Name	*Number*	*Builder*	*Completed*	*Status*
Austral Lightning (ex-**Lash Espana**)	T-AKB	Avondale Shipyards Inc, Avondale, La	14 May 1971	RDF
Austral Rainbow (ex-**China Bear**)	T-AKB	Avondale Shipyards Inc, Avondale, La	April 1972	RDF

Measurements Deadweight, 30,298 tons; Gross, 26,406 tons; Net, 18,706 tons
Length overall 820ft (249.8m)
Maximum beam 100ft (30.5m)
Maximum draught 35ft (10.7m)
Main machinery Two De Laval steam turbines
Screws/s.h.p. 1/32,000
Maximum speed 22.5 knots
Complement Not available

Built to the C8-S-81b hull design, these large cargo ships are presently based in or around Diego Garcia in the Indian Ocean, having been assigned to the Rapid Deployment Force (RDF). Acquired under bare-boat charter by the Military Sealift Command (MSC) on 6 October, 1981, (*Austral Lightning*) and 27 October, 1981, (*Austral Rainbow*), they both deployed on 13 October, 1981, loaded with ammunition and palleted cargo totalling 17,146 tons. These ships, which are fitted with two 500-ton capacity cranes, are not on the Naval Vessel Register. Classification given here is unofficial. (See page 234.)

Type: Vehicle Cargo Ships (AKR) — *Number/Class:* 2 Mercury

Name	*Number*	*Builder*	*Completed*	*Status*
Mercury (ex-SS **Illinois**)	T-AKR-10	Bath Iron Works, Bath, Me	1977	RDF
Jupiter (ex-SS **Lipscomb Lykes, Arizona**)	T-AKR-11	Bath Iron Works, Bath, Me	14 May 1976	RDF

Measurements Deadweight, 19,480 tons; Gross, 13,156 tons; Net, 7,603 tons
Length overall 684.7ft (108.6m)
Maximum beam 102ft (31.1m)
Maximum draught 32ft (9.7m)
Main machinery General Electric geared turbines
Screws/s.h.p. 2/37,000
Complement 54 total

Built to the Maritime Administration C7-S-95a hull design, these ships became available when the original owner, State Lines Inc, went bankrupt, and were acquired for Military Sealift Command by the Navy on 1 April, 1980, (*Mercury*) and 18 March, 1980 (*Jupiter*) for use in the Rapid Deployment Force (RDF). The purchase of *Mercury* was approved under the FY-1981 Programme at a cost of $93.1 million, and *Jupiter* in FY-1982 at a cost of $93.9 million. After loading at Wilmington, North Carolina, both ships deployed to Diego Garcia in July 1980.

Mercury (T-AKR-10) seen before deploying to the Indian Ocean to take up position with the RDF

Type: Vehicle Cargo Ship (AKR) — *Number/Class:* 1 Meteor

Name	*Number*	*Builder*	*Completed*	*Status*
Meteor (ex-**Sea Lift**, ex-LSV-9, AK-278)	T-AKR-9	Lockheed SB and Cons. Co, Seattle, Wash	25 Apr 1967	MSC

Displacement Light, 11,130 tons; standard, 16,940 tons; full load, 21,700 tons
Length overall 540ft (164.7m)
Maximum beam 83ft (25.3m)
Maximum draught 27ft (8.2m)
Main machinery Two geared turbines. Two boilers
Screws/s.h.p. 2/19,400
Maximum speed 20 knots
Complement 5 officers, 49 enlisted men

Originally authorised as *Sea Lift* (AK-278) in the FY-1963 Programme, this vessel was built to the C4-ST-67a hull design at a cost of $15.9 million. Reclassified LSV-9 on 1 June, 1963, she was laid down on 19 May, 1964, and launched on 18 April, 1965. Following completion she was transferred to the Military Sealift Command on 29 April, 1967, for service, being reclassified AKR-9 on 1 January, 1969. The ship was renamed *Meteor* on 12 September, 1975, to avoid confusion with the *Sealift* class Transport Oilers (AOT). Assigned to the RDF from 3 April, 1980, until mid-1981, she was then returned to general cargo service. *Meteor* has internal ramps, a stern ramp, and side openings for rapid roll-on/roll-off handling of general cargo or wheeled, tracked, and amphibious vehicles, and is fitted with two 70-ton, 14 15-ton, and two 10-ton cranes.

Radars are TM-1650/6X and TM-1660/12S.

Meteor (T-AKR-9). Note the stern ramp projecting above the transom *(US Navy)*

Type: Vehicle Cargo Ship (AKR)			*Number/Class:* 1 *Comet*	
Name	*Number*	*Builder*	*Completed*	*Status*
Comet (ex-LSV-7, AK-269)	T-AKR-7	Sun SB and DD Co., Chester, Pa	24 Jan 1958	TAA

Displacement Light, 8,175 tons; full load, 18,286 tons
Length overall 499ft (152.1m)
Maximum beam 78ft (23.8m)
Maximum draught 28.8ft (8.8m)
Main machinery One General Electric geared turbine. Two Babcock and Wilcox boilers
Screws/s.h.p. 2/13,200
Maximum speed 18 knots
Complement 73 total

This roll-on/roll-off ship was built to Maritime hull design C3-ST-14a as AK-269. Laid down 15 May, 1956, she was launched on 31 July, 1957, and transferred to the Military Sea Transportation Service on 24 January, 1958, following completion. Reclassified LSV-7 on 1 June, 1963, and then to AKR-7 on 1 January, 1969, *Comet* is ice strengthened for Arctic operations. Designed with ramp systems for rapid loading and unloading, and fitted with stabilizers, *Comet* accommodates up to 700 vehicles in two after holds and carries general cargo in the forward holds.

Radar is TM-1650/6X

Disposal: AKR-8 (ex-LSV-8) *Taurus*, which originally was the uncompleted *Fort Snelling* (LSD-23), was struck from the Navy List on 22 June, 1971, and sold commercially.

Comet (T-AKR-7), the Navy's first purpose built AKR

Type: Vehicle Cargo Ships (AKR) — *Number/Class:* 2 Lyra

Name	Number	Builder	Completed	Status
Lyra (ex-M/V **Reichenfels**)	T-AKR	Sasebo Heavy Industries Co, Ltd, Japan	30 Sept 1977	RDF
Cygnus (ex-M/V **Rabenfels**)	T-AKR	Howaldtswerke-Deutsche Werft, Kiel, West Germany	8 July 1977	MSC

Measurements *Lyra*, Deadweight, 15,175 tons; gross, 14,742 tons; net, 7,330 tons. *Cygnus*, Deadweight, 15,075 tons; gross, 14,190 tons; net, 7,170 tons
Length overall 633.9ft (193.1m)
Maximum beam 88.9ft (27.1m)
Maximum draught 29.9ft (9.1m)
Main machinery *Lyra*, two Kawaski-MAN diesels; *Cygnus*, two MAN diesels
Screws/s.h.p. 1/18,980
Maximum speed 21 knots
Complement 31 total

Both ships were originally built for the Hansa Lines of West Germany. *Cygnus* is the first western roll-on/roll-off ship to be fitted with a heavy slewing stern ramp, and both vessels are equipped with two 200 h.p. bow thrusters. They were bare-boat chartered by the Military Sealift Command from the Lykes Bros. Lines: *Lyra* on 17 May, 1981, and *Cygnus* on 28 March, 1981. *Lyra* was assigned to the Rapid Deployment Force (RDF) in mid-1981. Neither ship is on the Naval Vessel Register (NVR).

The Navy chartered *Lyra* (AKR) while she was in commercial operation as *Reichenfels* of the now defunct Hansa-Lines. The stern ramp is extensible outwards when lowered and can traverse about 15° to either side of the stern

Type: Oilers (AO) — *Number/Class:* 0+2+19 Henry J. Kaiser

Name	Number	Laid down	Launched	Commissioned	Status
Henry J. Kaiser	T-AO-187	Nov 1984		est. 1986	ORD
	T-AO-188				ORD
	T-AO-189/191				PROJ
	T-AO-192/195				PROJ

Builder Avondale Shipyard Inc, Westwego, La
Displacement Full load, 40,000 tons
Length overall 677.9ft (206.6m)
Maximum beam 97.5ft (29.7m)
Maximum draught 35ft (10.7m)
Main machinery Diesels
Screws/s.h.p. 2/Not available
Maximum speed 20 knots
Complement Not available

A new class of Oilers of commercial design, modified for fleet underway replenishment. Twenty-one ships are projected. The prototype was authorised in the FY-1982 Programme, a second unit was authorised in the FY-1983 Programme, with three more to be requested in the FY-1984 Programme, four in the FY-1985 Programme, four in the FY-1986 Programme, and six in the FY-1987 Programme. Construction cost of the ship approved in FY-1984 is $173 million. The contract for the construction of *Henry J. Kaiser* was awarded to Avondale on 12 November, 1982, with options on four more units (AO-188/191). The above characteristics are preliminary and are subject to change. These ships are to be civilian-manned and operated by the Military Sealift Command.

Cargo capacity: 180,000 barrels. (See page 234.)

Type: Oilers (AO) — *Number/Class:* 5 Cimarron

Name	Number	Laid down	Launched	Commissioned	Status
Cimarron	AO-177	18 May 1978	28 Apr 1979	10 Jan 1981	PA
Monongahela	AO-178	15 Aug 1978	4 Aug 1979	5 Sept 1981	AA
Merrimack	AO-179	16 July 1979	17 May 1980	14 Nov 1981	AA
Willamette	AO-180	4 Aug 1980	18 July 1981	18 Dec 1982	PA
Platte	AO-186	2 Feb 1981	30 Jan 1982	29 Jan 1983	PA

Builder Avondale Shipyard Inc, New Orleans, La
Displacement Light, 8,210 tons; full load, 26,110 tons
Length overall 591ft (180.2m)
Maximum beam 88ft (26.8m)
Maximum draught 35ft (10.7m)
Main machinery One geared turbine. Two boilers
Screws/s.h.p. 1/24,000
Maximum speed 20 knots
Armament Two 20mm (Mark 16) CIWS
Complement 135 total

This new class of Fleet Oilers was Authorised in the FY-1976 Programme (AO-177, -178), FY-1977 (AO-179), and FY-1978 (AO-180, -186). Their 120,000-barrel capacity is designed to provide two complete refuellings of a fossil-fuelled aircraft carrier and 6–8 accompanying destroyers. These ships are fitted with a helicopter platform aft. Fifteen units of this class were planned, but the remainder were ultimately dropped in favour of the AO-187 class on the grounds of insufficient cargo capacity.

Electronics comprise an AN/SPS-10 surface search radar, an OE-82 satellite communications antenna, and an SSR-1 receiver and WSC-3 transceiver.

Monongahela (AO-178) proceeding down the Mississippi River to conduct sea trials. The second unit of the five-ship *Cimarron* class, she has a 120,000-barrel capacity and three stations on each side *(US Navy)*

Type: Oilers (AO) — *Number/Class:* 6 Neosho

Name	Number	Commissioned/USN	Assigned to MSC	Status
Neosho	T-AO-143	24 Sept 1954	25 May 1978	MSC
Mississinewa	T-AO-144	1 Jan 1955	15 Nov 1976	MSC
Hassayampa	T-AO-145	19 Apr 1955	17 Nov 1978	MSC
Kawishiwi	T-AO-146	6 July 1955	10 Oct 1979	MSC
Truckee	T-AO-147	23 Nov 1955	30 Jan 1978	MSC
Ponchatoula	T-AO-148	12 Jan 1956	1 Sept 1980	MSC

Builders New York SB Corp, Camden, N.J. except AO-143: Bethlehem Steel Co, Quincy, Mass
Displacement Light, 9,553 tons; full load, 26,840 tons
Length overall 655ft (199.6m)
Maximum beam 86ft (26.2m)
Maximum draught 35ft (10.9m)
Main machinery Two General Electric geared turbines. Two Babcock and Wilcox boilers
Screws/s.h.p. 2/28,000
Maximum speed 20 knots
Complement 129 total

The largest Oilers, and first built (SCB-82) specifically for the Navy. They have a capacity of 180,000 barrels of fuel. All were authorised in the FY-1952 Programme, and all were originally fitted as flagships. The original armament was two 5in/38 mounts (removed in 1969) and 12 3in/50 mounts. Two of the twin mounts were removed from AO-143, -144 and -147, and a helicopter platform was installed. Those ships also have an additional superstructure installed forward of the after superstructure. Armament was removed from all of these ships as they were phased into MSC service.

Radars: RM-1650/12X and TM-1650/6X.

Mississinewa (T-AO-144) at sea off the coast of Cuba. Since this photo was taken the fleet oilers have had their hull numbers restored to the bow to distinguish them from those ships that serve as bulk carriers *(US Navy)*

Type: Oilers (AO)

Number/Class: 5 *Mispillion*

Name	Number	Commissioned/USN	Assigned to MSC	Status
Mispillion	T-AO-105	29 Dec 1945	26 July 1974	MSC
Navasota	T-AO-106	27 Feb 1946	13 Aug 1975	MSC
Passumpsic	T-AO-107	1 Apr 1946	24 July 1973	MSC
Pawcatuck	T-AO-108	10 May 1946	15 July 1975	MSC
Waccamaw	T-AO-109	25 June 1946	24 Feb 1975	MSC

Builder Sun SB and DD Co, Chester, Pa
Displacement Light, 9,486 tons; full load, 34,020–35,000 tons
Length overall 664ft (196.3m)
Maximum beam 75ft (22.9m)
Maximum draught 35.5ft (10.8m)
Main machinery Two Westinghouse geared turbines. Four Babcock and Wilcox boilers
Screws/s.h.p. 2/13,500
Maximum speed 18 knots
Complement 111 total civil service plus 21 total Navy

These Second World War Oilers were built to the T3-S2-A3 specification. *Waccamaw* was reclassified AOR-109 on 11 December, 1950, as a preliminary to being converted into the Navy's first Replenishment Oiler. However, the conversion was cancelled, and she reverted to AO-109 on 7 May, 1951. These ships were "jumboised", by cutting the ship in half and adding a mid-body, to increase cargo capacity to 180,000 barrels. A helicopter platform was fitted forward. This work was authorised (SCB-224) under the FY-1963 Programme (AO-106, -109) and FY-1964 Programme (AO-105, -107, -108). The first two ships were done at Lockheed SB and Const. Co, Seattle, Washington. AO-106 was begun on 27 May, 1963, and completed on 28 December, 1964; AO-109, begun on 10 June, 1963, was completed on 26 February, 1965. The work on AO-105, -107 and -108 was performed by Lorain SB Company, Lorain, Ohio. AO-105 was begun 30 March, 1964, and completed on 1 June, 1966; AO-107 was begun on 2 March, 1964, and completed on 15 December, 1965; and AO-108 was begun 1 June, 1964, and completed on 16 December, 1966.

In their enlarged form, these ships had four single 3in/50 gun mounts, but these were removed when the ships were transferred to the Military Sealift Command. A small detachment of Navy personnel remains on board for communications.

Radar: TM-1650/6X.

Passumpsic (T-AO-107) refuels Chicago (CG-11). All five units of this class were lengthened in the mid-1960s and transferred to MSC in the mid-1970s *(US Navy)*

Type: Oilers (AO) — *Number/Class:* 2 *Cimarron*

Name	Number	Commissioned/USN	Assigned to MSC	Status
Marias	T-AO-57	12 Feb 1944	2 Oct 1973	TAR
Taluga	T-AO-62	25 Aug 1944	4 May 1972	MSC

Builder Bethlehem Steel Corp, Sparrows Point, Md
Displacement Light, 7,470 tons; full load, 25,450 tons
Length overall 553ft (168.6m)
Maximum beam 75ft (22.9m)
Maximum draught 34ft (10.4m)
Main machinery Two Bethlehem geared turbines. Four Foster-Wheeler boilers
Screws/s.h.p. 2/13,500
Maximum speed 18 knots
Accommodation 150 total

Featuring the T3-S2-A1 Maritime Commission hull design, these ships are the survivors of the famous 26-ship *Cimarron* class Oilers, the work-horses of the American Fleet from the Second World War to the end of the Vietnam War. They were acquired from the Maritime Commission on 12 February, 1944, (AO-57) and 25 August, 1944, (AO-62), and of the 26, three were "jumboised", four (AO-28, -29, -31 and -33) were converted to escort carriers (CVE-26/29) during the war (and have since been disposed of), and the remaining 17 have been deleted.

These ships have a capacity of 145,000 barrels of liquid fuel. Original armament was one 5in/38 gun mount, four 3in/50 mounts, and up to eight 40mm gun mounts. The last were removed after the War. In 1972–1973 all remaining armament was removed when these ships were transferred to the operational control of the Military Sealift Command.

Taluga (AO-62) was scheduled to be taken out of service on 30 September, 1980, and transferred to the Maritime Administration

Reserve Fleet at Suisun Bay for layup. This was then put back until 30 September, 1983. *Marias* (AO-57) was taken out of service on 15 August, 1982, and transferred to the MARAD Reserve Fleet at James River, Va, on 22 November, 1982.

Disposals: *Sabine* (AO-25), *Chikaskia* (AO-54), and *Aucilla* (AO-56) of this class were struck from the Navy List on 1 December, 1976, and are retained in the Maritime Administration Reserve Fleet at James River. *Kennebec* (AO-36) and *Tappahannock* (AO-43), of the T2-A class Oilers, were struck on 15 July, 1976. *Kennebec* has been sold and *Tappahannock* is pending transfer to Taiwan.

Taluga (T-AO-62) at sea off the coast of Hawaii. She and her sister ship *Marias* are the only two units of the *Cimarron* class to survive in the standard configuration *(US Navy)*

Type: Oilers (AO) — *Number/Class:* 3 Jumboised *Cimarron*

Name	Number	Builder	Commissioned	Status
Ashtabula	AO-51	Bethlehem Steel Corp, Sparrows Point, Md	7 Aug 1943	MPR
Caloosahatchee	AO-98	Bethlehem Steel Corp, Sparrows Point, Md	10 Oct 1945	AA
Canisteo	AO-99	Bethlehem Steel Corp, Sparrows Point, Md	3 Dec 1945	AA

Displacement Full load, 34,040 tons
Length overall 644ft (196.3m)
Maximum beam 75ft (22.9m)
Maximum draught 35ft (10.7m)
Main machinery Two Bethlehem geared turbines. Four Foster-Wheeler boilers
Screws/s.h.p. 2/13,500
Maximum speed 18 knots
Armament Four single 3in/50 (Mark 26) gun mounts
Complement 20 officers, 300 enlisted men

These T3-S2-A1 hull designs were acquired from the Maritime Commission on 7 August, 1943, (AO-51), 10 October, 1945, (AO-98), and 3 December, 1945, (AO-99). Originally of the *Cimarron* class, and sisters to *Marias* (AO-57) and *Taluga* (AO-62), they were jumboised during the mid-1960s, having been funded in the FY-1965 Programme (SCB-706). An enlarged mid-body was installed, increasing the capacity to 184,524 barrels of liquid fuel. They can also carry 150 tons of ammunition and 100 tons of refrigerated stores. No helicopter platform is fitted. The stack was heightened, the superstructure extensively rebuilt, and an "M" frame was added.

Radars: AN/SPS-10 surface search, RM-1650/6X (AO-98 only).

Ashtabula (AO-51) was decommissioned on 30 September, 1982, and transferred to the MARAD Reserve Fleet at Suisun Bay, Cal, on 22 November, 1982.

Canisteo (AO-99). *Caloosahatchee*, *Ashtabula* and *Canisteo* of the *Cimarron* class were jumboised more extensively than the units of the *Mispillion* class, including the addition of an extra "M" frame *(US Navy)*

Type: Tankers (AOT)/Water Carrier Tanker (AWT) *Number/Class:* 4 *Ranger*

Name	Number	Completed	Status
Ranger	T-AO	May 1976	RDF
Rover	T-AO	June 1976	RDF
Courier	T-AO	27 Jan 1977	RDF
Patriot	T-AWT	Dec 1975	RDF

Builder Todd Shipyards Corp, San Pedro, Cal
Measurements Deadweight, 35,663 tons; Gross, 21,572 tons; Net, 16,489 tons
Length overall 711.3ft (216.7m)
Maximum beam 84ft (25.6m)
Maximum draught 34.5ft (10.5m)
Main machinery Four Fairbanks-Morse diesel engines
Screws/b.h.p. 2/14,000
Maximum speed 16 knots
Complement 26 total

All of these ships were built to a T6-M-98a tanker design with a 308,277-barrel capacity for commercial service. As an AWT, *Patriot* has a 9,000,000gal water capacity. She was chartered by MSC in June 1980, followed by *Ranger* on 16 October, 1981, *Courier* on 3 December, 1981, and *Rover* on 1 January, 1982. *Patriot* was assigned to the Rapid Deployment Force and deployed to Diego Garcia in July 1980, the remainder following in December 1981. These vessels are not on the Naval Vessel Register.

The commercial AO *Zapata Ranger*, later *Ranger*, in the English Channel. In December 1981 she and two sister ships, *Zapata Rover* (later *Rover*) and *Zapata Courier* (later *Courier*) were chartered to the Navy for operations with the RDF. A fourth sister ship, *Zapata Patriot* (later *Patriot*) was converted to a Water Tanker (AWT) (*Skyfotos*)

Type: Fast Combat Support Ship (AOE) — *Number/Class:* 0+(3) "ADE-6"

A new class of AOE is programmed to supplement and eventually to replace the *Sacramento* class. The prototype is to be requested in the FY-1986 Programme, followed by a second unit in the FY-1986 Programme. One more unit is planned for in the FY-1987 Programme, and a third unit follows in FY-1988.

Finalised characteristics are not yet available.

Type: Fast Combat Support Ships (AOE) — *Number/Class:* 4 *Sacramento*

Name	*Number*	*Laid down*	*Launched*	*Commissioned*	*Status*
Sacramento	AOE-1	30 June 1961	14 Sept 1963	14 Mar 1964	PA
Camden	AOE-2	17 Feb 1964	29 May 1965	1 Apr 1967	PA
Seattle	AEO-3	1 Oct 1965	2 Mar 1968	5 Apr 1969	AA
Detroit	AOE-4	29 Nov 1966	21 June 1969	28 Mar 1970	AA

Builders Puget Sound Naval Shipyard, Bremerton, Wash except AOE-2: New York SB Corp, Camden, N.J.
Displacement Light, 19,200 tons; full load, 51,400–53,600 tons
Length overall 793ft (241.6m)
Maximum beam 107ft (32.6m)
Maximum draught 39.3ft (12m)
Main machinery Two General Electric geared turbines. Four Combustion Engineering boilers
Screws/s.h.p. 2/100,000
Maximum speed 28 knots
Armament One Nato Sea Sparrow system (Mark 29) (AOE-1, -2, -4); four twin 3in/50 (Mark 33) gun mounts (AOE-3); two twin 3in/50 (Mark 33) gun mounts (AOE-1, -2, -4)
Complement 33 officers, 569–647 enlisted men

Designed to carry out the rapid replenishment of a wide variety of supplies and equipment, these ships combine the capabilities of the AF, AO, AE and AK types. AOE-1 was authorised in the FY-1961 Programme, AOE-2 in FY-1963, (both SCB-196), AOE-3 in FY-1965, and AOE-4 in FY-1966, (both SCB-711). A fifth unit, authorised in FY-1968, was cancelled on 4 November, 1969. Estimated cost of construction per ship is $70 million. Beginning with the FY-1984 Programme, each ship will receive a Service Life Extension Programme (Slep) overhaul.

These ships are fitted with a helicopter platform and a large hangar, and carry 2–3 H-46 *Sea Knight* helicopters for Vertical Replenishment. *Sacramento* and *Camden* are fitted with the main machinery from the uncompleted battleship *Kentucky* (BB-66). In addition to their liquid fuel cargo of 177,000 barrels, these ships can carry 2,150 tons of ammunition, 500 tons of dry stores, and 250 tons of refrigerated stores.

Electronics are as follows: AN/SPS-10B surface radar (AOE-1), AN/SPS-10F surface search radar (AOE-2-4), AN/SPS-40 air search radar (AOE-1), AN/SPS-40C air search radar (AOE-2), AN/SPS-6C air search radar (AOE-3, -4), AN/SPS-58A air search radar (AOE-1, -2, -4), one Mark 91 missile fire control system (AOE-1, -2, -4), OE-82 satellite communications antenna, an SSR-1 receiver and a WSC-3 transceiver. One Mark 36 Super RBOC Chaffroc is fitted to each ship.

▲ *Sacramento* (AOE-1). Note the Sea Sparrow launcher on the platform before the bridge *(US Navy)*

▼ *Seattle* (AOE-3) seen during vertical replenishment operations with *America* (CV-66) *(US Navy)*

Type: Gasoline Tankers (AOG) — *Number/Class:* 2 *Alatna*

Name	Number	Completed	Assigned to MSC	Status
Alatna	T-AOG-81	17 July 1957	10 May 1979	MSC
Chattahoochee	T-AOG-82	22 Oct 1957	24 May 1979	MSC

Builder Bethlehem Steel Corp, Staten Island, New York
Displacement Light, 2,366 tons (AOG-81); 2,275 tons (AOG-82). Full load, 7,300 tons (AOG-81), 5,720 tons (AOG-82)
Length overall 302ft (92.1m)
Maximum beam 60.9ft (18.6m)
Maximum draught 19ft (5.8m)
Main machinery Two turbo-electric diesel engines
Screws/b.h.p. 2/4,000
Maximum speed 13 knots
Complement 11 officers, 40 enlisted men

These small gasoline tankers were built to a Maritime Administration TI-MET-24a design for Arctic operations. The design includes a hull strengthened with an ice-resistant belt, and resembles the *Eltanin* class AK/AGORs. Fitted with a small helicopter platform, these vessels have a cargo capacity of 30,000 barrels. They were placed out of service and transferred to the MARAD Reserve Fleet at Suisan Bay on 8 August, 1972, and 22 February, 1972, respectively, for layup.

AOG-81 was re-acquired on 10 May, 1979, and AOG-82 on 24 May, 1979, for re-activation and modernisation as replacements for *Petaluma* (AOG-79) and *Rincon* (AOG-77). The work was carried out at the National Steel and SB Co, San Diego, Cal, beginning on 28 November, 1979. *Chatahoochee* was placed "in service" on 11 January, 1982, followed by *Alatna* on 3 February, 1982. Both ships were re-engined during their reactivation.

Both *Alatna* (T-AOG-81) (illustrated) and her sister ship *Chattahoochee* (T-AOG-82) are ice-strengthened. Each has a cargo capacity of 30,000 barrels

Type: Gasoline Tanker (AOG) — *Number/Class:* 1 *Tonti*

Name	Number	Builder	Completed	Status
Nodaway (ex-SS **Belridge**)	T-AOG-78	Todd Shipyards Corp, Houston	12 Sept 1945	MSC

Displacement Light, 2,100 tons; full load, 6,047 tons
Length overall 325.2ft (99.1m)
Maximum beam 48.2ft (14.7m)
Maximum draught 19ft (5.8m)
Main machinery One Nordberg diesel engine
Screws/b.h.p. 1/1,400
Maximum speed 10 knots
Complement 14 officers, 26 enlisted men

This ship was built to a Maritime Commission T1-M-BT2 hull design, and is the sole survivor of a class of five units. Laid down on 19 February, 1945, launched on 15 May, 1945, and completed on 12 September, 1945, she was acquired by the Maritime Commission on 7 September, 1950, and assigned to the Military Sea Transportation Service for operation. Laid up briefly, she was reacquired on 26 August, 1965, and reactivated. *Nodaway* has a capacity of 30,000 barrels.

Disposals: Class leader *Tonti* (AOG-76) was transferred to the Columbian Navy, and has since been deleted. *Piscataqua* (AOG-80) has been scrapped, and *Rincon* (AOG-77) and *Petaluma* (AOG-79) were leased to South Korea on 21 February, 1982.

Type: Replenishment Fleet Oilers (AOR) — Number/Class: 7 Wichita

Name	Number	Laid down	Launched	Commissioned	Status
Wichita	AOR-1	18 June 1966	18 Mar 1968	7 June 1969	PA
Milwaukee	AOR-2	29 Nov 1966	17 Jan 1969	1 Nov 1969	AA
Kansas city	AOR-3	20 Apr 1968	28 June 1969	6 June 1970	PA
Savannah	AOR-4	22 Jan 1969	25 Apr 1970	5 Dec 1970	AA
Wabash	AOR-5	21 Jan 1970	6 Feb 1971	20 Nov 1971	PA
Kalamazoo	AOR-6	28 Oct 1970	11 Nov 1972	11 Aug 1973	AA
Roanoke	AOR-7	19 Jan 1974	7 Dec 1974	30 Oct 1976	PA

Builders General Dynamics Corp, Quincy, Mass; except AOR-7: National Steel and SB Corp, San Diego, Cal
Displacement light, 13,000 tons (AOR-7); 12,500 tons (rest). Full load, 37,360 tons
Length overall 659ft (200.9m)
Maximum beam 96ft (29.3m)
Maximum draught 33.3ft (10.2m)
Main machinery Two General Electric steam turbines. Three Foster-Wheeler boilers
Screws/s.h.p. 2/32,000
Maximum speed 20 knots
Armament One Nato Sea Sparrow (Mark 29) system (AOR-3, -7); two twin 3in/50 (Mark 33) gun mounts (AOR-1, -5, -6); four single 20mm (Mark 67) gun mounts (AOR-3, -6, -7)
Complement 27 officers (except AOR-7, 30), 363 enlisted men (AOR-2/6), 381 (AOR-1), 427 (AOR-7)

A smaller but equally successful version of the *Sacramento* class AOEs. They were authorised in the following Programmes (SCB-707): FY-1965 (AOR-1, -2); FY-1966 (AOR-3, -4); FY-1967 (AOR-5, -6); and FY-1972 (AOR-7). The estimated construction cost of AOR-2 was $27.7 million.

These ships employ the latest methods for rapid replenishment at sea, and are fitted with helicopter platforms. A hangar is to be retrofitted. The liquid fuel capacity is 175,000 barrels, and there is capacity for 600 tons of ammunition, 425 tons of dry stores, and 150 tons of refrigerated stores. A Super RBOC Chaffroc (Mark 36) system is installed on AOR-1, -3 and -6, and the remainder of the class are also to be so fitted. This class will have two 20mm CIWS (Mark 16) mounts fitted on each ship.

Radars comprise; air search: AN/SPS-58 (AOR-7), AN/SPS-58A (AOR-3), surface search: AN/SPS-10 (AOR-1, -2), AN/SPS-10F (AOR-3-7).

Electronics fitted are one missile fire control (Mark 91) system (AOR-3, -7), to be fitted on remainder), an OE-82 satellite communications antenna, an SSR-1 receiver and a WSC-3 transceiver.

Milwaukee (AOR-2) *(US Navy)*

Type: Transport Oiler (AOT) — Number/Class: 1 Potomac

Name	Number	Builder	Acquired	Status
Potomac (ex-AO-181; ex-M/V **Shenandoah**; ex-USNS **Potomac** T-AO-150	T-AOT-181	Sun SB and DD Co, Chester, Pa	12 Jan 1976	MSC

Measurements Deadweight, 27,467 tons
Length overall 620ft (189m)
Maximum beam 83.5ft (25.5m)
Maximum draught 34ft (10.4m)
Main machinery Geared turbines; two boilers
Screws/s.h.p. 1/20,460
Maximum speed 18 knots
Complement Not available

This ship, or at least a part of it, has had an interesting career. It began life as *Potomac* (T-AO-150) of the *Maumee* class (AO-149). On 26 September, 1961, *Potomac* was virtually destroyed by a fire and explosion at Morehead City, North Carolina. The bow and midsection of the wreckage were salvaged and sold for scrap in March 1963, but the stern section, which was also raised, was refurbished and used in the construction of a virtually new ship, the SS *Shenandoah*. Upon completion, this ship was chartered 14 December, 1964, by the Military Sealift Command. Acquired by the Navy and re-instated on the Navy List as *Potomac* (AO-181) on 12 January, 1976, it is operated by the Trinidad Corporation for MSC. Cargo capacity is 200,000 barrels. It was reclassified T-AOT-181 on 30 September, 1978. She is to be replaced with new construction in the 1980s.

Radars: RM-1650/6X and TM-1660/12X.

Type: Transport Oilers (AOT) — *Number/Class:* 4 *Columbia*

Name	*Number*	*Delivered to owner*	*Acquired*	*Status*
Columbia (ex-AO-182; ex-MV **Falcon Lady**)	T-AOT-182	11 Mar 1971	15 Jan 1976	MSC
Neches (ex-AO-183; ex-MV **Falcon Duchess**)	T-AOT-183	4 Aug 1971	11 Feb 1976	MSC
Hudson (ex-AO-184; ex-MV **Falcon Princess**)	T-AOT-184	4 May 1972	23 Apr 1976	MSC
Susquehanna (ex-AO-185; ex-MV **Falcon Countess**)	T-AOT-185	13 Jan 1972	11 May 1976	MSC

Builder Ingalls SB Div, Pascagoula, Miss
Displacement light, 8,730 tons; full load, 46,600 tons
Length overall 672ft (204.8m)
Maximum beam 89ft (27.1m)
Maximum draught 34ft (11m)
Main machinery Two Pielstick diesel engines
Screws/b.h.p. 1/15,000
Maximum speed 16.5 knots
Complement 11 officers, 12 enlisted men

These merchant tankers were originally bareboat-chartered by the Military Sealift Command on the following dates: AOT-182 and -183 on 3 May, 1974; AOT-184 on 10 April, 1974, and AOT-185 on 17 April, 1974. They are operated under contract by the Trinidad Corporation. Each ship has a cargo capacity of 310,000 barrels.

Originally classified as Oilers (AO), they were reclassified Transport Oilers (AOT) on 30 September, 1978. This was done to distinguish them from the underway replenishment capable AOs and the point-to-point oil carriers which have no underway replenishment capability.

Type: Transport Oilers (AOT) — *Number/Class:* 9 *Sealift*

Name	*Number*	*Laid down*	*Launched*	*Completed*	*Status*
Sealift Pacific (ex AO)	T-AOT-168	29 Nov 1972	13 Oct 1973	14 Aug 1974	MSC
Sealift Arabian Sea (ex AO)	T-AOT-169	5 Mar 1973	26 Jan 1974	6 May 1975	MSC
Sealift China Sea (ex AO)	T-AOT-170	15 Oct 1973	20 Apr 1974	9 May 1975	MSC
Sealift Indian Ocean (ex AO)	T-AOT-171	30 Jan 1974	27 July 1974	29 Aug 1975	MSC
Sealift Atlantic (ex AO)	T-AOT-172	20 Apr 1973	26 Jan 1974	26 Aug 1974	MSC
Sealift Mediterranean (ex AO)	T-AOT-173	9 Mar 1973	9 Mar 1974	6 Nov 1974	MSC
Sealift Caribbean (ex AO)	T-AOT-174	23 July 1973	8 June 1974	10 Feb 1975	MSC
Sealift Arctic (ex AO)	T-AOT-175	6 Feb 1974	31 Aug 1974	22 May 1975	MSC
Sealift Antarctic (ex AO)	T-AOT-176	29 Apr 1974	26 Oct 1974	1 Aug 1975	MSC

The transport oiler *Sealift Pacific* (T-AOT-168) has a cargo capacity of 225,154 barrels *(Joseph J. Ernest/Todd Shipyard Corp)*

Builders Bath Iron Works, Bath, Me except AOT-168/171: Todd Shipyards Corp, San Pedro Div, Los Angeles, Cal
Measurements Dead weight, 27,500 tons
Length overall 587ft (178.9m)
Maximum beam 84ft (25.6m)
Maximum draught 32.6ft (9.9m)
Main machinery Two Colt-Pielstick turbo-charged diesel engines
Screws/b.h.p. 1/19,200 (controllable-pitch propeller)
Maximum speed 16 knots
Complement 30 total (civilian-manned) plus two Maritime Academy cadets

Because these vessels were built especially for long-term charter to the Military Sealift Command (MSC), there was no authorisation or SCB number. Estimated total cost of construction was $146.5 million each. They were assigned to MSC on completion. They are operated for MSC under charter by Marine Transport Lines. One ship of this class is always assigned to the Near-term Rapid Deployment Force, and is stationed off Diego Garcia ready to provide underway replenishment. Reclassified T-AOT-168/176 on 30 September, 1978.

These ships have a cargo capacity of 225,154 barrels. They are fitted with a bow thruster to assist in docking and undocking, and have an automated engine room.

Type: Transport Oiler (AOT) — *Number/Class:* 1 *American Explorer*

Name	*Number*	*Builder*	*Completed*	*Status*
American Explorer (ex-AO)	T-AOT-165	Ingalls SB Corp, Pascagoula, Miss	27 Oct 1959	MSC

Measurements Light, 8,400 tons; deadweight, 27,525 tons; full load, 31,300 tons
Length overall 615ft (187.5m)
Maximum beam 80ft (24.4m)
Maximum draught 32ft (9.8m)
Main machinery One De Laval geared turbine. Two Babcock and Wilcox boilers
Screws/s.h.p. 2/22,000
Maximum speed 20 knots
Complement 10 officers, 37 enlisted men

This ship was built to a Maritime Administration T5-S-RM2a hull design. Laid down on 9 July, 1957, it was launched on 11 April, 1958, and transferred upon completion to the Military Sea Transportation Service for service as T-AO-165. Operated by the Military Sealift Command under charter by Hudson Waterways Corporation, it was reclassified T-AOT-165 on 30 September, 1978. Cargo capacity is 190,300 barrels. She is to be replaced by new construction in the mid-1980s.

Construction of the first two of a new class of oilers (AO-166 and -167) was authorised in FY-1965, However, they were cancelled on 25 May that year. The ships were to be operated by the Military Sealift Command.

Type: Transport Oilers (AOT) — *Number/Class:* 3 *Maumee*

Name	*Number*	*Builder*	*Completed*	*Status*
Maumee (ex-AO)	T-AOT-149	Sun SB and DD Co, Chester, Pa	12 Dec 1956	MSC
Shoshone (ex-AO)	T-AOT-151	Sun SB and DD Co, Chester, Pa	15 Apr 1957	MSC
Yukon (ex-AO)	T-AOT-152	Ingalls SB Div, Pascagoula, Miss	17 May 1957	MSC

Maumee (T-AO-149) in Thule, Greenland. Each unit of this class has a 203, 216-barrel cargo capacity *(US Air Force)*

Displacement Light, 7,761 tons; full load, 32,953 tons
Measurements Dead weight, 25,000 tons
Length overall 620ft (189m)
Maximum beam 83.5ft (25.5m)
Maximum draught 32ft (9.8m)
Main machinery One Westinghouse geared turbine. Two Combustion Engineering boilers
Screws/s.h.p. 2/18,600
Maximum speed 18 knots
Complement 5 officers, 17 enlisted men

Originally a four-ship class, these ships were built to a Maritime Administration T5-S-12a hull design. *Maumee* was laid down on 8 March, 1955, and launched on 16 February, 1956; *Shoshone* was laid down on 15 August, 1955, and launched on 17 January, 1957; and *Yukon* was laid down on 16 May, 1955, and launched on 16 March, 1956. The fourth ship exploded and sunk in 1961 (see *Potomac*, T-AOT-181).

Delivered to the Military Sea Transportation Service on the indicated dates, they are operated for the Military Sealift Command under charter by the Hudson Waterways Corp, being reclassified T-AOT-149, -151 and -152 on 30 September, 1978. Their cargo capacity is 203,216 barrels. *Maumee* was fitted in 1969–1970 with an ice-strengthened bow for Antarctic operations. The entire class is to be replaced by new construction in the mid-1980s.

Radar: TM-1650/6X and TM-1660/12s.

Type: Transport Oiler (AOT) — *Number/Class:* 1 *Mission*

Name	Number	Builder	Completed	Status
Mission Santa Ynez (ex-AO)	AOT-134	Marineship Corp, Sausalito, Cal	13 Mar 1944	MPR

Displacement Light, 5,730 tons; full load, 22,380 tons
Length overall 524ft (159.7m)
Maximum beam 68ft (20.7m)
Maximum draught 31ft (9.5m)
Main machinery One General Electricturbine electric drive. Two Babcock and Wilcox boilers
Screws/s.h.p. 1/10,000
Maximum speed 16 knots
Complement 10 officers, 37 enlisted men

Last survivor of a 27-ship class (AO-111/137) built to the Maritime Commission T2-SE-A2 hull design, *Mission Santa Ynez* was laid down on 9 September, 1943, and launched on 19 December, that year. Acquired by the Navy on 22 October, 1947, she was operated by the Naval Overseas Transportation Service until 1 October, 1949, when she was taken over by the newly organised Military Sea Transportation Service as T-AO-134. On 6 March, 1975, she was transferred to the MARAD Reserve Fleet at Suisun Bay for layup, being reclassified AOT-134 on 30 September, 1978.

Type: Transport Oilers (AOT) — *Number/Class:* 5 *Suamico*

Name	Number	Commissioned	Status
Tallulah (ex AO-50; ex-M/V **Valley Forge**)	T-AOT-50	5 Sept 1942	MAR
Cache (ex AO-67; ex-M/V **Stillwater**)	T-AOT-67	3 Nov 1942	MAR
Millicoma (ex AO-73; ex-M/V **Conestoga**)	T-AOT-73	5 Mar 1943	MAR
Saugatuck (ex AO-75; ex-M/V **Newton**)	T-AOT-75	19 Feb 1943	MAR
Schuylkill (ex AO-76; ex-M/V **Louisberg**)	T-AOT-76	9 Apr 1943	MAR

Builder Sun SB and DD Co, Chester, Pa
Displacement light, 5,252 tons; full load, 21,880 tons
Length overall 523.5ft (159.6m)
Maximum beam 68ft (20.7m)
Maximum draught 33ft (10.1m)
Main machinery One electric drive turbine (Westinghouse, AOT-67, -75 and General Electric remainder). Two Babcock and Wilcox boilers
Screws/s.h.p. 1/6,000
Maximum speed 17 knots
Complement 52 total

Constructed as commercial tankers, these vessels were based on the T2-SE-A1 hull design. *Tallulah* (ex-M/V *Valley Forge*) was laid down on 1 December, 1941, launched on 25 June, 1942, and completed on 30 July, 1942. *Cache* (ex-M/V *Stillwater*) was laid down on 25 May, 1942, launched on 7 September, 1942, and completed on 28 September, 1942. *Millicoma* (ex-M/V *Conestoga*) was laid down on 4 August, 1942, launched on 21 January, 1943, and completed on 30 January, 1943. *Saugatuck* (ex-M/V *Newton*) was laid down on 20 August, 1942, launched on 7 December, 1942, and completed on 21 December, 1942. *Schuylkill* (ex-M/V *Louisberg*) was laid down on 24 September, 1942, launched on 16 February, 1943, and completed on 27 February, 1943. They were acquired by the Navy during the Second World War for service as Fleet Oilers, but were laid up after the war and stricken from the Navy List in 1946. They have a capacity of 134,000 barrels.

These ships, and some sisters, were reacquired on 28 April, 1950, for service with the Military Sea Transportation Service as point-to-point oil carriers, with their underway replenishment capabilities removed. They served as T-AOs until they were laid up in the MARAD Reserve Fleet, James River, on the following dates: *Tallulah* on 29 May, 1975; *Cache* on 6 May, 1972; *Millicoma* on 16 July, 1975; *Saugatuck* on 5 November, 1974, and *Schuylkill* on 8 September, 1975. They reclassified as T-AOTs on 30 September, 1978.

Sister ship *Chepachet* (T-AOT-78), laid up on 13 March, 1972, was transferred on loan to the Department of Energy on 13 October, 1978. Converted at a cost of about $25 million to serve as a test platform in the Ocean Thermal Energy Conversion experiments, she was renamed *Ocean Energy Converter* (OTEC-1). The project was cancelled, however, and the ship was returned to the Navy on 17 June, 1981, and laid up at Pearl Harbor for disposal. She had been struck from the Naval Vessel Register on 1 April, 1980.

Schuylkill (T-AO-76) (later T-AOT-76) seen from *Chipola* (AO-63). The two ships are about to combine fuel cargoes so that only one needs to return to port. *Schuylkill* and the other surviving units of the *Suamico* class were all replaced in the active fleet by the *Sealift*-class AOTs and are now maintained in reserve *(US Navy)*

Type: Transport (AP) — *Number/Class:* 1 *Barrett*

Name	*Number*	*Builder*	*Completed*	*Status*
Geiger	AP-197	New York SB Corp, Camden, N.J.	11 Sept 1952	MAR

Displacement Full load 19,600 tons
Length overall 328ft (99.9m)
Maximum beam 50ft (15.2m)
Maximum draught 14ft (4.3m)
Main machinery One General Electric geared turbine. Two Babcock and Wilcox boilers
Screws/s.h.p. 1/13,750
Maximum speed 19 knots
Complement 426 officers, 1,723 enlisted men, including troops

Geiger is the sole survivor of the US Navy's last class of "troopers". Built to a Maritime Administration P2-S1-DN3 hull design, she was acquired from Marad incomplete on 13 September, 1952, for operation with the Military Sealift Command. After almost 20 years of continuous service, she was withdrawn and transferred to the MARAD Reserve Fleet for layup at Suisun Bay on 27 April, 1971. Transferred to the Massachusetts Maritime Academy on 12 May, 1980, for use as a training ship, she was renamed SS *Bay State*, replacing ex-*Henry Gibbins* (AP-183). During her first training cruise in the summer of 1980, ex-*Geiger* suffered serious engineering damage in the mid-Atlantic. Towed to Norfolk, she was inspected and found unrepairable.

Sister ships *Barrett* (AP-196) and *Upshur* (AP-198) are currently employed as civilian training ships. *Barrett* was struck from the Navy List on 1 July, 1973 and transferred to the New York State Maritime Academy on 5 September, 1973, as SS *Empire State V*. *Upshur* was struck on 2 April, 1973, and transferred on the same date to the Maine Maritime Academy as SS *State of Maine*, replacing ex-*Ancon* (AGC-4).

Type: Transports (AP Unclassified Miscellaneous (IX) — *Number/Class:* 5 *Admiral W. S. Benson*

Name	*Number*	*Original USN name*	*Commissioned*	*Status*
General Alexander M. Patch	AP-122	**Admiral R. E. Coontz**	21 Nov 1944	MAR
General Simon B. Buckner	AP-123	**Admiral E. W. Eberle**	24 Jan 1945	MAR
General Maurice Rose	AP-126	**Admiral Hugh Rodman**	10 July 1945	MAR
(ex General William O. Darby ex-AP-127)	IX-510	**Admiral W. S. Sims**	27 Sept 1945	ASA
General Hugh J. Gaffey (ex-AP-121)	IX-507	**Admiral W. L. Capps**	18 Sept 1944	PSA

Builder Bethlehem–Alameda Shipyard Inc, Alameda, Cal
Displacement Light, 10,798–12,674 tons; full load, 22,574 tons
Length overall 609ft (185.6m)
Maximum beam 76ft (23.2m)
Maximum draught 29ft (8.67m)
Main machinery Two General Electric turbo-electric drive. Four Combustion Engineering boilers
Screws/s.h.p. 2/18,000
Maximum speed 21 knots
Complement 2,056, total (499 officers, 1,557 enlisted men (includes troops)

Originally a ten-ship class, these ships were built to a Maritime Commission P2-SE2-R1 hull design. After serving with the Navy from 1944 to 1946, they were transferred to the Army Transportation Corp, where they served until 1 March, 1950. On that date they were re-acquired by the Navy for operation with the Military Sea Transportation Service as T-APs. All the ships were renamed as indicated on 28 April, 1950.

General Hugh J. Gaffey (AP-121) was struck from the Naval Vessel Register on 9 October, 1969. On 1 November, 1978, she was reacquired by the Navy, instated on the NVR, reclassified IX-507 and placed "in service". She is now based at Bremerton Naval Shipyard, Washington, having been converted to a barracks ship. Only those spaces needed for service as an APL were activated.

On 27 October, 1981, ex-*General William O. Darby* (AP-127) was reacquired and reinstated on the NVR. She was towed to Charleston, S. C. where she was converted to a non-self-propelled barracks ship at the Braswell Corp. in the same manner as *Gaffey* (IX-507). Conversion began in November 1981, with completion in June 1982. Her first employment will be at Newport News, where she will house the crew of *Nimitz* (CVN-68) when that ship begins overhaul in June 1983. She was reclassified IX-510 on 1 July, 1982.

General Nelson M. Walker (AP-125), struck on 25 January, 1981, is scheduled for transfer to Life International, Inc. for conversion to a civilian hospital ship on the lines of the successful SS *Hope*.

AP-122 was transferred to the Maritime Administration on 26 May, 1970; AP-123 on 24 March, 1970, and AP-126 on 8 June, 1970. All three are laid up at James River.

General Alexander M. Patch (T-AP-122), one of five troopers of the *Admiral W.S. Benson* class remaining on the NVR

Type: Transports (AP) *Number/Class:* 3 General John Pope

Name	Number	Builder	Commissioned	Status
General John Pope	AP-110	Federal SB and DD Co, Kearny, N. J.	5 Aug 1943	MPR
General W. H. Gordon	AP-117	Federal SB and DD Co, Kearny, N. J.	29 June 1944	MAR
General William Weigel (ex-General C. H. Barth)	AP-119	Federal SB and DD Co, Kearny, N. J.	6 Jan 1945	MPR

Displacement Light, 12,601 tons (AP-110); 13,801 tons (rest). Full load, 20,175 tons
Length overall 623ft (189.9m)
Maximum beam 76ft (23.1m)
Maximum draught 26ft (7.9m)
Main machinery Two De laval geared turbines. Four Foster-Wheeler boilers.
Screws/s.h.p. 2/17,000
Maximum speed 20 knots
Complement 246 officers, 4,114 enlisted men (includes troops)

Three survivors of a ten-ship class built to the Maritime Commission P2-S2-R-2 hull design, these vessels were decommissioned in 1946 and laid up, with the exception of AP-119, which was transferred to the War Department for service. All were struck from the Naval Vessel Register (NVR). AP-110 was reacquired and reinstated on the NVR on 20 July, 1950, and transferred to the Military Sea Transportation Service, in which she served from 1 August, 1950, until 5 September, 1958, as T-AP-110. She was then laid up again, but was reacquired on 17 August, 1965, and reinstated on the NVR, where she served with MSC until being finally laid up on 23 April,

General John Pope (AP-110) (illustrated) and two of her sisters served as Vietnam troopers from 1965 to 1970, when they were laid up *(US Navy)*

1970, at the Suisun Bay MARAD Reserve Fleet.

AP-117 was reacquired and reinstated on the NVR on 8 November, 1951, as T-AP-117. She served with MSC until transferred to the MARAD Reserve Fleet, James River, on 23 April, 1970, for layup. AP-119 was reacquired and reinstated on the NVR on 20 July, 1950, as T-AP-119, for service with MSC until she was again laid up in the MARAD Reserve Fleet on 12 June, 1958. On 16 August, 1965, she was reacquired for service with MSC and reinstated on the NVR, serving with the MSC until she was laid up for the third and final time on 7 April, 1970, with the Maritime Reserve Fleet at Suisun Bay.

Type: Repair Ships (AR) — *Number/Class:* 4 *Vulcan*

Name	Number	Builder	Commissioned	Status
Vulcan	AR-5	New York SB Corp, Camden, N.J.	16 June 1941	AA
Ajax	AR-6	Los Angeles SB and DD Corp, Los Angeles, Cal	30 Oct 1943	PA
Hector	AR-7	Los Angeles SB and DD Corp, Los Angeles, Cal	7 Feb 1944	PA
Jason	AR-8	Los Angeles SB and DD Corp, Los Angeles, Cal	19 June 1944	PA

Displacement Light, 9,140 tons; full load, 16,160–16,380 tons
Length overall 529.3ft (161.3m)
Maximum beam 73ft (22.3m)
Maximum draught 23.3ft (7.1m)
Main machinery Two geared turbines (Allis-Chalmers, except AR-5; New York SB Corp.). Four Babcock and Wilcox boilers.
Screws/s.h.p. 2/11,000
Maximum speed 19.2 knots
Armament Four single 20mm
Complement 28/72 officers, 745/906 enlisted men

These were built to a modified design based on the *Fulton* (AS) and *Dixie* (AD) classes. *Vulcan* was funded under the 1939 Programme, and the remainder in 1940. *Vulcan* was laid down on 26 December, 1939, and launched on 14 December, 1940; *Ajax* was laid down on 7 May, 1941, and launched on 22 August, 1942; *Hector* was laid down on 28 July, 1941, and launched on 11 November, 1942; *Jason*, originally commissioned as a Heavy Hull Repair Ship (ARH-1), was laid down on 9 March, 1942, and launched on 3 April, 1943. She was reclassified AR-8 on 9 September, 1957.

These ships are well equipped with machine tools for a wide variety of ship repairs. The original anti-aircraft battery of four twin 40mm mounts was removed after the Second World War. *Vulcan* and *Ajax* are equipped as flagships.

Radar comprises an AN/SPS-10 surface search. Electronics comprise on OE-82 satellite communications antenna, an SSR-1 receiver and a WSC-3 transceiver.

Repair Ships (AR) disposals: Of the two ships of the *Delta* class, *Delta* (AR-9) was struck from the Naval Vessel Register on 1 October, 1977, but was retained indefinitely for use as station ship at the Bremerton Inactive Ship Facility. She was to be disposed of in FY-1983. *Briarus* (AR-12) was struck off on 1 January, 1977 and sold for scrap. Of the *Amphion* class, *Amphion* (AR-13) was struck off the NVR on 1 November, 1976, and sold to Iran on 1 March, 1977, having been on loan to that country since 1 October, 1971. *Markab* (AR-23) of the *Klondike* class was struck from on 1 September, 1976, and *Grand Canyon* (AR-28) of the *Shenandoah* class on 1 September, 1978. Both were sold for scrapping.

Battle Damage Repair Ships disposals: the last three units on the Navy List were struck off the NVR as follows: *Midas* (ARB-5) on 15 April, 1976; *Sarpedon* (ARB-7) on 15 April, 1976; and *Helios* (ARB-12) on 10 December, 1977, the latter being sold to Brazil, to whom it had previously been on loan, on 28 December, 1977.

The Repair Ship (AR) *Hector*, similar in design to the *Dixie*-class ADs and *Fulton*-class AS. No Repair Ship replacements are projected in the FY-1984–88 Five-Year Shipbuilding Programme, so this class will be active until the early 1990s at least *(US Navy)*

Type: Cable Repairing Ships (ARC) — *Number/Class:* 0 +1+(1) *Zeus*

Name	*Number*	*Laid down*	*Launched*	*Completed*	*Status*
Zeus	T-ARC-7	1 June 1981	30 Oct 1982	Jan 1984	BLDG

Builder National Steel and SB Co, San Diego, Cal
Displacement tons: Light, 8,370 tons, full load, 14,157 tons
Length overall 502ft (153.2m)
Maximum beam 75ft (22.9m)
Maximum draught 25ft (7.5m)
Main machinery Diesel electric drive
Screws/s.h.p. 2/10,200
Maximum speed 15 knots
Complement 88 officers and enlisted men (civilians), 6 USN personnel, 25 technicians

Two ships are planned for this class, replacing the already deleted *Thor* (T-ARC-4) and *Aeolus* (T-ARC-3). The first was authorised in the FY-1979 Programme, the second unit being scheduled for FY-1986. Estimated cost of construction for ARC-7 is $175 million. Upon completion, they will be transferred to, and operated by, the Military Sealift Command.

The engine room will be remotely controlled from the bridge. Two bow and two stern 1,200 h.p. thrusters will be fitted to enable the ships to "hover" while performing their basic mission.

These ships will be tasked with the repair of SOSUS cables and USAF communications cables in the Pacific.

Type: Cable Repairing Ship (ARC) — *Number/Class:* 1 *Aeolus*

Name	*Number*	*Laid down*	*Launched*	*Commissioned*	*Status*
Aeolus (ex-**Turandot** AKA-47)	T-ARC-3	29 Mar 1945	20 May 1945	18 June 1945	MSC

Aeolus (T-ARC-3). Originally built as *Turandot* (AKA-47), she was converted into an ARC in the mid-1950s along with her sister, the since stricken *Thor* (ARC-4)

Builder Walsh-Kaiser Co Inc, Providence, R.I.
Displacement Light, 4,910 tons; full load, 7,810 tons
Length overall 438ft (133.4m)
Maximum beam 58.2ft (17.7m)
Maximum draught 19.25ft (5.9m)
Main machinery Two Westinghouse turbine electric drive engines. Two Wickes boilers.
Screws/s.h.p. 2/6,000
Maximum speed 13 knots
Complement 33 officers, 217 enlisted men (civilians)

This ship was commissioned as *Turandot* (AKA-47). Built to a Maritime Commission S4-SE2-BE1 hull design, she was decommissioned, laid up and struck off the Naval Register in 1946, but was reacquired on 4 November, 1954, for conversion to a cable repair ship. *Turandot* was renamed and reclassified *Aeolus* (ARC-3) on 17 March, 1955. Converted at Bethlehem Steel Corporation, Baltimore, Maryland, she was recommissioned on 14 May, 1955. On 1 October, 1973 she was decommissioned and transferred to the Military Sealift Command for further service as T-ARC-3.

Aeolus is fitted with a helicopter platform aft, and has cable laying bow sheaves, a cable storage tank and cable repair facilities.

Radar: TM-1650/6X and TM-1660/12S.

Disposal: Sister ship *Thor* (T-ARC-4) was struck from the Naval Register on 20 December, 1977, and sold.

Type: Cable Repairing Ships (ARC) — *Number/Class:* 2 *Neptune*

Name	Number	Laid down	Launched	Commissioned	Status
Neptune (ex-SS **William H. G. Bullard**)	T-ARC-2	22 Jan 1945	22 Aug 1945	1 June 1953	TPA
Albert J. Meyer (ex-SS **Albert J. Myer**)	T-ARC-6	14 Apr 1945	7 Nov 1945	13 May 1963	TAA

Builder Pusey and Jones Corp, Wilmington, Del
Displacement 8,500 tons full load
Length overall 369ft (112m)
Maximum beam 47ft (14.3m)
Maximum draught 27ft (8.2m)
Main machinery Diesel-electric (General Electric). Two Combustion Engineering boilers.
Screws/s.h.p.2/4,000
Maximum speed 14 knots
Complement 105 total (Data are for *Albert J. Myer* as rebuilt).

These ships were built to a S3-S2-BP1 Maritime Commission hull design. ARC-2 was completed on 26 February, 1946, as SS *William H. G. Bullard*, being acquired by the Navy on 17 February, 1953, and commissioned on the indicated date. Decommissioned at Norfolk on 8 November, 1973, she was transferred to Military Sealift Command for further service.

ARC-6 was laid down on 14 April, 1945, launched on 7 November, 1945, and completed on 17 May, 1946, as SS *Albert J. Myer*. Both this ship and *Neptune* were laid up in the Maritime Reserve Fleet upon completion. *Neptune* was acquired from the Maritime Administration and commissioned as indicated. She was decommissioned on 8 November, 1973, and transferred to MSC for further service as USNS *Neptune* (T-ARC-2). ARC-6 was acquired on loan from the Army on the indicated date, and acquired permanently in September 1966. She is employed as a hydrographic research ship.

Neptune is fitted with a helicopter platform, and both ships are fitted with electric cable handling machinery and precision navigation equipment. Both have been "FRAMED". *Myer* was rebuilt at Bethlehem Steel Co., Key Highway Division, Baltimore, Md. between March 1978 and May 1980. *Neptune* was rebuilt at General Dynamics Co., Quincy, Mass. between February 1980 and February 1982. Modernisation included stripping the superstructure down to the main deck, gutting the hull, replacing the propulsion system, the wiring and the piping, and replacing the steel decks and superstructure with aluminium where possible.

Radar: RM-1650/6X (ARC-6 only).

Disposals: ARC-1 was *Portunus* (ex-LSM-275), and ARC-5 was the ex-USCGC *Yamacraw* (WARC-333). Both ships have been deleted.

Albert J. Meyer (T-ARC-6) seen in 1981 after reconstruction

Type: Landing Craft Repair Ships (ARL) — *Number/Class:* 1 *Achelous*

Name	Number	Builder	Commissioned	Status
Sphinx (ex-LST-963)	ARL-24	Bethlehem Steel Co, Hingham, Mass	12 Dec 1944	PR
Ex-**Indra** (ex LST-1147)	ARL-37	Chicago Bridge and Iron Co, Seneca, Ill	28 May 1945	None

Displacement Light, 1,625 tons; full load, 4,325 tons
Length overall 328ft (99.9m)
Maximum beam 50ft (15.2m)
Maximum draught 14ft (4.3m)
Main machinery Two General Motors diesel engines
Screws/s.h.p. 2/1,800
Maximum speed 12 knots
Armament Two quad 40mm gun mounts
Complement 34 officers, 227 enlisted men

Originally laid down as units of the LST-511 class, these vessels were converted during construction to ARLs. Originally there were 37 ships of this class, but now only *Sphinx* and *Indra* remain. Both were reclassified from LST to ARL on 14 August, 1944, and named. Recommissioned on 16 December, 1967, and in January 1968, respectively, for service in Vietnam, they were decommissioned on 30 September, 1971, and in April 1970, respectively, and laid up in reserve. *Indra* was struck from the Naval Register on 31 December, 1977, but is retained as station ship at the Inactive Ship Facility, Norfolk, Va.

These ships and their sisters were activated for the Vietnam War, and served as tenders for small amphibious minesweepers and riverine craft. They are fitted with machine shops, parts storage areas, and lifting gear including 60-ton booms.

Disposals of the *Achelous* class: *Egeria* (ARL-8) was struck from the Naval Register on 1 October, 1977; *Minotaur* (ARL-15) was struck on 1 November, 1976, and sold to South Korea on 31 January, 1977, having previously been on lease; *Satyr* (ARL-23) was struck on 15 June, 1975, and sold to the Philippines on 24 January, 1977, having previously been on lease to South Vietnam (30 September, 1971–30 April, 1975); *Askari* (ARL-30) was struck on 15 June, 1978, and sold to Indonesia on 22 February, 1979; *Bellerophon* (ARL-31) was struck on 1 October, 1977; *Krishna* (ARL-38) was struck on 15 September, 1979, and sold to the Philippines on 5 March, 1980; and *Quirinus* (ARL-39) was struck and sold to Venezuela on 30 December, 1977, having previously been on loan.

Sphinx (ARL-24) and five sisters were reactivated for Vietnam War service. Only *Sphinx* now remains on the NVR, though a second unit, *Indra* (ARL-37), is retained for use at the Inactive Ship Maintenance Facility, Norfolk

Type: Salvage Ships (ARS) — *Number/Class:* 0+4 *Safeguard*

Name	*Number*	*Laid down*	*Launched*	*Commissioned*	*Status*
Safeguard	ARS-50	8 Nov 1982		Oct 1984	BLDG
Grasp	ARS-51	30 March 1983			BLDG
	ARS-52				ORD
	ARS-53				ORD
	ARS-54				None

Builder Peterson Builders Inc, Sturgeon Bay, Wisc
Displacement Full load, 2,880 tons
Length overall 255ft (77.7m)
Maximum beam 50ft (15.2m)
Maximum draught 15ft (4.6m)
Main machinery Diesel engines
Screws/b.h.p. 2/4,200
Maximum speed 14 knots
Endurance 8,000 n.m. at 12 knots
Armament Two 20mm (Mark 67) gun mounts
Complement 87 total

A new class of Salvage Ships to supplement and then replace the 40-year-old *Bolster* (ARS-38) class. An improved *Bolster* class design, the prototype was approved in the FY-1981 Programme at a cost of $93 million, and two more in FY-1982 at a cost of $135.5 million each. A fourth unit was approved in the FY-1983 Programme at a cost of $50 million, and the fifth is projected for the FY-1984 budget. Each ship has a bollard pull of 65.5 tons.

Type: Salvage Ships (ARS) *Number/Class:* 6 *Bolster*

Name	Number	Builder	Commissioned	Status
Bolster	ARS-38	Basalt Rock Co, Napa, Cal	1 May 1945	NRF
Conserver	ARS-39	Basalt Rock Co, Napa, Cal	9 June 1945	PA
Hoist	ARS-40	Basalt Rock Co, Napa, Cal	21 July 1945	AA
Opportune	ARS-41	Basalt Rock Co, Napa, Cal	5 Oct 1945	AA
Reclaimer	ARS-42	Basalt Rock Co, Napa, Cal	20 Dec 1945	PA
Recovery	ARS-43	Basalt Rock Co, Napa, Cal	15 May 1946	AA

Displacement Light, 1,520 tons; full load, 2,040 tons
Length overall 213.5ft (65.1m)
Maximum beam 44ft (13.4m)
Maximum draught 15ft (4.6m)
Main machinery Four Diesel engines (Cooper-Bessemer in ARS-40, -41, -43, and Caterpillar Tractor Co, in ARS-38, -39, -42)
Screws/b.h.p. 2/3,060
Maximum speed 14.8 knots
Armament Two 20mm mounts (Mark 68 except ARS-39 and -41, Mark 67)
Complement 6/8 officers, 86/97 enlisted men

Second World War designed Salvage Ships, these craft differ only slightly from the earlier *Diver* class. Both classes are/were capable of salvaging ships of all types, and their shallow draught permits close-in salvaging and emergency repairs. This class is fitted with 10- and 20-ton booms. ARS-44 through -49 of this class were cancelled on 11 August, 1945. *Bolster* was decommissioned on 1 June, 1983 and assigned to the NRF.

Radars: AN/SPS-53 air search (ARS-38, -39, -42); AN/SPS-10 surface search (ARS-40, -41, 43).

Bolster (ARS-38). An improved version of this class is being built for fleet service *(US Navy)*

Type: Salvage Ships (ARS) *Number/Class:* 1 *Diver*

Name	Number	Builder	Commissioned	Status
Preserver	ARS-8	Basalt Rock Co Inc, Napa, Cal.	11 Jan 1944	NRF
Clamp	ARS-33	Basalt Rock Co Inc, Napa, Cal	23 Aug 1943	None

Displacement Full load, 1,970 tons
Length overall 213.5ft (65.1m)
Maximum beam 41ft (12.5m)
Maximum draught 13ft (4.0m)
Main machinery Four Caterpillar Tractor Co. diesel engines
Screws/b.h.p. 2/3,000
Maximum speed 14 knots
Armament Two 20mm (Mark 68) gun mounts
Complement 10 officers, 77 enlisted men

Preserver and *Clamp* are the last survivors of this class on the Navy List. A slightly less-capable version of the *Bolster* class, they have smaller-capacity booms (8- and 10-tons), but have the same capabilities. Both classes have compressed air diving equipment and are employed in salvage and towing operations. *Preserver* was transferred to the Naval Reserve Force on 1 November, 1979, and is assigned to Little Creek, Virginia. *Clamp* was struck off the Navy List on 1 July, 1963, but was reacquired by the Navy in 1973 for potential reactivation. However, this was

Now with the Naval Reserve Force, *Preserver* (ARS-8) is the last of the *Diver*-class units in the Navy *(US Navy)*

cancelled on the grounds of cost and the material condition of the ship. *Clamp* is to be sunk as a target in Harpoon or Tomahawk missile tests.

Radar: AN/SPS-53 air search (ARS-8 only).

Two sisters, ex-*Shackle* (ARS-9) and *Seize* (ARS-26), serve with the US Coast Guard as Medium Endurance Cutters. *Escape* (ARS-6) was transferred to the Coast Guard on 4 December, 1980. *Grapple* (ARS-7) was struck off the Naval Register on 1 December, 1977, and sold to Taiwan; *Cable* (ARS-19) was struck from the NVR on 15 April, 1977; *Curb* (ARS-21) (to be sunk as a target) and *Gear* (ARS-34) were struck on 30 April, 1981; *Deliver* (ARS-23) was struck on 15 August, 1979, and sold on the same date to South Korea; *Grasp* (ARS-24) was struck on 31 March, 1978, and sold on that date to South Korea; and *Safeguard* (ARS-25) was struck from the NVR on 28 September, 1979, and sold to Turkey on that date.

Type: Submarine Tenders (AS)

Number/Class: 2 *L. Y. Spear* and 3 *Emory S. Land*

Name	*Number*	*Laid down*	*Launched*	*Commissioned*	*Status*
L. Y. Spear	AS-36	5 May 1966	7 Sept 1967	28 Feb 1970	AA
Dixon	AS-37	7 Sept 1967	20 June 1970	7 Aug 1971	PA
Emory S. Land	AS-39	2 Mar 1976	4 May 1977	7 July 1979	AA
Frank Cable	AS-40	2 Mar 1976	14 Jan 1978	5 Feb 1980	AA
McKee	AS-41	14 Jan 1978	16 Feb 1980	15 Aug 1981	PA

Frank Cable (AS-40) on trials. Capable of handling modern SSNs such as the *Los Angeles* class or any succeeding types, she was built to a modified *Samuel Gompers* Destroyer Tender (AD) design *(US Navy)*

Builders General Dynamics Corp, Quincy, Mass (AS-36, -37); Lockheed SB and Construction Co, Seattle, Wash (remainder)
Displacement Standard, 13,000 tons (AS-36, -37); 13,840 tons (remainder). Full load, 22,640 tons (AS-36, -37); 23,000 tons (remainder)
Length overall 643.8ft (196.1m)
Maximum beam 85ft (25.9m)
Maximum draught 28.5ft (8.7m)
Main machinery One General Electric steam turbine. Two Foster-Wheeler boilers
Screws/s.h.p. 1/20,000
Maximum speed 20 knots
Armament Two single 40mm (Mark 19) gun mounts (AS-39–41); Four single 20mm (Mark 67) gun mounts
Complement 96 officers, 1,252 enlisted men (AS-36, -37), 50 officers, 1,108 enlisted men (AS-39/41)
Flag accommodation 25 officers, 44 enlisted men

As there are large numbers of fast, modern nuclear-powered attack submarines in the Fleet, the need for modern submarine tenders is vital. This class has been designed to meet that need; namely to support the *Los Angeles* class Attack Submarines (SSN) and succeeding classes. AS-36 and -37 were authorised in the FY-1965 and -1966 Programmes (both SCB-702), while AS-39/41 were authorised in FY-1972, FY-1973, and FY-1977, respectively, under a modified design (SCB-737). AS-38 was authorised in FY-1969, but was cancelled on 27 March, 1969, the funds being diverted to offset the cost overruns of other shipbuilding projects Estimated cost of construction of *McKee* is $260.9 million.

The hull is basically that of a modified *Samuel Gompers* class destroyer tender design. These vessels have a helicopter deck, but no hangar. AS-39 was placed in reduced commission on 23 March, 1979, and AS-40 on 20 October, 1979, for passage. They were placed in full commission on the indicated dates.

Electronics comprise an AN/SPS-10 surface search radar, an OE-82 satellite communications antenna, an SSR-1 receiver and a WSC-3 receiver.

Type: Submarine Tenders (AS) — *Number/Class: 2 Simon Lake*

Name	*Number*	*Laid down*	*Launched*	*Commissioned*	*Status*
Simon Lake	AS-33	7 Jan 1963	8 Feb 1964	7 Nov 1964	AA
Canopus	AS-34	2 Mar 1964	12 Feb 1965	4 Nov 1965	AA

Builders Puget Sound Naval Shipyard, Bremerton, Wash (AS-33); Ingalls SS Corp, Pascagoula, Miss (AS-34)
Displacement Full load, 19,934 tons (AS-33); 21,089 tons (AS-34)
Length overall 643.7ft (196.2m)
Maximum beam 85ft (25.9m)
Maximum draught 30ft (9.1m)
Main machinery One DeLaval turbine. Two Combustion Engineering boilers
Screws/s.h.p. 1/20,000
Maximum speed 20 knots
Armament Two twin 3in/50 (Mark 33) gun mounts
Complement 90 officers, 1,338 enlisted men (AS-33), 95 officers, 1,326 enlisted men (AS-34)

These tenders were specifically designed (SCB-238) for servicing ballistic missile submarines. In addition to repairing and/or replacing the missiles, as well as other systems, these ships can repair SSBN powerplants. Three submarines can be handled alongside at the same time.

AS-33 was authorised in the FY-1963 Programme and AS-34 in that for the following year. A third unit of this class (AS-35) was authorised in FY-1965, but when requirements for a fifth Fleet ballistic missile tender were cancelled, construction of AS-35 was cancelled in 1965. When the *Poseidon* (C-3) missile was fitted into the SSBN submarines, the conversion of the ships to give them a Poseidon capability was authorised in the FY-1968

Canopus (AS-34) is one of four AS designed to tend Fleet Ballistic Missile Submarines (SSBN). Each AS (FBM) carries spare Poseidon missiles *(US Navy)*

Programme (AS-34) and FY-1969 (AS-33), both under SCB-733. The work was assigned to Puget Sound Naval Shipyard, Bremerton, Washington. *Simon Lake* began conversion on 7 July, 1970, and was completed on 9 March, 1971. Conversion of *Canopus* began on 3 June, 1969, and was completed on 3 February, 1970. *Simon Lake* is the first SSBN tender to be homeported at Kings Bay, Georgia, the east coast Trident base.

Radars: AN/SPS-10 surface search. Electronics: OE-82 satellite communications antenna, SSR-1 receiver and WSC-3 transceiver.

Type: Submarine Tenders (AS) — *Number/Class:* 2 *Hunley*

Name	*Number*	*Laid down*	*Launched*	*Commissioned*	*Status*
Hunley	AS-31	28 Nov 1960	28 Sept 1961	16 June 1962	AA
Holland	AS-32	5 Mar 1962	19 Jan 1963	7 Sept 1963	AA

Builders Newport News SB and DD Co, Newport News, Va (AS-31); Ingalls SB Corp, Pascagoula, Miss (AS-32)
Displacement Standard, 10,500 tons; full load, 19,600 tons
Length overall 599ft (182.6m)
Maximum beam 83ft (25.3m)
Maximum draught 27ft (8.2m)
Main machinery Six Fairbanks-Morse diesel engines; diesel electric drive
Screws/b.h.p. 1/15,000
Maximum speed 19 knots
Armament Four single 20mm (Mark 67) gun mounts
Complement 144 officers, 2,424 enlisted men

The first class of Submarine Tenders constructed since the Second World War, and the first specifically designed (SCB-194) to support Fleet Ballistic Missile Submarines, these vessels were authorised in the FY-1960 (AS-31) and FY-1961 (AS-32) Programmes. Construction cost of *Holland* was $24,359,000.

The original 32-ton hammerhead crane aft became troublesome and was replaced by two 47-ton cranes. A helicopter platform is fitted, but no hangar provided. A large complex of workshops enables these ships to provide complete support of FBM submarines.

Conversion to handle the Poseidon C-3 ballistic missile (SCB-736) was performed by Puget Sound Naval Shipyard, Bremerton, Washington. *Hunley* (authorised FY-1973) began conversion on 1 April, 1973, and was completed on 22 January, 1974. *Holland* (FY-1975) was begun on 3 September, 1974, and completed on 20 June, 1975.

From 1975 to 1982 *Holland* (AS-32) served as tender at the Holy Loch, Scotland, SSBN base. Relieved by her sister ship *Hunley* (AS-31) in December 1981, she returned to the US for a much needed overhaul

Radar: AN/SPS-10 surface search. Electronics: OE-82 satellite communications antenna, SSR-1 receiver and WSC-3 transceiver.

Note Hull numbers AS-20/30 were Second World War construction and/or conversions, some of which were never completed.

Type: Submarine Tender (AS) — *Number/Class:* 1 *Proteus*

Name	Number	Builder	Commissioned	Status
Proteus	AS-19	Moore DD Co, Oakland, Cal	31 Jan 1944	PA

Displacement Light, 14,195 tons; full load 19,200 tons
Length overall 574.5ft (175m)
Maximum beam 73.3ft (22.3m)
Maximum draught 25.5ft (7.8m)
Main machinery Eight Allis-Chalmers diesel engines
Screws/b.h.p. 2/11,200
Maximum speed 15.4 knots
Armament Four single 20mm (Mark 67) gun mounts
Complement 84 officers, 1,210 enlisted men

Completed as a standard AS of the *Fulton* class, *Proteus* (AS-19) became the Navy's first AS (FBM) under the FY 1959 conversion programme. In 1981 she went to Diego Garcia, becoming permanent station ship there

Originally completed as a unit of the *Fulton* class submarine tenders, this ship was laid down on 15 September, 1941, launched on 12 November, 1942, and decommissioned at New London on 26 September, 1947, being placed in service as the Depot Ship with the Reserve Fleet there.

Proteus was selected for conversion to become the Navy's first FBM submarine tender (SCB-190). Authorised in the FY-1959 Programme, the work was performed by Charleston Naval Shipyard, Charleston, S.C. at a cost of $23 million. Conversion began on 19 January, 1959, and completed on 24 July, 1960. The main work entailed lengthening the ship by 44ft (13.4m) by inserting a six-deck mid-section, which added 500 tons to the displacement. The upper decks were extended aft for additional workshops. A mid-ship overhead rail crane was installed for transporting missiles to and from midships Polaris missile storage tubes.

Originally armed with four single 5in/38 mounts, *Proteus* had three of them removed during the conversion, as well as the original 40mm gun mounts. The remaining 5in gun mount was replaced by four single 20mm gun mounts in the seventies.

With the completion of the last Polaris (A-3) patrol on 1 October, 1981, and the decommissioning of Submarine Squadron 15 on the same date, *Proteus*' service as an FBM Tender ceased and her future became uncertain. At present, she is stationed at Diego Garcia providing support services to ships deployed to the Indian Ocean and the base there. She is equipped as a flagship.

Radar: AN/SPS-10 surface search. Electronics: OE-82 satellite communications antenna, SSR-1 receiver and WSC-3 transceiver.

Type: Submarine Tenders (AS) — *Number/Class:* 3 *Fulton*

Name	Number	Builder	Commissioned	Status
Fulton	AS-11	Mare Island Navy Yard, Vallejo, Cal	12 Sept 1941	AA
Nereus	AS-17	Mare Island Navy Yard, Vallejo, Cal	27 Oct 1945	PR
Orion	AS-18	Moore DD Co. Inc, Oakland, Cal	30 Sept 1943	AA

Displacement Light, 9,957–11,150 tons; full load, 16,230–17,020 tons
Length overall 530.5ft (161.7m)
Maximum beam 73.3ft (22.3m)
Maximum draught 25.5ft (7.8m)
Main machinery Eight General Motors diesel engines
Screws/b.h.p. 2/11,200
Maximum speed 15.4 knots
Armament Two single 5in/38 gun mounts (AS-17); four single 20mm (Mark 67) gun mounts (AS-11, -18); two twin 20mm (Mark 24) gun mounts (AS-17)
Complement 48/59 officers, 797-936 enlisted men

This class has the same basic hull design as the *Dixie*-class destroyer tenders and the *Vulcan*-class repair ships. These ships received a FRAM II modernisation in the early 1970s, which gave them the capability to service nuclear-powered submarines. Workshops were added and the existing ones upgraded to handle the sophisticated electronic equipment, weapons and powerplant. Originally there were seven ships in the class. *Proteus* (AS-19) was modified to FBM Tender. *Sperry* was decommissioned on 30 September, 1982, and struck from the Navy List. She is to be retained for the support of the remaining active units of the class. *Nereus* was decommissioned at Mare Island on 27 October, 1971, and laid up. These ships are all equipped as flagships.

Radar: AN/SPS-10 surface search (AS-11, -12, -18).

Disposals: *Howard W. Gilmore* (AS-16) was struck off the Naval Register on 1 December, 1980. One of the findings of the routine inspection conducted by the Board of Inspection Survey on every ship about to be decommissioned was that *Howard W. Gilmore* was the filthiest ship that any officer on the board could recall seeing in their entire naval service. *Bushnell* (AS-15) was struck from the NVR on 15 November, 1980, and will be expended as a target.

The *Fulton*-class AS *Orion*. Of the seven *Fulton*-class units built, she and *Fulton* are the only ships still active *(US Navy)*

Type: Submarine Rescue Ships (ASR) *Number/Class:* 2 *Pigeon*

Name	*Number*	*Laid down*	*Launched*	*Commissioned*	*Status*
Pigeon	ASR-21	17 July 1968	13 Aug 1969	28 Apr 1973	PA
Ortolan	ASR-22	22 Aug 1968	10 Sept 1969	14 July 1973	AA

Builder Alabama DD and SB Co, Mobile, Ala
Displacement Light, 2,725 tons; full load, 3,411 tons
Length overall 251ft (76.5m)
Maximum beam 86ft (26.2m) (see notes)
Maximum draught 21.3ft (6.5m)
Main machinery Four Alco diesel engines
Screws/b.h.p. 2/6,000

Pigeon (ASR-21), one of three operational catamarans in the Navy *(US Navy)*

Maximum speed 15 knots
Armament Two single 20mm (Mark 67) gun mounts
Complement 115 total (6 officers, 109 enlisted men). Staff accommodation: 14 total (4 officers, 10 enlisted men). Submersible operators: 24 total (4 officers, 20 enlisted men)

This class comprises two of the three catamarans built for the Navy (*Hayes*, AGOR-16, being the third), and is the first specifically designed and built for submarine rescue. These vessels were authorised in the FY-1967 (ASR-21) and FY-1968 (ASR-22) programmes, to SCB-721 design. The advantages of the catamaran hull are many. A large deck area is available, facilities for handling submersibles are improved as well as for operating underwater equipment, and there is greater stability while operating equipment at extreme depths.

Each hull of these ships is 251ft (76.5m) by 26ft (7.9m) with a 34ft (10.4m) wide well in-between. There is a 200-ton crane aft, and a helicopter deck but no hangar. Each ship is equipped with the McCann rescue chamber and a decompression chamber, and can act as a mother ship for a Deep Submergence Rescue Vehicle (DSRV), for major deep diving support, and as the flagship of a salvage operation.

Radar: AN/SPS-53 air search. Electronics: OE-82 satellite communications antenna, SSR-1 receiver and WSC-3 transceiver.

Space and weight has been reserved for installation of one bow thruster in each hull. The Navy had planned to build a total of ten of this class, but only two were funded.

Ortolan, sister ship to *Pigeon*. The large objects on each bow are flotation pontoons for submarine salvage *(US Navy)*

Type: Submarine Rescue Ship (ASR) — *Number/Class:* 4 *Chanticleer*

Name	*Number*	*Builder*	*Commissioned*	*Status*
Florikan	ASR-9	Moore SB and DD Co, Oakland, Cal	5 Apr 1943	PA
Kittiwake	ASR-13	Savannah Mach and Foundry Co, Savannah, Ga	18 July 1946	AA
Petrel	ASR-14	Savannah Mach and Foundry Co, Savannah, Ga	24 Sept 1946	AA
Sunbird	ASR-15	Savannah Mach and Foundry Co, Savannah, Ga	28 Jan 1947	AA

Displacement Light, 1,790 tons; full load, 2,320 tons
Length overall 251.5ft (76.6m)
Maximum beam 44ft (13.4m)
Maximum draught 16ft (4.9m)
Main machinery Four diesel engines (Alco: ASR-9, -15) and General Motors (remainder)
Screws/b.h.p. 1/3,000
Maximum speed 16 knots
Armament Two single 20mm (Mark 68) gun mounts
Complement 10–11 officers, 86–112 enlisted men

These large tug-boat type ships are equipped with heavy air compressors, rescue chambers and powerful pumps. They can no longer meet the demands of contemporary submarine salvage and/or rescue operations, but owing to a lack of suitable replacements the Navy is forced to retain them and make the best use they can of them. The original two single 3in/50 gun mounts were removed 1957–1958.

Radar: AN/SPS-53 air search.

Class notes: Originally a seven-ship class, construction on *Verdin* (ASR-17) and *Windhover* (ASR-18) was cancelled on 11 August, 1945; *Macaw* (ASR-11) was sunk on 12 February, 1944; *Chanticleer* (ASR-7) was struck from the NVR on 9 September, 1973, and scrapped; *Coucal* (ASR-8) was struck on 15 September, 1977. *Greenlet* (ASR-10) loaned to Turkey on 12 June, 1970, was struck off on 1 February, 1973, and finally sold to Turkey on 15 February, 1973, *Tringa* (ASR-16) was struck from the NVR on 30 September, 1977, and expended as a target.

Florikan, one of four survivors of the original seven *Chanticleer*-class ASRs. They are virtually obsolete, being retained only because of the lack of any suitable replacement

Type: Auxiliary Ocean Tugs (ATA) — *Number/Class:* 1 *Sotoyomo*

Name	Number	Builder	Commissioned	Status
Accokeek (ex ATR-108)	ATA-181	Levingston SB Co, Orange, Texas	7 Oct 1944	MAR

Displacement Light, 534 tons; full load, 860 tons
Length overall 143ft (43.6m)
Maximum beam 33.9ft (10.3m)
Maximum draught 13ft (4m)
Main machinery Two General Motors diesel engines
Screws/b.h.p. 1/1,500
Maximum speed 13 knots
Complement 5 officers, 44 enlisted men

The last survivor of a class of numerous steel-hulled tugs originally ordered as Rescue Tugs (ATR). Reclassified ATA on 15 May, 1944, and named in 1948, *Accokeek* was laid down 15 June, 1944, and launched on 27 July, 1944. Many sister ships serve in foreign navies and commercially. *Accokeek* was decommissioned at Norfolk on 2 July, 1971, and was then transferred for layup to the Maritime Reserve Fleet, James River, on 19 September, 1972, where she remains.

Disposals: *Kalmia* (ATA-184), struck from the Naval Vessel Register on 31 October, 1977, was sold to Columbia on 31 March, 1978, after being on loan to that country since 1 July, 1971; *Cahokia* (ATA-186), leased to Taiwan from 14 April, 1972, was struck on 15 April, 1976, and sold to Taiwan on 19 May, 1976; *Salish* (ATA-187) was struck on 14 February, 1976, and sold on the same date to Argentina, having been on lease since 10 February, 1972; *Samoset* (ATA-190), struck on 1 July, 1978, was sold to Haiti on 16 October, 1978; *Tillamook* (ATA-192), on lease to South Korea since 9 August, 1971, was struck on 15 April, 1976, and sold to that country; *Tatnuck* (ATA-195) was struck on 1 October, 1977; *Mahopac* (ATA-196) was struck on 15 April, 1976, and sold to Taiwan on 19 May, 1976, having been leased by that country since 1 July, 1971; *Sagamore* (ATA-208) was sold to the Dominican Republic 31 December, 1980, having been on lease since 1 February, 1972; *Catawba* (ATA-210), struck on 1 February, 1975, was sold to Argentina on 14 February, 1976, having been on lease to that country since 10 February, 1972; and *Keywadin* (ATA-213) was struck from the NVR on 1 June, 1980, and is now in the MARAD Reserve Fleet, James River.

Accokeek (ATA-181), sole US Navy survivor of the once numerous class *(US Navy)*

Type: Fleet Ocean Tugs (ATF) — *Number/Class:* 7 *Powhatan*

Name	Number	Laid down	Launched	Assigned to MSC	Status
Powhatan	T-ATF-166	30 Sept 1976	24 June 1978	15 June 1979	MSC
Narragansett	T-ATF-167	5 May 1977	12 May 1979	9 Nov 1979	MSC
Catawba	T-ATF-168	14 Dec 1977	22 Sept 1979	28 May 1980	MSC
Navajo	T-ATF-169	14 Dec 1977	20 Dec 1979	13 June 1980	MSC
Mohawk	T-ATF-170	22 Mar 1979	12 May 1980	16 Oct 1980	MSC
Sioux	T-ATF-171	22 Mar 1979	15 Nov 1980	1 May 1981	MSC
Apache	T-ATF-172	22 Mar 1979	28 Mar 1981	23 July 1981	MSC

Builder Marinette Marine Corp, Marinette, Wisc
Displacement Full load, 2,000 tons
Length overall 225ft (68.6m)
Maximum beam 42ft (12.8m)
Maximum draught 15ft (4.6m)
Main machinery One General Motors diesel engine
Screws/b.h.p. 2 (controllable pitch)/4,500
Maximum speed 15 knots
Complement 17 civilians, 4 USN communications contingent

These are the first Fleet Tugs to be built since the Second World War. The wartime *Cherokee* and *Abnaki* class tugs reached block obselescence, and it was planned to replace all of them with units of this class, but funding was dropped after only seven had been built.

Adapted from commercial standards, these tugs (SCB-744) were authorised in the FY-1975 (ATF-166–169) and FY-1978 (ATF-170–172) Programmes. The estimated construction cost has risen form $11.5 million (ATF-166) to $17.2 million (ATF-170–172).

The *Powhatans* are operated by the Military Sealift Command and are civilian manned. Habitability is to civilian standards. These ships have fire fighting and salvage capability, a bollard pull of 53.9 tons and can tow ships of up to 60,000 tons displacement. They have a 10-ton capacity crane, and 300 h.p. bow thrusters are fitted to aid manoeuvring. Included in the ship's complement is a salvaging and diving detachment. Although MSC ships are unarmed, space is provided for the installation of two single 20mm gun mounts and two .50 calibre machine guns.

Navajo (T-ATF-169) seen during the towing of *New Jersey* (BB-62) to Long Beach. Based on a commercial design, the seven-unit *Powhatan* class has proved quite successful *(US Navy)*

Type: Fleet Ocean Tugs (ATF) — *Number/Class:* 1 *Cherokee*, 7 *Abnaki*

Name	Number	Builder	Commissioned	Status
Seneca	ATF-91	Cramp SB Co, Phila, Pa	30 Apr 1943	MAR
Moctobi	ATF-105	Charleston SB and DD Co, Charleston, S.C.	25 July 1944	NRF
Quapaw	ATF-110	United Engineering Co, Alameda, Cal	6 May 1944	NRF
Takelma	ATF-113	United Engineering Co, Alameda, Cal	3 Aug 1944	NRF
Atakapa	ATF-149	Charleston SB and DD Co, Charleston, S.C.	8 Dec 1944	MAR
Mosopelea	ATF-158	Charleston SB and DD Co, Charleston, S.C.	28 July 1945	MAR
Paiute	ATF-159	Charleston SB and DD Co, Charleston, S.C.	27 Aug 1945	NRF
Papago	ATF-160	Charleston SB and DD Co, Charleston, S.C.	3 Oct 1945	NRF

Displacement Light, 1,235 tons; full load, 1,640 tons
Length overall 205ft (62.5m)
Maximum beam 38.5ft (11.7m)
Maximum draught 17ft (5.2m)
Main machinery One diesel engine (Alco in ATF-105, -113; Caterpillar Tractor in ATF-110 and General Motors [remainder])
Screws/b.h.p. 1/3,000
Maximum speed 16.5 knots
Armament Removed
Complement 5 officers, 70 enlisted men

These large ocean tugs are fitted with powerful pumps and salvage equipment. Although basically of one class, they are actually from two, the main difference between the classes being the type of external engine exhaust. *Mosopelea* and *Atakapa* served with the Military Sealift Command from July 1973 and August 1974, respectively until being transferred to the MARAD Reserve Fleet at James River on 1 October, 1981 for layup. *Seneca* was transferred to the MARAD Reserve Fleet, James River, on 18 November, 1971 for layup.

The following ships have been assigned to the Naval Reserve Force: *Moctobi* (ATF-105) on 1 January, 1977, at Everett, Wash; *Quapaw* (ATF-110) on 30 September, 1977, at Port Hueneme, Cal; *Takelma* (ATF-113) on 1 June,

1979, at San Diego, Cal; *Paiute* (ATF-159) on 1 February, 1977, at Maryport, Fla.; and *Papago* (ATF-160) on 1 August, 1977, at Little Creek, Va.

Four sisters were transferred to the Coast Guard for further service after the Second World War. *Ute* (ATF-76) and *Lipan* (ATF-85) were transferred on 30 September, 1980, joining their sister ships as Medium Endurance Cutters (WMEC).

Radar: AN/SPS-53 air search (NRF ships only). Electronics: OE-82 satellite communications antenna, SSR-1 receiver and WSC-3 transceiver in *Moctobi* only.

Disposals: *Kiowa* (ATF-72) was sold to the Dominican Republic on 31 December, 1980; *Bannock* (ATF-81) was struck off the Navy List on 1 December, 1977, and sold to Italy in May 1979 having previously been on loan. *Carib* (ATF-82), *Hidasta* (ATF-102) and *Jicarilla* (ATF-104) were sold to Columbia on 15 March, 1979, having previously been laid up in MARAD James River since being struck on 1 July, 1963. *Abnaki* (AFT-96), *Cocopa* (ATF-101), and *Hitchiti* (ATF-103) were sold to Mexico on 30 September, 1978; *Molala* (ATF-106) was sold to Mexico on 1 August, 1978. *Cusabo* (ATF-155) was sold to Ecuador on 30 August, 1978, having previously been on loan to that country. *Nipmuc* (ATF-157) and *Salinan* (ATF-161) were struck and sold to Venezuela on 1 September, 1978; *Shakori* (ATF-162) was sold to Taiwan on 29 August, 1980.

Takelma (ATF-113), one of eight surviving units of the *Cherokee/Abnaki* classes *(US Navy)*

Type: Salvage and Rescue Ships (ATS) — *Number/Class:* 3 *Edenton*

Name	Number	Laid down	Launched	Commissioned	Status
Edenton	ATS-1	1 Apr 1967	15 May 1968	23 Jan 1971	AA
Beaufort	ATS-2	19 Feb 1968	20 Dec 1968	22 Jan 1972	PA
Brunswick	ATS-3	5 June 1968	14 Oct 1969	19 Dec 1972	PA

Builder Brooke Marine, Ltd, Lowestoft, England
Displacement Full load, 2,929 tons
Length overall 282.6ft (86.1m)
Maximum beam 50ft (15.2m)
Maximum draught 15.1ft (4.6m)
Main machinery Four Davey-Paxman diesel engines
Screws/b.h.p. 2 controllable pitch/6,000
Maximum speed 16 knots
Armament Two twin 20mm (Mark 24) gun mounts (ATS-1); two single 20mm (Mark 68) gun mounts (ATS-2, -3)
Complement 100 total (9 officers, 91 enlisted men)

Originally rated as Salvage Tugs (ATS), these vessels were re-rated on 16 February, 1971, to Salvage and Rescue Ships (ATS). British-built ships, they suffer from spares problems because they need British-made components. Authorised in the FY-1966 (ATS-1) and FY-1967 (ATS-2 and -3) Programmes, they were built to SCB-719 design. ATS-4 was authorised in FY-1972, and ATS-5 and -6 in FY-1973, but their construction was dropped due to their size and escalating costs. Fitted with twin rudders, controllable pitch propellers and a 70-ton self tensioning towing winch, these ships achieve precise manoeuvring by means of a tunnel bow thruster. One 10-ton crane is forward, and a 20-ton crane aft.

Each ship can lift up to 267.9 tons from a depth of 120ft (36.6m). In addition to heavy ocean-towing, salvage, and fire fighting operations, these ships can carry the Mark 1 Deep Diving Systems, which can support four divers, working in two-man shifts, at depths of 850ft (258.9m).

Radar: AN/SPS-53D air search.

Though *Edenton* (ATS-1) has proved effective, supply problems resulted in the cancellation of additional units *(US Navy)*

Type: Guided Missile Ship (AVM) — *Number/Class:* 1 Converted *Currituck*

Name	Number	Builder	Commissioned	Status
Norton Sound (ex AV-11)	AVM-1	Los Angeles SB abd DD Co, San Pedro, Cal	8 Jan 1945	PA

Displacement Light, 10,310 tons; full load, 13,590 tons
Length overall 540.6ft (164.8m)
Maximum beam 71.6ft (21.8m)
Maximum draught 23.5ft (7.2m)
Main machinery Two Allis-Chalmers geared turbines. Four Babcock and Wilcox boilers
Screws/s.h.p. 2/12,000
Maximum speed 19 knots
Armament One twin Standard missile Mark 26 launcher (tests only)
Complement 86 officers, 664 enlisted men

First commissioned as a Seaplane Tender of the *Currituck* class, this vessel was laid down on 7 September, 1942, and launched on 28 November, 1943. Its conversion to a Guided Missile Test Ship by the Philadelphia Naval Shipyard took seven months (1948–1949). The familiar 30-ton capacity crane aft was removed and a helicopter deck was fitted forward. Provision was made for the complete handling and test-firing of missiles and rockets. Reclassified AVM-1 on 8 August, 1951, as an operational testbed *Norton Sound* has tested a wide variety of new weapons and electronic systems, including Loon, Lark, Regulus, Terrier, Tartar, the Aegis system, the lightweight 5in/54 gun mount, and the Sea Sparrow missile.

Further conversion was authorised in the FY-1963 Programme (SCB-233), and from 21 November, 1962, to 13 June, 1964, she was converted by the Maryland SB and DD Company, Baltimore, Md to serve an operational test ship for the *Typhon* missile system. *Typhon* was intended for the planned nuclear-powered Guided Missile Frigates, but this project was cancelled when it was found that the system would not fit the ships for which it was intended.

In 1968 AVM-1 was fitted with the new lightweight 5in/54 gun mount and its Mark 86 Gunfire Control System for testing and evaluation. This was followed by more modification to serve as the evaluation platform for Aegis, the advanced fleet defence system to be mounted on the *Ticonderoga*-class CGs.

Norton Sound is currently testing the new EX-41 eight-cell (two × four) missile Vertical Launch System (VLS) module, one of which was fitted in her bow in May–June 1982 at Ingalls SB Corp, Pascagoula, Miss. Tests are being conducted in conjunction with the already-installed AN/SPY-1A Aegis system. The EX-41 has a mixed load (Tomahawk and Standard (SM-2)) firing capability.

Radars: AN/SPS-40 air search and AN/SPS-10 surface search.

Note The Auxiliary Aircraft Landing Training Ship *Lexington* (AVT-16) is listed in the Aircraft Carrier chapter with the *Hancock/Intrepid* classes of aircraft carriers.

Norton Sound (AVM-1) pictured in 1974, when she was serving as a test platform for the Aegis (AN/SPY-IA) system, the antennae of which can be seen directly above the bridge. She is currently serving as a test ship for the EX-41 Vertical Launch Missile System (VLS) *(US Navy)*

SERVICE CRAFT
Dry Docks

Type: Large Auxiliary Floating Dry Docks (AFDB) (non-self-propelled) *Number:* 5

Name	Number	Status
Artisan	AFDB-1	Active: Sections B-E. Section F was struck from the Naval Register on 1 November, 1981, for use as a bombing target.
	AFDB-2	Active: Sections C, D, F, H and I joined with AFDB-1 to form *Artisan* Reserve: Sections A, B, E, G and J at Pearl Harbor.
	AFDB-4	Reserve: Sections A-G at Bremerton.
	AFDB-5	Reserve: Sections A-G at Pearl Harbor.
Los Alamos	AFDB-7	Active: Sections C-E and G at Holy Loch, Scotland. Reserve: Sections A and B at Philadelphia.

Displacement Light, 38,500 tons (AFDB-1, -2); 30,800 tons (remainder)
Lifting capacity 90,000 tons (AFDB-1, -2); 55,000 tons (AFDB-4, -5); 40,000 tons (AFDB-7)
Length overall 825ft (251.3m) to 927ft (282.4m)
Length on pontoons 398.8ft (121.5m) to 827ft (251.9m)
Maximum draught 67.3ft (20.5m) to 78ft (23.8m)
Light draught 8.7ft (2.65m) to 9ft (2.7m)
Over blocks draught 119.5ft (36.4m) to 133.6ft (40.7m) (clear)

These large dry docks, constructed of steel, were completed between July 1943 and March 1945. They are actually in two classes: AFDB-1 and -2, and AFDB-4, -5 and -7.

The large floating dry docks provide repair facilities in forward combat areas and support ballistic missile submarines at advanced bases. In addition, they supplement dry dock facilities at major shipyards. They can dock up to CV/BB size (AFDB-7 is used to dock SSBNs). The docks consist of seven to ten steel sections that are detachable for towing and maintenance. Each section is 256ft (78m) long and 80ft (24.4m) wide. Wing walls are 83ft (25.3m) high, and fold down when the sections are towed.

The active portions of *Artisan* (AFDB-1) and AFDB-2 are joined together to form one active nine-section dock named *Artisan* (AFDB-1). AFDB-3 was struck off the Navy List on 1 August, 1981, and donated to the State of Maine on 10 March, 1982.

This view of AFDB-1 illustrates the enormous size of these 10-section docks, which can accommodate an *Iowa*-class battleship *(US Navy)*

Los Alamos (AFDB-7) with *Robert E. Lee*, then an SSBN, high and dry inside *(US Navy)*

Type: Medium Auxiliary Floating Dry Docks (AFDM) (non-self-propelled) — *Number:* 9

Name	*Number*	*Status*
(ex YFD-3)	AFDM-1	Commercial lease to Todd Shipyards Corp, Galveston, Tex
(ex YFD-4)	AFDM-2	Commercial lease to Todd Shipyards Corp, New Orleans, La
(ex YFD-6)	AFDM-3	Commercial lease to Todd Shipyards Corp, New Orleans, La
Resourceful (ex YFD-21)	AFDM-5	Active: Subic Bay, Philippine Islands
Competent (ex YFD-62)	AFDM-6	Active: Pearl Harbor, Hawaii
Sustain (ex YFD-63)	AFDM-7	Active: Norfolk, Virginia
Richland (ex YFD-64)	AFDM-8	Active: Guam, Marianas Islands
(ex YFD-65)	AFDM-9	Commercial lease to Jacksonville Shipyard, Fla
Resolute	AFDM-10	Active: Norfolk, Virginia (placed "in service" on 2 June, 1981)

Displacement Light, 6,400–8,000 tons
Lifting capacity 15,000–18,000 tons (nominal)
Length overall 615.7ft (187.5m) to 622ft (189.5m)
Length on pontoons 544ft (165.7m) to 552ft (168.1m)
Maximum draught 31.8ft (9.7m) to 52.8ft (16.1m)
Light draught 5.7ft (1.74m) to 6.1ft (1.86m)
Over blocks draught 28ft (8.5m) to 31ft (9.4m)
Inside width 87.5ft (26.7m) to 93.1ft (28.4m) (clear)

These steel floating dry docks were completed between July 1942 and March 1945. One dock is formed by joining three steel sections together. Normally used to dock CG/DD types, they are divided into two classes: AFDM-1 (AFDM-1/3) and AFDM-5 (AFDM-5/10). Except for AFDM-10, all are former YFDs.

AFDM-7 was named on 9 May, 1979, AFDM-5 and -6 on 7 June, 1979, and AFDM-10 on 9 April, 1982.

Type: Medium Auxiliary Floating Dry Docks (ARDM) (non-self-propelled) — *Number:* 4+1

Name	*Number*	*Status*
Oak Ridge (ex ARD-19)	ARDM-1	Active: Kings Bay, Georgia
Alamagordo (ex ARD-26)	ARDM-2	Active: Charleston, South Carolina
Endurance (ex ARD-18)	ARDM-3	Active: Charleston, South Carolina
Shippingport	ARDM-4	Active: New London, Connecticut
—	ARDM-5	Bldg: Todd Shipyards, Seattle

Displacement Light, 5,200 tons (ARDM-1/3); 5,300 tons (ARDM-4); not available (ARDM-5)
Lifting capacity 8,000 tons (ARDM-1, -2); 5,500 tons (ARDM-3); 17,000 tons (ARDM-4); not available (ARDM-5)
Length overall 536.1ft (163.4m) (ARDM-1, -2); 512.6ft (156.1m) (ARDM-3); 492ft (149.9m) (ARDM-4, -5)
Length of pontoons 456.1ft (139m) (ARDM-1/3); not available (ARDM-4); not available (ARDM-5)
Maximum draught 42ft (12.8m) (ARDM-1/3); 33ft (10.1m) (ARDM-4); not available (ARDM-5)
Light draught 7ft (2.1m) (ARDM-1/3); not available (ARDM-4, -5)
Over blocks draught 31ft (9.5m) (ARDM-1/3); not available (ARDM-4, -5)
Inside width 59ft (18m) (ARDM-1, -2); 39.2ft (11.9m) (ARDM-3); not available (ARDM-4, -5)

Of steel construction, these dry docks can handle all submarines except the Trident SSBNs. ARDM-1 to 3 were completed between February 1944 and June 1944 as ARD-19, -26 and -18, respectively. ARD-19 and -26 were converted to ARDMs during 1961/1965, and ARDM-3 received a less austere conversion during 1968/1969.

ARDM-1 was commissioned in December 1963 as *Oak Ridge* (ARDM-1). ARDM-2 was commissioned in August 1965 as *Alamagordo* (ARDM-2), but sank at Charleston on 10 November, 1965, while docking a ballistic missile submarine (SSBN). She was raised, repaired, and recommissioned in June 1966. ARDM-3 was placed "in service" in October 1971.

ARDM-4 is of new construction, having been authorised in the FY-1975 Programme. A contract for construction was awarded to Bethlehem Steel Co., Sparrows Point, Maryland, on 23 October, 1975. Construction began on 19 July, 1976, she was completed on 4 January, 1979. Named *Shippingport* on 7 June, 1979, this floating dry dock was built specifically to service the *Los Angeles* (SSN-688) class submarines, and is the first US Navy dock constructed to handle nuclear-powered ships. ARDM-5 was authorised in FY-1983 and the contract awarded to Todd Shipyards, Seattle, on 13 October 1982. Construction cost is estimated at $32.7 million and completion is scheduled for 1986. The dock will then be assigned to San Diego Naval Station.

Type: Auxiliary Repair Dry Docks (ARD) (non-self-propelled) — *Number:* 3

Name	*Number*	*Status*
Waterford	ARD-5	Active: New London, Connecticut
West Milton	ARD-7	Reserve: Maritime Administration, James River, since 30 June, 1981
San Onofre	ARD-30	Active: San Diego, California

Displacement Light, 1,300 tons (ARD-5); 4,200 tons (ARD-7); 5,200 tons (ARD-30)
Lifting capacity 3,500 tons (nominal)
Length overall 485.7ft (147.9m) to 491.7ft (149.8m)
Length on pontoons 414ft (126.1m)
Maximum draught 32.6ft (9.9m) to 32.9ft (10m)
Light draught 5ft (1.5m) to 5.7ft (1.7m)
Over blocks draught 21.1ft (6.4m) to 21.6ft (6.6m)
Inside width 49ft (14.9m) to 59ft (18m) (clear)

These one-piece steel dry docks, normally used to dock LST and small DD/SSN/FF types, were completed during 1942/1944. Two classes are combined here: ARD-1 (ARD-5 and -7) and ARD-12 (ARD-30). Three sisters of the ARD-1 class have been converted to ARDMs (see ARDM Section), and ARD-20 became *White Sands* (AGDS-1), since disposed of. These units were named as follows: ARD-5 on 17 November, 1976, ARD-7 on 18 May, 1976, and ARD-30 on 7 March, 1978.

To facilitate towing, ARD-type docks have the forward end of the docking well closed by a bow-structure topped by a bridge.

Disposals: ARD-28 was sold to Columbia on 4 February, 1981, for scrapping, having previously been on lease. The following ARDs have been leased or sold to foreign navies for service: ARD-2, -6, -8, -9, -11 to -15, -17, *Windsor* (ARD-22), -23 to -25, *Arco* (ARD-29), and ARD-32.

San Onofre (ARD-30), one of three remaining ARDs in the Navy, is currently active at San Diego Naval Station *(US Navy)*

Type: Small Auxiliary Floating Dry Docks (AFDL) (non-self-propelled) — *Number:* 10

Name	*Number*	*Status*
Endeavor	AFDL-1	Guantanamo Bay, Cuba
Dynamic	AFDL-6	Active: Little Creek, Virginia
	AFDL-12	Commercial lease to SEA-TAC, Seattle, Washington
	AFDL-15	Commercial lease to Hendry Corp., Tampa, Florida
	AFDL-21	Commercial lease to Dillingham Shipyard Inc., Honolulu, Hawaii
Adept	AFDL-23	Active: Subic Bay, Philippine Islands
	AFDL-25	Commercial lease to Puerto Rico DD and Repair Co., San Juan, Puerto Rico
	AFDL-40	Commercial lease to Dillingham Shipyard Inc., Honolulu, Hawaii
Reliance	AFDL-47	Activation plans cancelled; transferred to Maritime Administration, James River, on 12 August, 1981, for layup
Diligence	AFDL-48	To be commercially leased (out of service 23 May, 1980)

Displacement Light, 800–13,000 tons (nominal)
Lifting capacity 4,000 tons (AFDL-48); 2,800 tons (AFDL-40, -41); 1,900 tons (AFDL-23); 1,000 tons (remainder)
Length overall 200ft (60.9m) to 489ft (148.9m)
Length on pontoons 200ft (60.9m) to 448ft (135.5m)
Maximum draught 28.5ft (8.7m) to 46.9ft (14.3m)
Light draught (3.2ft (0.97m) to 13.4ft (4.1m)
Over blocks draught 15.1ft (4.6m) to 26ft (7.9m)
Inside width 45ft (13.7m) to 70ft (21.3m) (clear)

Four separate classes grouped together. These units were completed between September 1943 and December 1944 (AFDL-48 completed June 1956). AFDL-1 class consists of AFDL-1, -6, -9, -12, -15, -21, -25 and -29; AFDL-23 is the sole survivor of the AFDL-7 class. AFDL-40 and -41 compromise the AFDL-35 class; AFDL-47 and -48 are one-unit classes. The AFDL-35 and -48 classes are constructed of concrete; the remaining AFDLs are of steel. A new construction dock, numbered AFDL-49, was authorised in FY1958 but never built. These small Auxiliary Floating Dry Docks are normally used to dock DD/LST/FF/ATA/ATF/MSO types. Unlike their larger counterparts, AFDLs are single sections. AFDL-1, -6, -23, -47 and -48 were named on 7 June, 1979.

The following docks have been struck from the Naval Register: *Ability* (AFDL-7) on 15 February, 1981; AFDL-37, -38 and -45 on 1 October, 1981; AFDL-2 on 15 November, 1981; AFDL-8 on 1 December, 1981, AFDL-16 on 15 May, 1982, AFDL-9 on 15 May, 1982, AFDL-19 on 28 April, 1983, AFDL-41 on 30 April, 1983, and AFDL-29 on 13 July, 1983. All were sold commercially. Many units of this type have been leased, loaned, or sold outright to foreign navies or are in commercial use.

Type: Yard Floating Dry Docks (non-self-propelled) (YFD) — *Number:* 7

Number	*Status*
YFD-23	Commercial lease at Lockheed SB and Construction, Co, Seattle, Wash
YFD-54	Commercial lease at Todd Pacific Shipyard, Seattle, Wash
YFD-68	Commercial lease at Todd Pacific Shipyard, San Pedro, Cal
YFD-69	Commercial lease at Port of Portland, Ore
YFD-70	Commercial lease at Todd Pacific Shipyard, Seattle, Wash
YFD-71	Overhaul at Guam, August 1981 to March 1984, then active at San Diego Naval Station (now **Steadfast** (AFDM-10))
YFD-83 (ex AFDL-31)	On loan to the US Coast Guard since January 1947. Based at Curtis Bay Shipyard, Baltimore, Md

Displacement Light, 800 to 8,400 tons
Lifting capacity 1,000 to 20,000 tons (nominal)
Length overall 200ft (60.9m) to 658.9ft (200.7m)
Length on pontoons 200ft (60.9m) to 587.2ft (178.9m)
Maximum draught 28.5ft (8.7m) to 49.7ft (15.1m)
Light draught 3.4ft (1.04m) to 8.2ft (2.50m)
Over blocks draught 15.9ft (4.8m) to 28ft (8.5m)
Inside width, clear 45ft (13.7m) to 98ft (29.9m)

A collection of a wide range of sizes, ranging from one-sectional steel to six-sectional timber docks. These were completed between July 1943 to July 1945 and constructed of steel with the exception of YFD-23 and 54, which are made of wood. This miscellaneous group can dock from the smallest of ships up to cruisers. The docks with two sections or more can be split to facilitate towing. All units are one-unit classes. Many YFDs have been converted to AFDMs. YFD-71, a one-section dry dock, was returned from commercial lease in January 1973 and placed "in service" for Navy use at San Diego (see page 234).

Disposals: YFD-8 was struck from the Naval Register on 15 November, 1981; YFD-9 was struck on 12 July, 1979. Both were sold commercially.

Self-Propelled Service Craft

Type: Unclassified Miscellaneous (IX)

Summary of Unclassified Miscellaneous Vessels IX-505 through 511.

IX-511 Originally commissioned on 5 January, 1943, as LST-399. Transferred to Military Sea Transportation Service (MSTS) in March 1952 for service as T-LST-399. She served with MSTS, later MSC, until 1 November, 1973, when she was stricken and transferred to the MARAD Reserve Fleet at Suisun Bay, Cal, for layup. Reacquired on 25 November, 1980, for use as a range tender and support ship at the Pacific Missile Range, Point Mugu, Cal. Reinstated on the NVR on 30 September, 1982, and reclassified IX-511 on the same date. Current status: active, in service, Pacific Fleet.

IX-510 Originally ex-*General William O. Darby* (AP-127). See under *Admiral William S. Benson* class APs for details.

IX-509 Originally Underwater Explosives Barge No. 1 and rated as "floating equipment". Classified IX-509 on 1 December, 1979, and instated on the Naval Vessel Register (NVR) on the same date. Displacement, 3,000 tons; length overall, 184ft (56.1m); extreme beam, 12ft (3.7m). IX-509 is based at the David W. Taylor Naval Ship Research and Development Centre.

IX-508 Originally LCU-1618. Reclassified IX-508 on 1 December, 1979, replacing IX-505 (ex YTM-759). Converted to a range support craft during September/November 1977 for the Naval Ocean Systems Centre (NOSC). The following major modifications were made: installation of a bow thruster, construction and installation of a bridge and pilot house, installation of a hangar-type enclosed storage area for support of the Centre's underway Recovery Vehicles CURV II and III, installation of a multiple torpedo tube mount and an HIAB crane. For basic characteristics, see under Amphibious chapter, "LCU-1610" class. Classified as "floating equipment" from September 1977 to 1 December, 1979.

IX-507 The transport *General Hugh J. Geoffrey* (AP-121) was instated on the NVR and reclassified IX-507 on 1 November, 1978. See under *Admiral William S. Benson* class in the Auxiliary Section for basic details on characteristics. Converted and based at Puget Sound Naval Shipyard, Bremerton, Wash.

IX-506 Originally YFU-82 of the "YFU-71" class. Reclassified IX-506 on 1 April, 1978. Assigned to the Naval Oceanographic Systems Centre. This craft is 125ft (38.1m) long; has a light displacement of 220 tons and a full load displacement of 380 tons. She is powered by two General Motors diesel engines (two screws/1,000 b.h.p.) and has a complement of two officers and ten enlisted men. Details of configuration not available.

IX-505 IX-505 was originally YTM-759. She was struck from the Naval Vessel Register on 1 December, 1977, and sold, being replaced by IX-508.

IX-509, seen while still rated as Underwater Explosive Barge No 1

Type: Unclassified Miscellaneous (IX) — *Number/Class:* 3 *Benewah*

Name	Number	Builder	Commissioned	Status
Mercer (ex APB-39; APL-39)	IX-502	Boston Navy Yard, Boston, Mass	19 Sept 1945	PSA
Nueces (ex APB-40; APL-40)	IX-503	Boston Navy Yard, Boston, Mass	30 Nov 1945	PSA
Echols (ex APB-37; APL-37)	IX-504	Boston Navy Yard, Boston, Mass	—	ASA

Displacement Full load 4,080 tons
Length overall 328ft (99.9m)
Maximum beam 50ft (15.2m)
Maximum draught 14.1ft (4.29m)
Main machinery General Motors diesel engines
Screws/b.h.p. 2/1,800
Maximum speed 12 knots
Armament Varies
Complement 13 officers, 180 enlisted men (as APB)
Troops 16 officers, 1,210 enlisted men (as APB)

These vessels have basic LST type hull and characteristics, but were built as self-propelled barracks ships (APB) to provide support and accommodation for small craft and riverine forces. All were originally classified as APLs, but were reclassified APB on 11 August, 1944, (APB-37) and 7 August, 1944, (APB-39 and -40). *Mercer* and *Nueces* were reclassified IX-502 and -503, respectively, on 1 November, 1975; *Echols* became IX-504 on 1 February, 1976.

Barracks ships have complete facilities for berthing and messing. They carry fresh water evaporators (40,000gal per day), and include living and working space and a 16-bed hospital with other medical facilities. *Nueces* and *Mercer* were recommissioned on 3 May, 1968, and 9 May, 1968, respectively for service in Vietnam. *Echols*, which was put in reserve in January 1947 right after trials, was scheduled to be commissioned in 1969 for Vietnam operations, but this was cancelled.

Those units recommissioned were again decomissioned on 13 March, 1970, at San Diego (IX-503) and 7 January, 1970, at Mare Island (IX-502). *Mercer* and *Nueces* were put back in service in 1974 and *Echols* in 1976 to relieve the shortage of berthing facilities at Bremerton and Groton. IX-502 and -503 are based at Bremerton and IX-504 is at Groton. They serve as "homes" for crews whose ships are in overhaul or under construction.

Disposal: *Benewah* (IX-311, ex APB-35) was struck off the Naval Register on 1 September, 1973, and transferred to the Philippines on 22 May, 1974 for service as a civilian hospital ship.

Mercer (IX-502) seen during her career as APB-39. Along with *Nueces* (IX-503), she serves as barracks ship at Puget Sound Naval Shipyard for crews of ships in overhaul *(US Navy)*

Type: Unclassified Miscellaneous (IX) — *Number/Class:* 1 *Elk River*

Name	Number	Builder	Commissioned	Status
Elk River (ex LSMR-501)	IX-501	Brown SB Co, Houston, Tex	27 May 1945	PSA

Displacement Full load, 1,785 tons
Length overall 229.7ft (70m)
Maximum beam 50ft (15.2m)
Maximum draught 9.2ft (2.8m)
Main machinery One General Motors diesel engine
Screws/b.h.p. 2/2,880
Maximum speed 11 knots
Complement 25 Naval personnel, 20 technicians

Originally commissioned as the Landing Ship Medium (Rocket) *Elk River* (LSMR-501), this vessel was reclassified IX-501 on 1 April, 1967, and taken in hand for conversion to a support vessel for the Navy's deep-diving submersible activities on the San Clemente Island range off the coast of southern California. Converted by Avondale Shipyards, Westwego, La. and San Francisco Naval Shipyard during 1967–1968, the following changes were made: the hull was lengthened and bulges added amidships to improve stability and provide additional workspace; an open well was provided amidships and a 65-ton capacity crane was fitted (on tracks). *Elk River* is also fitted with five anchors, including a bow anchor. An active positioning mooring system holds the ship in a precise location, enabling it to operate as a mother ship for deep diving salvage operations, as well as for deep diving for man-in-the-sea programmes; test and evaluation of submersibles; testing of underwater equipment; and deep mooring operations. She was placed in service, special, in January 1969, and in full service in January 1973.

Elk River (IX-501) serves as support ship for the Sealab III experiments *(US Navy)*

Type: Unclassified Miscellaneous (IX) — *Number/Class:* 1 "Barge Group"

Name	*Number*	*Status*
Unnamed	IX-310	Under operational control of the Naval Underwater Systems Centre, Newport, Rhode Island, but is stationed in Lake Seneca, New York, where she serves as a test ship.

This "vessel" consists of two barges held together with a deck housing running athwartships at the midship section, giving an "H" shape configuration as seen from above. It was placed in service on 1 April, 1971.

Note IX-309 was originally YW-87. Reclassified to Unclassified Miscellaneous in May 1969, it was again reclassified to YAG-61 (q.v.).

Type: Unclassified Miscellaneous (IX) — *Number/Class:* 1 *Mark*

Name	*Number*	*Builder*	*Acquired*	*Status*
New Bedford (ex AKL-17, FS-289)	IX-308	Martinolich SB Co, San Diego, Cal	1 Mar 1950	PSA

Displacement Light, 526 tons; full load 935 tons
Length overall 176.5ft (53.8m)
Maximum beam 32.8ft (10m)
Maximum draught 10ft (3.1m)
Main machinery Two General Motors diesel engines
Screws/b.h.p. 2/1,000
Maximum speed 10 knots
Complement 16 total

This ship was acquired from the Army on the indicated date for service with the Military Sea Transportation Service as an AKL, being instated on the Naval Register on the same date. Named *New Bedford* on 20 November, 1961, she was re-rated as "floating equipment" on 26 August, 1963, and her name was dropped. She was transferred to the Naval Torpedo Station, Keyport, Washington for further service. Her name was restored in February 1969, and she was classified IX-308 and reinstated on the NVR at the same time. Her status was changed to "in service" in October 1971. She is currently based at Keyport as a torpedo test ship.

Type: Unclassified Miscellaneous (IX) — *Number/Class:* 1 "IX-306"

Length overall 179ft (54.6m)
Maximum beam 33ft (10.1m)
Maximum draught 10ft (3.1m)
Propulsion Diesel engines
Maximum speed 12 knots

One converted Army ship type, formerly in service with the Army as FS-221, was acquired by the Navy in 1969 and instated on the Naval Register at the same time as IX-306. Placed "in service" in 1969, following conversion to a weapon test ship, this vessel conducts research for the Naval Underwater Weapons Research and Engineering Station, Newport, Rhode Island. Among the notable weapons tested was the Mark 48 torpedo. IX-306 is manned by Navy and civilian personnel and operates in the Caribbean Sea. The blue-painted bow is a prominent identification feature.

Disposal: *Brier* (IX-307) was stricken from the Navy List on 15 August, 1982.

IX-306 is based at Newport, Rhode Island, and serves as a weapons test ship. She was the major trials vessel for the new Mark 48 ASW torpedo. The door of her single internal torpedo tube can be seen in the notch just aft of the hull number *(US Navy)*

Constitution (ex-IX-21) ex-Unclassified Miscellaneous

Builder Hart Shipyard, Boston, Mass
Displacement full load, 2,200 tons
Length, on the waterline 175ft (53.3m)
Maximum beam 43.5ft (13.3m)
Maximum draught 20ft (6.1m)

The oldest active ship in the US Navy, *Constitution* represents the only USN ship which the Russians have not tried to copy or steal the plans for. Authorised on 27 March, 1794, and completed in 1798, she was overhauled and rebuilt at the Boston Navy Yard 1927/1930. After a nation-wide tour she was stationed in Boston as flagship of Commandant of the First Naval District. *Constitution* was placed in full commission in October 1971, having been "in commission, special" before that date. On 1 October, 1977, this ship was transferred to the control of the Director of Naval Historical Centre, Department of the Navy.

Sea duty for *Constitution* comprises an annual "sailing" out of Boston Harbor to be turned around and brought back pierside. This is done to provide even weathering of the masts.

The designation "IX-21" was assigned to this ship on 8 January, 1941, but was dropped on 1 September, 1975. As a result *Constitution* is the only ship on the Naval Vessel Register without a classification. Consequently her legal status is a bit confused, since it is technically illegal for a commissioned ship to be on the NVR with no classification.

The classification was dropped because it ". . . tended to demean and degrade *Constitution* through association with a group of insignificant craft of varied missions and configurations". The authors hardly think that such ships as *Constellation* (IX-20), the last sail-equipped warship to be built for the Navy; the former cruiser *Olympia*, flagship at Manila Bay; and the former Battleship *Oregon* (BB-3), all of which wore the "IX" classification at one time or another, are "insignificant". They may not have been used for the missions for which they were designed when classified as "IXs" but insignificant they were not.

Constitution (ex-IX-21), the dowager of the Navy, seen on her annual "turnaround" cruise. Permanently berthed in Boston Harbour, she is taken out once a year and turned round to ensure even wear of her hull *(US Navy)*

Type: Miscellaneous Auxiliary (YAG) — *Number/Class:* 1 "YAG-62"

Length overall 120ft (36.6 m)

Ex-M/V *Deer Island*. Acquired and placed on the Naval Vessel Register as YAG-62 on 15 March, 1982. Used in surface vessel noise-reduction tests. Based at Port Everglades, Fla.

Type: Miscellaneous Auxiliary (YAG) — *Number/Class:* 1 "YAG-61"

Displacement Light, 400 tons; full load, 1,390 tons
Length overall 174ft (53m)
Maximum beam 33ft (10.1m)
Propulsion One diesel engine
Maximum speed 7 knots

This unit was originally the Water Barge YW-87 of the "YW-83" class. Reclassified IX-309 in May 1969, it was converted to a mobile listening barge (called *Monob I*) for acoustical research. Its classification again changed, on 1 July, 1970, to YAG-61. This craft is based at Naval Research and Development Centre, Port Everglades, Florida. To be replaced by AG-195 in FY-1985.

Note YAG-60 (ex-*Butternut*, ANL-9) was struck from the Navy List on 1 July, 1971. The vessel still exists as a fire-fighting training hulk at Pearl Harbor, Hawaii.

Type: Diving Tenders, self-propelled (YDT) — *Number/Class:* 2 *Phoebus*

Displacement Light, 300 tons; full load, 650 tons
Length overall 133ft (40.5m)
Maximum beam 31ft (9.4m)
Maximum draught 8ft (2.4m)
Main machinery Union diesel engine
Screws/b.h.p. 2/600
Maximum speed 10 knots
Complement 1 officer, 10 enlisted men (YDT-14), 2 officers, 9 enlisted men (YDT-15)

The Navy has two self-propelled diving tenders, *Phoebus* (YDT-14, ex YF-294) and *Suitland* (YDT-15, ex YF-336). Completed during 1942/1943, they are used to support shallow water diving operations.

One non self-propelled diving tender is also in service, namely YDT-16 (ex YFNB-43).

Type: Covered Lighters, self-propelled (YF) — *Number/Class:* 3 "YF-852"

Displacement Light, 160 tons; full load, 650 tons
Length overall 133ft (40.5m)
Maximum beam 31ft (9.4m)
Maximum draught 10ft (3m)
Main machinery Two General Motors diesel engines
Screws/b.h.p. 2/1,000
Maximum speed 10 knots
Complement 1 officer, 10 enlisted men

There are only three self-propelled covered lighters on the Naval Register: YF-862, *Kodiak* (YF-866), and *Keyport* (YF-885). Only *Keyport* is active. These lighters are used to transport materials in harbours. All three units were completed in 1945.

Type: Ferry Boats, self-propelled (YFB) — *Number/Class:* 1 "YFB-83" 1 "YFB-87" 4 "YFB-88"

Displacement Light, not available (YFB-83); 390 tons (YFB-87); 200 tons (YFB-88/91). Full load, 773 tons (YFB-83); 500 tons (YFB-87); 375 tons (YFB-88/91)
Length overall 180ft (54.8m) (YFB-83); 162ft (49.3m) (YFB-87); 134.9ft (41.1m) (YFB-88/91)
Maximum beam 46ft (14m) (YFB-83); 59ft (18m) (YFB-87); 29ft (8.8m) (YFB-88/91)
Maximum draught not available (YFB-83); 12ft (3.7m) (YFB-87); 6.1ft (1.9m) (YFB-88/91)
Main machinery Two diesel engines (Cooper-Bessemer, YFB-83 and Caterpillar Tractor Co, YFB-87). Four Detroit diesel engines (YFB-88/91)
Screws/b.h.p. 1/400 (YFB-83); 2/860 (YFB-87); 2/1,000 (YFB-88/91)
Maximum speed Not available (YFB-83); 8 knots (YFB-87); 11 knots (YFB-88/91)
Complement 12/17 enlisted men

Ferry Boats used to transport vehicles and personnel across large harbours. All are active. YFB-83 was completed in 1949, YFB-87 in 1970, and YFB-88/91 between 1967 and 1971. YFB-88/91 were originally completed as LCU-1636 and 1638/1640 of the "YFB-88" class, and were reclassified YFB on 1 September, 1969.

Note *Aquidneck* (YFB-14) was transferred to the State of Washington on 23 December, 1975.

Type: Refrigerated Covered Lighters, self-propelled (YFR) *Number/Class:* 2 "YFR-443"

Displacement Light, 290 tons (YFR-888); 300 tons (YFR-890). Full load, 610 tons (YFR-888); 600 tons (YFR-890)
Length overall 133ft (40.5m)
Maximum beam 30ft (9.1m)
Maximum draught 9ft (2.7m)
Main machinery Two General Motors diesel engines
Screws/b.h.p. 2/1,000
Maximum speed 10 knots
Complement 1 officer, 10 enlisted men

Two YFR-888 and -890, remain on the Naval Vessel Register. Both were completed in 1945. YFR-888 has been laid up in reserve since October 1971; YFR-890 has been on loan to another Government agency since March 1972.

These lighters are used to store and transport food and other perishable materials requiring refrigeration.

Type: Covered Lighters (Range Tenders), self-propelled (YFRT) *Number/Class:* 5 "YFRT-257"

Displacement Light, 300 tons; full load, 650 tons
Length overall 133ft (40.5m)
Maximum beam 30ft (9.1m)
Maximum draught 9ft (2.7m)
Main machinery Two diesel engines, Union (except YFRT-287, Cooper-Bessemer)
Screws/b.h.p. 2/1,000 (YFRT-523); 2/800 (YFRT-287) and 2/600 (remainder)
Maximum speed 10 knots
Complement 1 officer, 10/19 enlisted men

These lighters were completed between August 1940 and September 1945, and five of the class remain on the Navy List, YFRT-287, -418, -451, -520 and -523. All are active except YFRT-418, which has been laid up in reserve since September 1961. YFRT-520 is fitted with a triple Mark 32 torpedo tube mount for tests.

Type: Harbour Utility Craft, self-propelled (YFU) *Number/Class:* 10 "YFU-71"

Displacement Light, 220 tons; full load, 380 tons
Length overall 125ft (38.1m)
Maximum beam 36ft (10.9m)
Maximum draught 7.5ft (2.3m)
Main machinery Two General Motors diesel engines
Screws/b.h.p. 2/1,000
Maximum speed 8 knots
Armament 2 50-cal machine guns
Complement 2 officers, 10 enlisted men

This class is a militarised version of a commercial lighter design, used for off-loading large ships in harbours and for ferrying cargo from one coastal port to another. Cargo capacity is 300 tons. These vessels were completed during 1967–1968, and the following units remain on the Naval Register: YFU-71, -72, -74 to -77, -79 to -81, and -83. All were loaned to the Army in 1970 for service in Vietnam, being returned to the Navy in 1973. They are now laid up in reserve, except for YFU-75 and -83, which are active, and YFU-82, which was reclassified to IX-506 (see previous section).

Note YFU-73 of this class was loaned to the Khmer Republic in April 1970 and YFU-78 was sunk in action in Vietnam.

YFU-72 of the YFU-71 class. These craft have proved to be very handy for harbour and coastal cargo-carrying duties *(US Navy)*

Type: Harbour Utility Craft, self-propelled (YFU)

Number/Class: 1 Converted "LCU-501"
3 Converted "LCU-1466"
4 Converted "LCU-1610"

Displacement Full load, 320/380 tons
Length overall 116/134.9ft (35.3/41.1m)
Maximum beam 29/34ft (8.8/10.4m)
Maximum draught 5/6.1ft (1.52/1.97m)
Main machinery Three diesel engines (YFU-50, -91, -94). Four diesel engines (YFU-97, -98, -100, -101). Not available (YFU-102)
Screws/b.h.p. 3/675 (YFU-50, -91, -94); 2/1,000 (YFU-97, -98, -100, -101); Not available (YFU-102)
Maximum speed 10/12 knots
Complement 14/20 total

All of these are conversions from the LCU-501, 1466 and 1610 classes. YFU-50 is ex LCU-1486; YFU 91 ex LCU-1608; YFU-94 ex LCU-1488; YFU-97 ex LCU-1611; YFU-98 ex LCY-1615; YFU-100 ex LCU-1610; YFU-101 ex LCU-1612 and YFU-102 ex LCU-1462. Of the 90 LCUs converted to YFUs, only these eight survive, surviving as harbour and coastal craft for cargo transport. One unit, YFU-83 (since deleted), duplicated the last unit of the built-for-purpose "YFU-71" Class. All are active except for YFU-50 and -94, which are in reserve.

Type: Fuel Oil Barges, self-propelled (YO)

Number: 16

YO-47 class
Displacement Light, 950 tons; full load, 2,660 tons
Length overall 235ft (71.6m)
Maximum beam 37ft (11.3m)
Maximum draught 15ft (4.6m)
Main machinery Two Enterprise diesel engines
Screws/b.h.p. 2/820
Maximum speed 10 knots
Complement 4 officers, 30 enlisted men

YO-65 class
Displacement Light, 440 tons; full load, 1,390 tons
Length overall 174ft (53m)
Maximum beam 33ft (10.1m)
Maximum draught 13ft (4m)
Main machinery One diesel engine, Union (YO-106, -129, -264); Fairbanks-Morse (YO-241); General Motors (remainder)
Screws/b.h.p. 1/560 (YO-106, -129, -264); 1/480 (YO-241); 1/640 (remainder)
Maximum speed 11 knots
Complement 1 officer, 22 enlisted men

YO-153 class
Displacement light, 370 tons; full load, 1,095 tons
Length overall 156ft (47.5m)
Maximum beam 30ft (9.1m)
Maximum draught 12ft (3.7m)
Main machinery 1 Fairbanks-Morse diesel engine
Screws/b.h.p. 1/525
Maximum speed 10 knots
Complement 2 officers, 14 enlisted men

These small liquid fuel carriers are employed fuelling ships in harbour where no pierside facilities are available. The following YOs are on the Naval Vessel Register: *Casinghead* (YO-47) and the unnamed YO-106, -129, -153, -194, -200, -202, -203, -220, -223 to -225, -228, -230, -241 and -264. All were completed during 1942–1946. YO-47, -153, -228, -230 and -241 are in reserve; the remainder are active.

The now stricken YO-205. These craft are used to fuel ships in harbours where pierside facilities are unavailable *(John A. Jedrlinic)*

Type: Gasoline Barges, self-propelled (YOG)

Number/Class: 8 "YOG-5"

Displacement Light, 440 tons, full load, 1,390 tons
Length overall 174ft (53m)
Maximum beam 33ft (10.1m)
Maximum draught 13ft (4m)
Main machinery One diesel engine, General Motors (except YOG-58, Union)
Screws/b.h.p. 1/560 (YOG-58); 1/640 (remainder)

Maximum speed 11 knots
Complement 1 officer, 22 enlisted men

The following units, all unnamed, are on the Naval Register: YO-58, -67, -68, -78, -79, -88, -93 and -196. All were completed during 1945/1946.

Copies of the YO design, these fuel barges carry gasoline and aviation fuels to ships moored in harbours or at piersides. YOG-78, -88 and -196 are active; the remainder are in reserve. YOG-196 is ex YO-196.

One of the three active YOGs. These craft are identical to the YOs except that they carry petrol and aviation fuels instead of fuel oil for ships *(John A. Jedrlinic)*

Type: Patrol Craft (YP) — *Number/Class:* 23 "YP-654", "YP-673" and "YP-676"

Displacement Full load, 68 tons (YP-673 Cl.); 69.5 tons (YP-654 Cl.); 85 tons (YP-676)
Length overall 80.6ft (24.6m) (YP-673 Cl.); 80.4ft (24.6m) (YP-654 Cl.); 108ft (32.9m) (YP-676)
Maximum beam 17.8ft (5.4m) (YP-673 Cl.); 18ft (5.7m) (YP-654 Cl.); 23ft (7m) (YP-676)
Maximum draught 5.3ft (1.6m)
Main machinery Two Detroit diesel engines (YP-668 to 672, -676) and four General Motors diesel engines (remainder)
Screws/b.h.p. 2/680 (YP-673 Cl.); 2/660 (YP-654 Cl.); 2/875 (YP-676 Cl.)
Maximum speed 12 knots (YP-676), 10 knots (remainder)
Complement 0–2 officers, 10–12 enlisted men (except YP-676, 2 officers, 2 officers, 4 enlisted men, 24 midshipmen)

The following units are on the Naval Vessel Register: YP-654/663 (completed in 1958); YP-664, -665 (completed in 1960); YP-666, -667 (completed in 1967); YP-668 (completed in 1968); YP-669 (completed in 1971); YP-670/672 (completed in 1972), and YP-673/675 (completed in 1979). A new class of seven YPs (YP-676/82) is to be built. The prototype was authorised in FY-1982 at a cost of $4,976,027. Construction contract was awarded to Petersen Builders Inc, Sturgeon Bay, Wisc, on 15 October, 1982. Completion is due in October 1984 and six more units are projected.

These vessels have wooden hulls and aluminium deckhouses. They are fitted with surface search radar, fathometer, gyrocompass, and UHF/MF communications. YPs are used for seamanship and navigation instruction at the Naval Academy in Annapolis, and at the Naval Officers Candidate School and the Surface Warfare Officers School at Newport, Rhode Island. YP-655 is also fitted for instruction in oceanographic research at the Naval Academy.

Type: Large Harbour Tugs (YTB) — *Number/Class:* 81 "YTB-752" and "YTB-760"

Name	Number	Name	Number	Name	Number	Name	Number
Edenshaw	YTB-752	**Nogales**	YTB-777	**Tamaqua**	YTB-797	**Hyannis**	YTB-817
Marin	YTB-753	**Apoka**	YTB-778	**Opelika**	YTB-798	**Mecosta**	YTB-818
Pontiac	YTB-756	**Manhattan**	YTB-779	**Natchitoches**	YTB-799	**Iuka**	YTB-819
Oshkosh	YTB-757	**Saugus**	YTB-780	**Eufaula**	YTB-800	**Wanamassa**	YTB-820
Paducah	YTB-758	**Niantic**	YTB-781	**Palatka**	YTB-801	**Tontogany**	YTB-821
Bogalusa	YTB-759	**Manistee**	YTB-782	**Cheraw**	YTB-802	**Pawhuska**	YTB-822
Natick	YTB-760	**Redwing**	YTB-783	**Nanticoke**	YTB-803	**Canonchet**	YTB-823
Ottumwa	YTB-761	**Kalispell**	YTB-784	**Ahoskie**	YTB-804	**Santaquin**	YTB-824
Tuscumbia	YTB-762	**Winnemucca**	YTB-785	**Ocala**	YTB-805	**Wathena**	YTB-825
Muskegon	YTB-763	**Tonkawa**	YTB-786	**Tuskegee**	YTB-806	**Washtucna**	YTB-826
Mishawaka	YTB-764	**Kittanning**	YTB-787	**Massapequa**	YTB-807	**Chetek**	YTB-827
Okmulgee	YTB-765	**Wapato**	YTB-788	**Wenatchee**	YTB-808	**Catahecassa**	YTB-828
Wapakoneta	YTB-766	**Tomahawk**	YTB-789	**Agawam**	YTB-809	**Metacom**	YTB-829
Apalachicola	YTB-767	**Menominee**	YTB-790	**Anoka**	YTB-810	**Pushmataha**	YTB-830
Arcata	YTB-768	**Marinette**	YTB-791	**Houma**	YTB-811	**Dekanawida**	YTB-831
Chesaning	YTB-769	**Antigo**	YTB-792	**Accomac**	YTB-812	**Petalesharo**	YTB-832
Dahlonega	YTB-770	**Piqua**	YTB-793	**Poughkeepsie**	YTB-813	**Shabonee**	YTB-833
Keokuk	YTB-771	**Mandan**	YTB-794	**Waxahachie**	YTB-814	**Negwagon**	YTB-834
Nashua	YTB-774	**Ketchikan**	YTB-795	**Neodesha**	YTB-815	**Skenandoa**	YTB-835
Wauwatosa	YTB-775	**Saco**	YTB-796	**Campti**	YTB-816	**Pokagon**	YTB-836
Weehawken	YTB-776						

Displacement Light, 268–311 tons; full load, 356–409 tons
Length overall 109ft (33.2m) except YTB-752 and -753; 101ft (30.8m) and YTB-760, YTB-761; 85ft (25.9m)
Maximum beam 30ft (9.1m), except YTB-752, -753 29ft (8.8m) and YTB-760,-761 24ft (7.3m)
Maximum draught 13.8ft (4.2m), except YTB-752, -753 16ft (4.9m) and YTB-760, -761 11ft (3.4m)
Main machinery One Fairbanks-Morse diesel engine, except YTB-752, -753 (Alco), YTB-761 (Detroit), YTB-799/802 (General Motors)
Screws/b.h.p. 1/1,800–2,000
Maximum speed 12 knots
Complement 4 officers, 6-12 enlisted men

Coastal and harbour tugs used for handling large ships during docking and undocking, these vessels are also used to tow non-self-propelled service craft. *Palatka* was rammed and sunk by *Nashville* (LPD-13) on 17 January, 1972, but was raised on 21 January, 1972, repaired and restored to service.

Completed as follows: 1959 (YTB-752), 1960 (YTB-753), 1961 (YTB-756/762), 1963 (YTB-763/766), 1964 (YTB-770, -771), 1965 (YTB-767/769, -776), 1966 (YTB-774, -775, -777/789), 1967 (YTB-790/793), 1968 (YTB-794, -795), 1969 (YTB-796/803), 1970–72 (YTB-808/815), 1972–73 (YTB-816/827) and 1974–75 (YTB-828/836). In addition, two units completed in 1975 (YTB-837, -838) were built for and transferred to Saudi Arabia.

Opelika (YTB-798) *(Marinette Marine Corporation)*

Type: Medium Harbour Tugs (YTM) — *Number:* 51

Name	Number	Name	Number	Name	Number	Name	Number
Toka	YTM-149	**Cochali**	YTM-383	**Taconnet**	YTM-417	**Migadan**	YTM-549
Dekaury	YTM-178	**Wannalancet**	YTM-385	**Nabigwon**	YTM-521	**Acoma**	YTM-701
Madokawando	YTM-180	**Winamac**	YTM-394	**Tutahaco**	YTM-524	**Arawak**	YTM-702
Nepanet	YTM-189	**Wingina**	YTM-395	**Wahaka**	YTM-526	**Moratoc**	YTM-704
Dekanisora	YTM-252	**Yanegua**	YTM-397	**Wahpeton**	YTM-527	**Yuma**	YTM-748
Hiawatha	YTM-265	**Natahki**	YTM-398	**Nadli**	YTM-534	**Hackensack**	YTM-750
Red Cloud	YTM-268	**Numa**	YTM-399	**Nahoke**	YTM-536	**Mascoutah**	YTM-760
Pawtucket	YTM-359	**Otokomi**	YTM-400	**Chegodega**	YTM-542	**Menasha**	YTM-761
Sassaba	YTM-364	**Coshecton**	YTM-404	**Yatanocas**	YTM-544	**Apohola**	YTM-768
Waubansee	YTM-366	**Cusseta**	YTM-405	**Accolanoc**	YTM-545	**Mimac**	YTM-770
Chanagi	YTM-380	**Kittaton**	YTM-406	**Takos**	YTM-546	**Hiamowee**	YTM-776
Chepanoc	YTM-381	**Porobago**	YTM-413	**Yanaba**	YTM-547	**Pocasset**	YTM-779
Coatopa	YTM-382	**Secota**	YTM-415	**Matunak**	YTM-548		

Displacement Light, 220–260 tons; Full load, 310–320 tons
Length overall 100–102ft (30.5–31.1m)
Maximum beam 25–28ft (7.6–8.5m)
Maximum draught 10–11ft (3.1–3.4m)
Main machinery One General Motors diesel engine, except YTM-189, -265, -268 (Enterprise)
Screws/b.h.p. 1/815–11,030
Maximum speed 13 knots
Complement 1–3 officers, 8–17 enlisted men

These harbour tugs are former YTBs completed in 1942/1945 and reclassified to YTMs in the mid-1960s. They perform similar functions to YTBs. YTB-748 and onwards are former Army tugs. Eighteen of these tugs are in reserve (two in Marad, James River), and the remaining 35 are active, but they are being slowly phased out owing to their age.

A sister, *Nanigo* (YTM-537), was presumed lost at sea on 7 April, 1973, after the line parted in rough seas while she was being towed by *Takelma* (ATF-113). She disappeared and is presumed sunk.

Type: Small Harbour Tugs (YTL) — *Number/Class:* 7 "YTL-422"

Displacement Light, 70 tons; full load, 80 tons
Length overall 66ft (21.1m)
Maximum beam 18ft (5.5m)
Maximum draught 8ft (2.4m)
Main machinery One Hoover, Owens, Rentsher Co, diesel engine
Screws/b.h.p. 1/375
Maximum speed 10 knots
Complement 1 officer, 4 enlisted men

YTL-422, -434, -438, -439, -583, -588 and -602 are the only craft of this type still on the Naval Vessel Register. They were completed during 1944/1946. YTL-434, -588 and -602 are active; the remainder are in reserve.

Type: Water Barges, self-propelled (YW) — *Number/Class:* 9 "YW-83"

Displacement Light, 440 tons; full load, 1,390 tons
Length overall 174ft (53m)
Maximum beam 33ft (10.1m)
Maximum draught 13ft (4m)
Main machinery One diesel engine, General Motors, except YW-83 (Fairbanks-Morse) and YW-86 (Union)
Screws/ b.h.p. 1/640 except YW-83 (1/400), and YW-86 (1/560)
Maximum speed 7 knots
Complement 1 officer, 22 enlisted men

The following YWs remain on the Naval Vessel Register: YW-83, -86, -98, -101, -108, -113, -123, -126 and -127. Similar in design to the YO and YOG types, these craft carry water to ships in harbours and roadsteads and at piers, where there is no access to fresh water. Four units are active and the remainder are in reserve.

Summary of Non-Self-Propelled Service Craft

As of 1 February, 1983, the following non-self-propelled Service Craft were on the Naval Vessel Register (NVR): 18 Barracks Craft (APL); 26 Ship Waste Off-loading Barges (WOB), 200 Open Lighters (YC); one Car Float (YCF); six Aircraft Transportation Lighters (YCV); six Floating Cranes (YD); 55 Covered Lighters (YFN); 16 Large Covered Lighters (YFNB); three Dry Dock Companion Craft (YFND); 15 Lighters, special purpose (YFNX); three Floating Power Barges (YFP); four Refrigerated Covered Lighters (YFRN); seven Garbarge Lighters (YGN); three Dredgers (YM); two Gate Craft (YNG); 13 Gasoline Barges (YOGN); 51 Fuel Oil Barges (YON); 13 Oil Storage Barges (YOS); five Floating Pile Drivers (YPD); 20 Floating Workshops (YR); three Repair and Berthing Barges (YRB); 27 Repair, Messing, and Berthing Barges (YRBM); four Floating Dry Dock Workshops (Hull) (YRDH); four Floating Dry Dock Workshops (Machinery) (YRDM); 14 Radiological Repair Barges (YRR); five Salvage Craft Tenders (YRST); 23 Sludge Removal Barges (YSR), and eight Water Barges (YWN).

Salvage Craft Tender YRST-1 is typical of the non-self-propelled service craft currently on the Naval Vessel Register *(US Navy)*

SPECIAL VESSELS

A number of Advanced Naval Vehicles (ANV) are being considered for the American Navy of the 21st century. The ANVs (not on the Naval Register) considered for future construction include airships, Small Waterplane Area Twin Hull (Swath) craft (see AGOS-13 class in Auxiliary section), Surface-Effect Ships (SES), air-cushion vehicles (ACV) (see Amphibious section), hydrofoils, and Wing-In-Ground effect (WIG) vehicles. Not all of the concepts are new; airships were used from the Second World War until they were discarded in 1962, hydrofoils are in production for the Navy after several years of experimentation, and the Navy is currently experimenting with three surface-effect ship designs.

In 1975 the Navy established ANV Concept Evaluation. This came about when its plans for the construction of the radically new 3,000-ton SES were gradually slowed down by a Defense Department order. This stated that the Navy should undertake a comprehensive analysis of all advanced platform concepts, to determine their potential roles and related estimated costs. The Navy had done this in detail some years previously, and had come up with the 3,000-ton design. It seems that the Navy was doing things properly in this case, but that someone in the Defense Department could not grasp the concepts. The Carter Administration finally scuttled the 3,000-ton design in December 1977. Nonetheless, the largest ANV effort, in terms of funding, is still the SES programme. The money allocated, however, is indeed paltry when compared with that devoted to research and development efforts in a number of other areas, and especially when compared with what the Soviet Navy is doing. Despite this, SES concept development continues.

Surface-Effect Ships (SES)

Type: Experimental Surface-Effect Ship (SES) — *Number/Name* 1 "SES-100A"

SES-100A at high speed *(US Navy)*

Weight 100 tons gross
Length 81.9ft (25m)
Maximum beam 41.9ft (12.8m)
Main and lift engines Four Avco-Lycoming TF35 gas turbines (12,000 b.h.p.); three lift fans and two water jet propulsion systems
Maximum speed 76 knots

Built by the Tacoma Boat Building Company, Tacoma, Wash, and developed by the Aerojet-General Corporation. Christened in July 1971, SES-100A was under way mid-1972; it is of aluminium construction with rigid sidewalls to contain the bubble of air, or "cushion".

The SES-100A has a cargo capacity of 10 tons and has accommodation for a crew of four to six. This craft is fitted with four TF-35 gas turbine engines, marine versions of the T55-L-11A developed for the CH-47C Chinook helicopter. On trials, the SES-100A is reported to have attained a speed of 76 knots. The craft was overhauled at NAS Patuxent River in 1978, and is now under the operational control of the Naval Sea Systems Command.

Type: 1 Experimental Surface-Effect Ship (SES); *Number/Name* 1 "SES-100B"

Weight 100 tons gross
Dimensions overall length, 78ft (23.8m) ;
Maximum beam 35ft (10.7m)
Main engines Three Pratt & Whitney FT-12 gas turbines (13,500 b.h.p.). Two semi-submerged super-cavitating propellers
Maximum speed 80 knots
Lift engines Three United Aircraft of Canada ST-6J-70 gas turbines providing 1,500 h.p.; eight lift fans

Developed by the Bell Aerospace Division of the Textron Corporation and built at the Bell facility in Michoud, Louisiana, SES-100B was christened on 6 March, 1971, and under way in February 1972. It was developed to compete with the SES-100A.

The aluminium hull has rigid side-walls to contain the cushion, and the craft has a cargo capacity of 10 tons. A crew of four plus six observers can be accommodated.

This craft set the current SES speed record of 87.5 knots during trials on 30 June, 1976. In the same year, while moving at 60 knots, SES-100B made a successful vertical launch of a Standard missile. Overhauled at NAS Patuxent River in 1979, it is under the operational control of the Naval Sea Systems Command.

SES-100B (illustrated) and SES-100A are based at the Patuxent River research facility

Type: Surface-Effect Ship (SES) *Number/Name* "SES-200"

Displacement Full load, 128 tons
Length overall 160ft (48.8m)
Maximum beam 54ft (16.6m)
Maximum draught On cushion, 7.5ft (2.3m); off cushion 12.5ft (3.8m)
Main engines Propulsion, two MTU 20V 956 TB92 diesels; lift, 2 MTU 12V 331 TC 92 diesels, two double-inlet centrifugal 40in-dia lift fans
Screws/b.h.p. 2/3,200 (propulsion); not available
Maximum speed 30+ knots
Endurance 5,000 nm at 30 knots
Complement 3 officers, 10 enlisted men

This is the largest surface-effect ship (SES) in the world. Developed by Bell Aerospace Textron and Halter-Marine from 1977, she was completed in early 1980. During February and March 1980 the Navy, in conjunction with the US Coast Guard and the Urban Mass Transportation Administration, ran tests of the type off Virginia. The results showed that the craft could operate in seas up to State 4 and perform well in all types of manoeuvres. Purchased in September 1980, she was designated SES-110BH. Transferred to Coast Guard operational control for joint Navy/Coast Guard trials, she was commissioned as USCG *Dorado* (WSES-1). After the conclusion of the trials, which were successful and led to the Coast Guard ordering three more units for duty in the Caribbean, she was decommissioned on 15 December, 1981, and returned to the Navy. After ten months of modification work at the Bell-Halter yard, New Orleans, which included the addition of a 50ft (15.2m) mid-section, she was returned to service in September 1982. The mid-section was added to increase the cushion length-to-beam ratio, permitting higher speeds. SES-200 currently operates from Patuxent River Naval Air Station, conducting advanced system development tests and operational evaluation of surface-effect ships in Navy/Coast Guard roles.

SES-200 is a waterborne, air-supported craft with catamaran-style rigid sidewalls. A cushion of air trapped between the sidewalls and flexible bow and stern seals lifts a large part of the hull clear of the water, greatly reducing drag. A portion of the sidewall remains in the water, adding to stability and manoeuvrability.

Type: 3,000-ton Surface-Effect Ship (SES)

$800–900 million was requested in the FY-1979 budget for construction of the prototype of this craft. However, the Carter Administration deleted the entire project from the budget in December 1977 in the name of economy. Despite this, Congress approved $80.0 million for further research and development. In FY-1980 no money was requested for the project and Congress did not approve any further funds. Again, in FY-1981, no further funds were requested, and thus the project died on the vine.

Submersibles

Type: Nuclear-Powered Research Vehicle

Number/Name 0+0+1 "HTV" (ex-NR-2)

In the early 1980s Admiral H. G. Rickover proposed the construction of a nuclear-powered hull research vehicle. This craft was to employ a nuclear plant similar to that of NR-1 (see next entry), but would have a greater depth capability. The HTV, originally referred to as NR-2, would be 153ft (46.6m) long and 14.5ft (4.42m) in diameter. The purpose of this vehicle is to check the feasibility of using HY-130 steel for submarine construction (SSN/SSBN) on actual production lines by production workers. Submarines cannot be massed-produced under laboratory conditions, so it is vital to determine whether HY-130 can be welded and handled by the workers who build the submarines.

The less advanced HY-80 steel was introduced into the submarine construction programme without the benefit of a hull test vehicle, and severe cracking problems were encountered in the shipyard. In 1978 it was planned to schedule a construction contract award for early 1980, with completion in 1985. HTV was to be built at General Dynamics, Electric Boat Division. Costing about $300 million, the vessel would be fully funded in the research development, test and evaluation programme, rather than under shipbuilding and conversion.

Type: Nuclear-Powered Ocean Engineering and Research Vessel

Number/Class: 1 "NR-1"

Displacement 400 tons (submerged)
Length overall 136.4ft (41.6m)
Maximum beam 12.4ft (3.8m)
Maximum draught 14.6ft (4.5m)
Propulsion One water-cooled nuclear reactor; electric motors; four ducted thrusters
Screws/Maximum speed 2/12 knots (submerged)
Complement 7 total (2 officers, 3 enlisted men, 2 scientists)

Built by General Dynamics, Electric Boat Div., New London, Conn. as a test platform for a small nuclear propulsion plant, NR-1 is the first and only nuclear-powered service craft to date. A second, the "HTV" design, is to be built. NR-1 was laid down on 10 June, 1967, launched on 25 January, 1969, and placed in service on 27 October, 1969. Estimated cost of construction was $99.2 million.

This highly successful research submersible is equipped with external lights, TV viewers, viewing ports, movie cameras, and retractable wheels. This last feature is unique and enables NR-1 to crawl about the sea bottom. It is fitted with a TV mast, but has no periscope. A surface mother ship is required to support NR-1.

This craft is driven by electric motors located on the outside of the pressure hull, which use power provided by a turbo-generator within the pressure hull, powered in turn by the reactor. Four ducted thrusters, two horizontal and two vertical, enable precise manoeuvring. NR-1 is active in the Atlantic.

Nuclear-powered research submarine NR-1 pictured in September 1969. The torpedo tube on the bow was removed in 1971. A second nuclear-powered research submarine is in design *(General Dynamics)*

Type: Deep Submergence Rescue Vehicles (DSRV) *Number/Class:* 2 "DSRV-1"

Number	*Builder*	*In service*	*Status*
DSRV-1	Lockheed Missile and Space Co, Sunnyvale, Cal	7 Aug 1971	PSA
DSRV-2	Lockheed Missile and Space Co, Sunnyvale, Cal	7 Aug 1972	ASA

Displacement Full load, 32 tons (in air)
Length overall 49.2ft (15m)
Diameter 8ft (2.4m)
Propulsion Battery powered electric motors, propeller mounted in a control shroud, four ducted thrusters
Screws/Maximum speed 1/3 knots
Operating depth 5,000ft (1.523m)
Complement Pilot, copilot, and rescue sphere operator. 24 survivors

These units, with the unofficial names *Avalon* (DSRV-1) and *Mystic* (DSRV-2), were built in response to the *Thresher* (SSN-593) disaster, at a cost of $41 and $23 million, respectively. They are designed to operate in all weathers, anywhere in the world, for rapid deployment to rescue survivors from sunken submarines. These two craft provide the US Navy with a deep-submergence rescue capability much greater than it previously had with the *McCann* rescue chamber, and greater than that of any other Western country. The DSRVs can operate deeper than the survival depth of any existing US Navy submarine. Six units were planned, but costs and construction delays limited the class to two units. DSRV-1 was activated for rescue duty on 4 November, 1977, followed by DSRV-2 on 1 January, 1978.

These vessels are transportable by road, aircraft (C-141 and C-5), surface ships (*Pigeon* Class ASRs), and submarines (*Hawkbill*, SSN-666, and *Pintado*, SSN-672) which were especially modified for the mission. One factor limiting their use is the serious lack of ships and submarines in the US Navy capable of transporting and supporting the craft.

DSRVs have elaborate search and navigational sonar and closed-circuit TV. Side-looking sonar can be fitted for search missions. The outer hull is made of formed glass fibre, within which are three interconnected spheres. Each sphere is 7.5ft (2.3m) in diameter and made of HY-80 steel. The forward sphere houses the vehicle control equipment and is manned by a pilot and copilot. The centre and after spheres accommodate the 24 survivors and a third crewman.

DSRV-2. The DSRVs were developed in response to the loss of *Thresher* (SSN-593) and the inadequacies in the field of submarine rescue which this disaster revealed *(US Navy)*

Type: Deep-Submergence Vehicles (DSV) — *Number/Class:* 2 Modified *Alvin*

Name	*Number*	*Builder*	*Status*
Turtle	DSV-3	General Dynamics, Electric Boat Div, New London, Conn	PA
Sea Cliff	DSV-4	General Dynamics, Electric Boat Div, New London, Conn	PSA

Weight 21 tons
Length overall 25ft (7.6m)
Diameter 8ft (2.4m)
Propulsion Electric motors, trainable stern propeller, two rotating propeller pods
Maximum speed 2.5 knots
Operating depth 6,500ft (1,980m)
Complement 1 pilot, 1 observer

Completed for the Navy in 1968–1969 with the unofficial classification Autec I and Autec II, respectively, these vessels were originally rated as "equipment". Both were instated on the Naval Register on 1 June, 1971, as DSC-3 and -4, retaining their original names, and were placed in service on the same date. DSV-3 was placed in commission (miscellaneous) in January 1973, and DSV-4 was placed in service (miscellaneous) in the same month.

These vehicles were intended for deep submergence research and work tasks. Twin-arm manipulators are fitted to each submersible. There were three spheres fabricated for the *Alvin* submersible programme, one for installation on *Alvin*, one for testing and the other as a spare. The second and third sphere were later used in the construction of DSV-3 and -4.

Turtle (DSV-3) is the only DSV still in commission *(US Navy)*

Type: Deep-Submergence Vehicle (DSV) — *Number/Class:* 1 *Alvin*

Weight 16 tons
Length overall 22.5ft (6.9m)
Diameter 8.5ft (2.6m)
Propulsion Electric motors, stern propeller, 2 rotating propeller pods
Maximum speed 2 knots
Operating depth 12,000ft (3,657.5m)
Complement 1 pilot, 2 observers

Alvin was built by General Mills, Inc., Minneapolis, Minn. in the mid-1960s, for operation by the Woods Hole Oceanographic Institute. It was rated as "equipment" when completed.

On 16 October, 1968, while conducting dives approximately 120 miles south of Cape Cod, *Alvin* accidentally sank. Raised on 28 August, 1969, the vehicle was rebuilt during 1970–1971 and instated on the Naval Register as DSV-2 (retaining her original name) and placed "in service" on 1 June, 1971. Assigned to the Atlantic Fleet, *Alvin* was originally configured to operate at a depth of 6,000ft (1,827.6m), but was subsequently refitted with a titanium pressure sphere to increase depth capacity. The vessel was again declared operational in November 1973.

Accidentally sunk in 1968, *Alvin* (DSV-5) was raised and rebuilt *(US Navy)*

Type: Deep-Submergence Vehicle (DSV) *Number/Class:* 1 *Trieste*

Displacement 84 tons (surface); 303 tons (submerged)
Dimensions Length overall 78.6ft (24m); **Diameter** 15.3ft (4.7m)
Propulsion Electric motors, three propellers aft; ducted thrusters forward
Maximum speed 2 knots
Designed operating depth 20,000ft (6,096m)
Operating depth 12,000ft (3,658m)
Complement 2 operators, 1 observer

Originally built for private use by Auguste Piccard by Castellammare of Italy early in 1954, *Trieste* was purchased by the US Navy in 1958 and named *Trieste* I. Rebuilt in the mid-1960s and renamed *Trieste* II, she was rated as "equipment" until 1 September, 1969, when she was designated a "submersible craft" and instated on the Naval Register as X-2, being placed "in service" on the same date. Reclassified DSV-1 on 1 June, 1971, the vessel was assigned to the Pacific Fleet and primarily used as a testbed for underwater equipment and to train DSV operators. Placed "in service" (miscellaneous) in January, 1973, she is operated by Submarine Development Group One, San Diego, California.

Trieste II was rebuilt at the Mare Island Naval Shipyard during September 1965–August 1966. A modified float, pressure sphere, propulsion system, and mission equipment were fitted, plus external TV cameras and a mechanical manipulator. A computerised digital navigational system was installed. The float is filled with gasoline to provide the necessary buoyancy.

Nemo (DSV-5) has been on loan to the Southwest Research Institute of San Antonio, Texas, since 1974. She was acquired in the mid-1960s and rated as "equipment". *Nemo* was instated on the Naval Vessel Register on 1 June, 1971, as DSV-5, retaining her original name.

The bathyscaph *Trieste II*. Note the two propulsion units on the stern and the single unit on the bow. The lattice framework on the bow supports a mechanical arm *(US Navy)*

MILITARY SEALIFT COMMAND

On 1 January, 1983, the Naval Overseas Transportation Service (NOTS) and its Army counterpart, the Army Overseas Transportation Service (AOTS) were combined to form the Military Sea Transportation Service (MSTS). As the word "Military" suggests, the functions of both of the former organisations were combined to achieve greater efficiency, improved economics, and less duplication of requirements, without changing the prime mission. The name was changed to Military Sealift Command on 1 August, 1970.

The basic mission for MSC ships is to provide ocean transportation for all branches of the Defense Department. The nucleus of the Command comprises ships that are employed in various missions as part of the Navy's operational forces (thus, a part of the Navy Department) and are carried on the Naval Vessel Register. However, none are in commission or armed and, with the exception of a small naval detachment on board they are manned by civilians. MSC ships are assigned and/or retain their standard Navy designation, but the prefix "T" is added to that designation. The "T" is not a formal part of the ship's classification, and merely indicates that the ship is under the Administrative control of MSC. In addition, to indicate that the ship is civilian-manned, the prefix "USS" is replaced by the prefix "USNS". For example, when the USS *Kilauea* (AE-26) was transferred to the MSC, she became USNS *Kilauea* (T-AE-26). MSC ships, except T-AOs, carry no visible hull numbers; their stacks are grey with blue, yellow, and black stripes at their tops. From 1979 /80 onwards, all T-AOs had their hull numbers restored to their bows to distinguish them from T-AOTs, which have no underway replenishment capability.

The Commander, Deputy Commander, and Area Commanders (Atlantic, Pacific, and Far East) are flag officers of the Navy on active duty. Transport Oilers (AOT) are operated under contract by commercial lines and are manned by merchant seamen. Some ships are configured to carry submarine-launched ballistic missiles and other supplies to support the Poseidon Trident submarines. Through the MSC, most of the US defence cargo is carried in commercial ships under charter to the Government. A list of the ships currently under charter appears at the end of this section.

Although the MSC is operated as one homogenous fleet – as a "fifth" fleet *per se* – there are three types of craft operated by the MSC in three specific roles. These are as follow: **1** The operation of ships and oilers to carry bulk goods and liquid fuels from point to point in support of Navy operations. **2** The operation of special mission and research ships. Although these ships are under the administrative control of MSC, they are under the operational control of the Navy or a Navy office, such as the Oceanographer of the Navy, or of a private organisation, such as Woods Hole or Scripps Institute. **3** On 17 July, 1977, fleet support became an added duty, and MSC began taking over underway replenishment ships to operate in support of the Navy's ocean-going forces. This group is known as the Naval Fleet Auxiliary Force (NFAF). Administrative control is under the MSC, but operational control remains with the Navy. Together these ships form the "nucleus fleet".

As of 1 October, 1982, there was a total of 86 "nucleus fleet" ships in the Military Sealift Command. Of that number, 76 were active and nine were in reduced operating status. Of the active ships, 28 were assigned to the NFAF.

The recently stricken *Pvt John R. Towle* (T-AK-240) on a supply voyage to the Arctic. She was replaced by *Northern Light* (T-AK-284)

Rigel (T-AF-58) in her MSC configuration

Pvt Leonard C. Brostom (T-AK-255). She and *Marine Fiddler* (T-AK-267) are the only two heavy-lift-capable AKs in the Navy

Nucleus fleet

Name	Number	Notes	Status
Kilauea	T-AE-26	Naval Fleet Auxiliary Force Ship	TPA
Rigel	T-AF-58	Naval Fleet Auxiliary Force Ship	TAA
Sirius	T-AFS-8	Naval Fleet Auxiliary Force Ship	TAA
Spica	T-AFS-9	Naval Fleet Auxiliary Force Ship	TPA
Kingsport	T-AG-164	Scientific Support Ship	TAA
Vanguard	T-AG-194	Scientific Support Ship	TAA
General Hoyt S. Vandenberg	T-AGM-10	Scientific Support Ship	TAR
Redstone	T-AGM-20	Scientific Support Ship	TAA
Range Sentinel	T-AGM-22	Scientific Support Ship	TAA
Observation Island	T-AGM-23	Scientific Support Ship	TPA
Lynch	T-AGOR-7	Scientific Support Ship	TAA
Mizar	T-AGOR-11	Scientific Support Ship	TPA
De Steiguer	T-AGOR-12	Scientific Support Ship	TPA
Bartlett	T-AGOR-13	Scientific Support Ship	TAA
Hayes	T-AGOR-16	Scientific Support Ship	TAA
Bowditch	T-AGS-21	Scientific Support Ship	TAA
Dutton	T-AGS-22	Scientific Support Ship	TPA
Silas Bent	T-AGS-26	Scientific Support Ship	TPA
Kane	T-AGS-27	Scientific Support Ship	TAA
Chauvenet	T-AGS-29	Scientific Support Ship	TPA
Harkness	T-AGS-32	Scientific Support Ship	TAA
Wilkes	T-AGS-33	Scientific Support Ship	TAA
Wyman	T-AGS-34	Scientific Support Ship	TAA
H. H. Hess	T-AGS-38	Scientific Support Ship	TPA
Furman	T-AK-280	Scientific Support Ship	TPA
Victoria (FBM)	T-AK-281	Naval Fleet Auxiliary Force Ship	TAA
Marshfield (FBM)	T-AK-282	Naval Fleet Auxiliary Force Ship	TAA
Northern Light	T-AK-284	Cargo Ship	TAA
Southern Cross	T-AK-285	Cargo Ship	TPA
Vega (FBM)	T-AK-286	Naval Fleet Auxiliary Force Ship	TPA
Algol	T-AK-287	Undergoing conversion to AKR	Conv
Bellatrix	T-AK-288	Undergoing conversion to AKR	Conv
Denebola	T-AK-289	In reserve, Bayonne, N.J. (MARAD custody)	MAR
Pollux	T-AK-290	In reserve, Pier 88, New York City (MARAD custody)	MAR
Altair	T-AK-291	In reserve, Pier 90, New York City (MARAD custody)	MAR
Regulus	T-AK-292	In reserve, San Francisco, Cal. (MARAD custody)	MPR
Capella	T-AK-293	Undergoing conversion to AKR	Conv
Antares	T-AK-294	Undergoing conversion to AKR	Conv
Comet	T-AKR-7	Vehicle Cargo Ship	TAA
Meteor	T-AKR-9	Vehicle Cargo Ship	TPA
Mercury	T-AKR-10	Rapid Deployment Force	TAA
Jupiter	T-AKR-11	Rapid Deployment Force	TAA
Taluga	T-AO-62	Naval Fleet Auxiliary Force Ship	TPA
Mispillion	T-AO-105	Naval Fleet Auxiliary Force Ship	TPA
Navasota	T-AO-106	Naval Fleet Auxiliary Force Ship	TPA
Passumpsic	T-AO-107	Naval Fleet Auxiliary Force Ship	TPA
Pawcatuck	T-AO-108	Naval Fleet Auxiliary Force Ship	TAA
Waccamaw	T-AO-109	Naval Fleet Auxiliary Force Ship	TAA
Neosho	T-AO-143	Naval Fleet Auxiliary Force Ship	TAA
Mississinewa	T-AO-144	Naval Fleet Auxiliary Force Ship	TAA
Hassayampa	T-AO-145	Naval Fleet Auxiliary Force Ship	TPA
Kawishiwi	T-AO-146	Naval Fleet Auxiliary Force Ship	TPA
Truckee	T-AO-147	Naval Fleet Auxiliary Force Ship	TAA
Ponchatoula	T-AO-148	Naval Fleet Auxiliary Force Ship	TPA
Nodaway	T-AOG-78	Gasoline Tanker	TPA
Alatna	T-AOG-81	Gasoline Tanker	TPA
Chattahoochee	T-AOG-82	Gasoline Tanker	TPA
Maumee	T-AOT-149	Transport Oiler; operated by Trinidad Corp	TWA
Shoshone	T-AOT-151	Transport Oiler; operated by Trinidad Corp	TWA
Yukon	T-AOT-152	Transport Oiler; operated by Trinidad Corp	TWA
American Explorer	T-AOT-165	Transport Oiler; operated by Trinidad Corp	TWA
Sealift Pacific	T-AOT-168	Transport Oiler; operated by Marine Transport Lines	TWA
Sealift Arabian Sea	T-AOT-169	Transport Oiler; operated by Marine Transport Lines	TWA
Sealift China Sea	T-AOT-170	Transport Oiler; operated by Marine Transport Lines	TWA
Sealift Indian Ocean	T-AOT-171	Transport Oiler; operated by Marine Transport Lines	TWA
Sealift Atlantic	T-AOT-172	Transport Oiler; operated by Marine Transport Lines	TWA
Sealift Mediterranean	T-AOT-173	Transport Oiler; operated by Marine Transport Lines	TWA
Sealift Arctic	T-AOT-174	Transport Oiler; operated by Marine Transport Lines	TWA
Sealift Antarctic	T-AOT-175	Transport Oiler; operated by Marine Transport Lines	TWA
Potomac	T-AOT-181	Transport Oiler; operated by Trinidad Corp	TWA
Columbia	T-AOT-182	Transport Oiler; operated by Trinidad Corp	TWA
Neches	T-AOT-183	Transport Oiler; operated by Trinidad Corp	TWA
Hudson	T-AOT-184	Transport Oiler; operated by Trinidad Corp	TWA
Susquehanna	T-AOT-185	Transport Oiler; operated by Trinidad Corp	TWA
Neptune	T-ARC-2	Cable Repairing Ship	TAA
Aeolus	T-ARC-3	Cable Repairing Ship	TPA
Albert J. Myer	T-ARC-6	Cable Repairing Ship	TPA
Powhatan	T-ATF-166	Naval Fleet Auxiliary Force Ship	TAA
Narragansett	T-ATF-167	Naval Fleet Auxiliary Force Ship	TPA
Catawba	T-ATF-168	Naval Fleet Auxiliary Force Ship	TPA
Navajo	T-ATF-169	Naval Fleet Auxiliary Force Ship	TPA
Mohawk	T-ATF-170	Naval Fleet Auxiliary Force Ship	TAA
Sioux	T-ATF-171	Naval Fleet Auxiliary Force Ship	TPA
Apache	T-ATF-172	Naval Fleet Auxiliary Force Ship	TAA

Ships chartered for the Rapid Deployment Force (RDF)

Name	Type	Charter Date
American Spartan	AK/C4	March 1982
American Titan	AK/C4	March 1982
American Spitfire	AK/C4	1 Sept 1981
Gulf Trader	AK/C4	Aug 1982
Austral Lightning	AKB/C8 (LASH)	6 Oct 1981
Austral Rainbow	AKB/C8 (LASH)	27 Oct 1981
George Wythe	AKB/C8 (LASH)	17 Sept 1982
Courier	AOT	3 Dec 1981
Lyra	AKR/Roll-on Roll-off	28 Mar 1981
Patriot	AWT (ex-AO)	9 Sept 1982 (renewed)
Ranger	AOT	16 Oct 1981
Rover	AOT	1 Jan 1982

Note All are based in or around Diego Garcia, Indian Ocean.

Ships Chartered by MSC

Name	Type	Chartered from	Effective date
Acadian Mariner	ATF	Acadian Marine	9 Dec 1981
Admiral William M. Callaghan	AKR/RO-RO	Sun Export	19 Dec 1981
American Corsair	AK/C4	US Lines	1 Sept 1971
American Monarch	AK/C4	US Lines	17 Sept 1981
American Ranger	AK/C4	US Lines	11 Sept 1971
American Reliance	AK/C4	US Lines	8 Aug 1971
American Trojan	AK/C4	US Lines	not available
Banner	AO	Grand Bassa Tankers	15 Oct 1981
Bay	AK/C3	Central Gulf	1 Apr 1980
Builder	AK/C3	Central Gulf	4 Mar 1980
Buyer	AK/C3	Central Gulf	1 May 1980
Cove Navigator	AO	Cove Tankers	15 Aug 1971
Cove Tide	AO	Cove Ship	12 Aug 1971
Cygnus	AKR/RO-RO	Lykes Brothers	28 Mar 1981
Dawn	AK/C4	Central Gulf	3 Mar 1980
Energy Service I	AGOR	Brazoport Marine	1 Nov 1978
Golden Endeaver	AO/T8	Ultramar Trident	10 Dec 1981
Gulf Shipper	AK/C3	Lykes Brothers	12 Mar 1980
Gulf Trader	AK/C3	Lykes Brothers	12 Mar 1980
Long Lines	ARC	Transoeanic Cable Ship	24 Aug 1981
Mallory Lykes	AK/C4	Lykes Brothers	24 May 1980
Mason Lykes	AK/C4	Lykes Brothers	16 June 1980
Monarch		British P & O	1 Nov 1981
New York Sun	AO	Sun Transportation	17 Dec 1980
Overseas Harriette	AKD	Ocean Bulk Ships	29 Jan 1981
Overseas Marilyn	AKD	Trans. Bulk Carriers	1 June 1980
Paul Langevin III	ATF	Tractor Marine	2 Nov 1981
Spirit of Liberty	AO	Charles Kurz	6 Oct 1968
Texaco Rhode Island	AO	States Tankers	6 Oct 1968
Texas Trader	AO	American Trading and Trans	15 Dec 1980
Transcolorado	AK/C4 (heavy lift)	Hudson Waterways	26 July 1968
Transcolumbia	AK/C4 (heavy lift)	Hudson Waterways	3 Oct 1968

Note *Golden Dolphin* (AO/T8), a ship on charter to MSC, exploded and sank on 7 March, 1982, while crossing the Atlantic.

US COAST GUARD

At the beginning of FY-1976 the Coast Guard listed 256 cutters of all types. By types, they were as follows: WHEC (7); WMEC (22); WAGB (10); WPB (77); WYTM (13); WYTL (15); WAGO (2); WLB (35); WLM (16); WLI (10); WLR (22); WLV (6); WTR (2) and WIX (2).

At the beginning of FY-1982 there were 249 cutters on the Coast Guard List, not including 13 under construction. They were as follows: WHEC (17); WMEC (30); WAGB (6); WPB (79); WYTM (9); WYTL (15); WTGB (6); WAGO (1); WLB (28); WLM (13); WLI (5); WLR (18); WLIC (18); WTR (1); WIX (1) and WLV (2).

The US Coast Guard is a highly efficient branch of the Armed Forces with a low profile. Established by an Act of Congress 28 January, 1915, it combined the old Revenue Cutter Service (est. 1790) and the Life Saving Service (est. 1848). The Act provided that the "Coast Guard shall be a service in the Treasury Department, except in war when it becomes part of the Navy". On 1 July, 1939, the Lighthouse Service (est. 1789) was transferred to the Coast Guard, followed by the Bureau of Navigation and Steamboat Inspection on 28 February, 1942. On 1 April, 1967, the Coast Guard was transferred to the newly-formed Department of Transportation. Currently there is a strong move to transfer the Coast Guard permanently to the US Navy, but the Coast Guard opposes this, as does the Navy Department. In times of war the Coast Guard has served the Navy heroically, with countless incidents of bravery and many dangerous missions to its credit. If there is a fault, it is that the Coast Guard is the most unsung branch of the Armed Forces and deserves more acknowledgement of its service to the country.

The US Coast Guard has instituted a policy whereby a large number of women officers and enlisted ranks/ratings are being deployed aboard combat craft. The wisdom of this policy is open to serious doubts. It is not a question of whether women can perform the assignments, for they would certainly do credit to the service. What is questionable is the *compatibility* of men and women during combat. A ship is a weapon of war, and its crew must work as one, for anything else than total teamwork can only lead to trouble. Can this be achieved with women on board? We think not, but time alone will tell.

Officially, the Coast Guard lists all classes of cutters by the vessels' length. For convenience to the reader, we will use the Navy system of listing by the lead ship's name.

Type: High-Endurance Cutters (WHEC) *Number/Class:* 12 *Hamilton* and *Hero*

Name	*Number*	*Laid down*	*Launched*	*Commissioned*	*Status*
Hamilton	WHEC-715	Jan 1965	18 Dec 1965	20 Feb 1967	AA
Dallas	WHEC-716	7 Feb 1966	1 Oct 1966	1 Oct 1967	AA
Mellon	WHEC-717	25 July 1966	11 Feb 1967	22 Dec 1967	PA
Chase	WHEC-718	27 Oct 1966	20 May 1967	1 Mar 1968	AA
Boutwell	WHEC-719	5 Dec 1966	17 June 1967	14 June 1968	PA
Sherman	WHEC-720	23 Jan 1967	23 Sept 1967	23 Aug 1968	PA
Gallatin	WHEC-721	27 Feb 1967	18 Nov 1967	20 Dec 1968	AA
Morgenthau	WHEC-722	17 July 1967	10 Feb 1968	14 Feb 1969	PA
Rush	WHEC-723	23 Oct 1967	16 Nov 1968	3 July 1969	PA
Munro	WHEC-724	18 Feb 1970	5 Dec 1970	10 Sept 1971	PA
Jarvis	WHEC-725	9 Sept 1970	24 Apr 1971	30 Dec 1971	PA
Midgett	WHEC-726	5 Apr 1971	4 Sept 1971	17 Mar 1972	PA

Builder Avondale Shipyards Inc, New Orleans, La
Displacement Full load, 3,050 tons
Length overall 378ft (115.2m)
Maximum beam 42.8ft (13.1m)
Maximum draught 20ft (6.1m)
Main machinery Two Pratt and Whitney FT-4A gas turbines; two 12-cylinder Fairbanks-Morse diesel engines
Screws/h.p. Two controllable pitch propellers; 36,000 s.h.p. (gas turbines), 7,000 b.h.p. (diesels)
Maximum speed 29 knots

Midgett (WHEC-726). These handsome vessels have proved to be very efficient, and with slight modification they would make excellent ASW platforms in wartime *(US Coast Guard)*

Armament One single 5in/38 (Mark 30) mount, two 40mm mounts, two 20mm (Mark 16) machine guns, two triple ASW torpedo tubes (Mark 32)
Aircraft One Seaguard (HH-52A) or Pelican (HH-3F) helicopter
Complement 15 officers, 149 enlisted men

The *Hamilton/Heros*' were originally designated Gunboats (WPG), but were reclassified WHEC on 1 May, 1966. They are the Coast Guard's only "long-legged boats" and possess good seakeeping qualities. These ships have a distinctive clipper bow and two funnels abreast, enclosing a helicopter hangar. An 80ft (24.4m) long helicopter deck is fitted aft. The superstructure is mostly of aluminium, and they are fitted with oceanographic laboratories, elaborate communications equipment, and facilities for gathering meteorological data.

Engine and propeller pitch controls are located in the wheelhouse, at the bridge wing stations, and in the engine room control booth. Bridge manoeuvring control is by use of an aircraft-type "joy stick" instead of a wheel. A 350 s.h.p. retractable bow thruster located abaft the sonar dome allows station keeping and precise manoeuvring.

The original Hedgehog ASW weapons have been removed, and the Mark 309 fire control system for the Mark 32 torpedo tubes has been installed.

Electronics comprise AN/SPS-29 and 64 search radars, the Mark 56 gunfire control system, and the AN/SPG-35 fire control radar and a bow-mounted AN/SQS-38 sonar.

Type: High-Endurance Cutter (WHEC) — *Number/Class:* 1 *Casco*

Name	Number	Laid down	Launched	Commissioned	Status
Unimak (ex-WTR-379; ex-WHEC-379; ex USN AVP-31)	WHEC-379	15 Feb 1942	27 May 1942	31 Dec 1943	AA

Builder Associated SB, Seattle, Wash
Displacement Standard, 1,766 tons; full load, 2,800 tons
Length overall 310.75ft (94.7m)
Maximum beam 41ft (12.5m)
Maximum draught 13.5ft (4.1m)
Main machinery Two Fairbanks-Morse diesel engines
Screws/b.h.p. 2/6,080
Maximum speed 18 knots
Armament One single 5in/38 (Mark 30) gun, two 20mm (Mark 16) machine guns
Accommodation 150 total (13 officers, 137 enlisted men)

Unimak is the last of the 18 former US Navy Small Seaplane Tenders (AVP) of the *Barnegat* class that were transferred to the Coast Guard during 1946/1948, *Unimak* being transferred on 14 September, 1948. Originally designated WPG, they then became WAVP's and finally were all changed to WHEC on 1 May, 1966.

Unimak was further reclassified WTR-379 on 28 November, 1969, and operated as a training cutter out of Baltimore until decommissioned there on 30 May, 1975. Reverted to WHEC on 15 August, 1977. With the Coast Guard in desperate need of more ships to patrol territorial waters, the ship was towed to Boston for reactivation. This was delayed by an engine room fire. She was finally recommissioned on 15 August, 1977. *Unimak* was overhauled during 1981/1982, and it is planned to keep her active until the first *Bear* (WMEC-901) class units are commissioned.

Sole survivor of the 18 *Casco*-class cutters, *Unimak* started life with the US Navy as a Small Seaplane Tender (AVP) *Unimak* will serve until the first of the new *Bear*-class WMECs are commissioned *(US Coast Guard)*

Type: High-Endurance Cutters (WHEC) — *Number/Class:* 4 *Bibb*

Name	Number	Laid down	Launched	Commissioned	Status
Bibb (ex-**George M. Bibb**)	WHEC-31	10 May 1935	14 Jan 1937	10 Mar 1937	AA
Duane (ex-**William J. Duane**)	WHEC-33	1 May 1935	3 June 1936	16 Aug 1936	AA
Ingham (ex-**Samuel D. Ingham**)	WHEC-35	1 May 1935	3 June 1936	12 Sept 1936	AA
Taney (ex-**Roger B. Taney**)	WHEC-37	1 May 1935	3 June 1936	20 Nov 1936	AA

Builders Philadelphia Navy Yard, Phil, Pa (except *Bibb*, Charleston Navy Yard, Charleston, S.C.)
Displacement Standard, 2,216 tons; full load, 2,656 tons
Length overall 327ft (99.7m)
Maximum beam 41ft (12.5m)
Maximum draught 15ft (4.6m)
Main machinery Westinghouse geared turbines. Two Babcock and Wilcox boilers
Screws/s.h.p. 2/6,200
Maximum speed 19.8 knots
Armament One single 5in/38 (Mark 30) gun mount, two 40mm/60 DP mounts, two 20mm (Mark 16) machine guns (WHEC-35)
Complement 13 officers, 131 enlisted men

Originally a class of seven, all of these vessels were commissioned as Gunboats (WPG), and all were reclassified High Endurance Cutters (WHEC) on 1 May, 1966. Soon after completion these ships dropped their first name and middle initial. *Taney* is the only Pearl Harbor attack survivor still on active duty. During the Second World War, all except the lost *Hamilton* (WPG-34) served as Amphibious Force Flagships. The midships structure was built up and one or two additional masts were installed. The fixed Hedgehogs and the two Mark 32 triple torpedo tubes that were installed after the war have since been removed. They are equipped with AN/SPS-64 surface search radar.

Deletions: *Hamilton* (WPG-34) was lost during the Second World War. *Spencer* (WHEC-36) was decommissioned on 1 February, 1974. She served as a stationary engineering school ship until 1981, when she was sold for scrap. *Campbell* (WHEC-32) was decommissioned for disposal in FY-1982.

Bibb (WHEC-31). Having seen long and strenuous service over a 45-year period, this class is on the way out *(US Coast Guard)*

Ingham (WHEC-35) departing the harbour at Norfolk, Va *(US Coast Guard)*

Type: Medium-Endurance Cutters (WMEC) — *Number/Class:* 1+12 *Bear*

Name	*Number*	*Laid down*	*Launched*	*Commissioned*	*Status*
Bear	WMEC-901	23 Aug 1979	25 Sept 1980	21 Sept 1983	PA
Tampa	WMEC-902	3 Apr 1980	19 Mar 1981	Dec 1983	BLDG
Harriet Lane	WMEC-903	15 Oct 1980	6 Feb 1982		BLDG
Northland	WMEC-904	9 Apr 1981	7 May 1982		BLDG
Spencer (ex **Seneca**)	WMEC-905	26 June 1982			BLDG
Seneca (ex **Pickering**)	WMEC-906	16 Sept 1982			BLDG
Escanaba	WMEC-907	1 Apr 1983			BLDG
Tahoma (ex **Legare**)	WMEC-908				ORD
(ex **Argus**)	WMEC-909				ORD
(ex **Tahoma**)	WMEC-910				ORD
(ex **Erie**)	WMEC-911				ORD
	WMEC-912				ORD
(ex **McCulloch**)					
(ex **Ewing**)	WMEC-913				ORD

Builders Tacoma Boatbuilding Co, Tacoma, Wash (WMEC-901/904); Robert E. Derecktor, Inc, Middletown, R.I. (remainder)
Displacement full load, 1,780 tons
Length overall 270ft (82.3m)
Maximum beam 38ft (11.6m)
Maximum draught 13.5ft (4.1m)
Main machinery Diesel engines
Screws/b.h.p. 2/7,000
Maximum speed 19.5 knots
Armament One 3in/62 (Mark 75) gun mount
Aircraft One Seaguard (HH-52A) or one Lamps III helicopter
Complement 13 officers, 85 enlisted men

Artist's impression of the *Bear*-class WMEC. These ships will replace the *Bibb* class, Unimak and the former US Navy ATFs and WHECs

This class was "launched" into a sea of troubles before the first unit was even commissioned. After the initial construction contract for the first four units of a projected class of 13 ships had been awarded to Tacoma Boatbuilding, the Coast Guard decided to exercise a contract option to award construction of the rest of the class to Tacoma. This was done on 29 August, 1980. At that time one of the original bidders, Robert E. Derecktor Corp., Middleton, Rhode Island, filed a law suit against the Coast Guard and Government, claiming it had been falsely disqualified as a bidder by the Coast Guard. With this threat hanging over them, the Coast Guard withdrew the contract for construction of WMEC-905/913 and re-awarded it to the Derecktor Corp. Tacoma Boatbuilding then filed suit against the Coast Guard for this action, which it ultimately lost. The interesting point is that the Derecktor Corp has no shipyard in Middleton, or anywhere else, where it can build these ships. During the company's recertification, the Coast Guard certified that the Derecktor facilities at the former Newport Naval Base/NAS Quonset, where it leases space from the state, were satisfactory. However, at no time has there ever been a shipyard in the area for the construction of large ships. There are Yacht Mariners, but they are not able to build 270ft-long Coast Guard cutters. To complicate matters further, the Coast Guard had played "musical chairs" with the naming of these ships (see Construction tables). All of these name changes and cancellations of names were effective on 30 September, 1981. No logical reason for any of this has been forthcoming. The *Bear* class is intended to replace the overaged WHEC/WMECs now in service.

WMEC-901 and -902 were authorised in the FY-1977 Programme; WMEC-903 and -904 in FY-1978; WMEC-905 and -906 in FY-1979; WMEC-907 to -909 in FY-1981; and WMEC-911 to -913 in FY-1982.

These ships will be employed on long patrols at low speeds, which is why diesel propulsion was chosen, instead of gas turbines for high speed operations. Space and weight has been reserved for the Harpoon missile system, the Phalanx CIWS system, and the Mark 92 fire control system. The Mark 36 Super Chaffroc RBOC is to be fitted. Each ship will be fitted with a Tactass towed-array sonar system as well. ASW weapons would be delivered by the ships' helicopters. Hull-mounted sonars will not be fitted. These vessels are easily recognised by their helicopter hangar and the Mark 92 weapons control antenna dome. They are the first cutters to have automatic command and control centres. Fin stabilisers are to be fitted.

Electronics: AN/SPS-64 surface search radar, Mark 92 weapons control system (radome above the bridge).

Type: Medium-Endurance Cutters (WMEC)
Training Cutter (WTR)

Number/Class: 17 *Reliance*

Name	Number	Launched	Commissioned	Status
Reliance (ex-WTR-615, WMEC-615)	WMEC-615	25 May 1963	20 June 1964	AA
Diligence	WMEC-616	20 July 1963	26 Aug 1964	AA
Vigilant	WMEC-617	24 Dec 1963	3 Oct 1964	AA
Active	WMEC-618	21 July 1965	17 Sept 1966	AA
Confidence	WMEC-619	8 May 1965	19 Feb 1966	PA
Resolute	WMEC-620	30 Apr 1966	8 Dec 1966	AA
Valiant	WMEC-621	14 Jan 1967	28 Oct 1967	AA
Courageous	WMEC-622	18 Mar 1967	10 Apr 1968	PA
Steadfast	WMEC-623	24 June 1967	25 Sept 1968	AA
Dauntless	WMEC-624	21 Oct 1967	10 June 1968	AA
Venturous	WMEC-625	11 Nov 1967	16 Aug 1968	PA
Dependable	WMEC-626	16 Mar 1968	22 Nov 1968	AA
Vigorous	WMEC-627	4 May 1968	2 May 1969	AA
Durable	WMEC-628	29 Apr 1967	8 Dec 1967	PA
Decisive	WMEC-629	14 Dec 1967	23 Aug 1968	AA
Alert	WMEC-630	19 Oct 1968	4 Aug 1969	AA

Builders Todd Shipyards (WMEC-615, -616, -617); Christy Corp (WMEC-618); Coast Guard Yard, Curtis Bay, Baltimore, Md (WMEC-619, -625, -628, -629); American SB Co, Lorain, Ohio (WMEC-620/624, -626, -627, -630)
Displacement Standard, 950 tons; full load, 970 tons (WMEC-616/619), 1,007 tons (remainder)
Length overall 210.5ft (64.2m)
Maximum beam 34ft (10.4m)
Maximum draught 10.5ft (3.2m)
Main machinery Two Solar gas turbines (WMEC-615/619 only); two turbo-charged Alco 251B diesel engines
Screws/h.p. 2/4,000 s.h.p. (gas turbines); 2/5,000 b.h.p. (diesels)
Maximum speed 18 knots
Armament One single 3in/50 gun mount, two 40mm (Mark 19) gun mounts
Aircraft One Seaguard (HH-52A) helicopter, when deployed
Complement 7 officers, 54 enlisted men

Cutters WTR-615 and WMEC-616/630 are basically to the same design and perform the same missions. The class is officially sub-divided into two classes, "A" (WTR-615, WMEC-616/619) and "B" (remainder) because of the difference in propulsion. Both classes have fire-fighting, fuel transfer and pumping capabilities. They can tow ships of up to 10,000 tons and have a high degree of habitability. The bridge has 360° visibility, there is a helicopter deck (but no hangar), and the engine exhaust vent is in the stern, eliminating the need for conventional stacks. Fitted with AN/SPS-64 surface search radar.

Originally designated WPC (Patrol Craft), all of these ships were reclassified WMEC on 1 May 1966. *Reliance* was reclassified from WMEC to WTR on 27 June, 1975, replacing *Unimak* (WTR-379). Back to WMEC in 1982.

▲ *Dauntless* (WMEC-624) *(US Coast Guard)*

▼ *Confidence* (WMEC-619). Unlike *Dauntless*, she is powered by gas turbine. Each ship of this class can tow ships of up to 10,000 gross tons *(US Coast Guard)*

Type: Medium-Endurance Cutters (WMEC) *Number/Class:* 3 Diver

Name	Number	Laid down	Launched	Commissioned	Status
Escape (ex-USN ARS-6)	WMEC-6	24 Aug 1942	22 Nov 1942	20 Nov 1943	AA
Acushnet (ex-WAGO-167; ex-WAT-167; ex-**Shackle**, ARS-9)	WMEC-167	26 Oct 1942	1 Apr 1943	5 Feb 1944	AA
Yocona (ex-WAT-168; ex-**Seize**, ARS-26)	WMEC-168	8 Sept 1943	8 Apr 1944	3 Nov 1944	PA

Builder Basalt Rock Co, Napa, Cal
Displacement Standard, 1,557 tons; full load, 1,745 tons
Length overall 213.5ft (65.1m)
Maximum beam 39ft (11.9m)
Maximum draught 15ft (4.6m)
Main machinery Two Cooper-Bessemer GSB-8 diesel engines
Screws/b.h.p. 2/3,000
Maximum speed 15.5 knots
Armament Removed
Complement 7 officers, 57 enlisted men (except WMEC-168, 65 enlisted men)

Steel-hulled salvage ships modified to cutter configuration, these vessels were transferred from the Navy to the Coast Guard 29 June, 1946 (WMEC-167), 28 June, 1946 (WMEC-168), and 4 December, 1980 (WMEC-6). WMEC-167 and -168 are permanent transfers; WMEC-6 is on loan. *Escape* is assigned to the drug patrol.

The first two ships were originally classified WAT (Tugs). In 1968, *Yocona* was reclassified WMEC and *Acushnet* was reclassified WAGO (Oceanographic Cutter). The latter was modified for handling environmental data buoys; she reverted to WMEC in 1980. *Escape* was overhauled and modernised at the Coast Guard Yard, Curtis Bay, in 1980/1981.

Electronics: fitted with AN/SPS-64 surface search radar.

Yocona (WMEC-168). *Yocona*, *Acushnet* and the newly acquired *Escape* (WMEC-6) were all built as Salvage Ships (ARS) for the Navy during the Second World War *(US Coast Guard)*

Type: Medium-Endurance Cutters (WMEC) — *Number/Class:* 5 *Cherokee/Abnaki*

Name	Number	Laid down	Launched	Commissioned	Status
Ute (ex-USN ATF-76)	WMEC-76	27 Feb 1942	25 June 1942	31 Dec 1942	PA
Lipan (ex-USN ATF-85)	WMEC-85	30 May 1942	17 Sept 1942	29 Apr 1943	PA
Chilula (ex WATF-153; ex-WAT-153; ex-USN ATF-153)	WMEC-153	13 July 1944	1 Dec 1944	5 Apr 1945	AA
Cherokee (ex-WATF-165; ex-WAT-165; ex-USN ATF-66)	WMEC-165	23 Dec 1938	10 Nov 1939	26 Apr 1940	AA
Tamaroa (ex-WATF-166; ex-WAT-166; ex-**Zuni** ATF-95)	WMEC-166	8 Mar 1943	13 July 1943	9 Oct 1943	AA

Builders United Engineering Co, Alameda, Cal (WMEC-76, -85); Charleston SB and DD Co, Charleston, S.C. (WMEC-153); Bethlehem Steel Co, Staten Island, N.Y. (WMEC-165); Commercial Iron Works, Portland, Ore (WMEC-166)
Displacement Standard, 1,240 tons; full load, 1,731 tons
Length overall 205ft (62.5m)
Maximum beam 38.5ft (11.7m)
Maximum draught 17ft (5.2m)
Main machinery One General Motors diesel; electric drive
Screws/b.h.p. 1/3,000
Maximum speed 16.2 knots
Armament One single 3in/50 gun mount, two 40mm gun mounts
Complement 7 officers, 65 enlisted men

Former US Navy Fleet Tugs (ATF), these ships were transferred to the Coast Guard as follows: *Cherokee* and *Tamaroa* on 29 June, 1946, *Chilula* on 9 July, 1956, and *Lipan* and *Ute* on 30 September, 1980. *Chilula, Cherokee* and *Tamaroa* originally classified WAT, then to WATF, and were finally reclassified Medium Endurance Cutters (WMEC) in 1968. All three were permanently transferred to the Coast Guard on 1 June, 1969. *Ute* and *Lipan* are on loan. The planned acquisition of *Hopi* (ATF-71) from the Maritime Administration was cancelled.

Electronics: all are fitted with AN/SPS-64 surface search radar.

Avoyel (WMEC-150) (ex-USN-ATF-150), a sister ship, was decommissioned in 1969 and sold to a private concern for commercial service.

WMEC disposals: Of the *Modoc* class, former USN Auxiliary Tugs (ATA), of the *Sotoyomo* class, *Comanche* (WMEC-202) and *Modoc* (WMEC-194), were decommissioned in 1980 and transferred to the Maritime Administration for disposal.

Cherokee (WMEC-165), with a *Reliance*-class cutter in the background. *Cherokee* and her four sisters were built during the Second World War as Fleet Tugboats (ATF) for the Navy, *Cherokee* being the class prototype. After over 40 years of service the class is only now being phased out of the US Navy *(US Coast Guard)*

Type: Medium-Endurance Cutter (WMEC) — *Number/Class:* 1 *Storis*

Name	Number	Laid down	Launched	Commissioned	Status
Storis (ex-WAGB-38; ex-**Eskimo** WAGL-38)	WMEC-38	14 July 1941	4 Apr 1942	30 Sept 1942	PA

Builder Toledo SB Co, Toledo, Ohio
Displacement Standard, 1,715 tons; full load, 1,925 tons
Length overall 230ft (70.1m)
Maximum beam 43ft (13.1m)
Maximum draught 15ft (4.6m)
Main machinery Three Cooper-Bessemer diesel-electric engines. One Westinghouse electric motor
Screws/b.h.p. 1/3,000
Maximum speed 14 knots
Armament One single 3in/50 gun mount, two 40mm (Mark 64) gun mounts
Complement 10 officers, 96 enlisted men

Completed as WAGL-38, this vessel was reclassified WAGB on 1 May, 1966, and to WMEC on 1 July, 1972. Strengthened for ice navigation and employed in Alaska for search, rescue, and law enforcement missions, *Storis* has been a long-familiar sight at Kodiak, Alaska, where she is stationed. Fitted with AN/SPS-64 surface search radar.

Type: Icebreakers (WAGB) — Number/Class: 2 Polar Star

Name	Number	Builder	Commissioned	Status
Polar Star	WAGB-10	Lockheed SB Co, Seattle, Wash	19 Jan 1976	PA
Polar Sea	WAGB-11	Lockheed SB Co, Seattle, Wash	23 Feb 1978	PA

Displacement Full load, 12,087 tons
Length overall 399ft (121.6m)
Maximum beam 86ft (26.2m)
Maximum draught 31ft (9.5m)
Main machinery Three Pratt & Whitney FT4A-12 gas turbines, six Alco diesel engines
Screws/h.p. 3 (controllable-pitch)/60,000 (gas turbines); 18,000 (diesel engines)
Maximum speed 13 knots
Armament Two 40mm machine guns (Mark 19)
Aircraft Two Seaguard (HH-52A) helicopters
Complement 13 officers, 125 enlisted men, plus 10 scientists and 15 flight crew

These are the largest Coast Guard icebreakers, and were built to replace the dated Second World War "Wind" class units. *Polar Star* was authorised in FY-1971, and *Polar Sea* in FY-1973. Originally, six units of this class were planned, but no more are to be built in the immediate future. Two 15-ton-capacity cranes, a helicopter flight deck and hangar are located aft. The *Polar Star*s have extensive laboratory facilities for Arctic and oceanographic research.

The conventional ice-breaking hull of this class has a cutaway bow and well-rounded body to prevent the ship being trapped in heavy ice. Controllable pitch screws on three shafts permit manoeuvring in heavy ice, minimising damage to the blades. Diesel engine propulsion is employed for normal cruising in field ice, while the gas turbines are used for "heavy work". These ships can break 6ft (1.83m) thick ice at slow speeds, and can ride up on to the ice to break up to 21ft (6.4m) ice packs.

For nearly two years after commissioning *Polar Star* experienced severe engineering problems, causing her to remain in port almost all of the time. Part of the problem centred on the shafts and the screws.

Electronics: Fitted with AN/SPS-64 surface search radar.

Polar Star (WAGB-10) pictured in February 1978 during her first deployment to the Antarctic. Ships of her class can break ice up to 21ft (6.4m) thick *(US Coast Guard)*

Type: Icebreaker (WAGB) — Number/Class: 1 Glacier

Name	Number	Laid down	Launched	Commissioned	Status
Glacier (ex USS AGB-4)	WAGB-4	3 Aug 1953	27 Aug 1954	27 May 1955	PA

Builder Ingalls SB Corp, Pascagoula, Miss
Displacement Full load, 8,449 tons
Length overall 309.6ft (94.4m)
Maximum beam 74ft (22.6m)
Maximum draught 29ft (8.8m)
Main machinery Ten Fairbanks-Morse diesel engines; two Westinghouse electric motors
Screws/b.h.p. 2/21,000
Maximum speed 17.6 knots
Armament None (see notes)
Aircraft Two Seaguard (HH-52A) helicopters
Complement 15 officers, 226 enlisted men

Originally built and operated by the US Navy, *Glacier* was transferred to the Coast Guard on 30 June, 1956. Part of her original armament, three twin 3in/50 gun mounts and four 20mm mounts, was removed before transfer, and the twin 5in/38 mount was removed in 1969. *Glacier* has a heavily armoured bow, a helicopter deck, and a small hangar. Two 40mm (Mark 16) machine guns are to be fitted.

Electronics: Fitted with AN/SPS-64 surface search radar.

Originally commissioned in the Navy in May 1955, *Glacier* was transferred to the Coast Guard in June 1956. She was overhauled in 1983.

Type: Icebreakers (WAGB) *Number/Class:* 2 *Wind*

Name	*Number*	*Builder*	*Launched*	*Status*
Westwind (ex-USS AGB-6)	WAGB-281	Western Pipe and Steel Co, San Pedro, Cal	31 Mar 1943	GLA
Northwind	WAGB-282	Western Pipe and Steel Co, San Pedro, Cal	25 Feb 1945	AA

Displacement Standard, 3,500 tons; full load, 6,515 tons
Length overall 269ft (82m)
Maximum beam 63.5ft (19.4m)
Maximum draught 29ft (8.8m)
Main machinery Four Enterprise diesel electric drive engines
Screws/b.h.p. 2/10,000
Maximum speed 16 knots
Armament Two 40mm (Mark 19) machine guns
Aircraft Two Seaguard (HH-52A) helicopters
Complement 135 total

There were originally seven ships in this class, five of which were delivered to the Coast Guard and two to the Navy. WAGB-281, along with two sisters since deleted, was loaned to the Russian Navy during the Second World War. The Russians astounded the Navy by actually returning them, albeit in filthy condition. Except for these ships and the ex-USS *Milwaukee* (CL-5), they have not returned any that were received under lend-lease.

These two ships were re-engined; WAGB-281 in 1973/1974, and WAGB-282 in 1974/1975, and they became known as the *Wind-R* class. They have helicopter decks and telescopic hangars.

They were originally completed with a third propeller shaft, which was located in the bow, but this was removed as it was frequently damaged in heavy ice.

Electronics: Fitted with AN/SPS-64 surface search radar.

Disposal: *Burton Island* (WAGB-283), of this class, was deleted on 9 May, 1978 for disposal.

Northwind (WAGB-282). Of the original seven ships in this class only the re-engined *Northwind* and *Westwind* survive *(US Coast Guard)*

Type: Icebreaker (WAGB) — Number/Class: 1 Mackinaw

Name	Number	Laid down	Launched	Commissioned	Status
Mackinaw (ex-**Manitowoc**)	WAGB-83	20 Mar 1943	6 Mar 1944	20 Dec 1944	GLA

Builder Toledo SB Co, Toledo, Ohio
Displacement Full load, 5,252 tons
Length overall 290ft (99.4m)
Maximum beam 74ft (22.6m)
Maximum draught 19ft (5.8m)
Main machinery Two Fairbanks-Morse diesel engines; Elliot electric drive
Screws/b.h.p. Three (one forward, two aft)/10,000
Maximum speed 18.7 knots
Aircraft One Seaguard (HH-52A) helicopter
Complement 10 officers, 117 enlisted men

This ship was specifically designed for Great Lakes ice-breaking duties. Originally classed as WAG-83, she was reclassified WAGB on 1 May, 1966. Two 12-ton capacity cranes are fitted, and there is provision for a helicopter area on the quarterdeck.

Electronics: Fitted with AN/SPS-64 surface search radar.

Great Lakes icebreaker *Mackinaw* (WAGB-83)

Type: Icebreaking Tugs (WTGB) — Number/Class: 6+1 Katmai Bay

Name	Number	Laid down	Commissioned	Status
Katmai Bay	WTGB-101	7 Nov 1977	8 Jan 1979	GLA
Bristol Bay	WTGB-102	13 Feb 1978	5 Apr 1979	GLA
Mobile Bay	WTGB-103	13 Feb 1978	6 May 1979	GLA
Biscayne Bay	WTGB-104	29 Aug 1978	8 Dec 1979	GLA
Neah Bay	WTGB-105	6 Aug 1979	18 Aug 1980	GLA
Morro Bay	WTGB-106	6 Aug 1979	25 Jan 1981	AA
Penobscot Bay	WTGB-107	June 1983		BLDG

Builder Tacoma Boatbuilding Co, Tacoma, Wash
Displacement Full load, 662 tons
Length overall 140ft (42.7m)
Maximum beam 37.6ft (11.4m)
Maximum draught 12.5ft (3.8m)
Main machinery Diesel-electric engines
Screws/b.h.p. 1/2,500
Maximum speed 14.7 knots
Complement 3 officers, 14 enlisted men

Built as replacements for the 110ft class WYTMs, these vessels were authorised as follows: WTGB-101 in FY-1976; WTGB-102/104 in FY-1977; WTGB-105 and -106 in FY-1978; and WTGB-107 in FY-1981. They have manoeuvrability and other characteristics suitable for harbours and other restricted waters, and are ice-strengthened for service on the Great Lakes, coastal waters, and rivers.

Electronics: Fitted with AN/SPS-64 surface search radar.

The class was originally designated WYTM, but was reclassified WTGB on 5 February, 1979. (More data on page 234.)

Icebreaking tug *Bristol Bay* (WTGB-102)

Type: Patrol Craft, Surface-Effect Ship (WSES) — *Number/Name:* 3 "Sea Bird"

Name	Number	Builder	Commissioned	F/S
Sea Hawk	WSES-2	Bell-Halter Inc, New Orleans, La	16 Oct 1982	AA
Shearwater	WSES-3	Bell-Halter Inc, New Orleans, La	16 Oct 1982	AA
Petrel	WSES-4	Bell-Halter Inc, New Orleans, La	17 June 1983	AA

Displacement Full load, 145 tons
Length overall 110ft (33.5m)
Maximum beam 39ft (11.9m)
Maximum draught 8.3ft (2.5m)
Main machinery Propulsion, two Detroit diesels; lift, two Detroit diesels; two double-inlet centrifugal 40in-diameter lift fans
Screws/b.h.p. 2/3,200 (propulsion); 736 bhp (lift)
Maximum speed 30+ knots
Endurance 1,250 nm at 30 knots
Armament Two 50-cal machine guns
Complement 2 officers, 16 enlisted men

Following the successful tests of USCG *Dorado* (WSES-1) the Coast Guard decided to order three modified units for use on the drug patrol in the Caribbean. The ships were ordered in June 1982 from Bell-Halter.

Their primary roles are the enforcement of maritime laws and treaties and search and rescue. The design includes a welded marine aluminium alloy hull comprising two sidehulls with connecting deck. The bow and stern have flexible seals to contain an air cushion, and the boat is supported by cushion lift as well as hydrostatic and hydrodynamic lift on the sidewalls. The bow seal consists of eight fingers, each of which is attached to the underside of the centre hull. The stern seal consists of three inflated lobes.

Each ship carries two Decca 914 surface search radars.

Disposals: USCG *Dorado* was decommissioned on 15 December, 1981, and returned to the US Navy, from which she was on loan.

Type: Patrol Craft, Large (WPB) — *Number/Class:* 26 *Cape* (A), (B) and (C)

Name	Number	Status	Name	Number	Status	Name	Number	Status
"A" class								
Cape Small	95300	PA	***Cape Gull**	95304	AA	**Cape Strait**	95308	AR
Cape Coral	95301	PA	***Cape Hatteras**	95305	PA	**Cape Carter**	95309	PA
***Cape Higgon**	95302	AA	***Cape George**	95306	AA	**Cape Wash**	95310	PA
***Cape Upright**	95303	AA	***Cape Current**	95307	AA	**Cape Hedge**	95311	PA
"B" class								
***Cape Knox**	95312	AA	***Cape Fox**	95316	AA	**Cape Newagen**	95318	PR
***Cape Morgan**	95313	AA	**Cape Jellison**	95317	AA	**Cape Romain**	95319	PA
Cape Weather	95314	AA				**Cape Starr**	95320	AA
"C" class								
Cape Cross	95321	AA	***Cape Shoalwater**	95324	AA	***Cape Henlopen**	95328	AA
***Cape Horn**	95322	AA	**Cape Corwin**	95326	PA	**Cape York**	95332	AA

* Modernised

Builder Coast Guard Yard, Curtis Bay, Baltimore, Md
Displacement Standard, 95 tons; full load, 105 tons
Length overall 95ft (29m)
Maximum beam 20ft (6.1m)
Maximum draught 6ft (1.8m)
Main machinery Four Cummings diesel engines, except in modernised ships (General Motors)
Screws/b.h.p. 2/2,324
Maximum speed 20 knots (21 knots, "C" class)
Armament Two–five machine guns
Complement 1 officer, 13 enlisted men

These steel-hulled vessels are designed for search and rescue operations and for port security. "A" class was completed in 1953, "B" class in 1955/1956, and "C" class in 1958/1959. Nine units of the "C" class were transferred to South Korea in 1968.

Cape Higgon, *Cape Hatteras*, *Cape Upright*, and *Cape Gull* were laid up for disposal in December 1972, but they were rein-

"Cape"-class Patrol Boat (WPB) *Cape Carter*. It was planned to replace this class with new construction in the 1980s, but costs rose and now these boats are to be modernised instead *(US Coast Guard)*

stated during 1979/1980 for reconstruction and modernisation. In fact, plans were made to dispose of all of the *Capes*, beginning in 1974, in favour of a new class, but when construction of the new class was cancelled an extensive modernisation programme was instituted in 1977. The cost of modernising each unit was $500,000 in 1976 dollars, but by 1980 the cost had risen to $2 million each. The programme, which will extend the useful life of each vessel another ten years, includes new engines, electronics, and deck equipment. The superstructure is modernised or replaced and habitability improved. An estimated eight months yard period for each vessel is required.

The *Capes* are fitted with AN/SPS-64 surface search radar.

Type: Patrol Craft, Large (WPB) — *Number/Class:* 53 *Point* (A), (C) and (D)

Name	Number	Status	Name	Number	Status	Name	Number	Status
"A" class								
Point Hope	82302	AA	**Point Verde**	82311	AA	**Point Thatcher**	82314	AA
			Point Swift	82312	AA			
"C" class								
Point Herron	82318	AA	**Point Estero**	82344	AA	**Point Stuart**	82358	PA
Point Roberts	82332	AA	**Point Judith**	82345	PA	**Point Steele**	82359	AA
Point Highland	82333	AA	**Point Arena**	82346	AA	**Point Winslow**	82360	PA
Point Ledge	82334	PA	**Point Bonita**	82347	AA	**Point Charles**	82361	AA
Point Countess	82335	PA	**Point Barrow**	82348	PA	**Point Brown**	82362	AA
Point Glass	82336	PA	**Point Spencer**	82349	AA	**Point Nowell**	82363	AA
Point Divide	82337	PA	**Point Franklin**	82350	AA	**Point Whitehorn**	82364	AA
Point Bridge	82338	PA	**Point Bennett**	82351	PA	**Point Turner**	82365	AA
Point Chico	82339	PA	**Point Sal**	82352	AA	**Point Lobos**	82366	AA
Point Batan	82340	AA	**Point Monroe**	82353	AA	**Point Knoll**	82367	AA
Point Lookout	82341	AA	**Point Evans**	82354	PA	**Point Warde**	82368	AA
Point Baker	82342	AA	**Point Hannon**	82355	AA	**Point Heyer**	82369	PA
Point Wells	82343	AA	**Point Francis**	82356	AA	**Point Richmond**	82370	AA
			Point Huron	82357	AA			
"D" class								
Point Barnes	82371	AA	**Point Carrew**	82374	PA	**Point Hobart**	82377	PA
Point Brower	82372	PA	**Point Doran**	82375	PA	**Point Jackson**	82378	AA
Point Camden	82373	PA	**Point Harris**	82376	PA	**Point Martin**	82379	AA

Builders Coast Guard Yard, Curtis Bay, Baltimore, Md (except 82345/82349: Martinac SB Co, Tacoma, Wash)
Displacement 67 tons ("A"); 66 tons ("C"); 69 tons ("D")
Length overall 83ft (25.3m)
Maximum beam 17.2ft (5.2m)
Maximum draught 5.8ft (1.8m)
Main machinery Two diesel engines
Screws/b.h.p. 2/1,600
Maximum speed 23.5 knots (22.6 knots for "D" class)
Armament 1/2 50-cal machine guns (some craft are unarmed)
Complement 1 officer, 7 enlisted men; or 8 enlisted men

Designed for search and rescue operations as well as for patrols, the *Points* were originally unnamed, but were assigned names in January 1964. "A" class was built in 1960/1961; "C" class during 1961/1967, and "D" class in 1970.

These craft are fitted with AN/SPS-64 surface search radar.

All 26 *Points* of the "B" class were transferred to South Vietnam in 1969/1970, and replaced by new vessels.

Point Baker (WPB-82342). Some 26 units of this class were transferred to South Vietnam in the early 1970s: 25 were captured by the North Vietnamese in 1975 and one disappeared in the South China Sea en route to the Philippines

Type: Buoy Tenders, Seagoing (WLB)/ Medium-Endurance Cutters (WMEC)

Number/Class: 31 *Balsam*

Name	Number	Launched	Status	Name	Number	Launched	Status
Cowslip	WLB-277	1942	AA	**Blackhaw**	WLB-390	1944	PA
Laurel	WLB-291	1942	PA	**Bramble**	WLB-392	1944	GLA
Clover	WMEC-292	1942	PA	**Firebush**	WLB-393	1944	PA
Evergreen	WMEC-295	1943	AA	**Hornbeam**	WLB-394	1944	AA
Sorrel	WLB-296	1943	AR	**Iris**	WLB-395	1944	PA
Ironwood	WLB-297	1944	PA	**Mallow**	WLB-396	1944	PA
Citrus	WMEC-300	1943	PA	**Mariposa**	WLB-397	1944	GLA
Conifer	WLB-301	1943	AA	**Sagebrush**	WLB-399	1944	AA
Madrona	WLB-302	1943	AA	**Salvia**	WLB-400	1944	AA
Mesquite	WLB-305	1943	GLA	**Sassafras**	WLB-401	1944	AA
Buttonwood	WLB-306	1943	AA	**Sedge**	WLB-402	1944	PA
Planetree	WLB-307	1943	PA	**Spar**	WLB-403	1944	AA
Papaw	WLB-308	1943	AA	**Sundew**	WLB-404	1944	AA
Sweetgum	WLB-309	1943	AA	**Sweetbrier**	WLB-405	1944	PA
Basswood	WLB-388	1944	PA	**Woodbrush**	WLB-407	1944	PA
Bittersweet	WLB-389	1944	AA				

Medium Endurance Cutter (WMEC) *Evergreen*, originally a *Balsam*-class Buoy Tender (WLB). She operates mainly in the North Atlantic Ocean and Labrador Sea *(US Coast Guard)*

Builders Marine Iron and SB Co, Duluth, Minn, and Zeneth Dredge Co, Duluth, Minn (except WLB-297; Coast Guard Yard, Curtis Bay, Balt, Md)
Displacement Standard, 935 tons; full load, 1,025 tons
Length overall 180ft (54.9m)
Maximum beam 37ft (11.3m)
Maximum draught 13ft (4m)
Main machinery Diesel electric drive engines
Screws/b.h.p. 1/1,000 (WLB-277, -291, -296, -301, -302, -292, -295, -300); 1/1,200 (remainder)
Maximum speed 12.8 knots (WLB-277, -291, -286, 301, -302, -295, -292, -300); 15 knots (remainder)
Armament Two 20mm gun mounts (WLB-297, -389, -393, -402, -405); none (remainder)
Complement 6 officers, 47 enlisted men

These were completed as seagoing buoy tenders 1943/1945. Although they are grouped together, there are actually three classes: "A" class (numbers -277, -291, -292, -296, -300, and -301); "B" class (numbers -297, -305 to -309); and "C" class (remainder)

The following vessels have undergone a nine-month major renovation at the Coast Guard Yard, Curtis Bay, Maryland: *Ironwood, Bittersweet, Hornbeam, Mariposa, Sedge, Spar, Sweetbrier*, and *Bramble*. The work included rebuilding the main engines and overhauling the propulsion motors, improving hability, and installing bow thrusters and hydraulic cargo-handling equipment.

The following have received austere renovations: *Basswood, Laurel, Buttonwood, Papaw, Planetree, Sweetgum, Iris, Mallow, Sagebrush*, and *Salvia*. In addition to the aforementioned, *Evergreen* is fitted with a bow thruster. *Spar, Blackhaw, Bramble, Sedge, Sundew*, and *Sweetbrier* are ice-reinforced. (See page 234 for more data.)

Citrus was reclassified to WMEC in June 1979, and *Clover* to WMEC in February 1980, both replacing the ex-USN *Sotoyomo*-class cutters. *Cowslip* (WLB-277) was decommissioned and sold in 1976 for commercial service. She was re-purchased in 1980 and recommissioned in October 1981 after overhaul and modernisation as a replacement for *Blackthorn* (WLB-391) (see below). *Sorrel* was decommissioned on 13 October, 1975, and laid up at Curtis Bay before modernisation.

All of these ships have 20-ton capacity booms and are fitted with AN/SPS-64 surface search radar.

Disposals: *Balsam* (WLB-62) was deleted and sold in 1978; *Tupelo* (WLB-303) followed in 1979. *Blackthorn* (WLB-391) sunk on 28 January, 1980, in a collision with SS *Capricorn* in the entrance to Tampa Bay. She was raised and later scuttled to serve as an artificial fishing reef.

Type: Buoy Tenders, Coastal (WLM) — *Number/Class:* 5 Red Wood

Name	Number	Launched	Status
Red Wood	WLM-685	1965	AA
Red Beech	WLM-686	1965	AA
Red Birch	WLM-687	1966	AA
Red Cedar	WLM-688	1971	AA
Red Oak	WLM-689	1972	AA

Builder Coast Guard Yard, Curtis Bay, Balt, Md
Displacement Standard, 471 tons; full load, 512 tons
Length overall 157ft (47.9m)
Maximum beam 33ft (10.1m)
Maximum draught 6ft (1.8m)
Main machinery Two Caterpillar D398A diesel engines
Screws/b.h.p. 2/1,800
Maximum speed 12.8 knots
Complement 4 officers, 27 enlisted men

These coastal buoy tenders can also perform search and rescue missions, law enforcement duties, and special assignments. They are fitted with controllable pitch propellers and a bow thruster, their steel hulls are strengthened for ice breaking, and a 10-ton capacity boom, is fitted. Steering and engine controls are located in the pilot house and on the bridge wings.

Coastal Buoy Tender (WLM) *Red Birch* (WLM-687). The engines are controllable from the pilothouse and bridge wings *(US Coast Guard)*

Type: Buoy Tenders, Coastal (WLM) — *Number/Class:* 7 White Sumac

Name	Number	Status
White Sumac	WLM-540	AA
White Bush	WLM-542	PA
White Holly	WLM-543	AA
White Sage	WLM-544	AA
White Heath	WLM-545	AA
White Lupine	WLM-546	AA
White Pine	WLM-547	AA

Displacement Standard, 435 tons; full load, 600 tons
Length overall 133ft (40.5m)
Maximum beam 31ft (9.5m)
Maximum draught 9ft (2.7m)
Propulsion Two Union Model 06 diesel engines
Screws/b.h.p. 2/600
Maximum speed 9.8 knots
Complement 1 officer, 20 enlisted men

Originally a class of eight ships, these vessels are former USN Covered Lighters (YF) completed in 1943/1944. All were transferred between July and December 1947 and modified for Coast Guard missions, fitments including the installation of a 20-ton capacity boom. Their machinery was upgraded in 1977. Former Navy hull numbers of the original eight units were YF-339, -341, -416, -417, -444 to -446, and -448.

The eighth ship of this class, *White Alder* (WLM-541), was sunk by collision on 7 December, 1968.

Disposals: *Fir* (WLM-212) and *Hollyhock* (WLM-220) of the *Hollyhock* class were decommissioned for disposal in 1982. *Walnut* (WLM-252) of the same class was decommissioned and transferred to Honduras on 1 July, 1982.

White Sage (WLM-544). Originally built as Covered Lighters (YF) for the Navy during the Second World War, the vessels of this class were transferred to the Coast Guard in 1947 *(US Coast Guard)*

Type: Buoy Tender, River (WLR) — Number/Class: 1 Sumac

Name	Number	Completed	Home port
Sumac	WLR-311	1943	Keokuk, Iowa

Displacement Full load, 404 tons
Length overall 115ft (35.1m)
Maximum beam 30ft (9.1m)
Maximum draught 6ft (1.8m)
Propulsion Three Caterpillar D-379 diesel engines
Screws/b.h.p. 3/960
Maximum speed 10.6 knots
Complement 1 officer, 22 enlisted men

Sister ship *Fern* (WLR-304) has been disposed of.

Type: Buoy Tender, River (WLR) — Number/Class: 1 Forsythia

Name	Number	Completed	Home port
Dogwood	WLR-259	1940	Vicksburg, Miss.

Displacement Full load, 230 tons
Length overall 114ft (34.8m)
Maximum beam 26ft (7.9m)
Maximum draught 4ft (1.2m)
Propulsion Two General Motors 8-268 diesel engines
Screws/b.h.p. 2/2,800
Maximum speed 11 knots
Complement 1 officer, 20 enlisted men

Class disposals: *Forsythia* (WLR-63) was sold on 12 August, 1977; *Sycamore* (WLR-268) was sold on 30 June, 1977; and *Foxglove* (WLR-285) was sold on 8 July, 1977.

Type: Buoy Tender, River (WLR) — Number/Class: 1 Lantana

Name	Number	Completed	Home port
Lantana	WLR-80310	1943	Owensboro, Ky.

Displacement Full load, 235 tons
Length overall 80ft (24.3m)
Maximum beam 30ft (9.1m)
Maximum draught 6ft (1.8m)
Propulsion Three Cummings VLA525 diesel engines
Screws/b.h.p. 3/1,000
Maximum speed 10 knots
Complement 1 officer, 19 enlisted men

The hull number policy of the Coast Guard is interesting with regard to the five-digit numbers. The first two numbers indicate the vessel's length.

Type: Buoy Tenders, River (WLR) — Number/Class: 9 Gasconade

Name	Number	Completed	Home port
Gasconade	WLR-75401	1964	Omaha, Neb
Muskingum	WLR-75402	1965	Memphis, Tenn
Wyaconda	WLR-75403	1965	Dubuque, Iowa
Chippewa	WLR-75404	1965	Hickman, Ky
Cheyenne	WLR-75405	1966	St Louis, Mo
Kickapoo	WLR-75406	1969	Vicksburg, Miss
Kanawha	WLR-75407	1969	Memphis, Tenn
Patoka	WLR-75408	1970	Greenville, Miss
Chena	WLR-75409	1970	Natchex, Tenn

Displacement Full load, 145 tons
Length overall 75ft (22.9m)
Maximum beam 22ft (6.7m)
Maximum draught 6ft (1.8m)
Propulsion Two Waukesha 6NKD diesel engines
Screws/b.h.p. 2/600
Maximum speed 10.8 knots
Complement 12 enlisted men

Buoy barges are assigned to units of this class.

Disposal: *Oleander* (WLR-73264), of the *Oleander* class, was sold on 1 June, 1977.

Type: Buoy Tenders, River (WLR) — Number/Class: 6 Ouachita

Name	Number	Completed	Home port
Ouachita	WLR-65501	1960	East Chattanooga, Tenn
Cimarron	WLR-65502	1960	Paris Landing, Tenn
Obion	WLR-65503	1962	Memphis, Tenn
Scioto	WLR-65504	1962	Leavenworth, Kansas
Osage	WLR-65505	1962	Sheffield, Ala
Sangamon	WLR-65506	1962	Peoria, Ill

Displacement Full load, 139 tons
Length overall 65.6ft (20m)
Maximum beam 21ft (6.4m)
Maximum draught 5ft (1.5m)
Propulsion Two Waukesha 6NKD diesel engines
Screws/b.h.p. 2/600
Maximum speed 12.5 knots
Complement 10 enlisted men

Buoy barges fitted with a 3-ton capacity crane are assigned to units of this class.

Type: Buoy Tenders, Inland (WLI)

Number/Class: 1 *Bluebell* (A)
1 *Buckthorn* (C)

Name	Number	Status	Name	Number	Status
Bluebell (A)	WLI-313	PA	**Buckthorn** (C)	WLI-642	GLA

Displacement Full load, 178 tons (*Bluebell*); 200 tons (*Buckthorn*)
Length overall 100ft (30.5m)
Maximum beam 24ft (7.3m)
Maximum draught 4ft (1.2m) (*Bluebell*); 5ft (1.5m) (*Buckthorn*)
Main machinery Two Caterpillar diesel engines
Screws/b.h.p. 2/440 (*Bluebell*); 2/600 (*Buckthorn*)
Maximum speed 9 knots (*Buckthorn*); 105 knots (*Bluebell*)
Complement 1 officer, 13 enlisted men (*Buckthorn*); 15 enlisted men (*Bluebell*)

Bluebell was completed in 1945; *Buckthorn* in 1963.

Azalea (WLI-641) of the "B" class was sunk as a target by the Navy on 31 October, 1978.

Type: Buoy Tenders, Inland (WLI)

Number/Class: 2 *Blackberry* and 2 *Bayberry*

Blackberry class			Bayberry class		
Name	*Number*	*Status*	*Name*	*Number*	*Status*
Blackberry	WLI-65303	AA	**Bayberry**	WLI-65400	PA
Chokeberry	WLI-65304	AA	**Elderberry**	WLI-65401	AA

Displacement Full load, 68 tons
Length overall 65ft (19.8m)
Maximum beam 17ft (5.2m)
Maximum draught 4ft (1.2m)
Main machinery Two General Motors 6-110 diesel engines
Screws/b.h.p. 1/222 (*Blackberry* class); 1/400 (*Bayberry* class)
Maximum speed 9 knots (*Blackberry* class); 11.3 knots (*Bayberry* class)
Complement 5 enlisted men

The *Blackberry* class craft were built in 1946, and are homeported at Southport and Hatteras, North Carolina, respectively. The *Bayberry* class craft were built in 1954; and are homeported at Seattle, Washington, (WLI-65400) and Petersburg, Alaska, (WLI-65401).

Disposal: *Tern* (WLI-80801), a one-unit class prototype fitted with an experimental gantry crane, was sold on 1 July, 1977.

Inland Buoy Tender (WLI) *Elderberry*. Note the small power boat carried forward for close-in inspection of boats or coastline *(US Coast Guard)*

Type: Construction Tenders, Inland (WLIC)

Number/Class: 4 *Pamlico*

Name	*Number*	*Home port*
Pamlico	WLIC-800	New Orleans, La
Hudson	WLIC-801	Miami, Fla
Kennebec	WLIC-802	Atlantic Beach, N.J.
Saginaw	WLIC-803	Mobile, Ala

Builder Coast Guard Yard, Curtis Bay, Balt, Md
Displacement Light, 413 tons
Length overall 160.9ft (49m)
Maximum beam 30ft (9.1m)
Maximum draught 4ft (1.2m)
Propulsion Two diesel engines; two screws
Maximum speed 11.5 knots
Complement 15 total

These were completed during 1975/1978. Unlike the old towboat-barge type that they replace, this class is of single-hull construction.

Type: Construction Tenders, Inland (WLIC) — *Number/Class:* 4 *Cosmos*

Name	Number	Completed	Home port
Cosmos	WLIC-293	1942	St Petersbirg, Fla
Rambler	WLIC-298	1944	Mobile, Ala
Smilax	WLIC-315	1944	Brunswick, Ga
Primrose	WLIC-316	1944	Atlantic Beach, N.C.

Displacement Full load, 178 tons
Length overall 100ft (30.5m)
Maximum beam 24ft (7.3m)
Maximum draught 5ft (1.5m)
Propulsion Two Caterpillar D353 diesel engines
Screws/b.h.p. 2/600
Maximum speed 10.5 knots
Complement 1 officer, 14 enlisted men

Primrose is fitted with a pile driver. Sister ship *Verbena* (WLI-317) was sold on 1 September, 1977

Type: Construction Tenders, Inland (WLIC) — *Number/Class:* 10 *Anvil, Sledge* and *Clamp*

Name	Number	Completed	Status
Anvil class			
Anvil	WLIC-75301	1962	Miami Beach, Fla
Hammer	WLIC-75302	1962	Fort Pierce, Fla
Sledge class			
Sledge	WLIC-75303	1962	Portsmouth, Va
Mallet	WLIC-75304	1962	Corpus Christi, Tx
Vise	WLIC-75305	1962	St Petersburg, Fla
Clamp class			
Clamp	WLIC-75306	1964	Galveston, Tx
Wedge	WLIC-75307	1964	New Orlenas, La
Spike	WLIC-75308	1965	Mayport, Fla
Hatchet	WLIC-75309	1965	Galveston, Tx
Axe	WLIC-75310	1965	Mobile, Ala

Displacement Full load, 145 tons
Length overall 75ft (22.8m); except *Clamp* class: 76ft (23.2m)
Maximum beam 22ft (6.7m)
Maximum draught 4ft (1.2m)
Propulsion Two Caterpillar D-353 diesel engines (except Waukesha F1905-DSIM in *Clamp* class)
Screws/b.h.p. 2/600
Maximum speed 10 knots
Complement 1 officer (*Sledge* class), none (remainder); 9 enlisted men

Each unit of this 75ft (22.8m) class of Inland Construction Tenders has a construction barge assigned to it.

Inland Construction Tender (WLIC) *Hammer*. She is used as a work platform for the repair and maintenance of fixed aids to navigation *(US Coast Guard)*

Type: Harbour Tugs, Medium (WYTM) — *Number/Class:* 6 *Manitou* and 3 *Arundel*

Name	Number	Completed	Status
Manitou (A)			
Apalachee	WYTM-71	1943	Curtis Bay, Md
Yankton	WYTM-72	1943	Portland, Maine
Mohican	WYTM-73	1943	Portsmouth, Va
Chinook	WYTM-96	1943	Curtis Bay, Md
Snohomish	WYTM-98	1943	Rockland, Maine
Sauk	WYTM-99	1943	Governor's Island, N.Y.
Arundel (B)			
Mahoning	WYTM-91	1939	Governor's Island, N.Y.
Raritan	WYTM-93	1939	Grand Haven, Mich

Displacement Full load, 370 tons
Length overall 110ft (33.5m)
Maximum beam 27ft (8.2m)
Maximum draught 11ft (3.4m)
Main machinery Ingersoll-Rand Type S diesel electric drive
Screws/b.h.p. 1/1,000
Maximum speed 11.2 knots
Complement 1 officer, 19 enlisted men

Arundel and *Raritan* are stationed inland; the remaining units serve in the Atlantic Fleet.

Disposals: *Kaw* (WYTM-61) and *Naugatuck* (WYTM-92) were sold on 17 June, 1979; *Objibwa* (WYTM-97) was struck on 6 May, 1980, and *Manitou* (WYTM-60) was struck in 1980 followed by *Arundel* (WYTM-90) in 1983.

Yankton (WYTM-72), currently based at Portland, Maine *(US Coast Guard)*

Type: Harbour Tugs, Small (WYTL) — *Number/Class:* 14 *Capstan, Bridle, Hawser* and *Bitt*

Name	Number	Completed	Status
Capstan (A) class			
Capstan	WYTL-65601	1961	Alexandria, Va
Chock	WYTL-65602	1961	Portsmouth, Va
Swivel	WYTL-65603	1961	Rockland, Maine
Tackle	WYTL-65604	1962	Curtis Bay, Md
Towline	WYTL-65605	1962	Bristol, R.I.
Catenary	WYTL-65606	1962	Gloucester, N.J.
Bridle (B) class			
Bridle	WYTL-65607	1963	Southwest Harbor, Maine
Pendant	WYTL-65608	1963	Boston, Mass
Shackle	WYTL-65609	1963	South Portland, Maine
Hawser (C) class			
Hawser	WYTL-65610	1963	Governor's Island, N.Y.
Line	WYTL-65611	1963	Governor's Island, N.Y.
Wire	WYTL-65612	1963	Governor's Island, N.Y.
Bitt (D) class			
Bollard	WYTL-65614	1967	New Haven, Conn
Cleat	WYTL-65615	1967	Gloucester, N.J.

Displacement Full load, 72 tons
Length overall 65ft (19.8m)
Maximum beam 19ft (5.8m)
Maximum draught 7ft (2.1m)
Main machinery One diesel engine (Caterpillar D375-D in *Capstan* class; Caterpillar D379-D in *Bitt* class; Waukesha LRD-BSM in *Bridle* and *Hawser* classes)
Screws/b.h.p. 1/400
Maximum speed 9.8 knots (10.5 knots for *Capstan* class)
Complement 10 enlisted men

All of these tugs are capable of providing assistance and performing towing, boarding, firefighting and light ice breaking duties.

Disposal: *Messenger* (WYTM-85009), 85ft (25.9m class), was reclassified "Boat" on 25 August, 1980, and continues in active service.

Type: Training Cutter, Sail (WIX) — *Number/Class:* 1 Eagle

Name	Number	Builder	Completed	Status
Eagle (ex **Horst Wessel**)	WIX-327	Blohm und Voss, Hamburg, Germany	1936	AA

Displacement Full load, 1,784 tons
Length overall 295.2ft (90m); waterline, 231ft (70.4m)
Maximum beam 39.1ft (11.9m)
Maximum draught 17ft (5.2m)
Propulsion One auxiliary M.A.N. diesel engine
Screws/b.h.p. 1/700
Height of masts Four and main, 150.3ft (45.8m); mizzen, 132ft (40.2m)
Sail area 25,351ft^2
Maximum speed 10.5 knots (diesel); 18 knots (under sail)
Complement 19 officers, 46 enlisted men, 180 cadets

Launched on 13 June, 1936, this former German Navy training vessels was ceded to United States Navy in January 1946 as part of war reparations, and then transferred to the Coast Guard for use as a training ship.

When the Coast Guard introduced the policy of using orange and blue marking stripes on the hulls of their cutters *Eagle* was originally exempted. However, the stripes and the words "Coast Guard" were added in 1976. The stripes greatly detract from the graceful lines of this beautiful ship. *Eagle* was extensively overhauled 1981/1982.

Electronics: fitted with AN/SPS-64 surface search radar.

Sister-ship *Albert Leo Schlageter*, was also ceded to the USA as war reparations, but was sold to Brazil in 1948. Resold to Portugal in 1962, she is still in service as *Sagres*.

Disposal: The Training Cutter *Cuyahoga* (WIX-157) was sunk in a collision on 20 October, 1978. She was raised and scuttled off Cape Charles on 19 March, 1979, to serve as a fishing reef.

The training barque *Eagle* (WIX-327), originally built for the German Navy in 1935–36. Her lines are spoiled by the stripes on her hull *(US Navy)*

Type: Lightships (WLV) — *Number/Class:* 2 "128ft"

Name	Number	Completed	Home port
Nantucket-I	WLV-612	1950	New York City
Nantucket-II	WLV-613	1952	New York City

Displacement Full load, 697 tons
Length overall 128ft (39m)
Maximum beam 30ft (9.1m)
Maximum draught 11ft (3.4m)
Propulsion One General Motors diesel engine
Screws/b.h.p. 1/550
Maximum speed 11 knots
Complement 1 officer, 15 enlisted men

Coast Guard Lightships have remained constant, but the names, until recently, changed according to their assignment. In recent years WLV-612 has been named *Nantucket, Portland,* and *Blunt's Reef*. Both of these ships were officially named as indicated in 1980.

Disposal: *Columbia River* (WLV-604) was sold on 13 December, 1979.

Addenda

I SUBMARINES

Page 16: *Los Angeles class* – The Tomahawk cruise missile system was installed in *Boston* (SSN-703), *Baltimore* (SSN-704), *Atlanta* (SSN-712) and *Houston* (SSN-713) in mid-1983 at Newport News SB & DD Co, Newport News, Va.

Page 22: *Ethan Allen class* – *Ethan Allen* (SSN-608) was decommissioned and struck from the Naval Vessel Register on 31 March, 1983, for disposal. *Thomas A. Edison* (SSN-610) of this class is to be decommissioned and stricken in January 1984, for disposal, after removal of her missile compartment.

Page 24: *George Washington class* – *Robert E. Lee* (SSN-601) of this class is to be decommissioned and stricken from the Naval Vessel Register, in January 1984, after removal of her missile compartment. Ex-*Theodore Roosevelt* (SSBN-600) and *Abraham Lincoln* (SSBN-602) were stricken from the Naval Vessel Register on 1 December, 1982, for disposal.

Page 30: *Skate class* – *Seadragon* (SSN-584) is to be decommissioned on 30 September, 1983, and laid up.

Page 36: *Tang class* – *Gudgeon* (SSAG-567) is to be decommissioned on 30 September, 1983, and leased to Turkey on the same date for further service.

II AIRCRAFT CARRIERS

Page 41: *John F. Kennedy* (CVA-67) was originally to be built with nuclear power (SCB-211A), but conventional power substituted when Secretary of Defense Robert S. McNamara refused to pay for the nuclear plant.

Page 44: The Service Life Extension Programme overhaul (SLEP) of *Ranger* (CV-61) has been indefinitely postponed. She was replaced in the programme by *Kitty Hawk* (CV-63), which is scheduled to be SLEPed at Philadelphia Naval Shipyard between 1 July, 1987, and 1 November, 1989. *Constellation* (CV-64), a new addition to the SLEP programme, is scheduled to be SLEPed at Puget Sound Naval Shipyard between 1 August, 1989, and 1 August, 1991.

III CRUISERS

Pages 58 and 59: Construction of the CGN-42 class has been shelved once again as has the plan to convert the *Virginia* class CGN's to an Aegis configuration. Hence, the projected force level of the *Ticonderoga* class CGs will remain at 30 units.

IV DESTROYERS

Page 73: *Arleigh Burke class* – DDG-60 through -111 of this class are projected for future programmes.

Page 77: *Charles F. Adams class* – The modernisation programme of this class has been reduced to just three units, namely *Tattnall* (DDG-19), *Goldsborough* (DDG-20) and *Benjamin Stoddert* (DDG-22). This is a shame as the class has been rated as the finest destroyer types built by the US Navy since World War Two. If the Navy is only going to modernise 3 of the 24 units of the class, it is the opinion of the authors that they might as well forget the programme completely.

Page 81: *Spruance class* – Construction of further *Spruance* class units, to replace the recently decommissioned *Forrest Sherman/Hull* class Destroyers is planned. One unit is planned for the FY-1988 Shipbuilding programme with further units planned for future programmes.

Page 82: *Hull* (DD-945) of the *Hull* class was decommissioned on 11 July, 1983, not 10 July, 1983.

Page 84: *Forrest Sherman class* – *Jonas Ingram, Manley* and *Du Pont* of this class were decommissioned on 4 March, 1983, followed by *Mullinnix* on 11 August, 1983.

V PATROL COMBATANTS

Page 101: *Asheville class* – On 16 May, 1983, *Tacoma* (PG-92) and *Welch* (PG-93) of this class were leased to Colombia as *Quito Sueno* and *Albuquerque* respectively.

VI MINE WARFARE

Page 106: *Avenger class* – The contract for the construction of MCM-2 was awarded to Marinette Marine Corp, Marinette, Wisc, on 2 May, 1983. A total of 21 units of this class are projected, with MCM-15/21 of this class scheduled to be authorised in future programmes. Problems with the design of this class are still being experienced.

VII AMPHIBIOUS WARFARE

Page 113: *LHD-1 class* – Cost to construct the prototype of this class is estimated at $1,379.9 million. The contract for long term lead items for this class was awarded to Ingalls SB Div, Litton Industries, Pascagoula, Miss.

Page 115: *Iwo Jima class LPHs and Austin class LPDs* – A programme has been initiated to give each ship of the two classes a Service Life Extension Programme (SLEP) overhaul that will extend the 30 year service life of the ships of the two classes by some 10–15 years each. The programme will begin in FY-1986 and conclude in the FY-1992 programme. The SLEP will be of the same type as that given to the *Forrestal* class CVs, but on a proportionately reduced scale.

Page 121: *Thomaston class* – The decommissioning schedule of the class has been revised. The US Marine Corp still doesn't like the schedule, but it is regarded by them as better than the schedule indicated in the notes on page 121. *Plymouth Rock* (LSD-29) and *Point Defiance* (LSD-31) of this class are to be decommissioned on 30 September, 1983, with the rest of the class to follow no later than FY-1989.

Page 126: *LCAC class* – The construction of LCAC-10/15 of this class is requested in the FY-1984 programme at a total cost of $169.3 million. LCAC-16/27 of this class proposed for the FY-1985 programme at a cost of $285.2 million with 12 units to follow each year thereafter. A total of 108 units of the class are planned, with 54 units to be assigned to the Pacific Fleet at Camp Pendleton, Calif, and 54 to be based at the Amphibious base at Little Creek, Va. Maximum cargo capacity of each craft is 60 tons. The well deck of each craft provides 1,800ft² (167.2m²) of cargo space.

VIII AUXILIARIES

Page 131: *Dixie class* – *Dixie* (AD-14) of this class was stricken from the Naval Vessel Register on 15 June, 1982, and transferred to the Maritime Administration for disposal.

Page 136: *Sirius class* – *Saturn* (T-AFS-10) (ex-RFA *Stromness*) has been at Bayonne, NJ since April 1983 with a skeleton British crew. She will remain there until the FY-1984 Shipbuilding and Conversion programme is approved in which there is $16.1 million requested to purchase the ship. Unlike her sister-ships, whose acquisitions were more urgent, the charter process has been avoided, the ship being purchased directly.

Page 136: *AFS-11 class* – A new class of AFS is projected. Funds for the construction of the prototype are requested in the FY-1987 programme with funds for a second unit of the class requested in the FY-1989 programme. Exact details of the class's characteristics and the exact number of units in the class are not available.

Page 140: *AG-51/65 class* – These ships were formally stricken from the Naval Vessel Register on 1 January, 1983, in order to "clear the books".

Page 146: *Robert D. Conrad class* – *James M. Gillis* (AGOR-4) was leased to Mexico on 15 June, 1983, for further service.

Page 153: *Algol class* – It is the intention of the Navy to reclassify this class, after conversion, as AKRs, but retaining their original AK numbers.

Projected capacities of this class have been revised and are as follows: Enclosed roll-on/roll-off and helo decks – 35,000ft^2 and roll-on/roll-off deck aft – 18,500ft^2. In addition, each ship will be fitted with twin 35-ton capacity cranes between the deck houses and two 50-ton capacity cranes aft.

Page 158: *Pvt Leonard C. Brostrom class* – On 25 October, 1982, *Pvt Leonard C. Brostrom* was transferred to Eastern Overseas Inc, New York City, NY, along with *General H.H. Arnold* (T-AGM-9), with Military Sealift Command (MSC) and Maritime Administration (MARAD) concurrence, for scrapping. This action was officially illegal as no US Naval Vessel can be disposed of without the Secretary of the Navy, or his accredited representative, first striking the vessel from the Naval Vessel Register. As of writing, this action had not been done.

Page 158: AKX class – Additional information on this class is as follows:

0 + (13) "Maritime Prepositioning Ships" Class: Vehicle Cargo Ships (AKR) (Ex T-AKX)

Name	*Number*	*Builders*	*Completed*	*F/S*
Waterman Steamship Co (A)				
SS **Charles Carroll**	T-AKR	Gen Dynamics Corp, Quincy, Mass	March 1983	CONV
SS **John B. Waterman**	T-AKR	Sun SB & DD Co, Chester, Pa	1981	CONV
SS **Thomas Heywood**	T-AKR	Sun SB & DD Co, Chester, Pa	Nov 1982	CONV
Maersk Co (B)				
M/V **Estelle Maersk**	T-AKR	Odenese Staalskibsvaerft A/S, Lindo	1979	CONV
M/V **Eleo Maersk**	T-AKR	Odenese Staalskibsvaerft A/S, Lindo	Apr 1979	CONV
M/V **Evelyn Maersk**	T-AKR	Odenese Staalskibsvaerft A/S, Lindo	Apr 1980	CONV
M/V **Emilie Maersk**	T-AKR	Odenese Staalskibsvaerft A/S, Lindo	Jan 1980	CONV
M/V **Emma Maersk**	T-AKR	Odenese Staalskibsvaerft A/S, Lindo	July 1979	CONV
General Dynamics Corp (C)				
	T-AKR	Gen Dynamics Corp, Quincy, Mass	March 1985*	BLDG
	T-AKR	Gen Dynamics Corp, Quincy, Mass	June 1985*	BLDG
	T-AKR	Gen Dynamics Corp, Quincy, Mass	Sept 1985*	BLDG
	T-AKR	Gen Dynamics Corp, Quincy, Mass	Dec 1985*	BLDG
	T-AKR	Gen Dynamics Corp, Quincy, Mass	March 1986*	BLDG

* Estimated

Characteristics:

Group (A) – **before conversion**
Measurement in tons 18,500 gross, 12,000 net, 23,500 deadweight
Dimensions in feet (metres) 692.6 × 105.4 × 33.0 (211.1 × 32.1 × 10.1)
Main machinery Two General Electric steam turbines; 32,000 s.h.p.; 1 shaft; 20 knots
Complement Not available

Group (B) – **before conversion**
Measurement in tons 13,706 gross, 6,856 net, 21,050 deadweight
Dimensions in feet (metres) 598.1 × 90.2 × 39.0 (182.3 × 27.5 × 11.8)
Main machinery Two Sulzer Bros diesels; 15,960 b.h.p.; 1 shaft; 18.5 knots
Complement Not available

Group (B) – **after conversion**
Displacement in tons 46,552 full load
Measurements in tons Not available
Dimensions in feet (metres) 755 × 90 × 32.9 (230 × 27.4 × 10.1)
Main machinery One diesel; 1 shaft; 17.2 knots
Range 10,800nm at economical speed
Complement 27 total civilians and a Navy communications team of 8 men

After conversion, the five Maersk operated ships will have a vehicle storage area of 122,380ft^2, provision for 306 containers for ammunition and refrigerated cargo, 1.3 million gallons of drummed or bulk petroleum products, 133,246 gallons of potable water and 595,087 gallons of fuel oil.

Group (C) – **as built**
Measurements in tons 22,700 deadweight
Dimensions in feet (metres) 671.2 × 105.5 × 29.5 (204.6 × 32.2 × 9.0)
Main machinery Two diesels; 26,400 b.h.p.; 1 shaft; 18.0 knots
Complement 70 total (30 ships crew, 7 MSC crew, 8 Navy communications team, 25 maintenance team)

The cargo capacity of each ship is as follows: 150,000ft^2 for vehicles; 100,800ft^3 for general cargo; 226,000ft^3 for ammunition; 1,523,000 gal for fuel (bulk); 2,039 drums of fuel; 81,250 gal potable water and 2 LCM-8s carried on deck. A helicopter deck will be fitted aft.

The Maritime Prepositioning Ship programme, originally called T-AKX, is designed to provide the capability for the prepositioning of equipment and supplies required to support three Marine Amphibious Brigades (MAB). All ships are to be initially chartered for five years with options for renewal. This programme replaces the programme to construct eight AKRs to a Maritime Administration C8-M-MA134J hull design which was cancelled in September 1981. An ultimate force level of thirteen ships is planned. This class and the eight *Algol* (SL-7) class will replace the seventeen ship Near-Term Prepositioned Ship (NTPF) force beginning in FY-1986 and will become the permanent portion of the Navy's contribution to the Rapid Deployment Joint Task Force (RDJTF).

While General Dynamics Corp will construct new ships to meet the requirements of the Maritime Prepositioned Ship (MPS) force, Waterman & Maersk will convert existing ships to suit the requirements. Waterman's contract is for three ships, each with a 1/4 MAB lift capacity. Maersk's contract is for five ships, each with a 1/5 MAB lift capability. The ships being built by General Dynamics will each have a 1/4 MAB lift capability. Initial contracts for this programme were let on 17 August, 1982, with all options in the initial contract being exercised on 14 January, 1983. A tentative conversion schedule is as follows:

TENTATIVE CONVERSION SCHEDULE

Name	*Conversion Yard*	*Started*	*Completed*
SS **Charles Carroll**	Nat Steel & SB Co, San Diego, Ca		Sept 1984*
SS **Thomas Heywood**	Nat Steel & SB Co, San Diego, Ca		Dec 1984*
SS **John B. Waterman**	Nat Steel & SB Co, San Diego, Ca		Apr 1985*
M/V **Estelle Maersk**	Beth Steel Co, Sparrows Pt, Md	Feb 1983	Aug 1984*
M/V **Eleo Maersk**	Beth Steel Co, Beaumont, Tx		Sept 1985*
M/V **Evelyn Maersk**	Beth Steel Co, Sparrows Pt, Md		Sept 1985*
M/V **Emilie Maersk**	Beth Steel Co, Beaumont, Tx		Sept 1985*
M/V **Emma Maersk**	Beth Steel Co, Sparrows Pt, Md		April 1985*

* Estimated

Page 159: *Mercury class* – *Mercury* (T-AKR-10) and *Jupiter* (T-AKR-11) were both instated on the Naval Vessel Register on 14 May, 1980.

Page 161: *Henry J. Kaiser class* – This class are commercialised versions of the *Cimarron* class AOs. AO-192/195 are scheduled to be requested in the FY-1985 programme, followed by AO-196/199 in the FY-1986 programme, AO-200/203 in the FY-1987 programme and AO-204/207 in the FY-1988 programme. Contract for the construction of

AO-188 was awarded to Avondale Shipyards Inc on 20 January, 1983.

Page 170: The following new class of ship should be counted as part of the Navy's Auxiliary Fleet:

0+5 "T-5" Type: Transport Oiler (AOT)

A contract was let on 29 September, 1982, to Ocean Carriers Inc, Houston, Texas, to construct two T-5 tankers for charter to the Military Sealift Command (MSC). An option for the construction of three more was exercised in May 1983. The tankers will be constructed by American Shipbuilding Co, Tampa, Fla, with major parts being fabricated in Lorain, Ohio, and Nashville, Tenn. The delivery of the first ship, to Ocean Carriers, is scheduled for November 1984 and the second in January 1985 with two more to follow in late 1985 and the last in 1986. The initial charter is for five years and the ships will be operated by Trinidad Corp, Philadelphia, Pa. These ships will replace the USNS *Potomac* (T-AOT-181), USNS *American Explorer* (A-AOT-165) and the three ships of the *Maumee* class AOTs. Cost to construct the first two units is $104.1 million total. Each ship will have a max deadweight tonnage of 30,000, diesel engines, a crew of 23 and an approx cargo capacity of 225,000 barrels.

Page 174: *Geiger class* – The engineering damage suffered during her first training cruise as SS *Bay State* was not repaired and the ship is to be replaced, probably by ex-USS *Tulare* (LKA-112).

Page 179: *Safeguard class (ARS-50/53)* – The projected fifth unit of this class (ARS-54) has been cancelled.

Page 188: *Cherokee/Abnaki class* – *Takelma* (ATF-113) of this class is due to be taken out of service on 30 September, 1983, and transferred to the Maritime Administration for layup. *Atakapa* (ATF-149) of this class is due to be transferred to Pakistan in FY-1984.

Page 187: *Sotoyomo class* – While conducting a search for a downed Argentine Canberra pilot on 3 May, 1982, during the Falklands War, *Alferez Sobral* (ex-USS *Catawba*, ATA-210) was discovered by a British Sea King helicopter and badly damaged by Lynxes firing Sea Skua missiles. Numerous sources report that *Commodoro Somellera* (ex-USS *Salish*, ATA-187) was in company with *Sobral* and was hit and sunk by two Sea Skuas.

IX SERVICE CRAFT

Page 191: The *Artisan* (AFDB-1) is for disposal.

Page 192: AFDM – YFD-71 was reclassified AFDM-14 on 1 February 1983 and was named *Steadfast* on 9 May, 1983.

Page 202: *YP-676 class* – The option for five more units of this class, to be numbered YP-677 through -681, was exercised on 29 May, 1983.

Page 202: *YTB-760 class* – 28 new YTBs are to be constructed as replacements for obsolete YTMs. To be classified YTB-839 through -864. Construction of YTB-839/841 was authorised in the FY-1983 programme. Seven additional units are requested in the FY-1984 programme with six more units to be requested in the FY-1985 programme and four units each in the FY-1986 through FY-1988 programmes.

Page 203: YTM – *Waubansee* (YTM-366) was stricken on 15 April, 1983, and transferred to the Massachusetts Maritime Academy for use as a training ship. *Toka* (YTM-149) and *Madokawando* (YTM-180) were stricken on 31 January, 1983, and transferred to the US Army for further service.

X SUBMERSIBLES

Page 207: HTV – With the departure of Admiral Rickover in early 1983, the status of this project is in doubt.

XI SHIPS CHARTERED TO THE RAPID DEPLOYMENT FORCE (RDF)

Page 214: Add the following ships to the table in this section:

Name	*Type*	*Chartered*
Bay	AE/C3	March 1982
Gulf Shipper	AE/C3	2 March 1982

XII SHIPS CHARTERED BY MSC

Page 214: Add the following ships to the table in this section:

Name	*Date chartered*	*Expires*	*Owner/Operator*
American Rapid (AK)	9 April 1982	9 April 1987	US Lines
American Rover (AK)	6 March 1982	6 March 1987	US Lines

XIII UNITED STATES COAST GUARD

Page 225: Cape class – *Cape Coral* was decommissioned in May 1983 because of engineering problems. She is to be cannibalised for spares.

Cape Carter, the latest of the class to be modernised, was recommissioned in June 1983.

The Coast Guard now officially classifies the modernised units of the class as the "R" series.

Page 227: Balsam class – *Evergreen* (WAGO-295) was reclassified as a WMEC on 1 May, 1982, and repainted black.

A total of 14 units of this class are to receive a SLEP overhaul. *Sorrel* (WLB-296), the first unit to be SLEPed, was recommissioned in January 1983. The second unit to be SLEPed, *Gentian* (WLB-290), was decommissioned on 19 March, 1976, at the Coast Guard Yard at Curtis Bay, Maryland, and laid up. She was removed from layup in late 1982 and taken in hand for her SLEP. Funds for three more units have already been appropriated. All SLEPs are being done at Curtis Bay. They take approx 16 months and cost $7.5 million per ship.

Classification of US Naval Ships and Craft

COMBATANT SHIPS

A WARSHIPS

1 AIRCRAFT CARRIERS

All ships designed primarily to conduct combat operations by aircraft which engage in attacks against airborne, surface, sub-surface and shore targets.

a CTOL (Conventional Take-Off and Landing Aircraft Carriers)

Multi-purpose Aircraft Carrier	CV
Multi-purpose Aircraft Carrier (nuclear propulsion)	CVN
ASW aircraft carrier	CVS

b V/STOL (Vertical/Short Take-Off and Landing) Aircraft Carriers

c Helicopter Carriers

2 SURFACE COMBATANTS

Large, heavily armed, surface ships designed primarily to engage enemy forces on the high seas.

a Battleships

Battleship	BB

b Cruisers

Gun Cruiser	CA
Guided Missile Cruiser	CG
Guided Missile Cruiser (nuclear propulsion)	CGN

c Destroyers

Destroyer	DD
Guided Missile Destroyer	DDG

d Frigates

Frigate	FF
Guided missile frigate	FFG

3 SUBMARINES

All self-propelled submersible types, regardless of whether they are employed as combatant, auxiliary, or R&D vehicles which have at least a residual combat capability.

a Attack Submarines

Submarine (conventional-powered)	SS
Guided Missile Submarine (conventionally-powered)	SSG
Submarine (nuclear-powered)	SSN

b Ballistic Missile Submarines

Ballistic Missile Submarine (nuclear-powered)	SSBN

c Auxiliary Submarines

Auxiliary Submarine	SSAG

B OTHER COMBATANTS

1 PATROL COMBATANTS

Combatants whose mission may extend beyond coastal duties, and whose characteristics include adequate endurance and sea keeping to provide a capability for operations exceeding 48hr on the high seas without support.

a Patrol Ships

Patrol Combatant	PG
Guided Missile Patrol Combatant (Hydrofoil)	PHM

2 AMPHIBIOUS WARFARE SHIPS

All ships having the organic capability for amphibious assault and which have characteristics enabling long-duration operations on the high seas.

a Amphibious Helicopter/Landing Craft Carriers

Amphibious Assault Ship (General Purpose)	LHA
Amphibious Assault Dock	LHD
Amphibious Assault Ship (Helicopter)	LPH
Amphibious Transport Dock	LPD

b Landing Craft Carriers

Amphibious Cargo Ship	LKA
Amphibious Transport	LPA
Dock Landing Ship	LSD
Tank Landing Ship	LST

c Miscellaneous

Amphibious Command Ship	LCC

3 MINE WARFARE SHIPS

All ships whose primary function is mine warfare on the high seas.

a Minelayers

b Minesweepers/Hunters

Minesweeper, Ocean	MSO
Mine Hunters	MSH

c Mine Countermeasures Ships

Mine Countermeasures Ship	MCM

AUXILIARY SHIPS

A AUXILIARIES

1 MOBILE LOGISTICS SHIPS

Ships which have the capability to provide underway replenishment to fleet units and/or provide direct material support to other deployed units operating far from home base.

a Underway Replenishment

Ammunition Ship	AE
Store Ship	AF
Combat Store Ship	AFS
Oiler	AO
Fast Combat Support Ship	AOE
Replenishment Oiler	AOR

b Material Support

Destroyer Tender	AD
Repair Ship	AR
Submarine Tender	AS

2 SUPPORT SHIPS

Ships designed to operate in the open ocean in a variety of sea states to provide general support to either combatant forces or to shore-based establishments. (Includes smaller auxiliaries which, by the nature of their duties, leave inshore waters).

a Fleet Support

Salvage Ship	ARS
Submarine Rescue Ship	ASR
Auxiliary Ocean Tug	ATA
Fleet Ocean Tug	ATF
Salvage and Rescue Ship	ATS

b Other Auxiliaries

Crane Ship	ACS
Miscellaneous	AG
Deep Submergence Support Ship	AGDS
Hydrofoil Research Ship	AGEH
Miscellaneous Command Ship	AGF
Frigate Research Ship	AGFF
Missile Range Instrumentation Ship	AGM
Oceanographic Research Ship	AGOR
Ocean Surveillance Ship	AGOS
Patrol Craft Tender	AGP
Surveying Ship	AGS
Auxiliary Research Submarine	AGSS
Hospital Ship	AH
Cargo Ship	AK
Vehicle Cargo Ship	AKR
Auxiliary Lighter	ALS
Gasoline Tanker	AOG
Transport Oiler	AOT
Transport	AP
Self-Propelled Barracks Ship	APB
Cable Repairing Ship	ARC
Repair Ship, Small	ARL
Guided Missile Ship	AVM
Auxiliary Aircraft Landing Training Ship	AVT

PATROL COMBATANT CRAFT

A PATROL COMBATANT CRAFT

1 PATROL CRAFT

Surface patrol craft intended for use relatively near the coast or in sheltered waters or rivers.

a Coastal Patrol Combatants

Patrol Boat	PB
Patrol Craft (Fast)	PCF
Patrol Gunboat (hydrofoil)	PGH
Fast Patrol Craft	PTF

b River/Roadstead Craft

Mini-Armoured Troop Carrier	ATC
River Patrol Boat	PBR

2 AMPHIBIOUS WARFARE CRAFT

All amphibious craft which have the organic capacity for amphibious assault and are intended to operate principally in coastal waters or may be carried aboard larger units.

a Landing Craft

Amphibious Assault Landing Craft	AALC
Landing Craft, Air Cushion	LCAC
Landing Craft, Mechanised	LCM
Landing Craft, Personnel, Large	LCPL
Landing Craft, Utility	LCU
Landing Craft, Vehicle, Personnel	LCVP
Amphibious Warping Tug	LWT
Side Loading Warping Tug	SLWT

b Special Warfare Craft

Light Seal Support Craft	LSSC
Medium Seal Support Craft	MSSC
Swimmer Delivery Vehicle	SDV
Special Warfare Craft, Light	SWCL
Special Warfare Craft, Medium	SWCM

3 MINE WARFARE CRAFT

All craft with the primary function of mine warfare that are intended to operate principally in coastal waters and may also be carried aboard larger units.

a Mine Countermeasures Craft

Minesweeping Boat	MSB
Minesweeping Drone	MSD
Minesweeper, Inshore	MSI
Minesweeper, River (Converted LCM-6)	MSM
Minesweeper, Patrol	MSR

SERVICE CRAFT

A grouping of navy-subordinated craft (including non-self-propelled) designed to provide general support to either combatant forces or shore-based establishments.

a Dry Docks

Large Auxiliary Floating Dry Dock (non-self-propelled)	AFDB
Small Auxiliary Floating Dry Dock (non-self-propelled)	AFDL
Medium Auxiliary Floating Dry Dock (non-self-propelled)	AFDM
Auxiliary Repair Dry Dock (non-self-propelled)	ARD
Medium Auxiliary Repair Dry Dock (non-self-propelled)	ARDM
Bowdock	YBD
Yard Floating Dry Dock (non-self-propelled)	YFD

b Tugs

Large Harbour Tugs (self-propelled)	YTB
Small Harbour Tug (self-propelled)	YTL
Medium Harbour Tug (self-propelled)	YTM

c Tankers

Fuel Oil Barge (self-propelled)	YO
Gasoline Barge (self-propelled)	YOG
Water Barge (self-propelled)	YW

d Lighters

Open lighter (non-self-propelled)	YC
Car Float (non-self-propelled)	YCF
Aircraft Transport Lighter (non-self-propelled)	YCV
Covered Lighter (self-propelled)	YF
Covered Lighter (non-self-propelled)	YFN
Large Covered Lighter (non-self-propelled)	YFNB
Lighter (special purpose) (non-self-propelled)	YFNX
Refrigerated Covered Lighter (self-propelled)	YFR
Refrigerated Covered Lighter (non-self-propelled)	YFRN
Harbour Utility Craft (self-propelled)	YFU
Garbage Lighter (self-propelled)	YG
Garbage Lighter (non-self-propelled)	YGN
Gasoline Barge (non-self-propelled)	YOGN
Fuel Oil Barge (non-self-propelled)	YON
Oil Storage Barge (non-self-propelled)	YOS
Sludge Removal Barge (non-self-propelled)	YSR
Water Barge (non-self-propelled)	YWN

e Miscellaneous

Barracks Craft (non-self-propelled)	APL
Deep-Submergence Rescue Vehicle	DSRV
Deep-Submergence Vehicle	DSV
Unclassified Miscellaneous	IX
Submersible Research Vehicle	NR
Miscellaneous Auxiliary (self-propelled)	YAG
Floating Crane (non-self-propelled)	YD
Diving Tender (non-self-propelled)	YDT
Ferry Boat or Launch (self-propelled)	YFB
Dry Dock Companion Craft (non-self-propelled)	YFND
Floating Power Barge (non-self-propelled)	YFP
Covered Lighter (Range Tender) (self-propelled)	YFRT
Salvage Lift Craft, Heavy (non-self-propelled)	YHLC
Dredge (self-propelled)	YM
Gate Craft (non-self-propelled)	YNG
Patrol Craft (self-propelled)	YP
Floating Pile Driver (non-self-propelled)	YPD
Floating Workshop (non-self-propelled)	YR
Repair and Berthing Barge (non-self-propelled)	YRB
Repair, Berthing, and Messing Barge (non-self-propelled)	YRBM
Floating Dry Dock Workshop (Hull) (non-self-propelled)	YRDH
Floating Dry Dock Workshop (Machine) (non-self-propelled)	YRDM
Radiological Repair Barge (non-self-propelled)	YRR
Salvage Craft Tender (non-self-propelled)	YRST
Seaplane Wrecking Derrick (self-propelled)	YSD

Index